GALE FORCE

GALE CINCOTTA

THE BATTLES FOR DISCLOSURE
AND COMMUNITY REINVESTMENT

by Michael Westgate
with Ann Vick-Westgate

George & Shizue

Michael

Best wishes!

HARVARD BOOKSTORE
CAMBRIDGE, MASSACHUSETTS

Cover Photo shows Gale Cincotta leading protesters and launching the campaign, "RECLAIM AMERICA." This was outside the American Bankers Association (ABA) Convention at McCormick Place, Chicago. Gale had planned to enter the convention but was told she could not attend. Columbus Day, October 13, 1980.

TABLE OF CONTENTS

INTRODUCTION

Gale Cincotta was a force to be reckoned with.

From modest beginnings with a tenth-grade education, with family obligations for her six sons and aging parents, Gale channeled her anger at the Chicago School Board in a way that mobilized thousands of mothers and others to demand improvements. She found that it was the real estate and banking interests fueling the racial imbalance that exacerbated the failing school system. The Federal Housing Administration aided and abetted unfair lending practices. She took them all on. Gale gained the grudging respect of Mayor Richard J. Daley and the vocal and tangible support of his son Mayor Richard M. Daley.

She was fearless in leading protest marches; discerning in what data she needed to back up her charges; incisive in using the media; and strategic in her timing, moving from protests outside to negotiations inside the board rooms of the nation's banks. The Chairman of the Federal Reserve Bank in Washington, Paul Volcker, acceded to her demands to meet—provided she remove the Loan Shark, borrowed from *Saturday Night Live,* from above the door of the Federal Reserve—and his staff took notes on what they learned from Gale in the ensuing meeting.

Gale's dream of a national balance sheet showing all lenders' sources and uses of capital, designed to point out the unmet borrowing needs of neighborhoods around the country, was an unfulfilled dream. But passage of the federal Home Mortgage Disclosure Act (HMDA) in 1975 and its better-known companion the Community Reinvestment Act (CRA) in 1977 were personal triumphs for her and Senator William Proxmire (D-WI). He called Gale "the mother of CRA". Had CRA and federal regulations been applied, as she advocated, to all mortgage lenders the worst excesses of the national and global financial crisis that began in 2007 might have been avoided.

Gale did not advocate a major direct role in lending for the federal government. She wanted every lender to have a direct stake in the loans they made. "Some skin in the game" is the term more recently applied. Nor did she believe that homeownership was a panacea for all.

Her rallying cry was "Full Disclosure." The market place, under public scrutiny and with appropriate regulation, could solve the major portion of the country's housing needs.

Gale took the fight for community reinvestment as far as she could before her death in 2001. It is the intent of this book to document her story and to inspire others to carry on, wherever economic injustices may occur.

Gale's work involved community organizers and community leaders. Some of her tactics were criticized as "not nice." Her retort was that the conditions they were protesting were "more not nice." The leaders and organizers came initially, like Gale, from Chicago, but it was a movement that spread across the country. Hers was a precursor to the popular movement that elected Barrack Obama to the presidency.

I worked with Gale in the 1970s in the formation of Neighborhood Housing Services of Chicago and kept in touch over the years as we both dealt with issues and implementation of the Community Reinvestment Act (CRA).

It is an honor to be able to tell Gale's story and I must tell it before people forget. At the National People's Action (NPA) Conference in May 2003, less than two years after her death, some young people I talked with did not know who she was.

Gale demonstrated how a few people in neighborhoods anywhere can make a real difference. If people can work, in unity, to redeploy existing resources across communities and across the nation, they can change the world.

Chatham, MA - March 2011

DEDICATION

This book is dedicated to the past generation of leaders and organizers represented by Gale Cincotta and Shel Trapp and to our three granddaughters, Sarah Vivienne Westgate, Cecilia Louise Pascual and Alison Zoe Westgate and the rest of their generation.

SOURCES

This book is based on primary sources: 859 pages of transcribed interviews of those who lived and worked most closely with Gale, as well as contemporaneous newspaper articles; issues of *DISCLOSURE* newsletter published by NTIC, particularly those covering the critical period 1974-78; and the complete files in the Ford Foundation archives relating to her work at the National Training and Information Center (NTIC).

There have been many books and articles written analyzing how the Community Reinvestment Act (CRA) came into being through the legislative process. This book will supplement those secondary sources, providing a primary record of some of the voices without which the Home Mortgage Disclosure Act (HMDA) and CRA would not have been enacted.

EDITORIAL NOTE

All of the quotations in this book come from the individuals listed in Appendix A, either drawn from transcripts of the interviews conducted for this book, or from cited printed sources. Quotations have mostly been left intact. To make the reading easier, there was minor editing inevitably required to continue the conversational flow. And, very occasionally, sentences have been gently rearranged to make the point clearer. But nothing has been taken out of context, only a word added here or there that the speaker inadvertently left out. What you read is what they said. These people, who knew Gale best, described her and the environment in which she lived impeccably.

This approach is based on the book about another high school drop-out, *A Reporter's Life, PETER JENNINGS*, edited by Kate Darnton, Kayce Freed Jennings & Lynn Sherr, published by Public Affairs, New York, 2007. The paragraph above is adapted from that book. Since the entire book is based on quotations, quotation marks have been dispensed with. Where books are cited, page numbers are provided.

CHAPTER 1

"I don't know why I should be intimidated."

GALE CINCOTTTA AND HER FAMILY

Michael Westgate: People ask how Gale got to be one of the most powerful and effective voices on behalf of neighborhoods heard in this country. This introductory chapter focuses on the private side of Gale as daughter, wife, mother and friend. Her commitment to family and friends was unwavering and formed the bedrock upon which she built her public role.

Gale, an only child born Aglaia Angelos in 1929, was raised in Garfield Park on Chicago's West Side. Many people thought her to be an

Theodore Angelos, Gale's father, with her, age 2, 1931.

Italian because of her married name, but she was Greek and Latvian and raised in the Greek Orthodox faith. She attended Greek school and church and spoke some Greek. As an adult, she visited the Greek village where her father was born. Gale learned from an early age about politics, what was right, and how to fight from her parents and grandparents.

As her family grew over the years, Gale placed all six of her sons in the Chicago Public Schools. She initially joined the Parent Teachers Association and then the Organization for a Better Austin (OBA) where she was recognized for her leadership potential. But she took parent engagement and community involvement to whole new dimensions, starting with her own neighborhood, then citywide, statewide and nationally.

Gale's youngest son begins her story:

Jimmy Cincotta: Her first name was Aglaia, one of the Three Graces, and means brilliance. She was baptized as a Greek Orthodox. Her parents owned restaurants, worked in them, sold them, then bought another. That's what first immigrants did.

My great-grandparents were farmers, living near Riga. They left Latvia in 1906 because of the Prussians. Everyone was being persecuted.

They came first to Cleveland, where they actually had a farm. You know what sharecroppers are? You don't really own your land, but you work it and you get a percentage of what you grow. They had a farm in Geauga Lake, which is now a big amusement park in Cleveland. My Uncle Charlie lives in a house next to where my great-grandparents lived.

When they came they were like indentured slaves, and they weren't getting the percentage they were supposed to. My great-grandfather John said, "I didn't come to America to be a slave again. It's supposed to be the land of opportunity." So he told his family, "Go off into the city. Take the car or the horse. Walk off into the city. I'll work the land—or whatever." …It was that idea that if someone is ripping you off, you do something.

My grandmother Amelia was ready to set off with her friends in 1927, so the three women bought a car together. They were going to drive from Cleveland and move to Los Angeles. On the way they stopped off in Chicago.

Gale as a young girl in the mid-1930s.

My grandmother stayed because she met my grandfather Theodore.

If you look at my mother's upbringing in the sense of working the land, and sense of family, and coming to a new country, you want to make something better for your family. Hence "Why are we living in this bad house when we were promised something better?" With my grandmother embracing being a woman in a new country, you can buy a car, you can smoke a cigar. You can take off. So it's that feeling, it's that sense, of being in a new country, that you can create what you are or create something better.

Michael Westgate: Gale resisted labeling herself or others. In school, where she was a straight A student, she insisted vehemently to a teacher who was trying to identify ethnic roots that she was not a hyphenated American.

Jimmy Cincotta: She would say she's an American. My mother actually got punished for saying that. She went to Marshall High School.

They were talking about origins and they asked, "Well, what's your origin?" She said, "I'm an American." And that's not the answer they wanted. She just said, "I'm an American." She saw herself as an American. And she got punished.

Michael Westgate: Gayle Brinkman, Gale Cincotta's best friend, moved into Austin on Chicago's West Side from the suburbs in 1967. She and her husband wanted to join the effort to revitalize this part of the city in transition. Gale moved to Austin in 1945 when she married Roy Cincotta at age 16.

Gayle Brinkman: Gale was an only child and said she was very happy if she could just play with her things and nobody bothered her. But if her mother made her share with some others, she had big temper tantrums.

In her father's restaurant, she remembered a lot of political talk. Gale's parents were Socialists but they were not very active. They voted for the Socialist party presidential candidate Norman Thomas. Gale was gregarious and grew up wanting to dance and to sing. She overheard adult discussions of what life was like, what issues they faced, what they might or might not do about them. In that regard, she got an education that stood her in good stead. She never had to unlearn what the system might have tried to teach her as a seventeen-year-old and beyond. She became a master. Between talent and instinct, she really taught people.

Helen Murray, a native Chicagoan who was one of the first female organizers hired by Gale. Her initial job was to put together the follow up meeting in Baltimore, Maryland after the first national housing conference: Their restaurant was on the West Side. I wouldn't be surprised if it was near Greektown. That area got destroyed by the Eisenhower Freeway which sort of wrecked that whole neighborhood.

Michael Westgate: While there are two versions of the way Gale and Roy met, there is no disagreement about the facts that Gale loved to dance and that Roy was an older man who charmed her.

Gayle Brinkman: Gale was a mature-looking young woman. She used to serve at the restaurant. Roy Cincotta went there because he was a colleague of her parents, her parents' age. She saw him as kind of a swashbuckler. He could ride a horse and lean over and pick up something from the ground. That impressed her. So

Gale, left, with a friend in the mid-1940s.

they fell in love. She was not yet out of high school. Gale married in 1945 at sixteen to Roy, an Italian-Irish gas station owner and operator.

Jimmy Cincotta: You know how they had ballrooms, like the social dancing clubs for the Army? She used to work in one of them, and that's how she met my father. He said he was ten years younger than he was.

She didn't finish high school. She was seventeen for the first child, eighteen, nineteen, twenty, four children like that. Each one was one step lower then the other in terms of height. So it was Tom, Ted, George, Chuck. Then there's a rest. Then there's Richard, and then there's me. I'm almost nine years after Richard. There was a stillborn in between.

Mary Volpe, veteran leader who lived in North Austin, worked with Gale at OBA on issues and later ran another neighborhood organization: I always used to kid Gale that she married her husband, who was older, to get out of the house, because she wasn't allowed to wear lipstick. You know how Gale loved her lipstick! She always had her hair done. The world could come to an end and Gale had to have that!

Alicia Mendoza, a Chicago Southsider who was hired by Gale in the early 1980's as her administrative assistant at NTIC. Alicia still works there: Gale had a beautiful red lipstick she used to wear all the time and mascara. And her hair was so pretty when she'd go to the beautician. I would compliment her.

Helen Murray: Roy was a skinny, small, quiet man. Probably when Gale was a young wife, with six kids, he was the grownup. When he was aging, and Gale had come into her prime, she was the boss.

Gayle Brinkman: Her family included four generations under one roof. Gale's whole upbringing was inclusive. Throughout her life, she was inclusive. That was one of the secrets to her success.

She was a strict mother. The boys were all very musical and she would dress them all in white and make sure they didn't get dirty. She was a good singer. She would have loved to be a piano-bar singer. She was also an artist. She painted and took art lessons with the other woman in our group, Betty. She painted some very nice paintings. She was multi-talented.

Jimmy Cincotta: I'm the baby. When I was a kid, my great-grandparents on my mother's side were living with us. They had owned their own farm, and they farmed other people's land as well. I know from stories and photographs that when my mother was a child in the summer they would ship her off to Cleveland to be on the farm. It was very much of an immigrant family where you took care of each other. So when they retired they moved in with us.

My great-grandparents spoke Latvian. So we had three languages – Latvian, Greek and English – in the house. Religiously, it was Protestant for the Latvians, Roman Catholic for the Italians, Catholic for the Irish, and

Greek Orthodox—all mixed together and the three languages. But my mother said, "How do you raise people one or the other?" So she said, "Forget it. Let's start new." So all the kids were raised Methodist!

I was born on Adams Street. We were right next to the Beltline on Adams Street. And then my parents bought the vacant lot next to them and made a larger space. After two years we moved to 5401 Monroe, near Central. That's where I grew up until my father died in 1976. He was a gas station attendant. At one point he owned them, like the one on Sacramento.

Michael Westgate: Gale's decision in 1952 to send her oldest son to first grade in Chicago's public schools was one of the moments which defined who Gale was and what she would go on to do. She became increasingly angry at what she saw in her sons' deteriorating schools and that anger fired her energy to challenge the system. It was her success working with others to win local victories over the Chicago School Board and for improved local city services that fueled the battles Gale went on to fight and win citywide, statewide and nationwide.

Jimmy Cincotta: Why did my mother get involved with schools? Well, she had so many kids in school. What do you do? You go to the PTA. And at that time it was May School that my brothers were going to.

When I was going to school, there was nine years age difference. When I was at Emmett, my brother was at Austin High School. There were like racial riots. The state troopers were on the school roof with guns. It was a riot between white and black kids. So it was at that time when things were racially changing and white people didn't want to be around black

Gale, age 19, with her first two sons, Ted age 1, and Tom age 2, in 1948. George was born later that year.

people. Big deal. It's like what's the difference? In Chicago it's still like that. It is so segregated. That's the one thing I don't like about Chicago.

Going with the PTA got her into the political stuff, like how organizations run and keeping your school okay. So her connection with OBA started with that.

I was only at Emmett for two years, which was kindergarten and first grade. And then I was switched to Oscar DePriest, which was on Central across the street from Columbus Park. There were already mobile "Willis wagons" [portable classrooms] there— derogatorily named after the school superintendent at the time. So that had to be my second grade.

Gayle Brinkman: Austin had a lot of rental units because most of the buildings where we lived were two-flats and three-flats. So lots of times there were families in the two-flats, but there were a lot of rental units. And there were a lot of single-family homes too.

Helen Murray: Austin was an old community, so you had the whole spectrum of ages. You had the old people. You had the single people. You had apartments with single people, single working people. What was happening in that tight market for blacks, because of the traditional segregation, was the first people coming were the people with kids. Immediately the people that were buying out of Austin were the older people with no kids. The schools were changing. They were setting up folding chairs and Gale's kids were in school.

Gale didn't have a racist bone in her body. That was an unusual perspective for a white leader, neighborhood leader or any other kind of leader. She saw it all as a people's issue and people got that real fast. She had people's respect.

Gayle Brinkman: Both of her parents lived in the same building. They lived on the first floor on Monroe, and she and her family lived on the second floor. Jimmy talked about how hard it was to have to put her father in a nursing home. After Roy died, Gale had to support everybody, her parents and her kids. And so they moved to North Austin, and her father used to get out onto the street. He would speak in Greek only and must have had Alzheimer's or some other form of dementia. They would have somebody come in and her mother still lived upstairs. But he evidently became too difficult, so both her mother and father went to a nursing home on the North Side. She visited and George, the police officer son, made it a point to come in uniform. Her mother went blind. Tommy, her eldest son, died and her two parents. She didn't cry at the time. She held it in; she said she was afraid that if she started crying, she wouldn't be able to stop.

Helen Murray: Gale would say that the pressures that be would always cause them to have to move. Because of the economics or whatever else, they moved three times. And when they got to Austin, she said, "That's the last time," because her grandfather was living with her and he couldn't find his way around the apartment because he was blind. "And that's enough. You got to quit pushing people." She would tell that story and that came right from her heart.

So where did she get her strength? God knows. But where did she get her anger? It came from that sense of having lived that Chicago history in a very intimate way. That grandfather story was very poignant. When do you stop pushing people around to play that whole marketing game? People can't find the bathroom when they're ninety because they've had to move once again to satisfy all those pieces. That was a poignant story.

Jimmy Cincotta: My father was never involved in the protests. Oh, God, no! He wasn't opposed. He would say, "I just don't want to get a phone call that you got arrested." Or "I just don't want to see your face in the newspaper." Which, of course, it was! In fact, when she got arrested, he flipped. Not because she got arrested. He said, "How come you didn't phone me?" The one phone call she was allowed wasn't to him. It was to Father Mike Rocheford at Resurrection, the Catholic church.

At that point my mother had issues with the Methodist minister. Because these Catholic priests were a bit radical—they cared about communities. They were doing God's work through the community, and not just reading scripture as one way of caring, but actually helping people in communities. So they're the ones that left the pulpit and moseyed into the neighborhood. Where the other guy, the Methodist, was a little bit more "I have my church. Here's my space." I would go with her to Baptist churches because there were meetings there and at the Catholic church. And there were also meetings at the Unitarian church. The Catholic priests later got punished by Cardinal Cody for what they did.

See, I never went to church services. And I'll tell you why. I had more fun protesting. Going to church was foreign – and the same thing about going to school. The only reason I went to school was because the truant officer would come and get me. But I remember the fun and the excitement of protesting. I wouldn't want to go to school because it was like alien. "I want to go with you and have fun." School was what we were protesting about anyway. So why would you go there? It's like selling out to the enemy. Protesting is much more real and quite educational.

When I was going to school, I would hide under the bed and my mother would take the end of a broom and try to jab me to get out. The school I went to was Emmett, a grade school in Austin, on Madison and Central. And there was a bus bench right out in front of it. I'm five. My mother would tell the story. I would say "Now you're gonna stay here. You're not gonna leave from this bench. You're going to stay here until I come out." What? Five hours later. And she would say, "Yes, Jimmy. I'm gonna stay here." As soon as I went off into the school she would walk away and do her work. But when I came out, she was sitting there and never left it. Right!

So you always had a blend of everything. Like you had a blend of cultures, a blend of religions, a blend of people. And it just made sense with the work she was doing because it's another blend. It's another Americanization. It's another "Let's do something new." And like the neighborhood we lived in was racially changing from European mix to black. And my parents didn't care about the change. All they cared about was "Is there a school to go to? Is there a grocery store down the street?" Who cares what the composite is, it's like there's always going to be a composite.

Roger Coughlin, a Roman Catholic priest, the retired director of research at Catholic Charities for the Archdiocese of Chicago, Roger continued to be a staunch supporter of community organizing and the visionary leadership of Gale, serving on the board of directors of NTIC until his death in 2010: This was what was the origin of Gale. Gale, she had six boys. She was not going to fool around with people abusing her kids by giving them lousy educations. So she was into the fray and that's how she began.

Gale Cincotta in an interview with Studs Terkel (July 15, 1982): As you got a little older, like myself, you made what you thought was a simple decision to live in the city of Chicago, where you were born, and send your children to a Chicago public school. My husband and I have six sons. What started to happen is you found out just because of where you were living, the kids weren't getting the kind of education they should be getting. And where you thought your job was taking care of the house, making sure they did their homework, getting to school on time and you have a good meal—and then a professional would take over. In this case it was teachers and principals.

What we found out is that nobody really cared if the kids learned to read. Nobody really cared if that school got the same amount of books as other schools in the city, or got regular teachers. People just cared if you got there on time and were clean and then the kids didn't open their mouth. What you found out very fast is that if you made that simple decision of living in the city and sending your kids to public school, you had to get involved. You had to care yourself because, even though those people were professionals, you were the professional who cared. And you better see yourself that way. Find out what's going on and, if you don't like it, do something about it and change it!

Michael Westgate: In a March 18, 1982 *Chicago Tribune* article, "She arose from grass roots to shake the tallest oaks," by Stevenson O. Swanson, Gale made many of the same points concluding, "To me they're people who are making decisions about my life, and I don't know why I should be intimidated."

Shel Trapp, the consummate community organizer who ended up as

Gale's lifelong colleague and fellow strategist, was the one who pushed hardest for her to become OBA's first woman president. With all those boys in the public school system, she became a vocal member of the PTA, and eventually crossed paths with Trapp, who had recently left the ministry to become an organizer. He long remembered their first encounter, in the basement of the Mandell Methodist Church.

Shel Trapp, master organizer and Gale's life-long collaborator: I was pretty nervous about this powerful person. So I go up and say, 'I'm Shel Trapp,' and she says, 'Well, who are you with?' and I say, 'It's a new organization that's just starting but doesn't have a name yet.' And she slaps her head and says, 'Oh Christ, not another one!'"

Gale Cincotta wrote in her own CV: My active community involvement began with issues of education at the local and citywide levels. I was instrumental in the formation of the Organization for a Better Austin and worked my way up through the ranks at OBA, between 1966-72, chairing the Education Committee, the Real Estate Practices Committee and the Finance Committee before becoming its President for two years.

Jimmy Cincotta: In terms of her leadership, what's inherited, learned, instinctive, how she related to other people, again it's the immigrant family. You have to be extraordinary to leave a country with nothing except your family. You do what you have to do to survive, with a lack of fear of the unknown. A lot of people talk about Gale as fearless. That ties in with the immigrant story. The other is the openness to change. There was so much change going on. The family was always changing. And the neighbors were changing. It didn't make a difference if you were black or white. You go back to the basics. What makes a community? That's like the farming people too. Farmers are stoic.

Bud Kanitz started his organizing career in Chicago with the Northwest Community Organization (NCO). Hired in 1997 as Director for Community Relations for the Comptroller of the Currency in Washington, Bud remained a favorite confidante of Gale: Gale's example is particularly good as a role model for immigrants or first generation people who don't think they can fight the system. That they're awed by the powers that be. I always in Chicago would hear, "Oh, hell. You can't organize Puerto Ricans like you organize Poles or white ethnics. You know, it's just not part of their culture." Well, the point is that you can organize anybody.

A lot of the problem is that working-class families are working a lot, many of them with two jobs, and they don't have time to go to community meetings. But the thing that people have to realize is that the example that Gale showed was you don't have to be awed by politicians or by bankers or corporate executives.

Jimmy Cincotta: All the work she was doing when I was very small was as a volunteer. When it became MAHA, the Metropolitan Area Housing Alliance, she had a job. And then when my father died, then it became work. I would never say it was a hobby but it was like "I'm working. I'm glad I'm making money." But when he died it then became, "I have to work. It's now a necessity." And at that point my grandparents were getting old too.

She was the breadwinner for everyone – for a generation older and a generation younger. That's why I withdrew a lot from her work. Because I'd always had a kind of love-hate relationship with it. Because I loved my mother and I wanted her to be around more, but her work took her away. But her work was important not only because of what she was doing, but also to make sure I was taken care of, her parents were taken care of, the dog was taken care of! I didn't see it that way, I just saw it as, "Quit your job...."

It was interesting going to one of those things at Lake Geneva. It must have been an organizers' conference...

Michael Westgate: Lake Geneva was the resort complex where the initial organizers met in 1974 to form what was to become the very successful Neighborhood Housing Services (NHS) of Chicago. There were about 55 people there, including Gale and myself. I had met with her several times over the previous year but here was where I first saw her in action.

Jimmy Cincotta: ...And people knew me. It was really funny. I remember someone came up – I must have been a young teenager – and said, "Are you going to follow in your mother's footsteps? Are you going to take over?" I'm thinking, "No." And then I'm thinking, "Not just no because no, that's her work."

It's not like you pass leadership on, you have to earn being a leader. You have to earn it. When Gale dies, no, I'm not going to step right into the corporation and become the new Joe Mariano. Joe moved in, but he's earned it. He's doing what Shel does in one way. Inez Killingsworth and the other women are doing what my mother does. They're the leaders. So you have to earn it. So I'm thinking, "No, I haven't done anything."

At that I thought I was quite spoiled in a lot of ways, making sure my life was better, fighting to get a better school, so I wouldn't be in a crowded school. So I felt the positive repercussions of the work she did, so, spoiled that way.

My brother Ted later worked insurance. He had some troubles with my mother because he worked for Allstate. Allstate was one of the enemies at the time. So he didn't really have troubles, but people couldn't understand how he knew the president of Allstate and he wasn't at the presidential level. "How do you know so-and-so?" "Because my mother sits on boards and committees of NHS", and you have different stakeholders. You have the bank president or whatever. You just knew different stakeholders. So that's how my brother got to know those people.

There's another brother Larry. He's not Gale's son biologically but it's like he's family. He had actually lived with us for years because we were just a "normal" family, or actually dysfunctional, which is normal in the States sometimes. We always had his picture up like one of the other sons, brothers. Because our family was normal for him and just lived. He would say, "You're normal. My family is crazy. I like you." And one brother is a policeman, yeah, a policeman, and that gave him trouble too because his mother was getting arrested—but never proven guilty.

Gale's parents, Amelia and Theodore Angelos, in the 1970s.

My mother was very practical. She said she raised all the boys as North Americans and sometimes she regretted that. She wanted to raise them more ethnic, because you're raised with different values. So she was by herself at that point, after having had a house that was constantly bubbling over with people. So we always had a duplex, so one generation, one floor and another generation, another floor.

Then she moved to Oak Park. She didn't want to move to Oak Park because she felt that she grew up in the city and she has to be identified with Chicago. She had a really hard time doing that. She actually had bought where she lived until she died as an investment. So she bought and rented it out for five years. Then she finally sold the house that we lived in. Every time a death happened she keeps moving because again you don't need the place above you.

Helen Murray: Between '76 and '85 was a very, very difficult time for Gale emotionally. Roy died in '76 of lung cancer. He was the least surprising; he was older. Her firstborn son Tommy died before Gale's dad or mom. That was rough. She got through that. Tommy had a very sudden illness and died very quickly. She and Roy had many years together. But then real close together the mom, the dad and Tommy. That was hard times.

Gayle Brinkman: Her husband Roy died in between her son Tommy

and her parents. Roy was supposed to come home from the hospital and he
died. She was shocked. He had cancer. They were all smokers. Terrible. And
he had gotten cancer of the larynx. They had given him radiation treatments,
and he had burns. He went back to the hospital, and he died from that. He
was a good deal older, 25 years at least.

Jimmy Cincotta: Tom was the eldest. It was a bad time, '84. It
was a bad, <u>bad</u> time. Because I left there was no one at home taking care
of the grandparents. Tom died very suddenly. He died of a very rare blood
disease – he must have been 35. He was gay. His partner Jerry always came as
part of the family. But that was the thing. You're just inclusive. Am I going
to love you less? And my mother was okay with that. It took her harder to
understand it, but I don't think it bothered her.

I left in the summer, like June. I don't remember much of July; it
was that much of a shock. I left for McGill, Montreal. My eldest brother, he
would take care at times, come over on the weekends and stuff like that. So
your support network fell apart.

So in June 1984 I leave. My brother dies. My grandmother
and grandfather, her parents, they're put into a nursing home. And she's
like hysterical, because she feels she failed them. Because your parents
are supposed to die in the house, that's what everyone else did. My great
grandparents they just… you wake up, they're dead. You're having breakfast
and they have a stroke. You don't push them away.

Michael Westgate: Gale persevered through all these deaths and
other family difficulties with minimal effect on her work.

We found an anonymously written, undated document titled *We've
Found the Enemy* in the Thomas Gaudette Papers in the von der Ahe Library
at Loyola Marymount University in Los Angeles which quotes interviews with
Gale capturing some of her motivation and her relationship with her family.

From *We've Found the Enemy*:

Gale Cincotta: When you look carefully at what's going on around
you, you have to get angry. I got mad, and that gave me courage. I was never
intimidated by people – the school board, for example. All I could see was
that these people were making decisions affecting my kids' lives. I guess I must
have thought enough of myself from the beginning to fight back, and not
worry about what people thought of me. Maybe that comes from having a
solid family, and my own strength, and a lot of friends.

If you do this kind of work, you can't be fretting about who likes you.
You've got to have your own base of support – be it your family or a network
of friends. Or when all else fails you have to at least be able to say to yourself,
"Well, I've got this big dog who likes me, and is glad to see me come home so

I can feed him!"

When I started doing this work, I found it doesn't really have to take away from other things. You can still have your family life and your friends. Some things have to give, of course. When I got busy, I taught my boys how to cook, how to sew, how to run the washing machine, and how to like Kentucky Fried Chicken! My youngest grew up going to organizing meetings. My husband might have liked me to stay home with the kids all the time, but he and the kids adjusted. The children learned to take care of one another. And my husband was always the steady one; he was like a clock – home the same time every day and on weekends. I made sure that birthdays were always celebrated and holidays, I was always home then.

And some things do change. When you get active like this, your outlook is different. You've started to control your life. Sure, it's hard work; it means long hours. But it's different from other kinds of work. My mother and father worked sixteen hours a day, but because it was their own business they didn't mind. With community organizing it's the same. It's different from working for a corporation, where you can always get fired, and where the end result is just a project – whatever it is they decide to make and sell.

Gayle Brinkman: Gale loved to dance. When she got arthritic and couldn't dance, she was very unhappy. Betty and Gale used to take art lessons Thursday nights. Then they and the art teacher would go to the Bar Double R, which was a country western bar downstairs, and dance. She and the family would always go out to Colorado for their summer vacation. Betty and her family were out there too. They were all very musical. They had a lot of fun. Four kids played instruments.

Gale liked bingo. She did like gambling and I do too, with annual trips to Vegas. And then when the boats came here we made a few trips out there too. She was good at gambling. She had to pay taxes on it. It's so much easier than parenting! It really is a thrill. And she never stopped giving to the Humane Society. She loved animals – and people.

Alicia Mendoza: The bingo attracted her. The riverboat, she'd go there once in a while. Myself, my brother, Jaci, Gale and Gayle Brinkman would go. We met Gale at her Oak Park apartment. Gayle Brinkman drove us all there to the Aurora Riverboat. It was on a Saturday. And we had a pretty good time.

Gale was just such a sharing person. I wasn't going to spend much because I didn't have much to lose. When we first get there, Gale says, "Here. Take this." She gave me a $20 bill. And I said, "No, Gale." She said, "Take it." "Okay, Gale. If I win, you're getting this back." Well, I did win. I was in shock. I think that day I won $700. I gave Gale back hers and then I bought

Gale (second from right) at Fox River, Summer 1978 with friends Joyce Gradel, Gayle Brinkman, Ruth Walther, and Janice Derrick

her lunch the next day.

To me Gale was in essence like a mother to all. It's just her charisma, the way she spoke. The way she thought and expressed her feelings to others just made everyone want to be a part of that particular effort. I didn't deal with Gale on various issues. I mainly dealt with Gale on little things as far as things she might have needed, like personal letters done.

She worked extraordinary hours, prior to my coming, really, really long hours. I've heard about those nights! And then they'd go dancing afterwards. Wonderful! During my time, she was traveling quite a bit when I first started, maybe the first ten years in the eighties, a quarter of her time to half.

She spent a lot of time on the phone with the troops talking to people from around the country. Gale would always take their calls. If someone from the neighborhood called in having a question about their home, she'd take it. Unless she was terribly busy she would talk to them and tell them exactly what they needed to do. To me that was just remarkable. Because in the past few positions I've had, they'd pass it on to someone else, "I'm too busy to talk with someone right now about their problems." But Gale wasn't.

Whenever she would speak with a person there would always be a jolly laugh in the comment. It never failed. But what really sticks out in my mind about Gale was she would always say, "Persistence pays. Keep on agitating and eventually you will get a resolution for either good or bad. You just continue to work on that. …"

Michael Westgate: Gale loved to travel. She continued to seek out her Greek roots, visiting her family home in the village of Examilia, near Corinth, Greece, several times. Gale also had the opportunity to travel professionally. She presented a paper, *From Redlining to Reinvestment, the Need for Eternal Vigilance,* before the 4th International Conference on Financial Services "European Monetary Union and the Regional Responsibility of Financial Institutions towards the Consumer" in Strasbourg, France, Sept. 27, 1996, urging that European governments learn from the battles fought for disclosure and community reinvestment in the U.S.

Gayle Brinkman: The time that we went to Greece and Italy that was the last trip that I took. She would take her kids to Greece and she would take George and his wife. She took Richard to Germany. Richard was along on the trip that I went to Greece.

Evidently she had a lot of frequent flyer miles and she said to one of her kids, "Okay. Let's go back to Greece." And they pretty much said, "What? Again?" And she said, "All right. Forget it." So she talked to her girlfriends and said, "I want to go to China. I will give you the frequent flyer miles to go to China if you will go for as long as I want to go." She wanted to go to the Far East. So we used to meet in Chinese restaurants and everybody would read their *Fodors.* Oh, it was so much fun. Each of us would have a book to read and then we'd talk about what we would do if we went there.

We ended up spending about eight nights in Hong Kong. We flew business class. She had enough miles. It was these four ladies in the back. The flight attendants loved us and gave us all kinds of little bottles of liquor to take with us. It was me and Ruth and Gale and Betty Knight. Gale would run very cold. She was afraid of getting infections. I shared her room and I'd run out and get her bottled water and that kind of stuff.

After our time in Suzhou and with a tour in Shanghai, we flew to Beijing, went out to the Great Wall, and on to Xian. Gale was really impressed by all the clay soldiers. Then we flew to Gualin and we took a one-day Li River cruise. We were gone a month. We went back to Hong Kong for another couple of nights. We ended up twelve nights in China, twelve nights total in Hong Kong. And then we went to Honolulu for five nights on the way home.

Alicia Mendoza: Gale would always, for Christmas, go to Florida. Charles lived there and she would always go there and be with them and stay almost a month. Then, of course, for her arthritis she would swim. It's a nice warm temperature there. She'd have a wonderful time – she <u>loved</u> to travel. Even if it was on work, she loved to travel – to be with the group.

Gale got her energy from people. She gave it to them, but she got it back. An exchange. It fired her up and then their excitement moved her, kind of a loop.

She got to and from home every day by cab. Jimmy was saying when they were coming here once that they were in a cab and the cab driver said, "Oh, you're the lady I used to bring here <u>all</u> the time." Flash Cab Company. They knew Gale. When I called for a cab, this time they gave me a number for her. And she says, "Oh, play it. You might win!" She said, "You can't win if you don't play!"

CHAPTER 2

"The System has to be changed."

AUSTIN AND CHICAGO IN THE 1960s-70s

Michael Westgate: Austin in the 1960s and '70s was, and it remains today, Chicago's largest neighborhood. If independent, it would be Illinois' third largest city. Like much of Chicago it is built on immigrants from all over the world, many from Eastern Europe, and increasingly elsewhere—Hispanics, Filipinos and others seeking a better life in America, as well as African Americans from the American South.

In the '50s and '60s there was strong demographic pressure in the Chicago area for more housing for African-Americans. Many were children and grandchildren of those who had come to Chicago in search of work during the Depression and World War II. They were part of the outward migration from center-city Chicago to its outer ring of former suburbs, seeking better housing and schooling for their families. This included Austin, which had a history of tolerance for people of color. Coupled with the construction of new middle-class white suburbs fostered by federal housing policy, notably the Federal Housing Administration (FHA), and fear mongering among realtors and others, Austin was an area susceptible to whites moving out to be replaced by blacks and other minorities.

The FHA was founded in 1934 to provide insurance to lenders and was most active in the suburbs until the 1960s when it turned to urban mortgage lending. Its services were often abused by a variety of lenders, notably in Chicago. Under a variety of scams, realtors scared whites, often elderly, into selling their homes at deflated prices. The realtors would quickly resell them, often to blacks, often at inflated prices. FHA guaranteed the new mortgages based on unjustifiably high appraisals. If the new family defaulted on their loan, the lender would foreclose on the property, get FHA to pay off 90% of the loan amount, and the process would be repeated, sometimes with the participation of the same realtors, lenders and appraisers. A few were prosecuted and spent time in prison. And as Gale pointed out it was the neighborhood, as much as the families, who suffered the consequences.

There was national recognition that lenders were discriminating in lending. In 1961, the U. S. Commission on Civil Rights had found that African-American borrowers were often required to make higher downpayments and pay off loans faster than whites. The federal Housing Act of 1968 declared, for the first time, a national housing goal of "a decent home and a suitable living environment within the next decade." The Housing Act of 1974 declared that we faced "critical social, economic and environmental problems arising in significant measure from inadequate public and private investment in housing."

That same year the Equal Credit Opportunity Act was passed. However, these laws all conveyed rights to individuals, not communities. It was only individuals who had the right to pursue redress if they felt denied credit and their lawsuits had to be based on specific criteria, initially race. Gale's fights were to be for the rights of neighborhoods who were being discriminated against.

Austin had the benefit of seeing how Woodlawn and other nearby communities failed to deal with racial issues. There was a core group of Austin activists that grew, through the Organization for a Better Austin (OBA), into a critical mass for political action, seeking control of its own destiny. Tensions were high in Austin with members of the competing Town Hall Assembly (THA) fighting a largely racial battle against integration of schools. OBA was finally barred from THA's meetings.

There was anger in Austin. Schools were deteriorating. City services were being scaled back. Whole sections of the community were being written off, redlined by lenders. The public sector and the private sector seemed to be colluding. Many of those able to move out were leaving, partly out of fear, but also for better schools. Older people, past childbearing age, were leaving, replaced by those with small children. Television advertising showing people "leading the good life" targeted those contemplating moving away. Background settings for ads showed the green grass, the new suburban house, cars and parking for each member of the family.

Austin's neighborhoods were among several thousand around the country seemingly written off by the financial establishment. But Gale Cincotta joined others who had decided that they were going to fight rather than flee. The story of Gale starts with her and some of the other mothers from Austin. Some of those who began the fight with Gale for better schools are still living in the neighborhood.

Classroom sizes grew as per pupil spending decreased. Over a period of three years enrollment in the Jimmy Cincotta's Austin school rose from 975 to almost 2,000. Parents boycotted in response.

Mary Volpe: Gale and I have been together since OBA days. Well, I've always felt that there are people like Gale that you're friendly with and at certain times you don't walk through her, you walk around her to avoid any conflict. Because Gale would grind you up if she's fighting, and I could not be fighting somebody that I'm working with in a way. Some leaders I go round because they'll cut you a different way. But Gale would come out like a street fighter.

I always talk about Gale when the blacks were going to infiltrate their children, bring them in from Marshall High School. And the Parent Teachers Association, the parent group from Austin, was waiting for them. By the way, Austin had been integrated in 1896. That was the first blacks that came through because I knew the family. But I mean really a big influx.

There were a whole slew of us that were coming up as leaders in those days. We were friendly but it was strictly on a business deal. We had no background. We had kids that were crawling all over. We'd take our kids on the picket line. My two girls were on the picket line at three and five years of age, sleeping in the back of station wagons.

George Knight: Schools, yeah. I mean Gale was a leading voice in the PTA.

Michael Westgate: Gale had the ability to capture people's energy and passion and, if people were angry, to give them a way of expressing it in a positive way. Where did she get that ability?

George Knight: Well, a lot of it was God-given. Some of it was just, as you know, the philosophy of that style of organizing. It's an educational process in many ways. It's how, as you talk about the issue, who do we think can deal with the issue, what are people comfortable doing? Which usually is writing a letter. And then it's really finding out that writing a letter was an absolute waste of time. And then, if not the letter, who do we go meet with? Then the progressively more difficult challenges, as you push up the institutional ladders, the institutional ladders are shifted from one institution to another, the front institutions or the back institutions.

How do you get in to see them? How do you really get the issue clear enough, because the time to meet shrinks and shrinks and shrinks. When you're face to face with Alan Greenspan, you've got two minutes. And if you can't get your point in in two minutes, not only the general injustice, but his role, what he can do to change things, in in that 30 seconds or that 45 seconds, you've wasted your time. You've wasted your meeting.

And I think Gale was always focused on the bottom line. It wasn't just a demonstration to get the meeting. It was to make a point.

Jimmy Cincotta: Like peeing in a bucket? No, I'm serious. There was a protest at Chicago City Hall. I must have been at least four. It was about overcrowded schools. It was one of the first things she got into: poor quality education. There's a photograph of my mother. I'm in it but you just don't see me because I'm a little bit lower than her. And she has her big white hair. I'm there.

But you just don't want to leave your protesting and, once you're in the chamber, if you leave you won't get back in. So you can't go to the public bathroom, you can't go to a private bathroom, so you just take the trash canisters, turn them up, take the garbage out, and that's where you pee. And that was it. You just can't leave. And then, as soon as you start doing this...

What I found, maybe in retrospect, with the organization no one really knew what they were doing to start off with. They didn't know what the whole strategy was. They just knew schools were overcrowded. You had poor quality of education. "Let's do something!"

And then you're in the City Council room, your kid's peeing and then all of a sudden people start panicking that "We have to get them out of here, so what can we do to get them out?" That was probably the most useful thing we could have done. The kids had a role! And then it's like they caught on. They tweaked on that "Oh, this is like a strategy!"

Fill your kids with cokes before the meeting starts. And then just bringing kids there too was a strategy. Because you had kids, police don't want to arrest kids. They don't want to arrest women. How can you arrest the mothers? What are they going to do with the kids? So I think that's why it started out with a lot of strong female leaders.

George Knight: Those were tactics that were all used. I mean kids were guaranteed to help bring results. It would be interesting in today's environment with the heightened security... Violence was never an option; it was never even considered. It was beyond the pale for all of us. But, as the '70s wore on and you had violence suddenly used by groups and physical attacks and weapons and things, then the context was so totally changed, it really required new thinking, new approaches.

From *We've Found the Enemy*:

Gale Cincotta: People tend to think that if you can't get a bank loan, there's something wrong with you; or if your kids aren't learning, there's something wrong with the kids. It's important to know it isn't you, or your kids—instead, there's something wrong with the system that has to be changed. When I first realized that, I got angry. The only alternative is to move—but what's the difference if you move? If you don't have the same problems there, you'll have other problems. So I think you have to come to a point where you stop and dig in and do something about the problems around you. When you look around your neighborhood, you start to see what's happening —people at school boards making decisions affecting your kids' education, realtors and banks controlling the community. Instead, you have to control your community.

What you figure out then is that the principal is worried about his job and his record in running the school and would rather have you be quiet so that he can look good. These people don't want to make waves; they've got their own mortgage to pay off and a couple kids in college to support, and they want that promotion. So you realize that people in their position are afraid to take responsibility. Either you're going to take the responsibility yourself and maybe end up very unpopular, or you have to move. I still didn't want to be pushed out of the city into the suburbs; I didn't want to send my kids to private school either.

Gayle Brinkmann: When we moved in, I would say it was a block-by-block change that was occurring. Laramie was three blocks east of us. The first black family moved in about the same time we did. If you define Austin as going to Cicero Avenue that was 4800 West and Laramie was 5200. And the black population was moving into the southeast corner of this neighborhood of about 130,000 people.

Mary Volpe: OBA started in the '60s. Austin goes all the way to Roosevelt Road. When the transition started we had different needs and different wants. Some of the people that joined, joined these organizations thinking that when you said, "We're going to stabilize the community" that stabilization meant white, American, English-speaking and Christian. No more newcomers: no way. So when you tried to explain to them stabilization means no matter who's in that area you have good schools, good housing, that anybody can come and go, a lot of people didn't want that.

We knew that transition was going to start coming. In cities like Chicago, you can tell where the transition's going to be. You can tell from the way city services go. It can be ten years coming. But you can see that the money isn't going into the park system. The change isn't there yet. Because I argue this with blacks especially, they say, "It's because we're here." I say, "No, it started before you came. You could see everything slacking down and going." You could see up north.

Jimmy Cincotta: I remember going to OBA. Austin was like a community; it was not part of Chicago at one point. So there is a town hall just north of the El, the Lake Street El, there's a library, there's a little plaza square. The first street on the left was office fronts and OBA was right there. My mother gave me money to buy cigarettes — with a note.

Shel Trapp: When we started, it was a Committee for a Better Austin. Gaudette had been there on the scene since June of '66. I had left the ministry about June, and he hired me in September of '66. In '67, May School was very overcrowded and we went to a meeting, both Gaudette and I, in the basement of Mandell Church [5010 W. Congress Parkway] and Gale was there. She had organized this meeting. It was a PTA meeting but it was bigger. She had gotten some neighbors there. And we introduced ourselves and just about the first words out of her mouth were, "Oh Christ, a bunch of other do-gooders!" That was our first meeting with Gale.

She was fighting it through the PTA and we started organizing on it. At that time in history the answer of the Chicago School Board was that they had three answers to blacks moving in. One was to move the boundary lines so that literally you had schools where their boundary line was like their east wall of the building. The school was still all white but half of the neighborhood might be 80% black. The other solution was what they called "Willis wagons." Willis wagons were temporary classrooms, named after School Superintendent Willis. Then the other solution was split shifts. And Gale said, "We're not going to accept any of that."

The split shifts were mixed black and white but it was still a holding action that they fought, school by school, against black migration. And obviously the schools did not stay integrated very long, maybe two, three years max, then it was all black. Whites put their kids into Catholic school and also an awful lot of people moved out because, you know, we're talking back in the '60s. First black on the block, fifteen "For Sale" signs would go up.

Michael Westgate: In a March 1, 1978 *Chicago Daily News* article, "Gale Cincotta: She wasn't the last angry woman. Chicagoan's fight to save Austin has grown to nationwide movement of neighborhood people who care," Marge McElheny reported that the boycotting mothers "won $30 million worth of new schools. Class size was cut in half."

Gale and others organized and succeeded. OBA had strong leadership and strong backing from some Catholic churches at the time. Cincotta set out in 1965 to unite PTAs, churches and grass roots organizations that could deal with the problems. She served key roles in the organization, as chair of OBA's education committee, then chair of the real estate practices and finance committees, and as elected secretary. With Trapp's help, Cincotta won election as OBA's first woman president, serving for two years, 1969-70.

From *We've Found the Enemy*:

Gale Cincotta: What we were told back then was that changing neighborhoods were a natural phenomenon. But we started to see that there was a lot of money being made in changing neighborhoods, and that they were being racially changed on purpose—targeted for change. First the realtors would come in, start on a block or two, and pass out leaflets, telling white people they had better get out or they would lose money. Then the banks wouldn't give mortgages and the insurance companies wouldn't write policies. Then police would be assigned somewhere else. In the meantime, people would deposit their money in the banks in these "changing" neighborhoods, but instead of investing the money back in the neighborhood, the banks put it into suburban tract development. There were ads in the papers telling you that you were practically un-American if you didn't move out there to the suburbs. There wasn't any money for loans if you wanted to buy here in the city, or rehab here, but for a low down payment and good terms, you could move somewhere else. *That's* no natural phenomenon!

Through the community organizing, people were able to identify who the enemies really were. They weren't the people moving in or out; they were the realtors, the banks, and the savings and loan companies.

Up until then, it was always the women who did the work, and the men who got elected. And even when I ran, although I was obviously qualified, people in the organization made a point of saying. "Do you want a man or a woman for president?" not "Who was smart, who could do the job, or whatever."

Ann Vick-Westgate: Does Chicago have a tradition of these strong woman leaders coming from the neighborhoods?

Mary Volpe: Not until that time. In the black community they had women that were strong. But there was a handful like the Nancy Jeffersons, the Illa Daggetts. I can name on the West Side maybe five, six of 'em that were really strong. But not like the whites who came out of the community movement.

Michael Westgate: What caused the community movement and the involvement of women to happen at that time, in the sixties? How did you get involved?

Mary Volpe: We were at a time that all of us stayed at home. Some of us were college grads. Some were not. They hadn't gone to school. They had their families. Jobs weren't open. Women were still considered not going back to work. If you weren't a schoolteacher or a nurse, you worked for Sears Roebuck or the telephone company. There weren't jobs that meant too much. And when you got married, you worked until you had your child. Or you stopped for a couple years after and stayed home and took care of the house. I think boredom made it happen.

Michael Westgate: There was also a shift in bankers' expectations of women. Even if a woman was working, I remember cases where her income would not be counted on a mortgage application if she was of child-bearing age. Between the 1960s and the 1980s there was a whole shift in perspective. One of the factors driving up the price of housing was the reversal from a woman's income being denied in computing the amount of an available mortgage. That denial even happened to a woman classmate of mine from Harvard Business School in 1971 when she and her husband-to-be sought a mortgage in suburban Virginia. The dynamic changed from denying a woman's income as too uncertain to a woman's having to work, to provide a two-income family, in order to afford a house. The long-term consequence of this factor alone was to increase the mortgage that could be supported and hence the price of housing rose at least 50%.

From *We've Found the Enemy:*

"Gale has encouraged more women to get involved," says one organizer, a man who has worked with her for several years. "Her own involvement has definitely had ripple effects, and has contributed to the growth of other groups around the country. Women were often active in these groups, but not as leaders. Today, much of the leadership of community groups is women, and Gale has done a lot to encourage that just by her example. She's also influenced many women going into community organizing as a career."

Mary Volpe: All of a sudden you get these organizers. And women start finding things, what's going on. Some of us didn't know who our elected officials were. Most of us didn't. We didn't know about interest and savings and loans. Dear God, who would have known?

The issues were dry. And all of a sudden they're educating you on interest rates. They put you in a position to go and educate an Illinois senator on the differences between a mortgage banker and a savings and loan. They didn't know when we had hearings. We had to tell 'em the difference. They said, "What do you mean? You mean savings and loans?" "No, mortgage houses." "What are they?" These were people that were government, governing us.

I had a book here that had the whole story of redlining. My son did a paper at Rosary. He went to Rosary for undergrad. The teacher said, "This is not how it happened." And my son said, "What do you mean?" "Well, it happened this way and this way and this way." And my son said, "But I sat at the meetings when the stuff was written. It didn't happen this way and this way and this way! My mother, my sisters were out on the picket line. What do you mean it didn't?" We write history too far apart.

We did pickets almost every day, sometimes two and three times a day with the kids. My son would say to me, "Mrs. Stump is here." "How do you know?" She had a station wagon and she'd go bang it on one side to make room, back and forth. And she'd have the cigarette hanging out of her mouth, a can of beer in her hand, eight in the morning. If there isn't a parking space, make one!

Gale, her staff was great. Her staff, they fed Gale. They had food waiting for her when she was crying, when she was angry, when she was happy. You knew you had to have food for Gale. She said to me one day, "You know, Mare, I have lost, since I've known you, at least 1500 pounds and I've gained

1500 pounds back." And I said, "Oh, shut up!" In later years she was always going to these health spas to lose weight. And she was on these crazy diets. I used to say, "Gale…" They would come up with a bucket of chicken and she would munch.

Michael Westgate: Weren't some of these issues ones that came to the forefront at a time when women didn't yet have to work? Because housing prices hadn't yet risen so high that the mortgage payments required both members of the household to work? Is there an issue of class?

Mary Volpe: That's why we could… and remember our class. When I talk about class, I shouldn't in America. But there is a class situation. We came out of a class, a working class family. My family's been in Austin since before the Civil War, so it's not that I was in a class coming from immigrants.

We came out of that class that we stayed at home. We also didn't go away to school and we didn't travel and we certainly didn't get apartments, because if you got an apartment you were nothing but a tramp. To go to college, away, you were a tramp. You stayed home and went to a local college. You lived in a big city. There were places for you to go, to attend. You stayed home until you got married or went to the convent. There was nothing in between. And same thing with the boys, they went to the Army. They could go away to school.

I was the first generation. I'm 70. I was the first generation that the boys had college education and that came from the war, getting the G.I. Bill. My mother had planned for me to go to college from the day I was born. But when I entered a lot of my companions thought me unusual.

Michael Westgate: The most important part of Gale's life from the perspective of writing this book is the time when she got started, because we're hoping that this book will show other people how they can get started.

Mary Volpe: I think what happened to a lot of us, we had no place to go. Most of us were bright. We had no interests. I had worked a little with the civil rights movement, much to a lot of people's dismay. But I had never gotten into it that deep. You know, I was always on the outskirt. I didn't get too much into the war work or movement. I really thought when I went I was a strange person. I had been in the house raising kids. And my husband decided, when I was two months' pregnant with my last kid, he didn't want to have a family anymore. So, you know, he could have thought of that three months' earlier!

But in those days you could eat off my floors – from all three floors. The garden was etched. Everything was perfect. That's all I had to do. I got to the point I never went out. My mother would pick up the food and buy it for me. I'd go to church or school and help out there. I taught preschool for the nuns. You know, helped out here and there for nothing. I'm a great nothing worker, I tell you. I'm paid nothing for a lot of things.

But there was no place to go and no place to stimulate your brain to work. I think that was why. People were learning. You learn. It's like when women go to the PTA. At one time that was the first plan, years ago before women worked. That was where women learned and got educated. *Robert's Rules of Order.* How to put an agenda together. They were taught!

The Austin Women's Club is defunct now. My mother was president of it. She was in the national and all that other stuff. She was their parliamentarian. That generation learned through the women's clubs' groups. They're no longer around. This was a learning tool for the women that were at home. The men were retiring and they had nothing else to do and they were tired of just playing cards with the guys and puttering in the yard. You taught the men who were their officials, who was responsible. Women didn't go to the aldermen for welfare. You didn't go to your state rep to get the hole in your street fixed.

Michael Westgate: Where did the tactics come from for the protests and for the marching? Was it something you created together?

Mary Volpe: When we were attending an Aldermen's meeting one of my kids said… They were all short that one year, the guys that were on city council. And my two girls… And one of them had a mouth – the one that's a priest now. Still has a mouth. "Where is Snow White? I see the dwarfs." Real loud. In city council. "Shut up!" The alderman walked over and said, "Volpe, what's with your kid? What are you here complaining about?"

That meeting was against redlining. We didn't want the money to go into the banks from the city without checking what the banks were doing. And my kid, couldn't have been more than five, six years old, told them what it was all about. Because the kids learned.

There was a hole on the next block. And that block, right down the middle was two wards. And the hole was over to one side. And, naturally, the alderman that I could scream at at two in morning, my alderman, it wasn't his side of the street.

So I found out that this guy… You learn a lot, you know all the dirt. You knew who he was playing around with and his wife was out of town. So somebody's office gave me his girlfriend's telephone number. So about two, three o'clock in the morning I called. I could call <u>my</u> alderman. And I said, "Put your friend on the telephone."

And she hemmed and hawed, "He's not here." I said, "Put him on or I go to the newspaper." He got on the telephone. I said, "Hi, Alderman, this is Mary Volpe. When are you fixing the pothole on the thirteen-and-half hundred block of Vermont?" He goes, "What the…" And I said, "Well, I would suggest that you fix it. I understand your wife's coming back next week for summer." Hung up. The next morning the truck was here.

I think of some of the things I did. It was just ridiculous. I had to have that pothole fixed so I could prove to the two blocks on each side of here and there that I had power, that we had power. Because it wasn't my power, it was people power that we used to stress.

Rats were in the neighborhood, vermin. We'd catch 'em and we'd freeze 'em. And the priest at the office got real tough. "I don't want 'em in the freezers down here where the food is." I'd say, "Yes, Father." And we'd freeze 'em anyway. Then we took this whole bag of rats and we went on a Monday night, which in those days the old time ward bosses they had open house.

So we'd showed up with all these frozen rats. And we walked in, "I live in the community." They're all, "You got a complaint?" "Yeah. We got problems with Streets and San [Sanitation]."

Michael Westgate: Are people too busy working today? What can you get people to come out for?

Mary Volpe: People are working. You try to explain things to them. They don't want any problems. Politically everybody wants to be friends with all these people. They might go to PTA or parent groups. They <u>might</u>. But they're all busy. They don't want to take the time. They might come out for a police deal, a pothole deal. When you run a local, you can't just have the large issues. You have to have the little issues. I call 'em "pothole fixing."

You have to have something that you draw a group of people together. It might be on this block, on the corner, or on somebody's front lawn. I believe in block clubs. I helped write the community policing and I went all over. But after the mayor changed it, the policing is not the same way that we wrote it.

The block clubs used to meet on the front lawns, in the back yards, on the street corners. If there's a pothole that had to be fixed, we'd get it fixed within a week or we'd do an action. A fast action onto the aldermen, to the Department of Streets and San, that you'd get it done and they're happy. It's a victory. They can see it.

It's not a victory ten years later like the CRA [Community Reinvestment Act]. You're still fighting it—since 1970. I mean the average person doesn't want to fight that over and over. They want to see things done right away.

Helen Murray: Gale gave courage and encouragement to women in organizing. It was okay to be a woman leader, but it wasn't okay to be an organizer [into] this kind of holding meetings, kind of military talk, kind of tough stuff.

In the first days that we were having these meetings, there were only about 30 or 35 local organizers in Chicago from the West Side Coalition, and, besides myself, there was one other woman out of thirty-five. And Gale, her very presence… The guys might have given us a hard time, but they weren't going to give us a hard time and get Gale pissed off too.

From The Ford Foundation Archives
HTIC Technical Assistance Proposal **(March 5, 1975):**
    After seven years of experience in local community organizing, dealing with a multitude of urban issues, Gale Cincotta and Shel Trapp organized the Westside Coalition in 1969. This coalition was made up of brown, black, and white ethnics, and focused on the issues related to neighborhood decline and deterioration. The Westside Coalition won significant reforms: prosecution of unscrupulous realtors, change in FHA procedures to benefit consumers, specific reinvestment commitments and review process of rejected applications from local financial institutions. At this point in the Coalition's development, it became evident to Ms. Cincotta and Mr. Trapp that they were dealing with issues that needed a broader base of support and understanding if neighborhoods, not only in Chicago, but across the nation, were to be saved from decay.

    Gayle Brinkmann: Gale was great. She was so smart; she was a genius. She was very political and she knew how to distill issues in a way that they could be understood by everybody. I remember saying, "I never ever thought we could pull people out and the issue was the Federal Home Loan Bank Board!" This is a whole different thing from your schools, your garbage, the slum on the corner. It was a very exciting time. It was a real education for a liberal from the suburbs.

From the *Chicago Daily News* (March 5, 1976)
Women taking over the reins in fight to save neighborhoods
By Karen Hasman
    Gale Cincotta: "It made me damn angry that anyone could have power over you – to be able to make decisions for you," Mrs. Cincotta said. "Women see that all the time.
    Women have always been the workers in community organizations. Men were usually the leaders. But finally the women decided to compete for the leadership. I'd never been told at home that I shouldn't do such things."

    Michael Westgate: It takes a lot of troops to effect change. The pools which typically provided the people-power during this period were non-working mothers and college students. They were motivated largely by self-interest, wanting a better education and living environment for their kids, but also by idealism.

Today those with time on their hands—and boredom—are the retired. Will they become the most involved in the future? Their perspectives are different. Will they return to the idealism some of them had in the 1960s and '70s or will they be looking out for their own self-interest in the '10s? Will they push for better education, with higher taxes, or will they push just for lower taxes? Will they respect the aspirations of immigrants and others or will they try to close the door behind them?

There are now much more sophisticated ways of alerting large numbers of people very quickly over the Internet. But does this make it easier or harder to galvanize enough public opinion to start to change public policy, be it predatory lending or rats in the neighborhood? Everyone likes to quote the former House Speaker Tip O'Neill, that "all politics is local." Politicians respond to the local base that elects them. Women made the difference in Chicago and continue to with National People's Action. Who will be the leaders and community organizers of the future?

Bud Kanitz: When Gale campaigned to become president of OBA, it was a knockdown, drag-out fight from what Gale told me. Because [the other candidate] Justin McCarthy asked, "Do you really want to have a woman head your organization?" It was just brutal. And, of course, Alinsky himself was a sexist. Gale met Alinsky a couple of times and, it seems to me, even got into it with Alinsky.

Justin McCarthy was active in Austin begnning in the 1960s and served as president of Organization for a Better Austin: I was born in 1912. We came back to Chicago in 1922 when St. Thomas Aquinas Church [5112 W Washington Blvd, closed in 1998] was being built. I started working at the *Sun Times* in 1936. I worked with the printers, making up the newspaper and writing headlines. I wound up being a fulltime worker as unit chairman of the *Sun Times* newspaper guild. In 1963 I got my house for $18,000. I still had the $10,000 I'd saved up by being four years in the United States Coast Guard.

I met Gale as a result of the Organization for a Better Austin. There was a convocation of people from the parishes and the schools and from the parent-teachers organization. And there were people in this area who were very active and very upset about the transition thing that was going on here. Gale was very militant and a well-organized organizer. She was very deeply versed in the parent-teachers organizing and so she was a natural to be a part of this convention of people from all over the Austin area.

Ann Vick-Westgate: So what were the things that made Gale effective? What did she do, either tactics or qualities she had?

Justin McCarthy: Well, her militant passions and her eloquence in bargaining and representing a voice of the people. The way a union negotiator talks when he talks to the company's managers, he can swear at 'em and make some kind of an argument. They'll have to answer in words but it'll show up that they're only interested in keeping the employees' wages down. But she was a natural. She was really <u>born</u> for the role she played in this organization and later on, she and Shel Trapp. They had something that was pure and it grew and it's still going. Gale was a natural and she was a natural fighter.

Bud Kanitz: Gale respected Alinksy's tactics if not necessarily agreeing with some other things. She respected his whole framework. A lot of people assumed or thought that Alinsky was some raving communist. He was actually such a red, white and blue American and believer in the capitalist system and everything. But it was interesting that his major contention was that when you get to the source of problems in the U.S. society, what you track them to is the banking system. Now Gale never knew that when she started the redlining fight. But it's a specific example of what Alinsky said coming true.

George Knight: I first met Gale at NCO [Northwest Community Organization], because we were trying to get the leadership between the organizations together. There were off and on attempts by the Industrial Areas Foundation [IAF, Alinsky's organization] to get the different groups that were IAF-affiliated together, sometimes through beer. Which I guess is instructional too.

Most of the organizations, we met late at night, after the community meetings so that staff meetings were typically from 10:00 p.m. to 1:00 a.m. But we didn't start again until 10:00 or 11:00 a.m. And Saturdays were half-days. We got to go home by 5:00 or 6:00 p.m.

Gale would not have billed herself an Alinsky affiliate. And they weren't. I don't think they were when they started. But I think the churches hired IAF to start NCO and Gaudette was the IAF employee. I came in right as Gaudette was leaving and Bob Johnsen was coming in.

Ed Bailey, past president of Organization for a Better Austin: I've been in the neighborhood for 35 or so years. I moved into the neighborhood in 1966. I've been president of the South Austin Coalition for around 25 years... Prior to 1966, there was a lot of excitement in the community, which brought on people anticipating blacks going to move in and ruin the neighborhood. Well, it was very serious business.

Now, the movement of blacks on the West Side, it started somewhere east of here. After it got up to Kedzie, then they probably advanced to Kostner. So they were held at bay for a good while at Cicero. They got up to the east side of Cicero. The resistance was stopping them at Cicero. Resistance: people didn't want them to advance into their community.

Now we had a crucial point there. I remember well one weekend, in 1966, when one or two families moved in across on the west side of Cicero, on this side. There was a rumor, "Well, the blacks done broke the barrier." And that started the whole stampede of whites moving out and blacks moving in.

Now OBA was an organization that, from all practical purposes, their mission was to stabilize the community and absorb the migrants. Not tear up the neighborhood, but keep the neighborhood viable. In addition to people moving in, keeping people in. That was about that time I moved in. Then I was invited to join OBA. I figured I'm going to join them. A lot of people joined black and white. We had a convention. OBA was set up something like the way the government is set up. We had districts and various precincts. Various sections where this group was the head of this and that was the head of that. We generally had our convention at Austin High School and we filled the place up, standing room there. They had good speakers. One year they had the State's Attorney.

They were responding to the conditions, to the redlining, to realtors coming in and spreading fear. They got a name for that: panic peddling. Also they were responding to the City. I do say the City and I mean it. The way the City responded to the in-migration by just really cutting off services, and schools were part of it. They just abandoned the neighborhood. I can't think of it any other way. Because there was Austin High School, one of the top high schools in the city. All these schools had very high standings. Right after that, here they are, everything began. Curriculum and everything began to get a little lower, a little lower.

It was told to me by reliable sources that wherever they had really good equipment —you know what it was then – high tech then was typewriters, mimeographs and all that, they would move it out. The faculty would leave. You had quite a turnover in faculty. Then, on the other hand, there's a lot of the faculty that wanted to stay. Now I want to be perfectly clear on that. Not every white person wanted to leave. Lots of white people bought into OBA's idea of "Let's stay here and keep the neighborhood nice, we can live with this situation." And become neighbors. A lot of them felt that way about it.

Bud Kanitz: After the education fights, the big issue in OBA was "panic peddling" or "block busting." And that was essentially the block-by-block change from a white neighborhood to a black neighborhood. And FHA was part and parcel of all of this.

I remember in the NCO neighborhood that all of a sudden there were a whole bunch of "For Sale" signs in a neighborhood we called NWCA, bounded by North, Western, California and Armitage Avenues. These were wooden houses. When they were originally built, they were just outside of the city limits, so therefore didn't have the brick and stone code requirements that a lot of other neighborhoods inside the city had. Well, it turned out that

FHA had just declared that four square block area eligible for FHA loans. So therefore the realtors, panic peddlers, went in there and started putting up flyers and panicking people. You know, "Better sell your house now when you can still get a good price."

That issue not only affected OBA but it also affected NCO and, obviously, Our Lady of Angels. That was why it was natural for the West Side Coalition that Gale put together to attack panic peddlers and also go after FHA. This was something that seemed to be happening in lots of other cities too.

Michael Westgate: OBA was not without its critics. In a December 5, 1971 article entitled "The battle tactics of the OBA," Franklin Dunlap, a reporter for the *Chicago Tribune*, describes OBA's confrontations, led by Gale, with father and son realtors, Frank and Jerry Rustin, including a march on the elder Rustin's home and 250 people turning out for a meeting with him in a church basement. Cincotta, "an articulate and firey woman," lectures Rustin on the morality of their actions and threatens extended legal action if his son does not halt speculation in Austin real estate.

In a counterpoint Dunlap concludes with Eilene McCaffrey, a leader of the Austin Town Hall Assembly (THA), who attacks OBA for demoralizing the community with their negative descriptions of the neighborhood and their picketing. She accuses OBA and their partners of creating problems to provide training opportunites for organizers and to raise money, calling Alinsky and Gaudette "parasites preying on the problems of the people."

There was clearcut redlining and blockbusting in Chicago. The real estate system fueled and was fueled by racial intolerance. Not that these practices did not happen elsewhere, but they were deeper and more widespread in Chicago than in many other cities. The brokers and others working with them would buy up real estate at depressed prices then sell them, often at inflated prices, to minorities. Entire residential blocks in Chicago were changing hands on this basis in the 1960s-1970s.

From *Journal of Urban History*, vol. 29, no. 4, pp. 394-420 (2003) article by Amy E. Hillier quoting her own University of Pennsylvania electronic dissertation (2001): "Redlining in the Home Owners' Loan Corporation"

Redlining is a practice of denying credit to certain neighborhoods because of their racial or ethnic composition. The origin of the term can be traced to the color-coded "Residential Security Maps" of major American cities produced by the Home Owners' Loan Corporation (HOLC), a New Deal agency created in 1933. Each map had four different classifications ranging from most to least desirable: green, blue, yellow, and red.

Most desirable were the green areas. They were ethnically "homogeneous" and worthy of loans in "good times or bad." The second and third grade areas were blue and yellow. Least desirable were the red areas. According to the maps, they had "detrimental influences in a pronounced degree" and an "undesirable population [disproportionately black] or an infiltration of it." During the late 1930s, the Federal Home Loan Bank Board (FHLBB) used the maps as a basis for its loans. It rarely gave loans to red areas, hence the term redlining. The federal government provided the maps to banks and developers who often used them as a basis for their own loan ratings.

Gayle Brinkmann: We owned a house in the suburbs. We listened to Tom Gaudette and we were activists and we thought that this would be a good thing to do. So we sold our house and moved onto the West Side. The church was not active; the parsonage was for rent so we rented there. And three weeks later the first black family moved west of Laramie.

We had foster children at the time and the foster child that we had was mixed race. We invited the new family over for dinner, very nice, but the neighbors were not very happy with us. By that time some of the people knew us, and they warned us to keep our kids' beds away from the windows. And they parked their Cadillacs out in front. There were Greek neighbors.

Paul Brinkmann, Gayle's husband: They firebombed the black family's home.

Gayle Brinkmann: And some of the neighbors hung an effigy on their porch too. So it was tense there. There were a lot of blockbusters. OBA wanted the people that lived there to recognize who the real enemies were. They weren't the other people looking for a house or the people afraid of their property values falling. The enemies really were this whole real estate system and the housing markets and the schools. So there were a lot of neighborhood meetings and we got involved. And that's how I first met Gale.

I got very interested in the OBA staff meetings that would be held in the evening. There would be meetings all the time, every day. So I started going to the staff meetings and listening to them all talk. Gale lived about three blocks from us so I would give her a ride home because she did not drive. So we just got to be friends. And I got to be friends with a lot of the staff people there too. Ruth Walther lived about a block from us and she was a very conservative lady. So we ran the spectrum of political beliefs. It really was a community that was focused on where the real enemies were, as opposed to each other.

Ed Bailey: What made Gale a good leader of these kinds of organizations is that Gale was always very aggressive, very on top of the issues, very enthused. And she was always making a very good talk wherever. Then, as Secretary, she didn't shy away from taking hold of an issue. She would fight an issue to the very end. That's how she emerged as that person that we were willing to follow. Even after she left here, we were willing to follow her.

Gayle Brinkmann: We had a friend named Mary Wallace who had four kids. We used to go down and meet with the School Board staff and she would always bring her kids and they were supposed to do as much as they could to disrupt things. She said if she could teach them to throw up on call, she would have done that too. It was guerilla tactics. They didn't ignore us, but if it had only been a few people, they could have.

We used to go down to Housing Court and we would get into elevators that they didn't want us to and go up to their offices. And pretty much make a lot of trouble for them so that they would sit down and meet with people from the community. We had the issues and, when you looked at them, we were on the right side. So it was just a matter of getting everybody's attention and having them sit with you and talk. And know that, if they weren't interested in that, we might just bring that whole crowd out to their house. So there were a lot of guerilla tactics.

Alinsky was probably the source for some of the tactics. They were all discussed in the staff meeting. A lot of the staff were young people, young men, and later more women got into it. Most of them had not organized before, so it was probably Tom Gaudette knowing it. The way they processed their history sometimes it came from other people, but you really knew that probably this was in the back of their minds. The men were off earning a living. This was the time when there was one worker in a lot of families, or the women were working part-time.

Michael Westgate: Gaudette was a veteran community organizer who founded the Organization for a Better Austin (OBA). Tom moved to the OBA turf from his position as the founding community organizer, with Msgr. Jack Egan, of the Industrial Areas Foundation (IAF) Chicago organizing project called the Northwest Community Organization (NCO). At that time, he was still a part of Alinsky's IAF.

From *The Chicago Reader* (Dec. 21. 2001)
The Good Neighbor: Community activist Gale Cincotta's work was never done, by Christopher Hayes

Back in the 70s, when Gale Cincotta first began organizing her Austin neighbors to fight for better housing policy, the Organization for a Better Austin decided to take a local slumlord to the city's housing court. The OBA spent weeks building its case, prepping the witnesses, and negotiating with the defendant's attorney, but when the big day arrived, the judge found an error in the case and dismissed it on a technicality.

"We left the courthouse befuddled, bewildered, like sheep without a sheepdog," recalls Shel Trapp, Cincotta's long-time colleague. "Then Gale became our sheepdog." They should go directly to the state's attorney's office and demand that the suit be filed again. As she led her posse of 30 residents toward the office, a young lawyer spotted them and tried to slam the door shut. Trapp got his foot in the door, and he and the lawyer wrestled back and forth. "I stand for law and order!" the flustered young attorney exclaimed. "Get away from my door!"

Cincotta cleared Trapp away and then slammed into the door shoulder first, knocking the attorney to the floor. As the group filed into the office, Cincotta stood over the bewildered attorney and yelled, "You stand for shit!"

Helen Murray: Shel was Gale's main strategical teacher. But I think she learned a lot from Tom Gaudette when she first started, when OBA first started. Absolutely. But he was at his peak at that point. Then it was Shel more. The tradition of sit-ins or hits on people's houses or offices was our organization's style. I used to think that it was Alinsky style, because I'd been taught all that stuff about Alinsky and everything. Then you'd watch the films on Alinsky and he would go into town and talk. I was shocked. We were always told as organizers, "The worst thing you can do is have your name in the paper! The leader had their name in the paper, and you were... dah, dah, dah." Then I watched this old black and white film of Alinsky when he was up at Eastman Kodak and he flies in on a plane. After talking to people and telling them what to do, he talks to the press. It was like, wait a minute!

So I think his was different. It was more institutional. He would come in and he'd say, "You have to do this, this and this. And your organizations can get together and you do this." Whereas we were really in the grassroots.

So Gale and Shel were bringing in a new style. Gale and Shel more than Tom. Tom was brilliant in a sense of strategy, but Tom started NCO for Alinsky. Then Tom went out and started OBA, and Alinsky said, "It'll never work in a mixed neighborhood." So they had this big fight. They didn't talk for years. It was great stuff. I mean it was like a soap opera.

Austin was a neighborhood that didn't have solid institutions. This was a neighborhood that its institutions were in flux. In the Back of the Yard, Alinsky was working with unions. And at TWO [The Woodlawn Organization], he was working with black churches and black businesses. At NCO [Northwest Community Organization], he was working with churches. And then here, you go out there and they're in flux. The churches that are in those neighborhoods are not black churches. They're white churches. And the neighborhood was changing radically. It was a very working class, middle class community in the beginning. The first black people coming in were working class, middle class people with kids... But you don't have an institutional base out there. Gaudette had moral or ethical values and not just organizing. He really wanted to make integration work. A lot of us did.

Ed Bailey: There's always another problem creeping in. I don't know what the people'd do in this community if you didn't have a community. And the community's got to be strong. You can't be weak. Now I'm not one to get close to the City because I'm like Lincoln. Lincoln was a very strong, hefty man and he took one guy and threw him out of his office one day. And another guy said, "Mr. Lincoln, why'd you throw that man out?" And Lincoln said, "Got too close to my price!" So the guy was almost about to bribe him and he just got him and throwed him out of his office. So I try to keep track. I don't want to try to get too close to the price.

That temptation is always out there. The alderman is always doing something good. Just like we're getting a new facility here. Well, I've probably got to deal with that now because they will probably want us – "Now that we did this for you, what are you going to do for me?" And all like that. You rub my back. You got to watch that. You expect to advance your people but you guys got to watch that because after a while, after so long a time, you'll be part of the establishment. And when you become part of the establishment, who are the people going to look to you?

Michael Westgate: The problems with the schools were largely race-based. The school population was directly linked to where people lived. It was the dynamics of the housing market which determined who could and would live where. So it was a natural progression for Gale and other leaders to move from school issues to housing issues. Although there may have been earlier references to redlining, OBA was the first group in the nation to organize against bank redlining

From Case Study by Hallahan (11/7/91)

Kirk Hallahan: In 1972, redlining as a term was virtually unknown. Cincotta claims that she and her group popularized the term, although NPA might not have been the first to coin the phrase. (5)

Shel Trapp: Bruce Gottschall [retired Executive Director, Chicago Neighborhood Housing Services] was starting to get into the FHA stuff and then in '71, this is how the whole redlining thing started. I was in the office at NCO and this Italian guy comes in, and he is just ripshit. His son had just gotten out of the military and he wanted his son to buy a house that was for sale on the block. He had visions of his son having a family and he'd be real close to his grandkid. They'd gone to National Security Bank, which was the bank right here on the corner of Ogden, Chicago and Milwaukee.

The banker said, "Well, we don't make loans in that neighborhood." But they were investing in a development in Schaumburg and he talked the kid into buying a house in Schaumburg. So the Italian father, he was one of our leaders, just ripped, "What the hell is NCO going to do about that?"

What the hell are you going to do? Of course the banks aren't going to make loans in this neighborhood because at that time this neighborhood was an asshole. I mean it was really the shits. Property values were going down, and when people would inherit a house, they wouldn't even put it on the market. That's why we had so many homes that we had to knock down. They'd just walk away from them. Maybe rent it for a year or two and then it would be so torn up they'd just leave it.

Well, then as the Great Spirit would give you gifts, a couple days later this Puerto Rican guy comes in and he's ripped 'cause he's got a very good small business on Division Street and he'd gotten to the place where his business was big enough he wanted to buy the storefront next to him so that he could expand. And he'd gone to National Security for a loan and they'd said, "Absolutely not. Division Street's a riot area." And it's because Hispanics had businesses on Division Street that it was a riot area. He wanted to know what the hell was NCO going to do about this. And he was one of my Puerto Rican leaders. I thought, "Oh fuck! I don't know nothing."

Then somebody brought it up at a board meeting. "Oh yeah, National Security Bank. They suck." "Oh, they turned my brother down for a loan." I knew we had to do something. So I said, "Okay." We got a group of leaders together, went over to the bank, had an appointment – very nice – with the president. And at that time there was no branching in Chicago, so a group from the neighborhood wants to meet with the president of the bank, no big deal. The president sat there all day long.

Italian guy tells his story; Puerto Rican guy tells his story, all very low-key. Just what is this problem? Bank president – I could have kissed the son of a bitch – said, "Well, of course we don't make loans in this neighborhood. Haven't you looked around? It's a slum!" I thought, "Oh, I love you."

Suddenly this very low-key meeting erupted, people screaming and hollering for fifteen minutes. We storm out and go back to NCO offices. "What are we gonna do?" "We're gonna kill that guy!" So then nobody knows what the hell to do. "Let's picket!" NCO's famous for pickets. We had a very tough, powerful organization. "Alright."

So the next Saturday we show up with about a hundred and fifty pickets. We're outside, and people going in and out of the bank said, "It's great somebody's doing something." "Man this is marvelous!" Several squad cars and a paddy wagon were there. I think we might even have had some press. People had a great time. Go back home. No reaction out of the bank. That was before we'd learned about storming in and taking over.

"Okay. We're going to go back next Saturday." We go back next Saturday and we've got about sixty to seventy people. And people went, "Oh, that's great. Keep it up." They're going in and out. "These are bad guys." Go back home. It's getting rough.

For some reason – I'd been to many slum landlords' homes – I never thought of going to a bank president's home. So we go back the third Saturday and we've got about thirty people there. "Oh, fuck. This thing's dying in front of me." We go back to the office. "Okay. What are we gonna do?" Someone says, "Alright. Let's hit 'em where it really hurts. Let's all take our money out." I'm looking around the table and I'm thinking, "Yeah." So I got a bunch of sheets of paper and said, "Everybody put what we got in the bank on a piece of paper. Don't sign your name. Fold it over." So we did it, got the adding machine out, totaled her up. It was something like $19,000. Forty-four million in assets, we have $19,000 to hit 'em where it hurts!

I said, "I don't think that's going to bother them too much." And we're talking along. Jo Koziel said -- she's still alive. I always call her what Rosa Parks was to the civil rights movement Josephine Koziel was to the redlining issue – "We've got one or two blacks, four or five Hispanics, five-six Italians, five-six Polish." That's the way NCO was then, a real mixed community. She says, "Well, why don't we have a bank-in?" I said, "Well, Josephine, some folks here might not be familiar with that." I didn't say, "Including me." "Why don't you explain that to us." She turns to the blacks and Hispanics and says, "Well, you people are doing it all the time! You're sitting in here, laying in there."

Michael Westgate: Under Illinois unitary banking law, each bank could only have one branch. The bank president was not far removed from his customers.

Shel Trapp: We started talking about what a bank-in would look like. So the next Saturday we had the first ever bank-in. I think they had five teller windows. We had about five people lined up to go to each teller window and they'd come up and say, "I want to put a dollar in my savings account." That's when you still had a passbook. And the teller would ring it up. "Oh, I'm sorry. I meant I want to take a dollar out of my account." The teller had to go back and do it. The next person would come up, "I want a dollar worth of pennies but I don't trust your rolls. Count 'em out for me." "Well, lady, our rolls are perfectly…" "No. Count 'em out. I don't trust 'em. I was cheated here once last week." Teller would count a hundred pennies. The person would go to the back of the line, come back up, "I want to put this into my savings account but, you know, I got so many pockets, I don't think there's a hundred of 'em left here. So you're gonna have to run 'em through the change machine or count 'em."

In that day in history, drive-in windows were new phenomena—a marvelous thing when somebody had a drive-in window. The bank had just put in one drive-in window. That was all they had but it was a great new phenomenon. So we had a school bus and we pulled that up there and had five people on the school bus doing the same thing. People started to get into it. One thing we've found out in the fight, everybody instinctively hates banks. I don't think I've ever met a person that likes banks yet except maybe bankers. And people were standing in line behind our people and seeing this thing going on, "Here's my paycheck. I'd like it in one dollar bills." People just joined in!

"Also I'd like ten dollars in quarters but I don't trust your rolls. Count out the quarters." So they started joining in. They didn't go to the back of the line but they did slow things down. So pretty soon the whole lobby's full. But I'm starting to really get antsy 'cause this has been going on about an hour now. Man, I could tell the folks were burning out on this thing. "Oh geeze, how do we get out of this damn thing with dignity?" And I can't come up with anything. Josephine is mucking around with a couple bucks worth of pennies. And she was standing in the middle of the bank and looking at her pennies, "Ah shit!" And throws them on the bank floor.

I didn't think anything of it. Bank guards come running from all over. "What the hell's all this about?" And then it hit me. It's like if the priest had just blessed the sacrament and thrown it on the floor! Oh dear, here's the sacrament on the floor! So they scoop 'em all up, put them in her hand. And Josephine, who at that time was in late fifties, early sixties, and the guard was probably the same age, maybe older. She looks at the guard and says, "Young man, I said, 'Ah, shit!'" and throws 'em on the floor. And I'm thinking, "Okay, something's going on here. I don't quite know what, but it's looking good." And so I went to another person, I said, "Is your money in pennies now?" "Yeah." "Throw it on the floor and yell, "Ah, shit!" "I don't know why. Do it!"

So about two or three people did this, and suddenly the bank president's door opens up. Runs out, "What's going on? Who's in charge?" So he said, "Okay. What do you want?" "We want a meeting with you this afternoon and your board of directors at two o'clock." And he said, "Alright, alright." So we stop the action and go back to the office and I'm thinking, "What the hell are the demands? We don't have any damn demands! We just want to talk about this thing." So we're sitting there, "Okay. How about four million in first mortgages and four million in small business loans? How about that for a demand?" "Okay. That sounds good." And then, as we're getting in the cars to go back for the meeting, somebody said, "Let's put in a thousand dollar contribution to NCO." At that time we were tight on money. A thousand dollars then was a big chunk of change. So we go back. I should have asked for five thousand but I wasn't smart enough then.

Did we specify interest rates? We knew nothing about it. I didn't. Just whatever the going market was. Any loan was better than no loan. We didn't think about speculators or anything. Go in. Board is there. Had the meeting. We walked out. Four million first mortgages, four million small businesses, a thousand dollars to NCO. We actually brought the check back with us to the office. And that was it. We had a big party and thought, "Okay. That's terrific. The issue's all over." No monitoring committee. Nothing. I'm clueless if one loan ever went out.

So we're back to our usual issues of housing, and somebody in the neighborhood at Milwaukee and Damen, where we had another power base, called up and said, "I heard about that thing you guys did down there with National Security. Can we do the same thing at Fairfield Savings and Loan?" "Yeah. Sure you can. Why not?" "They're not making any loans in our neighborhood either. We don't like that." So I sent a couple leaders up there to teach the folks there how to do it, and they had a bank-in at Fairfield. And it just kind of spread that way.

It was shortly after that that we formed the West Side Coalition: that was NCO, Our Lady of Angels Parish Committee and OBA. Because Gale and I had sat down and said, "Look. We're working on the same issues here. Why don't we do something, get something bigger?" And so we got some leaders from OBA, Our Lady of Angels. That was very interesting because Our Lady of Angels was a parish group. This guy that I had trained started it. It was basically an all-white Italian group, basically keep-em-out racists. Father Dodaro was the priest there.

So we got leadership from all three groups. This is pretty interesting. Gale would roll in with black leaders. I'd come with Italian, Polish, Hispanic, and occasionally a black. We had a very small black area in NCO. Then all these white guys who just hated blacks and Hispanics. OBA was pretty much all black because the real guts and power in OBA was South Austin. And whites would come occasionally but very seldom. And so there we'd be. And Al Velto who was the staff for Our Lady of Angels he just laughed, "My guys really hate those meetings, but as they say, 'We need them niggers.'" And so we formed this very tough coalition and started fighting.

Our first fight basically was FHA. We hadn't really started on the banks yet, but it was FHA. We could produce close to a thousand people, the three of us, three organizations together. Our first issue actually was the panic peddlers, Sky Realty. I had fought him back in Austin when I was there and then at Our Lady of Angels he was starting on their southern end to panic peddle there, and he was on the southern end of NCO [Northwest Community Organization] panic peddling. So that was our first issue. We got together, "What are we going to do with this guy?"

We decided four nights in a row to picket, and he had several offices. Tuesday, Wednesday, Thursday, and those three nights each one of the organizations would take a night. We started out with the weakest one, which was Our Lady of Angels. They went the first night, the OBA went, then we went. Then on Friday night we all went and marched down Belmont Avenue. He lived a block off Belmont. We marched down; we basically just shut the street down.

We were aiming for his house and started on the corner of Austin and Belmont which was an all-white area. There's a Catholic

Picketing realtors was a standard tactic in Austin in the 1960s.

high school. We marched two blocks east then on Belmont and then one block south. We had close to a thousand people. And cops were going nuts, "You can't block the street." "Well, talk to the leaders. Don't talk to us." So we got to his house and all the neighbors are, "What the hell is going on?" I mean the whole street is wall-to-wall people. He's terrified. He agreed to no solicitation and that was basically our demand. But that really welded the group together, in that we had blacks, whites, Latinos and they suddenly saw, "Hey. We're not so bad. We need each other."

Michael Westgate: The issue is not initially who is moving in so much as it is who is moving out. With a fully built-out neighborhood, where there is no new construction possible, if no one moves out, there are no buildings for anyone to move into. It is sometimes the closest-knit communities, Jewish or Greek for example, where a group mentality may set in and people make a collective decision either to stay or to disperse or to move to another community. People move out and others move in, often in waves.

Mary Volpe: You work in waves. You're a usually white European area that most of them are senior citizens living there, an older area. And then the first wave comes in. It's usually Asian, Filipino in our area. And then they move them in gradually all around. People don't have the problems with the Filipinos coming in. They sell. And you get an abundance of real estate people. We had 300 driving around here, working out of their cars. The next wave comes in is Spanish, Latino or something like that. And the Filipinos remained for them. And then the realtors won't show any whites anything for three miles away, two or three miles square. They jump to the next thing. They'll push.

Michael Westgate: The profits in the real estate industry are associated with change. New construction provides employment and profit for developers, construction firms, realtors, mortgage brokers, lawyers and others, some operating on a commission basis. But in older neighborhoods like Austin there is little new construction; it is a change in ownership of existing buildings that provides the greatest opportunity for profit. There was discrimination, steering and block busting, all of which fueled change.

Mary Volpe: You can come in with the same size family as a black. In my organization we did testing. We'll send a black family in. We'll send different families with the same structure, same amount of kids, same income. They won't show them anything there. All of a sudden they cut off Filipinos and move them to another location and Spanish to another location. They manipulate the whole setting, to maximize the turnover because they're paid on a commission.

And then you get the voices in the middle of the night threatening, "You've got a daughter and we're moving in" with a heavy black dialect. You know, scare treatments. It doesn't have to be a black on the telephone. It's just somebody with a dialect. For some reason this country will accept people from other lands before they'll accept American blacks that have been here since the start of the country. Which is ridiculous.

Michael Westgate: Later, as they discovered these issues were not confined to Austin or even to Chicago, Gale and Shel and others shifted their focus and their organizational base from their neighborhood to citywide and to national, founding and utilizing Metropolitan Area Housing Alliance (MAHA), National Training and Information Center (NTIC) and National People's Action (NPA) and involving groups from around the country, as well as Chicago, who wanted to take action in addressing the problems they all confronted. Gale had a genius for seeing a few isolated problems and saying "I think that is a national problem."

By the early 1970s, Americans began to realize that both the public sector and the private sector were abandoning the country's urban centers. Federal programs had funded highway systems facilitating the move out to suburban areas where land was cheap. Gas prices were lower than European countries due to favorable tax rates for oil companies and low taxes at the pump. Public transportation had been allowed to sink into disrepair and disuse or in some cases had been bought out, as was Los Angeles' excellent trolley system by General Motors.

Austin was a microcosm illustrating the dynamics which had led people to escape problems in Europe, moving first to the eastern U.S. then further and further west, and repeated on a smaller scale as people moved further and further out from older center cities into the countryside. Both the banks and particularly the Federal Housing Administration (FHA) were offering favorable rates and terms for home mortgages in the suburbs. Brokers, appraisers, loan officers and bank regulatory officials all reinforced each others' attitudes in establishing a system which favored those who had money and were white, to the detriment of the less affluent and minorities. Policies and procedures, whether by design or not, whether consciously racial or not, influenced many of the upwardly mobile toward the suburbs. Seemingly innocent rules, such as those at the Federal Home Loan Mortgage Corporation (FHLMC, now Freddie Mac, part of the Federal Home Loan Bank System when I was there) required appraisers to determine whether or not their appraisal was within 10% of surrounding properties on a per square foot basis. Rules like this threw up appropriate red flags in the relatively uniform suburbs but raised real questions about loans in cities where diversity of buildings as well as population were the norm. Discriminatory practices made it difficult if not impossible for minorities even of the same income to compete with whites for better housing, better neighborhoods, and better schools.

In some cities, Chicago being the most blatant I am familiar with, racism was pervasive. The *Chicago Tribune* reported on a poll in late 2008 which concluded that Chicago was still the most racially divided city in the U.S. ["Chicago, America's most segregated big city. Racial lines were drawn over the city's history and remain entrenched by people's choice, economics," by Azam Ahmed and Darnell Little, December 26, 2008]

Caught in a combination of racial change and mismanagement, fourteen Chicago savings and loan associations insured by the Federal Savings and Loan Insurance Corporation, FSLIC, went bankrupt in the early 1970s. I was the Assistant to the Director of FSLIC and I saw, first-hand, racial attitudes and epithets, apartment buildings foreclosed on by FSLIC where all the pipes had frozen literally because rocks had been delivered among the coal, ruining the equipment feeding the furnaces. Sheer, sometimes deliberate, mismanagement was rampant.

FSLIC was the sister agency to FDIC. We insured depositors at Savings and Loan Associations in the same way that FDIC insured those at commercial banks. It was created under the National Housing Act of 1934 and dissolved in 1989 when its responsibilities were merged with FDIC in 1989 in the wake of the S&L debacle.

In the '70s Chicagoans were growing more and more angry. Middle class working neighborhoods were declining rapidly. Bankers were largely correct in saying they could not, individually, responsibly, make conventional loans if no one else did. FHA loans were almost the only ones, besides some mostly unscrupulous private lenders, being made within red lines overtly drawn in bankers' and insurance company's offices. Between ineptness and fraud, a huge number of homes in poor condition were sold to unsuspecting homebuyers. The buyers were not the only ones to suffer. More recent studies have documented how foreclosures relate to housing values in neighborhoods. For each foreclosure in a neighborhood, overall values decreased by up to 1.8%, according to a 2005 study by the Woodstock Institute, *There Goes the Neighborhood: The Effect of Single-Family Mortgage Foreclosures on Property Values* by Dan Immergluck and Geoff Smith.

Austin, on Chicago's west side, had one advantage over many of the other neighborhoods in Chicago. It had been a separate city until 1899 and had its own city hall, shopping area, traditions and identity with which people could identify. But Austin was in the throes of change when the Organization for a Better Austin (OBA) was formed by residents who wanted to change the way business was done. They wanted to retain Austin's character while welcoming newcomers.

Chicago was and is a very dynamic city – for better and for worse. Politics was and is fierce. If you were an ally of the Mayor (Richard Daley the first) and his establishment, there was access to employment with the city and other public agencies. Through your alderman, you could call on city services. If you were not an ally – or particularly if Daley and his operatives perceived you as an opponent – doors would be closed. Gale knew this. She respected power but was not awed by it. She was completely unafraid to call on the school committee and city hall when they were not providing what her community, Austin, needed.

Racism was overt. The Mayor used it to his advantage, sometimes playing off whites, blacks and Latinos against each other. Daley "knew" that initiatives involving blacks, Latinos and whites working in concert could never stick together for any protracted period or for a multi-layered agenda. Gale was to prove him wrong.

Great demographic changes affected Chicago, with blacks continuing to move north from the South in search of better employment and a better life. Those who came in the earlier movements, during the Depression and World War II, had children and grandchildren, for whom succeeding generations of parents wanted better living conditions and schooling. While the whites emigrated to the suburbs for similar reasons, that was an option denied to blacks and other minorities. Austin was one of their better alternatives.

George Knight: Because OBA and NCO almost abutted along the east/west axis of Chicago really the battle was around blockbusting. OBA was much more aggressively blockbusted than NCO, although there were several attempts and we blocked those attempts very, very vigorously. But OBA was really much heavier on the blockbusting stuff. But, nevertheless, we had an alderman, Tom Keane, who was close to the mayor. So there were a number of reasons why NCO was involved in the thing from Gale's perspective.

Churches were involved. They had to be. The Catholic Church was home to many of the Eastern Europeans who formed a majority of Austin's population in the 1960s. Their parishioners were moving out. Some of the more radical priests embraced various forms of community organizing to deal with the changes in their parishes. The support the priests received from the Cardinal varied enormously. Sometimes the priests were more in step with the Vatican than the Cardinal was.

Cal Bradford, former Professor of Sociology at Northwestern University, public policy expert on housing and banking issues, and board member of NTIC: I was in graduate school and we were all smart folks in graduate school. I was in sociology, so we were especially smart. We all knew that you couldn't organize in racially changing neighborhoods because redneck whites and upwardly mobile blacks… the whole analysis. And that's all OBA and NCO did. Every neighborhood they organized in initially was racially changing. They did what we knew couldn't be done. That's one reason why John McKnight said, "Go down and watch these people. Because you're not going to believe this."

That's one reason that Daley didn't see them as a threat because nobody had ever successfully organized groups like that. And a lot of the neighborhoods they were in were the neighborhoods Daley and company had written off. Daley had this plan that Jim Downs, the consultant, gave him. He was Anthony Downs' son. There's actually this plan. John McKnight is more expert on it than I am.

But the original Daley when he first got to be mayor and the city had all these racial tensions, he commissioned RERC, Real Estate Research Corporation, Downs' outfit, to create this plan. And they actually had this plan and it was a triage plan. It said these are the neighborhoods that are likely to stay white. Put all your organizing in there. These are the ones that are black. You just write them off. And here are the ones that are racially changing, sort of in the middle. And you got to decide what to do with those.

But you didn't write off the black neighborhoods if the leaders were Catholic. You can't understand the Daley machine without understanding that the Catholics and the orthodox Jews could work together because they both understood authority structures. But you couldn't work with the evangelical blacks. That was a really interesting notion that really permeated the machine.

Michael Westgate: HUD, the Department of Housing and Urban Development, in Washington, also had plans drawn up by RERC, Real Estate Research Corporation, a Chicago-based consulting firm specializing in valuation, outlining the stages in decline of urban neighborhoods nationally, showing at what stages HUD would cease supporting local initiatives to rebuild housing or infrastructure.

Joe Mariano worked for NTIC for 20 years and took over as the second NTIC Executive Director after the passing of Gale in 2001: Anthony Downs was a nationally recognized urban planner who came up with the controversial concept of special deconcentration. He purports that having more than a certain percentage of African American or low-income people in a neighborhood is not a good thing.

Cal Bradford: If you looked at all the early blacks who got into power in Chicago, the fire chief, Irwin France, and all these people, they were all Catholics up until maybe almost the time Daley died... A machine has to have a sense of order. And those people grew up with a sense of respecting authority and order. And so did the orthodox Jews. So early on there are several Jews in his administration and they're orthodox Jews. That's just my own sort of sociological thing. But it's an interesting way to look at it.

The neighborhoods that Gale was organizing in, a lot of them, these were neighborhoods where the Catholics were leaving and evangelical blacks were moving in. So, to the Daley machine, they were neighborhoods that were moving to being written off. So you didn't stop the organizing...

The original Daley, he just saw this and he didn't quite understand it. One of the brilliant things about his son is his son really likes these organizations. Of course, his son loves Chicago. Even though there are still remnants of the machine hanging around and a lot of sweet deals to people, Daley the son really loves that city and he loved Gale.

Gale's relationship with the original Mayor Daley wasn't warm at all; sometimes it was confrontational. I think there was some respect there eventually. It took Daley a long time to understand. Partly it was hard for him to understand that she wasn't interested in politics. His son, young Dick, he understands it's the neighborhood people who are concerned about the neighborhoods. And once in a while one of them runs for alderman, but really they don't do that. They're not a threat in that sense.

They're trying to preserve his neighborhoods. I don't think his father ever really understood that. So anybody who did anything in a neighborhood was a threat to the machine. I don't think he understood how to deal with them ever. And didn't develop much respect for them even though they were trying to save his neighborhoods. Those were mostly neighborhoods he'd written off anyway.

I don't recall a lot of personal things about Gale's relationship with the elder Daley. But it was not cordial for the most part. She would invite him and he probably went on a couple tours. He did have some respect for what she was doing. I think he came to understand what she was doing; it just took him a long time. Which is unfortunate because, during the FHA issue, she was the strength that he didn't realize he had, to deal with a lot of serious issues in the city.

Later on, Dick Daley got a lot of pretty good housing people, even before Harold Washington was mayor, ones that were really committed to the neighborhoods. But there were some pretty good people in the planning and housing departments in Chicago and they helped. When they went around trying to plan <u>for</u> the neighborhood, they didn't get along with the organizing groups too much. But when they had to give out block grant money and they had to have people's participation that was always a big issue. So that created a lot of tension with the City because that was <u>all political in Daley's mind</u>, and it was <u>about neighborhoods in her mind</u>.

But I think there was eventually a much higher level of respect when he saw what the neighborhood groups were doing. A lot of it was that they began to do development corporations and had a really incredibly successful Neighborhood Housing Services program. And that was Gale's person. That was Bruce. Bruce worked for her rather than for them. The city had to fight real hard then to do multifamily stuff with NHS, which was really focused on single family. They kept saying, "No. We're not going to do it that way in Chicago." Because the city had to get involved with funding and because the banks were involved, I think NHS was one of the things that made the political relationship better with Daley.

See that's what I think about that sense of redemption. There's always that sense. That's why they drag people, bankers and others, into these neighborhoods. Gale said, "These people were terrified. I know these people were terrified to go in my neighborhood. And, yet, that's the most important thing we can do." People they give awards to, today, people from Harris Bank, those people they had to drag out to those neighborhoods. After a while, all these CRA officers who ended up being the ones who were in charge of these programs at the banks, they always said they were never going to be president of the bank because it was not a line position, but they had more fun than anybody else at the bank. They liked what they did. They're probably happier than anybody else at the banks. They got to do all this neat stuff. There's a lot of fear there.

The foundations have sort of withdrawn. They like to give to development groups. They like to feel they're part of the economic progress. They don't value organizing very highly. Maybe some of their board members don't like what organizing does. So that's part of the problem. So those resources have been taken away. You also had VISTA. The other thing that you had back in the early days was you had government programs where all these young folks from college were sent out into these neighborhoods and they were paid for by federal funds.

Warm, idealistic bodies who wanted to do things. Most of these people were fairly humble. I met a lot of students from different cities who were in these programs and they were sort of radicalized people, but they weren't particularly arrogant. That allowed them to work with the neighborhood people. Because you had to be pretty humble to work with the neighborhood people. You wouldn't survive long if you thought you were Jesus and you were going to save them.

The Church today is a problem for them because it's become more conservative. The powerful evangelical churches are not supportive. And Congress is not either. The staff tells me, they go to Congress, talk to a congressman and they have to start out praying before they do anything. It's scary. They have to show that they're faith-based. Even though they are largely faith-based…

Gale figured it out. It was a good sense of economics she had which was, "Well, economics is about making money. It's not about economic theory. That's just crap… People are out there to make money. Just like the Woodward and Bernstein kind of thing. Follow the money." So that's all we did, none of us having a background in economics either.

We said, "Well, how do you make money?" So we made up this set of actors, of diagrams. Well, mortgage bankers make money. They make money on the sale of the house. So, of course, they're going to screw your neighborhood because they have no other investment because it's fully insured by the government. So, as soon as they make the loan, they get their commission. Loan goes bad, who cares? And that's what Gale was finding out.

So we listened to Gale and we talked and we'd read our own literature. And we said, "Okay." And we just sort of made this little model of how it worked and that would help people think about, "Well, who should I intervene with? Who are the pivotal people to make this work?" And that's how it eventually got to Fannie Mae and Freddie Mac. Because you could see, well, the people who buy the mortgages, the ones who invest in the mortgages, they're the ones that make the flow of money work. So as long as Fannie and Freddie would buy a mortgage, it could work.

And initially Fannie Mae only bought FHA and VA. They didn't buy the conventional loans. They were responsible for a lot of the construction in the city because they were the ones that bought all the loans, unquestionably. Fannie Mae and Ginny Mae would essentially guarantee the payments to the investors. Nobody had any risk. Of course they were wiping out your neighborhoods.

Gale would say, "We want the bankers in there because the bankers have a risk." At the time she said to me, "That's why you need the bankers in your neighborhood. Not because we want to beat them up and make them make loans." She always felt some community groups who got involved in reinvestment never understood that. They just wanted loans. She said, "No. I want good loans. I want the banker to take their sense of risk, and the fact that they have to make money, and figure out how to make that work in my neighborhood."

Michael Westgate: Gale had figured out that the best way, better than any insurance plan, government or private, to ensure healthy neighborhoods was to have financial institutions invested in neighborhoods themselves. Then they would act in self-preservation. That dynamic was systematically diluted, with disastrous results, in the late 1990s-early 2000s as the ultimate risk-takers were almost totally removed from the neighborhoods, sometimes even from the United States. Fannie Mae, Freddie Mac and Wall Street were all culprits in the process.

Paradoxically, Gale demonstrated that there was money to be made, making loans in the inner city. But then unscrupulous lenders and complicit bankers moved in, making loans they knew or should have known were beyond the means of the borrowers to repay. From the pre-CRA times of no loans in redlined districts, we moved to unaffordable sub-prime and predatory loans by lenders unregulated by CRA.

Cal Bradford: Gale always said. "What I want, I want you to take the private creativity of your economy and put it in my neighborhoods." In the sixties everybody thought that activists were pro-government. And sort of left-wing people wanted the government to run things. Gale said, "Really, we hate the government. We don't want the government in our neighborhood. We're trying to get FHA out. We want the private economy to come in our neighborhood and do what it does – except with us."

To her, redlining was sort of this conversion experience. "You don't understand our neighborhoods. You should be in there. There are good opportunities in our neighborhoods to do homeowners' insurance, to make loans, to start businesses. We want to show you what they are. And we're gonna beat the hell out of you to get you to come in our neighborhoods. But it's because we respect the skills that you have as a banker, as a lender. Because we don't know how to do that; we don't want to do that."

She was always sort of against these people who wanted to have too many development corporations that were run by the community groups. She said, "Have someone else do the development corporations. We do the political things, the structural things, because we don't want to learn all that stuff, and we can't do both…"

I learned that was the brilliance that Gale had, you could see right from the beginning. The government was death to your neighborhood. So they always had this funny relationship in Washington. Because, in Washington, it's "Let's see. The pro-business people are the conservative Republicans. And the left-wingy Democrats, they always want the government to run everything." And as long as people thought that way, there was no way to understand NPA. Because it acted radically, but what it had in mind was pretty conservative. It said, "I want you to do all those things for me and get your government control the hell out of my neighborhood." They knew that if you had a neighborhood based in welfare, it wasn't going to work. You had to have jobs; you had to have investment.

From Gale's thinking, people like the Center for Urban Affairs, who did some really creative thinking about neighborhoods and economic development, and the South Shore Bank people who started there, it was out of Gale's movement that those people could see that what she was talking about was replacing the government economy in the inner city neighborhoods with the private economy. The key thing the government had to do was learn how to make investments, not maintenance payments, but investments. Because nobody wants to invest in a neighborhood where no one's got a risk because there's no return. So Gale always believed in risks. It was really a fascinating thing. And she believed that everybody could make money in those neighborhoods. It wasn't always true but…

Liberals didn't quite understand her because she didn't want the government to solve stuff. She was beating up on the government all the time. And the conservatives didn't understand her because she acted radically. But, interestingly enough, when she got inside the meeting hall with Paul Volcker, or with Standard Oil, or with a bank in Chicago, they'd realize that she was talking things they could understand.

At one time there was set of grants that Ford gave where ACORN and NPA and Woodstock, that bunch of people, had to work together. One of the things that drove Gale crazy was that, when you got to a meeting, the ACORN people kept chanting when they got around the table. And she said, "You're in the castle now. Once you get inside, you stop chanting. Now's the time to talk business." It just drove her nuts. "Don't you know how to talk business?" The purpose of organizing was to get the meeting. When you got the meeting, the purpose of the meeting was to move business forward. And, if you didn't understand the difference, she had no time for you because you'd accomplished what you wanted.

Michael Westgate: It was, in large part, Shel's job to get the meeting. It was Gale's job to move business forward. One without the other would have gotten nowhere.

Cal Bradford: They had these radical tactics for people who wouldn't come and talk to them because they worked. Because you could actually beat 'em up and get 'em to the table and embarrass them or something. But their philosophy is very conservative, maybe not reactionary, but it's very conservative.

Gale and Proxmire shared a lot in terms of philosophy. They really got along. That's interesting to see how. And the staff got along really well. Bob Kuttner came out a lot to Chicago and he drafted the Home Mortgage Disclosure Act and the Community Reinvestment Act, the first drafts.

Michael Westgate: In a *Christian Science Monitor* article (October 14, 1977) "A Nation of Neighborhoods: Chicago's West Side – How a community won the redlining battle" Stewart Dill McBride reports how a Federal Home Loan Bank study alerted the West Side Coalition to the facts that their neighborhood and other older inner city neighborhoods got three cents in loans from every $1 they deposited while suburban neighbors got 30 cents of each dollar. Austin's success in fighting this trend "not only proved a neighborhood could stop the 'inevitable' downward spiral predicted and perpetuated by real estate and lending institutions, but it worked as a buffer for neighboring communities."

In the meantime, the tactics employed by Gale and OBA were seen as a threat by the establishment. The Red Squad was a division of the Chicago Police Department actually formed in response to the Haymarket Affair in 1886, and particularly active after the two world wars when Chicago, like the rest of the nation, developed a great fear of Communism.

Shel Trapp: In my Red Squad files, the report says, "Subject preached integration." I never used the word "integration." We were talking about busing, but that was to get our kids a good education 'cause the kids were in rooms seventy kids per classroom, and when we bused 'em out and won, they were in groups of twenty-five.

In the bylaws of OBA, it was two or three years you could be president and then you had to step down. So Gale was stepping down and I'd come over to NCO, but then OBA called me back to be acting director. So I was director at NCO, acting director over there because Gaudette had left.

I was running both organizations and trying to figure out who the hell we're going to run for president. Number one, how do you ever match what Gale did?

We'd had this young black guy who was very articulate, really sharp. And wasn't working. So he was available for daytime meetings. I could never figure that out. He said, "Well, I'm a vet. I'm going to school on the G.I. Bill and they pay me enough that I don't have to work. And so I study and I'm available." Man, this is great! This is marvelous.

So we organized like hell and got him elected president. About a year later I get a call from Anne-Marie and she says, "We just got a call from the *Tribune* and they're going to call you at home tonight." "What do they want?" "Do you not know that Mark Sloane is on the Red Squad?" I said, "What?"

"Oh, Jesus Christ! And I busted my ass off organizing to get him elected president."

The *Tribune* called. So the best way I knew how to deal with it was to treat it as a joke. I said, "Jeeze, if the Red Squad…" Mark Sloane had been very involved with MAHA, Metropolitan Area Housing Alliance, also and a couple meetings had just blown up. There were meetings with the police on crime issues and Mark really screwed up. I attacked him afterwards. "Oh, I lost it, Trapp. I'm sorry. I apologize." "Okay." So that just didn't fit 'cause he was usually right on the issues.

Michael Westgate: In a November 1978 article for *Mother Jones*, "Blackjacking the City Redliners," John Conroy validates Shel's story, "The Chicago police assigned one cop to spy on OBA; eventually he was elected president, and the group seemed to lose its vitality after that." Conroy further cites police ticketing MAHA cars while they were meeting with the mayor, sign up sheets being taken to identify participants at gatherings and elevators being stopped to trap people heading to confront violators and others.

Shel Trapp: I remember TV cameras came out to our little office on Division about Mark Sloane and all that. I went to a file drawer and I said on camera, "Well, if the Red Squad wants to come out, they're free to come and see anything we have here in our files. I don't think we're subversive but they're open." And the police just dove for a foxhole. We just smeared egg all over their face. Of course, Mark Sloane stepped down as president. The organization threw him out. And that's when OBA started to die. We couldn't recover from that.

SACCC [South Austin Coalition Community Council] is basically – even though they claim a much bigger turf – their power base is still my Washington Boulevard Council and my South Austin Council. Then all the other ones started out as white civic groups on the North Side, Mid-Austin Council, Northeast Austin whatever, Northwest whatever they call themselves. They were all civic groups within OBA, and they split off by themselves.

Bud Kanitz: Marcus Sloane, he was a guy from the neighborhood. His mother was active in OBA. He got active in OBA and he ultimately succeeded Gale as the president of OBA. Guess what? He was an undercover cop!

At the same time there was the Red Squad of the Chicago Police Department that was tailing all of us. Now for NCO we had two assigned, Barney Lohan and Tom Mitten were the cops. In subsequent years there was a lawsuit against the Chicago Police Department and the disposition was that they, the Chicago Police Department, had to make their files available, at least to the people that they were spying on.

So I went down to the Chicago Police Headquarters and asked for my file. I made a xerox of it. It is the most complete information that I have of my organizing days at the Northwest Community Organization! Absolutely beyond belief! It had originals, not copies, originals of flyers.

We were in the midst of a huge, huge battle against the Department of Urban Renewal. We organized about twenty neighborhood hearings. So this was, of course, taking on the local politicians, all of whom wanted to tear down the neighborhood and redevelop it. There were my handwritten drafts of flyers or letters that were in this file in the police department. They were not wrinkled up or torn apart and pasted back together or anything like that. They had to go into our office to get the original, handwritten documents; we never could figure out who the spy was. I assume if they had as much as they had on me that they probably have a whole lot more on Gale.

But going back to the Chicago Red Squad connection, it was interesting because after one protest, I had parked substantially farther away 'cause I couldn't find any parking spot nearby the highrise. As I'm walking back to my car here is a Chicago Police van and in it is officer Mario Irrizary who was the community relations cop from <u>my</u> district. Not from Lake Shore Drive but West Town, the NCO area. And I said, "What the hell are you doing here?" Well, he was there; they were spying on Gale. So it shows you the depth of the operation. It was just interesting to me that they imported this guy from the 13th District, Division Street District. He was keeping tabs on what Gale was up to on Lake Shore Drive.

Mary Volpe: You get to know when you're being infiltrated. I was on the list for the Red Squad. Mayor Daley and his police department, along with the federal agencies, decided to put a squad together to infiltrate "unAmerican people." And guess who the unAmerican people were? Anyone giving the mayor a hard time! I got along with Dick Daley in later years. He was the type of man that if he said, "This was green," it was green. He never backed off of it. So you could deal with a man who's honest about that. You might not agree with him but you knew where he stood. Daley also was a prude. You knew that you didn't go meandering off with somebody else's wife or anything. Because he was a family man right down the middle. And his handshake meant something.

He made a lot of politicians. He was the one that made Stevenson. He made presidents and everything. Very brilliant man and he never forgot who you were. You could have been on the picket line throwing eggs at him and five minutes later, he'll be stopping you on the street and saying, "How's your kids, Mare?" There were no hard feelings.

The infiltration went on with people like Gale, people like myself. I had the Feds, she had the Chicago Police Department. You know when your kid comes and says, "Momma, why is that man in that suit going through our garbage? Why are they taking pictures of me in kindergarten?"

Our phones were bugged for four years. Gale said, "Do you have the same Fed watching your family as I have mine?" It was a status symbol. There was a whole slew of us. The problem is right now many of us have died. What's going to happen is some of the laws that we fought against about bugging are back.

It's a law in the city now that you can't picket without getting a license. You can't have a demonstration without a license. Since when did you ever tell where you're going? If you're going to have a demonstration, why do you have to notify them? You don't notify your enemy. Little by little we're being pushed back and we're back to square one.

These cops would be at every meeting with us. They would say, "What clothes are you going to wear tonight so I know how to dress?" This one guy, still a lieutenant over here, he used to say, "How can you stumble so well?" I'd fall on the guy and pat him up and down to find out where his gun was! I knew that he was a plant from the Feds.

We did a lot of things. I took five busloads to Milwaukee. We went in there and there were busloads from all over. They closed the banks in Milwaukee that day and everything. They had the storm trooper police in Milwaukee in those days. I don't know how they are now. But they'd just as soon hit the seniors with a club. So on the way home we stopped at the breweries. And all of a sudden one of the guys in the breweries got on and said, "The Feds are here!" And I said, "Oh? Where?" "They're posing as husband and wife. They showed us their thing." And he swung off. And I said, "Get up. Swing on the other buses and tell 'em so we know where we're standing." They were just bouncing all over the place....

We used to jam the bugging. We'd sit down at a table and go like this (shaking the table) all the way down so, if the table was bugged, it would break the damn thing. Now they can be a mile away and bug you without any little thing. You don't have a chance! There they are outside going and feeling around. I said, "Those days are gone. They all could be down a block somewhere. What are you doing?"

Helen Murray: Oh, God. Marcus! We didn't even know there was a plant then. That didn't come out until later. We just knew there was this nice, great, young guy who came back from Vietnam and had his eyes opened as to "I've got to do more in my community." I mean it kind of fit in. I always thought with Mark Sloane that a part of that was true. Marcus Sloane wasn't that whacked but he really hurt a lot of people. People really liked Mark. He really hurt people. He really damaged the organization. That was the final blow for OBA. And he's a judge now.

George Knight: You could get Gale's police file. That would be the Red Squad. She undoubtedly had an FBI file too.

We used to laugh on the phones. Sometimes the phones would be so heavily tapped that you couldn't hear the other person. You'd say, "Come on, guys. Someone get off the phone. We can't carry on a conversation for you to record if you're all of you on the phone!"

Michael Westgate: The Red Squad, used by Mayor Richard J. Daley and his regime to keep tabs on everyone they considered potential troublemakers, continued in operation until declared illegal by the courts in 1984. According to the website of the Civic Knowledge Project (CKP), the community connections branch of the Division of the Humanities at the University of Chicago, the Red Squad collected information on hundreds of thousands of leftist activists, civil rights leaders and other political dissenters.

CHAPTER 3

"Gale would have been nothing if it wasn't for the Catholic Church."

ROLE OF THE ROMAN CATHOLIC CHURCH

Cal Bradford: I tell you quite frankly I don't think NPA or the neighborhood groups in Chicago at least – and that's where the organizing started – would have existed without the Catholic Church. In the late sixties and early seventies you had a lot of young priests who really wanted to become involved. And they were out of synch with the Church in Chicago, but they were in synch with Rome at the time. They were tolerated. And most of the organizing took place in church basements. They were mostly Catholic church basements because the white neighborhoods that were undergoing racial change were Catholic neighborhoods. They were Eastern European for the most part, white neighborhoods. And the Catholic Church was the center of that community.

That was the main institution because the diocese is all-exclusive. There's a boundary, there's a church, and everybody inside that area goes to that church. So it wasn't like the Protestant stuff where people moved all over the place. It gave you a natural organizing base. The Church supplied a lot of equipment, the mimeo machines, the paper. And a meeting place.

Then there was Catholic Charities. At that time the early money for [Gale's work] came from Catholic Charities. Their first large office, significant office, was in the Catholic Charities building in Chicago on the North Side by the Cathedral. Without that it never would have existed. They had good organizers. You had people come out of the 60s with the organizing background and a sort of a political savvy. But the real resource in the neighborhood was the Catholic Church. That doesn't happen today. It's an unfriendly situation today.

From *An Alley in Chicago: The Ministry of a City Priest*
Margery Frisbie: Popes as far back as Leo XIII in 1891 had written encyclical letters urging Catholics to concern themselves about the plight of the poor and the rights of working people.

Ann Vick-Westgate: What role did the Catholic Church play in Austin?

Justin McCarthy: Oh, they were banking the organization. They were supporting the organization. They also provided meeting places. The pastors of the parishes, just like the Protestant ministers, were active in the OBA.

St. Thomas Aquinas when I was going to school there had like 2500 families. And now the parish is about 300 families and that is supposed to represent four parishes here. There was a big fight around here about which of the four parishes was going to be the one parish. Some of them wanted to keep just a little small group, but it winded (sic) up with just one small parish in numbers.

There were a lot of these pastors who were in the organization while Gale was president. They gradually had to fold up. The reason was race. They were white parishes. A lot of the Catholic parishes were the same way. My married life started in Help of Christians Parish. That now is one of five parishes that have been subsumed by the old St. Thomas Parish which is now Martin de Porres Parish [6423 South Woodlawn Avenue.]

Ed Bailey: The Cardinals in the Catholic Church [in Chicago] took a position on the role of the churches when they were active. Now the one before Cody, Meyer [Albert Cardinal Meyer, 1958-65], he was very into the community, very into doing away with a lot of prejudices. Cody [John Cardinal Cody, 1965-82] came in with a high reputation that he did some stuff in New Orleans on integration. But he didn't follow through to a great extent after he got here.

Now Father Phelan was at Resurrection Church. I was with Father Phelan all the time. I don't talk about Father Phelan too much now because I get too emotional. But I have never seen a man that was so sincere about helping his fellow man as Father Phelan. That's what you might call an "unsung hero." He'd been there since after he came out of school, about 1940, right up into the '80s. Gale, Father Phelan, Father Murray, all of them were tight. And they believed in her too. They believed in her because she would get funding from various Catholics' groups like Catholic Charities.

The only car that Father Phelan ever owned was a 1967 Pontiac that somebody died and left it to him. Everything that he had he put it into the struggle, paying salaries for the staff people and all. Phelan was at Resurrection. That's right around the corner here. But he was not very liked. Cardinal Cody didn't like him. Catholics had a lot of groups. Gale was well into that. Well into with Father Phelan, well into the Catholic set-up so she knew where the money was.

Michael Westgate: The Catholic Church had an enlightened self-interest in preserving Austin as a vibrant community. The more Catholic the neighborhoods stayed, the better for the Church. Hispanics, of course, were primarily Catholic. But blacks tended not to be.

It was to the consternation of some of the clergy who had raised money from their own parishioners that 50% of the people attending OBA's first convention in 1967 were black, particularly as they represented only 15% of the population then. It is clear that the actions of Tom Gaudette and Shel Trapp far exceeded the mandate that the clergy had given them to organize the community. But, had the Church really wanted to stop their efforts, they could have cut off the funding they were receiving from the churches and denied them the use of the parish halls where most of the meetings took place.

Some priests even went on picket lines themselves. The Church under Samuel Cardinal Stritch, Archbishop of Chicago (1946-1958) and Albert Cardinal Meyer (1958-65) was supportive. Cardinal Cody (1965-82) overturned much of the progress made in Austin and elsewhere, banishing Father Jack Egan, a leader of the progressive priests, to Notre Dame.

By its very organization, unlike other churches, the clear boundaries between every Catholic parish are delineated in a way that everyone knows which parish they belong to. Even Jews and others refer to their own neighborhood in Chicago as "in St. Peter's Parish" for example. OBA organized in some respects like the Catholic Church.

Ann Vick-Westgate: What do you see as the role of the Catholic Church in terms of OBA? You said that the parish priests had to fight the Church establishment to keep their parishes open in a changing neighborhood.

Helen Murray: Gale was very close to those guys. They were great supporters of her. But I think they were the outsiders. They were trying to keep those parishes open and make a transition and provide for the kids coming in. The downtown office, Cardinal Cody, was like, "They're not Catholic anymore, white anymore." Those guys were not popular.

George Knight: NCO (the Northwest Community Organization) was 100% Catholic, both diocesan and Polish national church – and one Lutheran church for ecumenical purposes. OBA though was a little more even, but it was mostly Catholic. Jack Egan, Monsignor Egan, played a huge role. Jack and Gale were very close. The churches played a huge role. Even though Gale was Greek Orthodox.

Kathy Desmond, program officer for the national Campaign for Human Development of the Catholic Church and wife of George Knight: When Gale originally organized in the schools, it was out of her kitchen. One of the things she always admired about the Catholic Church was that it was very neighborhood-based. It was very locally based. For Gale her [Greek Orthodox] church was sort of that way, but not explicitly. Her kids were in a Methodist church and it also wasn't so geographically neighborhood-based.

George Knight: Well, that's because the entire West Side was Catholic, so to assemble enough Orthodox or Protestants, except for the

Russian Orthodox enclave at NCO, the Ukrainian Orthodox people, was difficult. You have to understand that. Ask a Chicagoan where they're from and they'll tell you the parish.

Kathy Desmond: The parish priests who were in poor or declining areas generally would have been more open to what I call the "Alinsky model" of organizing because it was directly related to the people and what they were threatened with… But the Geno Baronis, the Jack Egans, these are order priests who never worked in a parish or they had other positions. They were on diocesan commissions. They worked in the diocese where you had a bishop that tolerated or supported some of this stuff. They also were very influential – in the '70s and '80s – in letting what was happening with the local bishops happen and getting money to have the church-based organizing like PICO in California. A lot of that was a combination of some social justice priests who were not working on a parish level, but who were working on either a diocesan committee level or were tagged on some way to a university. Look at where Jack Egan ended up, tagged on to Notre Dame when the bishop didn't work. Geno did the same thing. They established bases for themselves. They were another layer.

George Knight: But the parish-based priests, they were a separate structure. The Polish National Catholic structure and the Ukrainian Orthodox that were all in the neighborhood… Neighborhood was critical. That was the key thing. When I was an organizer one of our supporters, a tiny little S&L down in the Ukrainian district, got slapped by the Federal Home Loan Bank of Chicago for over-concentration of loans. This project got handed to me.

This was a thrift that was open four hours after Sunday Mass. It was such a simpler, less complex time. It was a notch different than a credit union. I went and met the gentleman who ran it at a Ukrainian restaurant. We had a wonderful meal. And he said, "Well, let's go upstairs and talk about this because I don't know what to do about this."

We went up and there's a map. And it's a map of a handful of blocks. And he said, "This is who we're lending to." And he's got pins, just pins on a map, that was it. And he pointed to a pin and he said, "This is…." and he names a name. "Now his father lives here. His maternal uncle lives there. His wife's family lives…" and he's pointing to these places. "That loan's not safe?" And he points to another. From his perspective, "I'm lending to people I know, to people who are known in the community." He says, "Why should I lend in the suburbs? I don't know anybody in the suburbs. I've never lost a nickel."

So then I went to the Federal Home Loan Bank of Chicago and I said, "What was this concentration of lending? What was the problem with this?" Eventually they backed off because I suspect some examiners said, "This isn't worth the hassle." Or maybe they came out and looked and had the conversation and said, "We're never going to move these Ukrainians."

But all of that was neighborhood focused. So that was always Gale's perspective, that it started from how does it play on the block, how does it convey in the kitchen. And, if it doesn't convey in the kitchen, it doesn't count.

The other thing on Chicago and race that was always a challenge for us, and a challenge certainly in Austin, at NCO and with parish priests, was that African Americans were not Catholic. So African Americans moving into the neighborhoods was the death knell for parishes, for a diocesan church, because they weren't Catholic and the parishes didn't attract from outside their boundaries.

There was also great, great animosity between the Polish community and African Americans. There was the competition for jobs. There was an uncertainty of position in Chicago. Many of the Polish who had come to Chicago had come as immigrants and refugees before the war, after the war, uncertain of their position, scared, uncertain economically. The blockbusting was an economic catastrophe. It'd be like people today discovering through a set of circumstances that their $550,000 house is now on the market for $250,000. They're bankrupt. They're finished. There is no way they can cover $300,000 and keep on living someplace else if they were forced to sell.

So it was a very complex stew there between [them and] the African American community on the West Side that was expanding west. And Austin dipped down right into the path, whereas the rest of us were north of the IC tracks, the big railroad/industrial complex that runs east/west through that part of Chicago. It ends before it gets to Austin. So Austin was right in the path.

Roger Coughlin: I took the summer to spend a lot of time up at NCO and that's where I met Tom Gaudette. So when I finally came out of school [the School of Social Work at the University of Chicago] I knew that somehow or another the Catholic Charities was going to be in community organizing. This is a traditional type of agency that deals with government and all those kinds of things, not the kind that has community organization of the type back then in the '60s. The community organizations stood for confrontation. That was the standard procedure. They started out realizing they didn't have any good cards in their hand, so they couldn't play it dependent upon their cards with these people with money and political control and what have you. They went in there ready to unload on them. So I was up there and I wouldn't. I held back.

Tom [Gaudette]'s idea of running a community organization was that you worked all night, then you came back starting at twelve o'clock to two o'clock in the morning and you rehashed the whole day's work. And you sat there with a bottle on the table and the cans of beer on the table. I mean I had to get up at 5:30 in the morning. So I'm sorry. That wasn't my bit.

But, at any rate, I certainly knew that this was it. So when I was in the position, I hired. I was in charge of the Family Care Department, but I had a very benevolent boss, and by the time I got through explaining something, it really was sanitized. And it was safe. So I had these positions. Three of the first people I hired had come out of the University of Illinois. I called it "Department of Family and Community Services". That sounds about as safe a name as you can come up with.

OBA was made up of two populations, one south of the El tracks and the other north. North was white; south was black. I had one staff member who was working with the Resurrection parish, which was south. Al Velto became a problem for the organization because he organized more people and brought twice as many people to the meetings as those who were working on the north side up there. Well, the problems were the same. The war cry was against redlining and against the mortgage bankers. Predatory lending continues to be a problem there.

From memorandum signed by Russell A. Rau, Assistant Inspector General for Audits on "Challenges and FDIC Efforts Related to Predatory Lending" (Report No. 06-011) dated June 6, 2007:
Although there is no universally accepted definition, predatory lending typically involves imposing unfair and abusive loan terms on borrowers, often through aggressive sales tactics; taking advantage of borrowers' lack of understanding of complicated transactions; and outright deception.

Roger Coughlin: I had a fellow once who had worked for me and I said I had to let him go because I had given only a couple of rules, but he ignored one of them. One of them was that you can't have a parish, ever, and be an incorporator in a community organization, because there are too many people, funny people, who get involved in community organizations. The parish can't be legally responsible for what some unusual people do.

But this fellow one day led a whole group of people into breaking up a meeting of mortgage bankers. I mean that is a high point in stupidity because you can only do an action against people who have a reputation and who are political, with visibility or a banker. Mortgage bankers, they come out of the sewer. You can't embarrass them. So the next day they instigated a $1 million lawsuit against the Archbishop of Chicago. Even though he had nothing to do with me. I didn't have anything to do with him. He hadn't worked for the Catholic Charities for at least two years. And they sued. That's how the Archbishop began to find out about some of the things that were going on over in his Catholic Charities. It was sad. Yeah. That was it. That was the beginning of the end. The Archbishop at that point was John Patrick Cody.

NTIC office space? Oh, that's another story! They were over on Division Street. It may have been only 50-foot across and was maybe 60-foot depth. So they were all jammed in there. And over here in our building, the second floor was vacant. We'd taken over this building and this building was St. Vincent's Infant Hospital and Orphanage. So in '71 the State, wanting to have its own empire for children, really destroyed this institution, St. Vincent's. So I made the pitch to the Sisters that we just couldn't let this building go down the drain and be knocked down by a ball and a big high-rise come up here. There's something better in life. So it's a kind of a shrine to the past.

Gale in the second HTIC office, housed in the former laundry facility behind Catholic Charities at 121 West Superior Street, in 1976. The offices were provided free thanks to Father Coughlin.

So we had the building. But what had been the laundry, over the garages, I put the guys from NTIC in out there. And right across the street from this was the 18th District Police Station. It took some time but, after about six months or so, the police began to understand that these people who were trying to barge into Mayor Daley's office, they're coming from right across the street from us! And who owns it? The Catholic Charities! So we're going to start complaining.

At any rate, I had to sit them down, "Guys, the days are over. We got to find another office." And, unfortunately, they didn't go peacefully into the night, some of them, a couple of wild men. You ever heard these stories about any of the wild men? They didn't help me. They probably thought it was funny, but it wasn't funny as far as my bosses were concerned.

Ed Bailey: So the key people in OBA were the pastors of the churches. Mandell, it was all-white; white was in control. Mandell had a white pastor. We called him "Bud". Mandell was Methodist. And I'm a member of Mandell today. The area was predominantly Catholic, but you had a few Protestants here and there. Bud was part of the pastors, the group of pastors.

Then we had Resurrection, right here on Jackson, big church, big operation. Father Francis Phelan. He was an anchor in the works of stabilizing the community, a key leader. He was probably high up in OBA. Not only were people like Father Phelan members, they also gave financial support. The Catholics gave a lot of support to the community organizations at that time. There was St. Thomas. Then we had the Protestant Lutheran Church which is right around the corner here. Gale was able to parlay that all over.

Then we ran into the crux of the change which was the redlining. The neighborhood was treated rather badly by the City, by everybody, by the banks, by institutions around here. Just about everybody except the churches. Gale Cincotta, she recruited me to join. She was one of the first that asked me to join. At that time Gale was a young woman and she was the elected secretary of OBA. Also she went out in the field and worked a whole lot. Gale's work as an advocate was like a rebel.

To get the city government to start bringing services back in, we were what you might call a protest organization. We would protest, carry picket signs. Make a lot of noise. And once in a while they'd take some of us to jail. They'd always turn them loose! But they'd arrest them once in a while. A lot of people were arrested, to get their point across. But we were a very aggressive, aggressive protest group. Most of the times one of the priests would be the leader. A lot of the times, what we found out, was that collar meant a lot. That collar would get you in a lot of places. Some of the priests really were a tremendous help. There were Catholic priests and Catholic policemen!

But I think they lost some support too because among the well-heeled financial people there were white people who had money and who didn't particularly care for integration. A lot of them withheld some of their support to the Catholic Church. They lost something there too. But that didn't stop them. They never ceased to help us get better conditions. Every priest that came in here, you could always depend on him. I have to give them credit. I like them today for that. I appreciate them.

The neighborhoods were organized all around their local churches. All the churches were involved and you had your little block clubs and all. All of us would meet at Mandell. And a lot of them over there would meet at Resurrection. They had it pretty well sectioned off, OBA did.

So the block clubs had their own issues and their own meetings. Then you had your big meeting. That would emanate from the small meetings. I tell you the truth – and I don't know how they did it – but they had just about every block in this community organized. They were some terrific organizing people—as a force.

We've never been able to duplicate that. We've never been able to do as good a job in organizing the blocks as the people with the OBA. I credit that with the churches being overwhelmingly involved. After so long a time, we got a fluctuation among the churches. The black church moved in and, with all due respect to them—and I want to give them credit for all the good that they do and did – they were not as forceful as the white church, as the priests, as the Catholics.

People go to church less nowadays than they used to. They're not all members of churches and they don't go to the church. The church isn't as much a center. They are not as involved from the pulpit as it was then, because then you would get up. Somewhere in there the community person would make an announcement in the church. At Mandell one time I was the community person that brought the news on Sunday what was going on, part of every Sunday. After I gave that up, another lady – she's long gone now – she would give the news of the block. All that is cut out now. That was part of the consolidating force that we had at that time. But we lost it. We did lose it after Gale Cincotta left.

From An Alley in Chicago:

Margery Frisbie: In the end, it took a Jack Egan backed by the carefully progressive Samuel Cardinal Stritch and trained by that inspiring but repressive seminary rector, Monsignor Reynold Hillenbrand. An English contemporary described Jack Egan's circle of seminarians. "When they emerged from the seminary, they had already had a kind of formation that no priests in the U.S. had. There had never been a seminary like this." These young priests, maybe a dozen of them, were part of a group of priests and lay people who created what Jack Egan looks back on as a Golden Age in the Chicago Church. That was the decade before John Cardinal Cody arrived. It was the decade when Chicago led the Church in the United States.

Jack Egan with his leprechaun zest, silver-tongued like early labor organizers of the same heritage, ingratiating, and convinced the Church's place was beside the poor, took the most public positions. (2-3)

Alinsky insisted his organization be creative. Creative, inspirational, and funny. And this is what their allies in community development saw in Alinsky and Egan: creative imaginations able to conceive of a better future for the people in the city's neighborhoods. They saw ways to change neighborhoods of which others despaired. At a surface level, it was clear how Alinsky and Egan benefited each other. Egan was Alinsky's funnel to the archdiocesan moneybags. Alinsky was the archdiocese's handle on how to organize neighborhood communities facing societal change. (122)

Archdiocesan leaders hoped that Saul Alinsky and his organizers could somehow modulate the population shifts taking place at a disruptive pace. They knew they couldn't stop the changes. What they hoped for was the integration of black Chicagoans into formerly all-white parishes without violence. They wanted to see the outflow of Chicagoans to the suburbs stemmed – for the good of the city and the good of the parishes. (123)

Michael Westgate: The Catholic Church had a big stake in Austin. People do not widely recognize that the Church was thoroughly involved in industrial as well as residential community organizing. The companies also had a stake in keeping their workforce who lived nearby.

Bud Kanitz: I was at NCO in '67 and worked there until '71 as a street organizer. Then I went over to a spin-off group that was started by NCO, which was called the Industrial Council of Northwest Chicago, which got some federal Department of Commerce money. It was an association of businesses, industrial companies, factories, that were at the south end of the NCO area, basically along Lake Street. And they were companies that were redlined also. Because sometimes when they wanted to get loans, they had difficulty.

Monsignor Geno Baroni characterized the Industrial Council as the only business group, certainly of factory associations, that was affiliated with a community organization. It was interesting how the company presidents supported NCO. A lot of them were Catholic, so there was synergy when Father Tony Janiak, who was the founding president of NCO, went to meet with some of the company heads that helped the partnership, the alliance, the coalition.

So the priests surely played a critical role initially. With all the hoopla these days about church-based, faith-based, church-based organizing, well, NCO was as church-based as you could possibly get. But it was a different kind of organizing. That was really out there in community change. A lot of George Bush's faith-based organizations, to me, are pushing hot meals and proselytizing, not really dealing with community change. They're basically service providers and they're not organizing or advocating on behalf of the 'hood.

After Cardinal Cody came in [1965] then, of course, Monsignor Egan was banished to Notre Dame. So there was still a lot of connection in terms of organizing in the NCO neighborhood in relation to the churches, but it was primarily in relation to using church basements as meeting halls. I always describe Gale as someone that started out leading her neighborhood residents. She started in a church basement but ultimately became very comfortable in a corporate boardroom meeting with bankers.

But Father Tony Janiak was the first president of NCO and then Reverend Lyle Franzen, who was a Presbyterian minister, was the second. When the Cardinal approached Alinsky, the story was that Alinsky insisted that Protestant churches be brought in too. Because Alinsky felt that in Back of the Yards, which was supported a lot by the Catholic churches, it became anti-Protestant. Yes, it was the thing to promote Catholic parishes and it wasn't an ecumenical kind of an effort. So as a result there were mainline Protestants involved right from the beginning.

The Protestants funded a little bit but mostly the money came from their denominational headquarters as opposed to the local parishes, which was where the Catholic money came from. Just in the NCO neighborhood it came from 22 Catholic parishes. That was a lot of money in 1961-62.

Mary Volpe: You know, Gale would have been nothing if it wasn't for the Catholic Church because of funding and building her up and location. The Catholic Church really made Gale. So all of a sudden they brought funding in '71-'72. They seeded. And how they seeded!

Remember the guys that were with the SDS group? They were all on the lam from the Feds. And all of a sudden they made great organizers. All of a sudden they were showing up and they talked to the priest and every parish was getting a group. The Church gave a big $4000 a year. Right? And that was to hire somebody and do all the stuff.

Well, those kids were trained how to do organizing the rough way. Great organizing. I haven't met any of them that didn't know how to really organize. They knew how to share their equipment. They knew how to go back and forth to each. Like if I have a printing press, you have a printing press type deal. Everybody shared.

They were not afraid of the Spanish. They thought that the Spanish would retain the Church. I'm Catholic and I know the politics of the Church. They were there to protect their property because so many of our constituents might move out.

So when these parishes were falling, they didn't get it that the second highest, second largest group of religion in the black community is Catholicism. On my block most of them were trained in Catholic schools. Their kids go to Catholic schools. But they'd never get wined and dined like the other groups get wined and dined. So the problem is they don't bring them back into the local church. When they move into a new neighborhood, they don't come into that church. They go back to the old parish.

So they put $4000 a head on it [per parish]. And it was for a three-year period of time. And by that time they had really organized. That took away from OBA because the whole of Austin belonged to OBA. So all these members that belonged to OBA in this area went to St. Peter's. The ones in the west of us went to St. Angela's. It was like parish by parish. The north end had a huge group. We could turn out 1500 in a morning meeting because people were interested. I don't know what was in their mind, if they thought this was going to save their souls.

So the church or the parish organizations were working at the same time OBA was working. See it broke down OBA. All of a sudden the parish organization here, the organizers, started working with other denominations and brought them in, into their area, and they used the parish boundaries. I really don't know if part of the intent was to weaken OBA. You know, when you're starting out something new, you can be awfully dumb. And I was awfully naïve in those days.

But we split up and it was OBA on the south end of Austin because all these other groups were against them. Then Gale started MAHA – Metropolitan Area Housing Alliance. She was still sticking to Chicago in those days.

Michael Westgate: Sometimes it is hard to say whether the Church was using the community organizations for its ends or vice versa. Shel Trapp had a particular attitude toward not just the Catholic Church but toward his own Methodist Church, where he had served as an ordained minister for seven years. He and some of the clergy had a distain for the Catholic hierarchy, particularly Cardinal Cody who did not support the clergy's activist role as his predecessors Cardinals Stritch and Meyer had.

Shel Trapp: Cody just came in in 1965 and went, 'Ugh. What is this?' I can remember meeting with Father Ahern [1924-2001]. Cody had just been mugged. I was so happy. Well, Ahern had been an NCO leader, and was the pastor of St. Sylvester's, where we had the national conference. We were getting ready for another one, so I was meeting with him. "Gee, Father, too bad about the Cardinal." The Cardinal had been in an accident. "Too bad. That was too bad. They should have killed him." So I thought, "Okay. We're on common ground!" Father Ahern was a pretty straight guy. He liked what we did, and he went on a picket line or so. "Yeah, you're on my team right now."

He didn't have a high enough profile that he would have gotten booted out, like Egan.

He ran a good tight parish. They paid their bills. He wasn't one to cause any ripples. So he stayed through Cody. He either moved to another parish or retired out of there. He was a nice solid guy.

I'm not sure that Coughlin was ever on a demonstration. He was just like the Rock of Gibraltar. I remember at one time when we were in really tough financial shape. The Ford Foundation had promised us a $100,000 grant. Kept pushing it back. "No problem. It's in the works." So we just kept spending money thinking, "Okay. We got $100,000." The reserves were just about gone. This had been going on for about five months. And, you know, we obviously sent out a desperation phone call, and they said, "No. You're not getting it." "Holy fuck!" And so, September, just about the whole NTIC office went on unemployment.

We were just scraping enough to pay the heat and the lights. The rule was anybody with another spouse working had to go on unemployment. So I was on unemployment. Anne-Marie was on unemployment, five or six of the rest of the staff were on unemployment. And we get to Christmas time and historically, when we had our Christmas party, NTIC would give everybody a bonus of $100 or something like that.

I remember early December, Coughlin called and he said, "Well it's been a rough year, huh?" "Yes, Father, it really has. The thing that pisses me off the most, I can't give the staff the usual Christmas bonus." "That's too bad. What do you usually give?" "I usually give 'em a hundred apiece." Pulls out a check and writes on the check, "How many staff you got to give it to?"

That was long enough ago that a hundred dollars was not like a small amount. It was still not a monstrous amount, but when you got a hundred dollar bonus at Christmas, "Hey, I got something. I can do something different now." That really meant a lot to the staff. It meant a hell of a lot to me. But that was the kind of guy that Coughlin was. Never up front.

The first national conference, Father Coughlin was a little pissed. He'd never said anything publicly. Just we were good, well, we are good friends. We were out having some drinks sometime afterward. Baroni had hit *Time* magazine. "That fucking Barroni. I pay the bills. He flies into town and he gets his picture in *Time* magazine." We could not have had the first national conference if it hadn't been for Coughlin.

Michael Westgate: Geno Baroni, a Roman Catholic priest and director of the Washington D.C. based National Center for Urban Ethnic Affairs, was "one of 200 faces to watch for the future" cited in the July 15, 1974 issue of *TIME* magazine.

From *GENO: The Life and Mission of Geno Baroni*

Lawrence O'Rourke: Granted all Baroni's weaknesses – he was incompetent as a manager; he was inarticulate as a writer and thinker; he stole others' ideas shamelessly; he was bound by personal insecurities – he was also a brilliant strategist and political analyst; a genius at connecting people and ideas; a deeply religious man who suffered on a lonely but ever-onward pilgrimage for justice. (116-117)

Baroni did not see his institute serving only Catholic interests. He regretted that the church had been so inadequately prepared for the great migration of blacks into white neighborhoods in the 1960s and 1970s. The flight of the white Catholics to suburban parishes, leaving the cities behind in a swamp of racial hostility and poverty, was a scandal to Baroni. (297)

He was the pioneer of many things, particularly effective advocacy of the legitimate grievances of urban ethnics and the revitalization of their neighborhoods. (299)

It was always the Baroni thesis that people of ethnic backgrounds had to come to grips with their ethnicity before they could deal with other problems, particularly those linked to the movement of blacks into their neighborhoods and schools and as challengers to their jobs. (179)

Shel Trapp: And then with the Catholic Charities thing, that gave me enough staff to build a real power base in Chicago, so that everybody was looking to Chicago: "My God, those guys are just kicking ass all over the place. We'd better scramble to catch up with them." We built a reputation so then Baroni hired me to do consulting and training with his groups. Which got us into another whole other network too.

Kathy Desmond: My tie-in was through the Campaign for Human Development (CHD). Geno may have been how I met Gale. But we were funding Gale and NTIC. So I got involved with her a little later on in the story. The Catholic bishops as a whole were trying to do their first statement on women. So I was invited to put a panel together about women and poverty and got three CHD grantees—one black, one Hispanic, one white—dynamic woman leaders. The black woman, Ruby Johnson, was a welfare rights organizer. The Hispanic woman, former migrant worker, was with the co-op movement out in California. And then Gale was the white woman.

It was the first time I saw Gale cowed. That was the interesting thing. She who could stare down any banker, any Congressman. I think it was because they were bishops. She said, "I just don't know." She really was getting me to do a power analysis of who was going to be in the room when she walked in and where were they coming from. Which was her usual way of doing information. But she was nervous about meeting with the bishops ahead of time. But she did great.

George Knight: Once in the water she could swim.

Kathy Desmond: The Geno/Gale relationship is very important. The Geno/Jack Egan nexus was how she got at least CHD funding and exposure nationally through CHD. It was Geno's thing about white ethnics. His friend, Ed Marciniak, formed a whole organization on the issue of white ethnics. And Gale was on that board. That was key in terms of getting Gale on a national level. ["Marciniak was involved in the formation of a score of organizations like the Christian Family Movement, the Cana Conference, the Catholic Social Action Conference, and Chicago Inter-Student Catholic Action. And they provided a powerful Chicago presence to national initiatives, including the Catholic Worker Movement, the Young Christian Workers, the Young Christian Students, the Catholic Committee on Urban Ministry, and the National Conference on Interracial Justice." – *National Catholic Reporter*, September 3, 2004.]

Michael Westgate: Is community organizing on the agenda today for Catholic Charities?

Roger Coughlin: No, it isn't. I got introduced to community organizing in the summer of 1963 when I was up near OBA. The second half of the sixties we began organizing.

Michael Westgate: What led to its becoming o.k. for Catholic Charities to get involved in community organizing?

Roger Coughlin: My demand. By the time you heard my description of it, you would think it was something that was written down in the Bible. See it was never called – never called – community organizing. These were people who were there to help parishes organize programs, self-help programs for their parish and their community. And I still think that there's a chance that could come back.

NTIC is recognizing that there are other strategies. Basically I think that while there's a lot of scummy people in this world, there's a lot of good people. And a lot of good people would be willing to get in there and help, provided you give them a strategy that will fit for them as a company or a bank or whatever it is.

They realized early on that it's as House Speaker O'Neill said all politics is local. Well, all organizing is local also. So it can't be just a question of great strategies. You got to get down there. And if you're not able to get down there and walk through and kick around in the garbage, you'll never understand what it's about. And so anything that's done where you're helping communities to play a role in their own lives and in their communities has to be founded in this.

You still can't ignore the fact that people do need a stoplight here. They've had four kids killed at this corner and they're not going to put up with it. And, by God, I don't care if it costs $60,000 to put up a stoplight, they're going to put up a stoplight here. So you've still got to be involved in that. But it can't just be the issues of the local community. It can be that, but you've got to be able to bind those people together to see the big picture. The reason why we haven't got any money for streetlights is because the cities have become accustomed to federal money. Like organizations get contracts, and we become partners and we become accustomed to that, so do cities. Now that money isn't there, it's a shell game. You would listen to the speeches, but in reality it isn't there. It can't be there when you spend $2 billion a week over there in Iraq. There's no money for the cities! The city has no money for the streetlights. There is no end to it.

I'd see Gale at our annual meetings and it was always a delight to be with her. She made you feel good. And the fact that there was a foot of snow out there didn't seem to matter. She would come in and she'd laugh and she would grab up that food. But I always felt it was a personal privilege of mine to have known such people as Gale and those people and to have them think I was a good guy.

Ann Vick-Westgate: You stepped in at some critical moments.

Roger Coughlin: Well, maybe I did. But it's the fact that they thought I was a good guy. So I'm on their board, but I'm really there to sit there in amazement at all the things they do. I have very little I can contribute any more to them.

Michael Westgate: Some people say they never could have gotten started the way they did without the support of the Church.

Roger Coughlin: Well, that's right. That's true. Okay, you'd have to go backwards on that one. You have to go back to Saul Alinsky. You can't tell the story without telling them about the Irish, Germans and Poles. You really can't understand the Chicago story here without understanding Saul Alinsky and Saul Alinsky's relationship with Cardinal Stritch [from 1940-58] who was very supportive of him.

What gave me this courage is the fact that historically the Ordinary [the Archbishop] of Chicago would have thought what I was doing was good. Archbishop Stritch would have thought what I was doing was good. And he ordained me. I came into the city at the time that there was lots of excitement, lots of excitement going on in Chicago. Everybody really looked to Chicago to find out what the Church in Chicago was doing.

I say it was this relationship that got The Woodlawn Organization (TWO) going. That was certainly supported by Cardinal Stritch. [Founded in 1960, TWO's mission is to build community through advocacy, social service programs and community development initiatives.] He supported Saul in that. Then, when NCO wanted to organize up here one of the bishops came out to the first meeting with the pastors. He told them, "This is a good thing. Involve your people and support this organization. You need the community organizations because otherwise you're ignoring the crap that your people have to live with." So there always was that, historically, there was that.

Right when I came back from school, my boss… See times had already changed, but I didn't know. I wasn't that conversant maybe. He asked me if I had any idea of what the Catholic Charities might be doing. He had stuck me up there on the third floor administration. "You got any thoughts?" So I whipped out this plan I had done for a paper at the University of Chicago when I was in school there. And I dressed it up and put in more particulars, basically saying that we ought to support an organization west of NCO, the whole area that would go particularly from west of Humboldt Park.

My boss looked at that and he saw all kinds of problems. Particularly, he never wanted the pastors of the diocese thinking that Catholic Charities was telling them how to do their business. So he opened the floor and kind of threw me down. I'm accustomed to that. But the next boss was the one who supported all these ideas. But it had to be done.

When I was ordained, it was Stritch. I was here by the time Meyer came on [1958]. So it was Stritch and he was the one that was supportive of the work. I think Meyer would have been too and he probably was. Meyer was another one of the good guys. He was very intelligent.

Michael Westgate: There are differing reports as to whether or not the priests were supportive and how supportive they were and why they were supportive.

Roger Coughlin: Well, the pastor of Resurrection was supportive, period. Now the parish just to the north of them, St. Thomas, that's the kind of place where they weren't sure whether the sun was rising or setting. Then going north of that, you would have a pastor there who probably didn't know a great deal about it. He was the kind of person who really did a lot of his own thinking. If your agenda didn't fit into his agenda, you could strong-arm him into making your idea his idea. So, I don't know, but I mean I had workers out there. I had a worker out there.

Ann Vick-Westgate: Were there any pastors that were opposed to the black in-migration?

Roger Coughlin: Oh, my god, yes. Oh! I put a worker, one of these workers that didn't work out, in the parish at W. 80th and S. Wood Street because the pastor would support anything. He really thought that if he gave a million dollars' worth of sermons – that was his expression – that the people would stay like they were in Mayor Daley's ward. So he had these priests saying Mass in the people's homes on the blocks, doing everything. He had recruited in more priests for all this service than you could imagine. It was like a diocese! But all you needed was one woman to get beat up at 82nd and Marshfield and they were leaving.

Now, certainly, the parish to the east of us had a wonderful pastor. But we didn't have strategies that would be able to protect him. So, fighting the battle over redlining and over the mortgage bankers, it was never going to be enough. In the best of all worlds, could we have been blessed with the kind of people who were so smart that they would come up with the kind of big strategies that the world needs? I mean we're living at a time now when there is a complete absence.

The best people aren't going into politics. And I don't see the best people going into the Church either. We don't have any Monsignor Hillenbrand. There's no Jack Egan. There's no Walt Imbiorski. We don't have those kinds of people. And, when you do have them, they're someplace where they'll be safe.

There's no group like Roosevelt had, that he gathered during the Depression, to come up with strategies to help people. We haven't got those people. So we just aren't blessed with the people that we need. The people with all the brains are going into creating Internet sites or they're running Google or something. That's where all the geniuses are. They're not where they could be so much used. The world can be changed. Our nation is going to be tremendously changed. We're just not keeping up.

Michael Westgate: You said that you thought community organizing might come back in terms of something that the Church could be supportive of?

Roger Coughlin: You're talking about a solution. Community organizing is a solution. But what is missing is there is no recognition of all the crap that's lying on the sidewalk. Until we become cognizant of that, community organizing for the sake of community organization just doesn't make any sense. Now if we have a problem that we need to rally the folks for, something that they sense, they see we have a reason. I don't hear many people crying about things. You would think that everything is fine almost. They think that the whole thing is involved in some political scam or something.

Ann Vick-Westgate: There isn't the anger that was there in the '60s and the '70s.

Roger Coughlin: No, there's not. No anger, no anger. It's a kind of a depression.

From *DISCLOSURE* #5 (February 1975)
Catholic Charities Leaders Strategize

On February 17th, 1975, top-level leadership of Catholic Charities from sixteen cities attended a two-day strategy session to map out plans for coordination of their local efforts to save their urban and rural communities. Issues discussed included the problem of redlining, mandatory disclosure, and reinvestment programs.

One result of the conference will be the addition of a one-day educational session on disinvestment at the mid-year meeting of Catholic Charities Directors in Chicago on April 8th-9th. In the meantime, participants strategized how to locally pursue state and city anti-redlining regulations and legislation, in addition to visiting banks and S&L's to determine their willingness to disclose.

To increase coordination of such local efforts, plans are being made for several state conferences to precede and follow the Fourth Annual National Housing Conference in Chicago on April 19th-20th, 1975. States that are working on regional conferences include: California, Indiana, Michigan, Nebraska, New York and Washington.

Roger Coughlin, Director of Chicago's Catholic Charities, points out that, "This conference was tied to a decision made by the Charities Directors last September in Boston to develop a national strategy for an anti-redlining campaign in urban and rural areas. Recognition of the problem is growing. Now we are all committed to working on disinvestment until it is cracked."

CHAPTER 4

"It always helps if you can identify the enemy."

HOW GALE CINCOTTA AND SHEL TRAPP
LED AND ORGANIZED

From Tom Gaudette tapes, 1990, found in the archives at Loyola Marymount University, Los Angeles. Interviewer unknown.

Tom Gaudette worked for Saul Alinsky at the Industrial Areas Foundation (IAF), then Organization for a Better Austin (OBA), then founded Northwest Community Organiztion (NCO) (p. 79): The first time I heard Alinsky speak was the first time I ever heard this whole concept of power, of people banding together to cause change. Prior to hearing Alinsky, I felt motivation and values were what caused change. In 1961, Alinsky asked me to join him.

Saul's style was to react, which is the style I've often used rather than "here's the package" which is the way it's done today. Which was a great freedom. In other words, you'd go out and screw it up or whatever you'd do, but he would react and give you some advice. That was the training. In the conversation some of these things occurred, the words, power…

Saul said organizing cannot be taught. You've got to go out from your own experience and find out what needs to be done: strategy. He's a great strategist. We'd play a lot of games about how to get into City Hall. And when I watch it today and see how academic it is, it's almost like computer training. And then the numbers that go on. "Oh, yeah, we had a meeting last night at the church, 800 people." I'm sitting there saying, "What did you accomplish? What are the issues?" They don't talk that way. See that's the old style. That's the Alinsky style. We don't work on issues anymore. You work on building relationships. Once you work on relationships and people are empowered, then you get on the issues.

Somehow or other I stepped back and became a little—I don't know if the word is— conservative, but controlled the anger, directed it. That's what Alinsky talked about many years later. That's why a lot of the stuff Alinsky brought up I understood because I went through it. "Wild, crazy anger is nothing but violence," Alinsky said, "We got to have anger, but it's got to be directed and controlled." That's what I was doing. I didn't put those words together, but that's what I was doing. Alinsky reacted to what we did. He didn't tell us. He would 'build the web' illustrating where the power was and who knew who ("Who's he got? Who's with 'em? Who's against 'em?") showing his organizers they knew these things but had never thought of it in that manner.

In 1966, I left him and went out to Austin. The last time I saw Alinsky was at a dinner we had in the early 1970s, Alinsky said he felt that all neighborhood organizing had failed. I disagreed.

I still worry about the community. I'm not in the business of saving the Church. I was able to take people from a church experience and logically interpret it into the community so they logically, every night when they got home from work, would be up and talking to the non-church people and ringing the door bells... In terms of staff, either staff adopts the value system developed by the people they serve or you fire the staff.

Shel Trapp: Gaudette was trained by Alinsky and he started NCO. NCO is dead now. But he started NCO in 1960. Alinsky had a theory, a rule: "Three years and out for a director," because Alinsky still was operating under the myth that you could train somebody from the neighborhood to take over an organization. So Gaudette started in 1960. In '63 Alinsky wanted Gaudette to go to Kansas City because one of his projects there was in trouble. And Gaudette wouldn't go, and he fought Alinsky for basically three years. And then in '66 they split over the issue of three years and Gaudette went out to Austin.

Gaudette was very tight with Monsignor Egan, and Monsignor Egan went with him and they got the Catholic pastors together. And at that time the Church had a lot of money and had some priests who were inclined to get involved and a Cardinal [Meyer] who'd back them up. So Egan basically went around the room and said, "Okay. St Thomas, you'll put in $5000. Resurrection, you'll put in $4000. St. Peter Canisius, you'll put in $7000." Just assigned numbers to them. Checks just like that. Pastors ruled. No parish councils in those days or anything else. So Gaudette started it and he was looking for staff. I had heard about community organizing and I had actually met Gaudette when I was still a minister. I was very impressed with him. So I went and asked him for a job because I'd heard he was hiring.

Gaudette wouldn't leave NCO. Basically I think he didn't mind leaving NCO; he didn't want to leave Chicago. He had deep ties to Chicago and he just wasn't going to do that. So he was able to start this thing in Austin. And it worked out very luckily for both of us that I applied for a job, not having ever organized anything really. So he basically trained me. He was the director.

So Gale and I got together through working under the OBA [Organization for a Better Austin]. Justin McCarthy was the first president. There was quite a battle when Gale ousted him as president. I basically got Gale elected because I had backed her.

Now we were not a church-based organization. We started with funding from the churches and there were a lot of churches there. The Catholics were there and Protestants were there too. Obviously, in Chicago, the Catholic churches were the power.

Basically at our first OBA convention [in 1967] we had about 1200 people there. This was the first convention of OBA. NPA didn't even exist then. That first convention we had 1200 folks. Probably six to seven hundred of them were blacks that I had produced because I formed block clubs and on top of that I formed what I called street clubs and then I formed civics. So I had three layers of organization.

Each block club was each block facing you. The way Chicago is laid out on a grid, every four blocks there's a major thoroughfare. So from like Cicero to Laramie would be a street club and then Cicero to Laramie, Madison to the Expressway was what I called a civic. All of those layers would meet once a month. So I had like probably 50 block club meetings a month. Usually about three to four street clubs a month. I had over a hundred meetings a month. So every night there was four or five block club meetings. Then once a month the street club would also meet. And once a month the civics would meet and the civics would deal with bigger issues.

The reason I started the street clubs was because the block clubs usually started around one bad building or a pothole, something very small. As soon as that's done, it usually becomes a social club. I didn't want to deal with that, so then I formed street clubs so we could keep dealing with issues. I formed the civics so we could deal with issues that covered the whole area, whether it was crimes, bad buildings, panic peddling, whatever.

So we had very deep penetration in the block club meetings. I mean I could go out walking and couldn't walk a block without meeting two or three people that I knew on a first name basis. We delivered heavy to the first convention. Then the second convention was where we elected Gale. But that was a big thing to have a woman president. Gale was the first woman president of any Alinsky-style organization. Well, through the whole busing fight she and a black lady [Illa Daggett] had become the heroes of South Austin.

Michael Westgate: Racism and panic peddling had been a problem in Chicago for decades. The Chicago Real Estate Board expelled realtors who sold across racial lines in the early 1900s, and guidelines in the 1950s still stated that any realtor who sold a house to a black in a block that didn't yet have a black in it would be expelled from the realtors' association.

From *American Pharoah: Mayor Richard J. Daley -- His Battle for Chicago and the Nation* by Adam Cohen and Elizabeth Taylor (2000).

White Chicagoans worked to prevent the migrants from moving into white neighborhoods. One South Side neighborhood association captured the exclusionary spirit sweeping white Chicago when it declared that "there is nothing in the make-up of a Negro, physically or mentally, which should induce anyone to welcome him as a neighbor." In April 1917, the Chicago Real Estate Board met and — concerned about what officials described as the "invasion of white residence districts by the Negroes" — appointed a Special Committee on Negro Housing to make recommendations. On this committee's recommendation, the board adopted a policy of block-by-block racial segregation, carefully controlled so that "each block shall be filled solidly and . . . further expansion shall be confined to contiguous blocks." Three years later, the board took the further step of voting unanimously to punish by "immediate expulsion" any member who sold property to a black on a block where there were only white owners (pp. 32-3).

Shel Trapp: You had an awful lot of shady realtors at that time. Shady? They were fucking crooks! So Gale and I started working together in late '67 and worked together ever since. Gale at this point was president of OBA. She was never paid at OBA. Our other big fight was panic peddling. And we really did a lot. It was a very touchy issue then because most everybody that came out against panic peddling was white groups. There was always a fight. It was never organized in Chicago but several organizations tried to start "blacks out." Basically that was the clergy's motivation for hiring Gaudette. And the reason I left the ministry. But Gaudette did not buy into that. No. And they said it very blatantly, "You've got to keep them out. Keep these neighborhoods stable," meaning "keep them white."

The way I got into organizing was I'd left the ministry because I'd gone down to Mississippi, got arrested down there and spent a week in jail. When I got back, my boss told me, "You keep doing things like that, you'll never get a suburban church." So I went home that night and said to my wife, "We're out of the church" [United Methodist in Lakeview].

So I was very committed to civil rights and I remember Gaudette saying to me when we went to the meeting, "You're going to hear some things here. Just keep your damn mouth shut."

Egan was using the pastors. I mean there's no way, at that time in history, you're going to stop racial change in Chicago. It's impossible. So Gaudette's response was, "We've got to build a strong organization, keep the neighborhood stable." His comment was always, "Guarantee you we'll give you an organization that represents the community." And at that first OBA convention they shit bricks when they saw 50% of the people here are black.

Well, it wasn't at all the community! As far as Austin would go at that time I would say maybe 15% was black. But because I'd built such a power base in the south part, when they saw 50/50 black and white, they went ape shit. Gaudette said, "That's what I promised you. It represents the community." Of course I'd just done a hell of lot better job in delivering my troops than staff in the white end did.

But panic peddling was an issue. We did a very good job of slowing panic peddling down through confrontation. We declared that the law in Austin was that a realtor could not solicit. We said it often enough that people really started to believe it was the law. So people would set up a realtor, "I want to sell my house. Could you come out and take a look at it?" And we'd have 20-30 people in the basement. After the guy had looked 'round, "Oh, let's go to the basement." He'd come down there and we'd say, "Get the fuck out of here." And surround him so he couldn't get up the stairs. Sometimes I was a little nervous that we were going to get assault charges. It got pretty testy.

Other things people did would be to call and say, "Could you come out and appraise my house?" And the guy would come out and we'd have folks hiding behind trees and bushes throw eggs and tomatoes at him. Then every Friday night we had a "For Sale" sign stripping, and we'd go through the community and tear down "For Sale" signs. So it slowed it down. We knew we weren't going to stop it, but we wanted to slow it down.

Anyway to be against that was walking a very fine line, because that's what white communities had always done. So very quickly I got some of my blacks into it. So we had a good balance, whenever we picketed a realtor or went to a realtor's home, we had blacks and whites. Blacks were in this group too because realtors would buy a house one day from a white family for $20,000, next day sell it to a black family for $30,000, plus taking the commission from the white family. So both sides were getting screwed. That was our battle cry, "Look. Whites aren't the enemy. Blacks aren't the enemy. The realtor is the enemy. We get him out of here, nature will take its course, and nobody will get screwed."

And so basically we wiped out panic peddling in South Austin. People still sold. Panic peddling only works because of racism. But we were able to slow that down enough that I could build block clubs so that people would know each other. 'Cause that's what tears the community down, when there's no network. So we were able to quickly rebuild a network of all black from the all white network on the blocks and throughout the community.

"Trust isn't given, it is earned." You can quote Shel Trapp. And it was always, "Blacks aren't the enemy. Whites aren't the enemy. It's the slum landlord. It's the City, or it's the School Board of Education, or panic peddlers."

Michael Westgate: Shel Trapp was responsible for recruiting Gale to leadership of OBA. After years of working together there, they moved onto progressively larger stages to build the Metropolitan Area Housing Alliance (MAHA), working first in the Chicago area and then statewide at the capital in Springfield. But they also discovered that they needed to work at the national level with HUD and Congress to effectively address the issues they encountered locally. They used the building blocks and experience gained at each level to become effective at the national level—and at the national level to increase their leverage locally.

As Shel points out, there must first be a local problem identified by a couple of neighbors who want to do something about it. There must always be an element of self-interest, whether it is parents seeking better schools, rallying to the needs of the neighborhood to rid it of rats, to get better sanitation, to end destructive real estate practices, or just to fix potholes.

It then comes to the attention of someone who sees it as part of a bigger picture, in some cases a community organizer. If there is no block group, one is formed. But that problem is not allowed to be the only item on the agenda. There has to be a larger, dynamic agenda to which other items can be added. The organizer seeks out other block groups to build an alliance. A number of block groups gather together periodically. They invite politicians to address their concerns. Tactics vary depending on the response from those responsible.

It takes manpower to organize. It also takes a certain amount of money. In Austin it was the churches, particularly Catholic, that contributed funds on a parish-by-parish basis. If and when an organization gets well enough established, with nonprofit status, it can seek foundation funds. But most community organizing remains on a shoestring basis.

From Case Study by Hallahan (11/7/91)

Kirk Hallahan: From the outset, neighborhood was probably the most powerful symbol and served as the chief warrant why action was needed. Indeed, redlining was a neighborhood-based issue that was steeped in historical traditions and that conjured up a sense of a community of caring, interdependent people looking out for one another. Neighborhoods were worthy of preservation. (23-24)

Equality played an equally significant role in the discourse, representing the democratic premise that individuals should have equal access and that credit was a community resource that should be shared, especially if the funds came from within a neighborhood. This was a matter of fairness that piggybacked on the heightened sense of equality that emanated from the civil rights movement. (24)

Michael Westgate: It is often most effective if the problem can be personalized. Victims are identified and presented as examples. But statistics are equally important, to show that it is not just one or two cases. Then the case needs to be made that the problem can be solved and that there are particular individuals who can be held responsible for correcting it. The "target" of neighborhood organizing may be a public figure, either elected or appointed, or it may be a private figure, in the case of Austin, often a realtor. As Gale told me years later when she visited the agency I headed, Chelsea Neighborhood Housing Services in Massachusetts, "It always helps if you can identify the enemy."

Shel Trapp: Gale's column in *DISCLOSURE* was entitled "The Next Move." I learned that from her very early in my organizing career. After an eight-month organizing drive in 1966 we were sure that we had the votes we needed from the Chicago Board of Education to pass a resolution to bus 500 black kids to the Northwest side of Chicago. One of our lock-in votes became confused and voted the wrong way. We lost the vote.

The bus ride back to the community was very silent. When we got back to the drop-off place for the busload of people, I quickly got into my car and drove to the organization's watering hole, with the intent of getting totally smashed. Deep into my third drink, the bartender shouted out, "Is there a Shel Trapp here? There is a very angry woman who wants to talk with you." Getting on the phone, Gale screamed at me, "Get your ass over here or you're fired."

Gale had not let the folks from the losing event go home, but had gathered them in the church basement. By the time I got there, she had convinced them that there was a way the Board of Education could call an emergency meeting. With the backing of the group, she called the Superintendent of Schools and we had an emergency meeting of the Board of Education for next week. We won that vote and 500 black kids got bused out of classrooms of 75 to classrooms of 25 only because Gale was always ready to take "The Next Move."

Joe Mariano: In terms of how Shel and Gale divided the work, Trapp was the one that was out there doing the local organizing, working with the local organizations helping them do a better job. His role around here sometimes was neglected, because he was out and about. Something would happen or he'd have to come back and deal with it. So he liked to be on the road. Part of the reason I came back to Chicago in '94, I came back here to help Trapp by going out on the road.

Michael Westgate: Gale, like others, depended on successes. Successes at the school committee level led to new battles, with realtors and lenders, as well as with City Hall. Successes at the Austin level fed into new crusades at the metropolitan Chicago level, Illinois and nationwide.

At critical points, she was able to access funding to move to the next level. Money was always a problem. Energies were devoted first into getting people together – staff and volunteers, leaders and organizers. Gale, Shel and others were masters at convening conferences of 1000 people and more, both at the local level and nationally. Funding was always a lower priority, addressed at least in the early days only insofar as bills needed to be paid.

Eventually, Gale was able to force a number of unlikely sources to support her operations. These included first the churches, then foundations, eventually the very banks she was fighting to change their ways, the insurance companies, even Fannie Mae (FNMA). There was a maturing process. As operations became larger and more sophisticated, more money was needed. They were quite successful in the 1970s in getting foundation funding and even the venerable Ford Foundation became a supporter.

But they never entered the political establishment by running for office themselves. They felt they could accomplish more goading the politicians into action than becoming one of the many on the "inside" of politics. They never lost their local base.

They were astute in recognizing that no single organization could fill all their needs. Over the years they developed a network of organizations in Chicago, under the umbrella of an amorphous organization, MAHA.

Cincotta and Trapp had a powerful symbiotic relationship. Neither could have done what they did solo. How did this unlikely pair work together? Who did what to make it work?

Ann Vick-Westgate: What <u>was</u> the relationship between you and Gale? How did you work together?

Gale with Shel Trapp in the 1980s. They were indispensable to each other.

Shel Trapp: Love-hate.... One year we had an influx of new staff. It was probably five that had been with us only maybe six months. We were coming up to NPA. Things always get very tense around here right before the NPA annual conference in DC. Gale and I had some disagreement. I am clueless what it was over. We're just screaming and screaming with the staff all around. I'm swearing like hell at her and she's swearing back at me. Just on and on and on. Usually those things came to just a loggerhead, and we just went and sat down at our desks. I left and shortly after I left Gale left.

The staff all came up to Anne-Marie and said, "Does that mean we're calling off the conference?" She said, "Oh, no. That's just Trapp and Gale. They'll be in tomorrow morning and nothing will have happened." "Oh, I don't think so. It was so terrible the things they were saying to each other." And the next morning we're in, "Hi, Gale." "Hi, Trapp." You know, we'd go on like nothing had ever happened. And the staff couldn't fathom that. It just was the way we worked.

I spent a lot of time on the road, selling the issues, making the issues make sense to local groups. So that they could see why they should buy in, so that I could provide a power base behind Gale. When we got to negotiations, very seldom did I ever go into those. That was her arena. She dealt with that. "I'll get the door open. You take care of it in there." She and the leadership then would deal with that.

Our minds worked so differently. She could be in a meeting and somebody would say something, and she could turn it back on that person in a split second. It was just unreal the way her mind worked. Whereas with me, I hear something like that and I got to go back and think about it awhile so I could think out the strategic plan and how we could deal with it. What's the self-interest that I can get all these groups from around the country to come to this damn conference, so that they'll be willing to fight to get the door open? When the door is open, I want out of there. My mind doesn't work that way.

Then when Gale would come back and say what had happened, then I'd just get away from her for a little bit and think about, "Okay. How do I sell this on the road? They said that or this or whatever. Okay." Then I would have my story for the troops. So that basically I did the work out here and Gale did the work up here. And the way her mind worked, just any little miniscule idea suddenly would blossom into this monstrous oak tree I had never even thought of. So our minds were really well suited for each other 'cause it was really a ying-yang. We looked at the world two different ways.

But I could figure out how to put all the pieces together out there on the turf with the troops. She could figure out how to use one banker against another. Take the words that he had meant something and just twist round so that he was eating 'em. So that was a very good working relationship. So when I went out, I worked with the staff, with the organizers and with the leaders.

From Trapp's book, *Dynamics of Organizing: Building Power by Developing the Human Spirit* :

Shel Trapp: I first met Gale Cincotta in the basement of Mandell Methodist Church at the beginning of the busing fight. She became my work partner for more than thirty years, and together we started both National People's Action and National Training and Information Center. She was the toughest, smartest, quickest-thinking person I have ever had the privilege to work with. She had grown up in the neighborhood, went to Austin High School, and got to OBA as president of the Parent Teacher Association at May School, where Jimmy, the youngest of her six sons, was going at the time. The school, at 512 S. Lavergne, had been built for eight hundred but had about sixteen hundred students. Feeding time at the lion house was quiet compared to May School. There were seventy-five kids to a room, classes in janitor closets, outdated textbooks, and more. Cincotta was angry about it. From day one, she was always angry, in a good sense – angry and motivated to create change.

Cincotta was a very intimidating woman. She had been fighting overcrowding on her own, but because she didn't have an organizer behind her, she didn't quite know how to mobilize more troops. After she hooked up with OBA that started to change. (27)

George Knight: Shel and Gale's relationship was like a stormy marriage, as Shel's probably told you.

Ann Vick-Westgate: We asked him to describe the relationship. He said, "Well, love-hate."

George Knight: I think that's fair. I think that's fair. They each brought something to the relationship.

Kathy Desmond: She would not be managed. And one of the tenets of organizing is you strategize ahead of a meeting. I mean this is what I loved about her. I had done an Industrial Areas Foundation training and you would agree on who was going to do what. Gale felt not bound by any of those pre-agreements. Which is why she was so good.

George Knight: Gale would ask people certain questions when she was talking to them: "Well, what do you want…? What are we fighting for…? What's the issue…? What can they do reasonably…? Who can do it…? And will the public accept it or embrace it…?" I mean those are critical questions.

Ann Vick-Westgate: I get the impression that in the relationship between the organizer and the leader that Gale got into the organizing as well. She wasn't just in the leader role.

George Knight: That's right. Certainly as the years went along she moved much more into the organizing, thinking role. But she never gave up the theory that the leader was in charge and there were times when, at least in my view, Shel had given that theory up.

Ann Vick-Westgate: He was telling us how his mother used to get infuriated at all the coverage Gale was getting and nowhere was there mention of Trapp. And he said, "That's the way it's supposed to be. Everywhere you see 'Cincotta' read Trapp."

George Knight: Yeah. But I do think at times that would get to Shel.

Joe Mariano: Gale and Shel had some epic fights in front of the staff. There was lots of moments like that. To me, nothing was that big of a deal. Later, Trapp was getting tired, fighting with Gale all the time. So there was less fights.

What I found is that Gale would come to me and say, "What's wrong with Trapp? Why is he in a bad mood?" I'd say, "Gosh, Gale. What do you mean?" She'd lay it out, "Well, he's always so negative. Anytime I say something, he's negative." "I'll talk to him." So I became a kind of a messenger in between them.

Without any concept of what the work involved, Gale could come up with grand schemes. I don't think Shel wanted to be around here sometimes because there was always some problem that had to be dealt with. He was actually much better on the road, and he enjoyed that. Whereas here you've got to deal with, "Okay, some person's not doing their job" or Gale is complaining about a staff member saying to Trapp, "Get rid of that person." It's not a particularly pleasant task to have to do that, or listen to Gale about that. Both of them did the hiring and firing.

There were experiences where Trapp would be delegated to fire somebody. When they fired [Tom] Fox, it was both of them. That scene was pretty heavy. They called Fox in and said, "Okay. You're fired." Gale could be ruthless on stuff. Fox says, "First of all, I got two questions. Is this a joke #1? And, #2, why?" And she said, "No, it's not a joke and we don't have to tell you why." In her moments she could just be brutal. He was out the door that quickly. No two weeks' notice.

If there's a dark side to her, Gale could be completely ruthless if she wanted to be and that was the way it was. When she felt she had been wronged, for whatever reason, sometimes it was the wrong reason. But with Fox I could see that coming. Fox was there one minute and he was gone the next. It's like the belief evangelicals have that people go up to heaven. What do they call that? "The Rapture." There's just nothing left. And somebody says, "Well, what happened? Where's Fox?" "He doesn't work here anymore." Like that. [Snaps fingers.] Ten o'clock in the morning, Fox is gone. So that was an instance where she could be real tough and brutal and ruthless.

Kathy Desmond: In another case Gale could reach across the racial divide at times when that was really, really difficult. I mean at the Campaign for Human Development we did a lot of work about balancing funding to Hispanics, funding to blacks, working people to be on committees that were the advisory committees about which grants were made, in other words a lot of things that were trying about that relationship.

I didn't know Gale that personally except for a couple of times that I met her one-on-one. But there was some anniversary we were all in Estes Park, Colorado. It was a CHD meeting where the grantees were coming. And it turned out to be a disaster because it was at a high elevation. And Gale was hefty, as were some of the black women from Baltimore. I remember meeting them out walking on the first night. Did Gale smoke?

Michael Westgate: Like a stovepipe.

Kathy Desmond: Right. So that's what they were out doing. They were trying to get a smoke at this place [high in the Rockies in Colorado]. First of all, they're overweight, they're smokers. So they were complaining to me. How could we have ever chosen a place like that? And here Gale was in the middle of these three big, black organizers. At least one of them was from Baltimore. The other one might have been Ruby Johnson. But she had established sisterhood over smoking, being in this god-awful place that we all thought was wonderful. They said, "We can't sleep. There're no sirens at night." She had that ability in the first half hour that she was in a new place she's with the black women and has established a bond. So whatever issues were being debated in the next three days' meetings, she had human ability to find whatever it was. "We can't walk up here. We can't sleep up here. We can't breathe up here. Who chose this god-forsaken place?"

Pablo Eisenberg, founding Executive Director of the Center for Community Change in Washington: Shel's relationship with Gale was "love-hate." And a little sort of "mother-son." But they played off each other superbly. Neither of them would have been effective without the other. It's hard to believe now that in some cases Gale played the "velvet glove" to Shel's "iron mace." I never saw her in that role except behind the scenes.

Shel Trapp: When we first started out Gale was not much up for traveling 'cause she had all these kids too. Her husband died. Her parents were living upstairs from her. We started out going together, couple places. But we got two different styles and we'll end up competing with each other. And that's stupid. It's also very expensive. So let's split it up. So then we started going individually to places. And it worked very good from my perspective. I did not mind at all that when I saw Gale Cincotta's name in the paper, I read "Gale Cincotta and Shel Trapp." And it didn't bother me a bit. My mother was a different story. She was very upset by that. That's the organizer's role. It just was a strange mix of chemicals that jelled, that lasted for decades. It went back to '67.

So when it came to doing testimony on the Hill, it was Gale. I'd strategize with her beforehand and help build the troops to come. In the early days we did some role-playing but then she was so good, I just stopped that. She'd usually just get an envelope out and make some notes. Whenever I give a talk even to this day for a training session, I've got to talk off a manuscript. I may not follow it, but that's my security blanket. She'd have this thing, turn it over, I'd say, "Okay, Gale. Is Anne-Marie going to type that up for you?" "Oh, I can't do that. I got it here. In my head." She'd go up on the stage. That would be her notes for her speech.

Michael Westgate: Did Gale have an early gift for speaking or did she develop it over time? She also had an extraordinary ability to see patterns. She could see two or three things happen and translate it to a broader context, "a national problem." She could see something down the road well before others could.

Shel Trapp: She was always very vocal. From the very first time I met her she was always talking, but she certainly became very proficient as a public speaker. In all my organizing, there's not another organizer ever who could have found a better leader than her. I mean just how sharp her brain was. She could remember so much shit.

Michael Westgate: Where did Gale draw her energy from, and where did you draw yours from? You both had a lot of energy.

Shel Trapp: I really don't know where the energy came from. We both used to say, "You know, you can't do this work unless you're angry." And, you know, that's always what I'd tell my young organizers even to this day. "If you're not angry about people getting screwed then, fuck, go be a banker so you can screw people." It was just there.

My father was a minister. I was a minister for seven years. I had always believed that the Gospel was about revolution and about social change. To this day I still believe the Gospel, if it's read right, which very few people do, is a very revolutionary and radical document. I don't believe all the other horseshit about heaven and hell. But I believe that's it's a revolutionary doctrine that the Church has totally screwed up. And I still feel that there is a good share of that that motivates me even to this day.

In the Catholic Church in the '70s there was a strong group of people that were doing things, Baroni and the whole liberation theology group. And they got tamped down pretty thoroughly. Of course, John Paul II, now that he's packed the College of Cardinals, we're not going anywhere. Except backwards.

Lawrence O'Rourke: Geno Baroni talked about his deepening involvement in social issues in Washington. That involvement was evident when in 1966, Cardinal O'Boyle appointed Geno executive director of the archdiocese's Commission on Urban Affairs. A big part of the Commission's job was to improve the quality of urban life. One way to go about that, Baroni said, was to provide decent housing for the poor. (64)

"When I first came to Washington, I wanted to save the world. Then I wanted to save the country. Then I wanted to save the city. Then I realized that if you wanted to save the world and the country and the city, you had to start right in the neighborhood where people lived." (65)

Ann Vick-Westgate: What made Gale unique as a leader?

Shel Trapp: Gale was also very sensitive. And it was always people clamoring. One of my jobs after a plenary session was to get her through the crowd 'cause it was even worse than a politician speaking, where everybody wants to say, "Oh, gee. I shook the President's hand." It was more than that. "I want to talk to Gale." Or, "I got a problem." People looked to her as the godfather. I mean, "She can solve my problem. If I talk to Gale, my problem, then it'll get solved." Whereas if they come to me I'd say, "Can you get twenty people together?" They didn't want to hear that. Gale would solve their problem.

I remember a lady phoning in for "Gale Cincotta" once. Gale and I would always say, "Boy, that name sounds familiar." She was somebody that had been a leader out in Austin, not a major leader, but had been involved in Austin. And her husband had died, she'd lost her income, and she was gonna lose the house. And could Gale help?

Gale's probably got a senator or two expecting a call back and a banker. We got five other things going on that she should be dealing with. I'm sitting there thinking, "Christ's sake. She's dealing with this." So Gale's talking with the lady and says, "Well, do you have mortgage insurance where, if one of you dies, your mortgage is paid up?" And the woman says, "I don't know." "Well, look for it." And told her what to look for. "And if it's there, your mortgage will be paid up. And call the bank and tell them this."

So, a week later the lady calls back and says, "God, it's in there. I called the bank but they said it's not gonna work." Gale picks up the phone, dials the number, "I want to speak to the president. This is Gale Cincotta, chairperson, National People's Action. It's in his best interest to speak to me." He comes on. "This is Gale Cincotta. And you know who I am." "Yes." "Your bank is holding the mortgage on Mary Smith's house." "Well, I don't know anything about that." "Well, you are. And there's a clause in her mortgage that says if one of the partners die, the mortgage will be paid up. Her husband died. You take care of that right now, because she's getting jerked around by your bank. And if I don't get a phone call from her in an hour saying that it's been cleared up and her mortgage is paid up in full, you are gonna rue this day. Goodbye." Twenty minutes later, the lady called,

"Gale, what did you do? They called, all apologetic. They were so sorry. Was there anything else they could do for me?"

Gale would put that call above the two senators that were waiting. Just the kind of person she was. If that lady were to call me, I'd say, "Well, let's get some neighbors together, and go hit the bank." I wouldn't "social work" it through like Gale did. But actually that saved a lot of time because, "Okay. That's done with now." Now she gets back to the senators and the bankers.

My organizing instincts are, "I'm not going to solve the problem for a person. I'll get some folks together and we'll solve it together." But Gale would use her power that way, to benefit the people. Which I'm not gonna argue with at all. Better that than she loses her home.

Michael Westgate: Shel, from an organizer's point of view, needed to have problems persist as the basis on which to organize. Gale, as a leader, wanted to solve problems, to have successes to point to. They complemented each other. Neither could do what they did as effectively without the other doing what he or she did. They also both knew that Gale was much more effective working outside mainstream politics, as she did, than she could have been as one of many legislators or commissioners.

Shel Trapp: I can't remember the number of times that people locally from the Democratic and Republican parties were in, asking her to run for office. It would be for county commissioner or state legislator. A lot of leaders that I have had over the years saw that as an option to power or as an avenue, a way to get into the inner circle. Gale was just smart enough to realize she had more power outside than she would inside. She has always said, "Not interested. You're wasting your time. I'm not interested."

From *The Builders: Houses, People, Neighborhoods, Governments, Money* (1978) by Martin Mayer:
Meanwhile, Chicago had produced the striking figure of Gale Cincotta, a very large housewife in a Mother Hubbard, with a round red face under an aureole of curly white hair – and (on the rare occasions when there is no cigarette between the lips) the most glorious politician's smile of the 1970s. Mrs. Cincotta had become an activist while leading a crusade to get a new junior high school for her children (among others) in the Austin section of Chicago. She understood both instinctively and intellectually the secrets of successful community organization, which are two: (1) you stay on the outside, forcing the authorities (local and national) to take complete responsibility for the performance of the task you set them; and (2) you always win, because even if nothing comes of the meeting or the protest you can always claim to have brought the people's grievance to the attention of some powerful figure who would otherwise have ignored it. "We won that junior

high school fifty-two times," Mrs. Cincotta said with reminiscent pleasure, "before they actually agreed to build it."

Michael Westgate: Community organizing is a profession. The terminology and the actions to be taken by community organizers are different from those of leaders. Did Gale see herself as an organizer? To what extent did each of you follow Alinsky-style tactics?

Shel Trapp: Gale was tough as nails. She would use the word "organizer"; I would not use the word "organizer" for her but that's just semantics. She had no problem being very aggressive, very tough. And using power which the people gave her against whomever, wherever.

She went from the very early days when we were going after a panic peddler. We went to schools where the kids of this panic peddler attended. We passed out flyers at the school saying, "Little Jimmy Jones' daddy is a panic peddler moving blacks into Austin. Westchester's next." Westchester was the suburb where he lived. She had no problem passing those flyers out around the kid's school. I had no problem either. If there was a way to crack the enemy, Gale and I were on the same page. In that regard, it was Alinsky-like tactics.

But she differed and I differed with Alinsky. I mean Alinsky never would have gone as far into development as NTIC was. Like working with Aetna Life and Casualty, he would have never done that. The guy who trained me, Gaudette, never would have done that. Back in Austin, a slum landlord wanted to give the organization a building. Gale and I both wanted to take it. It probably was good we didn't. But Gaudette said, "No. That's not what we're about. Get slumlords to fix 'em up; we don't manage properties." But I had seen what Bickerdike Redevelopment Corporation could do at NCO. The way it really started to change the whole neighborhood and the perception of the neighborhood. So I saw the importance of that kind of thing linked with organizing. I didn't want to get involved in that, but I knew that we could be of help to Bruce Gottschall [at Neighborhood Housing Services of Chicago] when he ran into problems, and he could be of help to us by putting houses strategically on blocks which basically became anchors on those blocks.

Michael Westgate: It is a constant dilemma for community-based organizations. Should an organization based on community organizing take on development? Should a CDC [Community Development Corporation] or an NHS [Neighborhood Housing Services] organize the community? It does dilute the mission of the organization to do both. It is difficult for the same organization simultaneously to picket a bank and ask it for donations or for a large loan for a project. Foundations are also difficult to deal with, as some will fund only community organizing, others only bricks and mortar.

The best solution may be, as there was between NHS of Chicago and NTIC, a relationship where a Bruce Gottschall and a Gale Cincotta could call on each other to take those actions or make those phone calls which might be unseemly if made by the other. Some CDCs, like Urban Edge in Boston, insert into the capital budget for each project funds for community organizing. Such funds can also be provided to an allied community organizing group rather than hiring staff internally to do the community organizing.

In Chelsea, in retrospect, I should have tried to formalize relationships with another non-profit where they would be strictly the organizing group and Chelsea Neighborhood Housing Services would have been the one only implementing housing, rather than mixing roles. Most professionals in this arena agree that community organizing has to be done by someone, either inside or outside the community-based housing organization, to maximize the effectiveness of the agency. Building community is more than bricks and mortar. It requires pressure on the lenders, and on the city and on the school system to make them respond to needs. In the Chicago model, OBA [Organization for a Better Austin], then MAHA [Metropolitan Area Housing Alliance], then NPA [National People's Action] and its affiliates provided the pressure. NHS [Neighborhood Housing Services of Chicago] delivered the goods. None of them could have been as effective without the others.

Shel Trapp: So our minds were, again, like Vince Lombardi's, "Winning isn't everything; it's the only thing." How we got to winning we didn't care, just so long as we won. We were not that particular about what form that victory would take. Whether we would get into bed with Aetna and get reinvestment with them or what it would be. So long as it worked and the neighborhood got better, who cares how it happened.

A lot of the purists argued with us. "Go get on our boating shoes. Having sold out before we started NPA, we're no longer tied to the grassroots." That was a bunch of bullshit. I was on the road 20-25 days a month, all out. I was not dealing with NTIC issues. We started a group in Denver on stray dogs. That's how that organization got started. Those were the kind of issues I dealt with.

Bud Kanitz: Gale and Trapp's relationship was a classic Alinsky organizer-leader relationship. Gale told me about a bald-headed guy that came out in the 'hood and he was organizing on education, and she already had been active in doing this. You know it was basically "What the shit is this guy doing in my neighborhood?" He was a minister, too, a Methodist. She told me Trapp said, "Well, if you're gonna have a meeting, you have to get together some flyers and get the word out." And her response was basically, "I've been doing that all along anyway. You're not teaching me anything new." Part of her instinct was doing the right thing, even though she'd never really had a "teacher" to teach her how to organize.

Gale got very little from Alinsky because she only met him a couple of times. She probably got a lot from Tom Gaudette. Gaudette was a kind of a guy that always would push you, push the envelope. He would challenge, challenge the leaders. But most of what Gale did was just instinctually correct. She just had the right instincts. Her being a leader was not something she learned out of a book. It just came natural.

I remember Gaudette telling the story that Trapp had applied for the organizer job at OBA. And he said every time that he called Trapp, Trapp never was home. And he said, "Well, this is the guy that I want to hire. 'Cause all he does is work." So that's what happened.

Gaudette had an uncanny ability to find really top-notch organizers and work 'em to death. Our tradition at NCO, which was started by Gaudette, and then Gaudette did it at OBA, was midnight staff meetings. I mean late at night, eleven o'clock or midnight, because that was when all the neighborhood meetings were finished. So you'd meet until one or two in the morning and then get up the next morning to get some neighborhood leaders and go down to Housing Court to testify against a slum landlord at nine o'clock.

So Gaudette created OBA and then recruited people. One of who was Gale. She was already active in the education fight prior to OBA's starting. Gale just started on her own in this education fight for self-interest. Her sons were all being penalized basically because of overcrowding in the neighborhood schools.

Gale and Shel just absolutely were the ying and yang. They worked together. And I remember Trapp telling me that when Gale first started getting interested in national public policy stuff he said, "You do the politics; I'll do the organizing." So that was the way it worked.

Then, in 1971, NCO hired Shel Trapp as its executive director. It was out of the NCO office that the planning, the initial organizing, happened to put together the first [meeting of] what is now NPA, which happened in '72.

I remember hearing from one of the local priests, "There's this guy in Washington named Geno Baroni." I suggested to Trapp, "You know, this guy, he's doing exactly...National Center for Urban Ethnic Affairs, that's NCO. If there is any kind of a neighborhood, and a neighborhood organization, that reflects what Geno is all about, it's NCO." So Geno was asked to be the speaker at the annual congress when all the NCO member organizations got together on an annual basis.

I was then assigned by Shel to be Geno's driver. So I took him around to see the neighborhood. And then he had an interview with some talk show host. I remember the talk show host saying, "And what do you think about abortion?" And Geno would always change the subject back to the neighborhood. It was that relationship that brought some money in. Geno had some Ford Foundation money and Geno put some of that money into the first NPA conference. [The National Center for Urban Affairs had been created in 1971 with funding from the Ford Foundation.]

So at the point Shel and Gale met he was a staff organizer at OBA and he became NCO's executive director in '71. Prior to that he was at OBA working for Tom Gaudette.

George Knight: There was an Italian place the staff used to go on Monday nights and have spaghetti and beer. And there were a lot of Chicago police. Shel at the time was out at OBA. So Shel would join us or Shel and Gale would join us or some of our leaders and you'd just be sitting around talking about what was going on in the neighborhoods, what the issues were, what were you struggling with. I mean the issues sound so terribly pedestrian. We wanted a swimming pool in the community. We wanted our own day in court, which we got eventually, Housing Court. So we could take just cases related to NCO on one day.

Michael Westgate: But that's a huge victory. That's the kind of thing that we can point to and that people in their twenties today seeing some real outrages in their own community can say, "Gee. Getting one day a week in the courts and then videotaping something we can bring before the judge."

George Knight: I remember a bunch of years ago, when the FBI files first became available, Bud Kanitz went and got our Chicago Red Squad files. He and I spent a couple of nights over beer laughing about them. The thing that staggered me was that they collected all this crap and held it. You would have agendas from a local civic meeting where the top item for discussion was a stop sign!

Kathy Desmond: And no context. That was the thing I've heard from other people who got their files. There's just no context and it's episodic, one agenda but not the next one. It was very episodic. Still, the stuff they have is just pretty amazing. But this was the trivia of daily organizing.

George Knight: But most of the stuff we were dealing with was just small. Literally it was stop signs, trash pickup, abandoned cars, schools, helping the local parish to get a sign that said you couldn't park here on Sundays or you were allowed to park here on Sundays. All the Catholic churches ran carnivals in the summertime, so it was getting street closings. It was all that kind of stuff. A lot of it was very, very small stuff, but it was all helping people get better skilled at who do we approach, how we do it, are we in agreement, who writes the letter. It was all building skills and abilities so that, when it did come to a blockbuster or it did come to a slum landlord, people would be willing to go to court and testify. People would be willing to say, "No, we've written to him five times."

We used to hold an annual meeting in February or January, some cold month, where we'd pull in all the slumlords that we'd been focusing on and try and get them to come and talk and picket them and take pictures of them and all that stuff. They sound so trivial.

Kathy Desmond: How would you get slumlords to come to a meeting?

George Knight: Oh, we'd sucker them in. The world was much more unsophisticated in those days. You'd say, "Well, Mr. Westgate, there are a few of us going to be meeting at St. Fidelis Church on Saturday afternoon. We know you collect rent on Saturdays. Would you mind coming by?" He'd say, "Oh, I don't know where St. Fidelis is." "Well, we can pick you up at such-and-such address." And he'd say, "Okay. That would be fine." Then there would be 300 people.

Ann Vick-Westgate: How would you get him to come back?

George Knight: Oh, they hardly ever did. I can remember seeing the photographer one year getting knocked down by one guy who was so angry. He was swinging at the camera but caught me too.

Ann Vick-Westgate: What made Gale an effective leader?

George Knight: She never minded doing that stuff. Even after she got a national presence, she didn't mind doing that stuff. She was always up for dealing with that stuff because that's where she started, the little stuff. She never lost touch with the base and what the issues were. But it was that ability to switch from a policy discussion to mechanics. "Have you talked to your committeeman? Have you talked to the alderman? How many of you talked to the committeeman? Do you think you can get five neighbors to go with you to talk to the committeeman?"

The committeeman was an elected position, Democratic Party position, for each ward who sat on the Central Committee. So they were the ones that put up the alderman. And sometimes they were identical, but sometimes they were different. But the committeeman was the more powerful one.

But Gale would always be willing to do that. And she was funny. I can remember one of our Neighborhood Reinvestment meetings she came and spoke. It was when the Kemp folks had just come in. She read an imaginary letter that she was writing to the Secretary suggesting that they not fire the current HUD employees. She'd made some comment and gotten in trouble. "Just gather them all on two floors of the HUD building, but feed them corn because they are turkeys." It was typical. And she'd refer to HUD as the "turkey farm." She was so out and out funny about some stuff. Outrageous.

Joe Mariano: I first met Gale coming to Chicago from Cleveland where Trapp was our consultant. And Trapp said, "Come. We're having this meeting at St. Sylvester's Schwinn Hall and people from all over the country are coming in to talk about bank redlining." And that was the first time I had seen Gale in operation.

I later realized that there was this competition between the two of them in a weird way. Trapp wanted to hire <u>his</u> staff and Gale wanted to make sure she had <u>her</u> people. Gale also had a love-hate relationship with organizers through the years. She felt they'd gotten away sometimes and they were too much into the <u>process</u>. You know, the fancy agenda and *Robert's Rules*. She said, "I tell you it's very simple. You just get people together and figure out what you want and go get it. You don't need a professional to tell you how to do that." So that was always at the basis of their relationship.

There was implicit trust but there was also that Trapp represented a different way of thinking that Cincotta felt was always an impediment. That as organizers we knew too much. We stood in the way sometimes and we had to forget what we knew and connect with people in different ways.

It's the organizer's role to be in the background. In the later years we tried to get Shel up front, like at the NPA conference, and he'd be more visible. He was open to that, to help the office and help the organization, but he was never comfortable being up in a role. They were like partners in this whole thing.

They'd always hash out these ideas and talk things through and argue about stuff. But Gale was clearly the one that was always up front. Gale would come up with the ideas and make the organizers do them. Do the writing, do everything. And then Gale would read it and say, "I don't like this and I don't like that. I don't understand what you're saying. Write it again." Gale was a speaker not a writer. She would talk about her column, "Next Move" in *DISCLOSURE* newsletter and then the staff person, for many years Ted Wysocki, would write it. She knew stuff. She read a lot. But you gave her something and she said, "Well, I don't understand what this means" or "What are you saying here?" or "That's not me. I don't talk like that." So that was it.

Alicia Mendoza: Gale sat at the front of the office. And then at the other two locations I was at with them, she sat at the front also. No separate office or anything. She sat where she could see everybody. Shel was in the desk along the window. It was the same way in the other offices as well. Gale would be here and Shel would be right here and then of course Anne-Marie— the three, from the beginning.

Helping other people was her goal. Of course, CRA [the Community Reinvestment Act] we know that. Just wherever she could in whatever way possible with the information she was able to obtain, to help others to live a better life. She always had a researcher.

Gale spoke, and from that, staff would write. She had no need to. She never used a typewriter. She never used any machines except the copy machine. She had no need to, really. She had everyone else to assist. And she didn't like any kind of electronic stuff, no new stuff. Never wanted, as you probably heard, a computer.

She did know how to use the phone. I don't think she would have approved of a cell phone and she would never have done email. So if people needed to reach her, they either showed up or they got her by phone.

So for her column "Next Move" she would give somebody the ideas and then they would write it and then she'd do the final edit. She would speak. But then she would say, "I don't talk like that! It doesn't sound like me at all." So she would edit it her own way.

Joe Mariano: She had no idea what people did. She had this notion. She said, "Well, I want to go door-to-door and floor-to-floor in Congress." I started to say, "Gale, do you how big all these offices are?" And she didn't want to hear that. "Well, there's no reason why we can't do that." I said, "Fine, Gale. We'll go door-to-door and floor-to-floor." So we did something like that. And she'd go into her meetings with a group of leaders and she'd see some other leaders wandering the halls. We did have a presence but it was clear we didn't hit every single door in every single floor.

But that's how she operated. She had some outrageous idea and then all the work would be done. And people somehow would show up. But that's what we got paid to do in Gale's mind. We were all these hotshots. "Okay. Here's the idea. Go do it." Like "Reclaim America" was a crazy idea. It was kind of the nadir of the neighborhood movement and it was starting to go downhill.

I started here in January of '82. I didn't know what I was going to do. Trapp's idea of an orientation was he'd take you around and he would say, "This is the photocopier. I don't know how it works. Talk to Alicia. This is the message box over here and we put your messages in here. Check it every day. This is your mailbox. This is where you're going to sit. Here's how the phone works. Go talk to people." Then he'd go out of town.

I worked in Cleveland from 1974 through 1981 so all that time I had been coming out to Chicago for staff meetings. Trapp would convene staff people and talk about, "What do we think we should do nationally? Where should we go?" Sometimes Gale would be a part of those meetings. And because I was in a position to deliver people out of Cleveland to NPA – Cleveland was one of the stronger cities at the time; they knew we had a good group of staff and leaders there through the years – I got to know Gale.

People like Joe Fagan, myself, Barb Bush, we'd be the ones to come in and talk about, "Just where are things at? Where do we see organizing going?"

Gale would give her analysis about, "There's really no such thing as middle class. We're all working class." It was fascinating to hear some of those stories that Gale would tell about growing up with her family and her grandfather burning the farmhouse. You know that those kinds of things are like, "Wow!" So how I got to know Gale was through these years coming to Chicago and seeing her here.

Michael Westgate: Who recruited you?

Joe Mariano: Well, they both recruited me. Trapp said to me, "I know you're going to be making a move soon. And we'd like you to consider NTIC, etc, etc, etc." I finally said yes to Trapp because he was the one that would always be coming to Cleveland to be the consultant. About a week later Gale calls me and says, "I've heard through the grapevine that you're thinking about where you're going to go next. We'd like to have you come to Chicago." And I said to her, "I had this conversation with Trapp several months ago and I told him last week that I was willing to start. Have you talked to Trapp about this?" And she goes, "No."

Ted Wysocki, founding editor of NTIC's *DISCLOSURE* and writer for Gale's speeches and Congressional testimony: Gale always had this open room office, and so her desk faced everybody, I learned, intentionally. If you wanted to get work done, you actually faced the same way Gale's facing so that, if you need to, you can swivel your chair and see if she's available, but otherwise you weren't making eye contact. If she wanted you real bad, she'd call your name. So as everybody would look at Gale or whenever you turned around to look at Gale, on the front of her desk was the sign that said, "WE WORK MIRACLES HERE – IT'S PART OF THE PROGRAM." That was the staff motivation.

Where did she get her energy from? Besides the cigarettes? I don't know -- the cigarettes, coffee and Coke or whatever. It was obviously contagious. Part of it is the way the office is set up and it's still set up that way. You are in this together. No private offices. There are private conference rooms. And it's jam-packed people elbow to elbow. There are rows of desk, and all working away.

And these 11:00 p.m. staff meeting or whatever, 10:00 at night. That would go on. But the late night meeting was mostly Shel. That wasn't Gale. That was back also when there were more of the organizers that were deployed, whether it be in churches or whatever the home bases were for the different communities.

Cal Bradford: John McKnight is one of the more brilliant people I ever met. He is on the NTIC Board. He was at the Center for Urban Affairs at Northwestern University. Before that, he was director of the regional Civil Rights Commission for the Upper Midwest. He had a long history working with civil rights issues. He's probably the only full professor at Northwestern who never had anything more than a bachelor's degree. So John brought that sort of perspective of questioning the professional dominance with him. When he heard about these community groups, John understood what they were up to right away. And he knew Saul Alinsky. I was there as a graduate student and he said, "You should go down and watch what's going on there. This is going to be really interesting stuff."

At the time Gale wasn't dealing with lending; she was just dealing with the schools. She started off trying to deal with the kids in the "Willis wagons." So we went down and watched this thing. We saw this guy Trapp because he hovers around in the back, and we were in the back. That's where you see him. When I saw Shel, I figured, "Well, it's going to be like Alinsky." It was going to be like me and my friends because we figured, "We're gonna go help these neighborhoods' folks. We got this great education. We have this great social conscience. We're gonna go save all these people." And Trapp's attitude and Gale's was always, "No. The only people can save us is us. You can help us and we'll tell you what we want you to do. But, otherwise, you just get out of our way."

We went down there and watched. Trapp never stood up in front of the group. Sometimes at the NPA meeting people would ask him to say something. And one time he gave a speech because someone was sick and they made him do it. He hated it. But he believed in his leaders.

I'd go down to the NTIC office and it was fascinating. Gale would go off to some trip somewhere and she'd come back and Trapp would go over and pull up his chair to her desk and she would say what everyone was thinking about doing. Trapp would figure out the strategy for how to organize around it. But the trust that developed between the two of them was just fascinating.

They'd argue a lot of times, but they had a lot of respect for each other and you could see that happen. I've never been involved in another organization where the organizers really respected the leaders and thought of them as leaders, not as sort of puppets. I mean most organizers – I got to be honest – sort of think of themselves as puppeteers. They have the ideas. They know what they're going to do, and they're gonna get those leaders out there to do it for them, so push them out in front.

But that's not the way it worked with Gale or the people who are part of it now. It's just to me a fascinating organization because of that structure and also because Gale insisted that they wouldn't go [move] to Washington, D.C. I always thought that was one of the more brilliant moves. Everyone thought it was stupid at the time. She said, "No. If you go to Washington, D.C., then you're going to be worried about your relationship with this Senator and this staff. And you're going to always think that whatever you're doing is the most important thing. The power is in the people. And if you're not someplace where you're directly connected to that, then whatever you do it's not going to be connected to people. People have to understand it and be part of it for it to make a difference to them."

I used to say, "Well, Gale, this is what we need to do with Fannie Mae and Freddie Mac," for example. She said, "Yeah. You're probably right, Calvin. But we're not doing that now. We're not doing that now unless the people decide that that's what needs to be done next." Because the whole point of the organization is you work with each group. And if they see the reality, how it affects their neighborhoods, they deal with these people face to face and <u>then</u>, if they need to go to the next level, then they'll do that. It's not an efficient system, but it's the only one that really empowers people. The other ones don't empower anybody. And, later on, whatever solution you have is gonna fall apart because there's no base to protect it. It was always that attitude she and Trapp had.

Michael Westgate: There was brilliance in how Gale could perceive and enunciate problems, and Shel could see how to mobilize the troops around the issues. There was also a respect for the troops that Saul Alinsky did not show. Gale knew how to recognize what issues people wanted to deal with and when. It was Gale's sense of timing that allowed Shel to maximize people's involvement. It was also her uncanny insight about when to get the bankers and others she had been targeting through demonstrations and protests to sit down in the boardroom and make a deal.

Shel Trapp: When I went on the road I always told groups, "I work for you. I'm here to deal with dog shit, dogs, pigeon shit. I don't care what the issue is; I'll work on that." And before I'd leave I'd say, "You know, have you heard about this thing, redlining?" And start trying to plant some seeds. In a month or two, I'd come back there. Usually after about the third trip somebody else was saying, "Gee, the banks don't seem to be doing much." Suddenly I had a CRA fight going. I didn't go in preaching it. Work on what you got first. People learned to trust me and understand, "Hey, he does know one or two things about organizing, and how to win. Maybe we can take this next step."

Gale started traveling, too, after her kids got older and her parents died. She did a lot of speaking stuff. Maybe once or twice I spoke at local conventions. She did some strategizing, not to the extent that I did. We complemented one another.

Joe Mariano: I started in Cleveland before Inez Killingsworth. We started with a project in the East Side of Cleveland where there was Hungarians, Slovaks, Italians, blacks, and Trapp was the consultant to the project. The first issue was dogs.

The Buckeye-Woodland Community Congress was the first organizing project in Cleveland that was based on the neighborhood model. It was an attempt to bring together all these different groups who literally were at war with one another. I mean the whites were bailing out and were afraid of the blacks and buying guns. And the blacks were moving in from the so-called "ghetto" in the late sixties. There was a lot of tension.

I also worked with the United Farm Workers, with Cesar Chavez in California. I grew up in Newark, New Jersey. The reason I went to California was I didn't know how you did this thing called organizing. People said, "Well, Chavez is training organizers." I had no idea what an organizer did. I went out there and people said to me, "Well, why are you leaving Newark? There are a lot of problems here." I said, "Yeah, there are tremendous problems, but I don't know what to do about them."

I was born in Newark, grew up in Belleville, N.J., which is adjacent to Newark. It's a working class suburb. You went to Newark for the culture and for the movies, for the shopping. But it all changed abruptly after the riots.

In the sixties I was there when the rioting was taking place. The National Guard had surrounded the city. It was pretty scary times. I was involved with the Lutheran Church and teaching school at the time. The response was, "Well, let's get together and have these racial dialogues and do a march in the city or something like that." And it just left me cold. It didn't seem like it was making any difference. I would take these suburbanites on tours of the ghetto, "sensitivity training." I just would come away with these incredible headaches. How overwhelming it all seemed with people in bad housing and all the rotten health clinics and abandoned cars.

In the Lutheran Church, literally these older folks – maybe in their seventies – were saying, "This is a church that was founded by German immigrants in Jersey City. Look at these beautiful stained glass windows. These lousy kids next door, all they do is throw rocks at our windows and there are abandoned cars outside. What the hell's happening in this neighborhood?" I'm thinking to myself, "Man, is this the future of the church?" There's no connection with the neighborhood. It just was like a little fortress. I didn't know what to do with myself.

So I was into non-violent direct action and I went out to California to learn about organizing. Actually I interviewed. In those days they hired volunteers at five dollars a week. They gave you room and board. So I had tenure as a schoolteacher in Maplewood, New Jersey, which is a very rich, white suburb of Newark, at the junior high school. I was going to change the world as a schoolteacher. 'Course long story short, it didn't happen. So I was trying to figure out, "Okay. What can I do to make a difference?" I left a tenured teaching position to go out there and people basically thought I was nuts. And I was wondering if I was sane too at that point.

I was scared shitless. Going from a place I had grown up all my life to a totally different environment with migrant farm workers, California, away from family, friends. And during the time at the end of the grape boycott, getting involved with the strike in Salinas in 1970 which was very violent and crazy because there were 10,000 workers on strike which the union wasn't prepared for. Actually the union was going to go in to fight Sunkist; that was the next big campaign 'cause they had the big label.

I was around with the boycott, going around the country. And I was there in 1970. Then I left to go on to Philadelphia, New York City, Atlanta, Georgia on the boycott, on five bucks a week. Had to raise your own budget too for the use of the unions. But the farm worker experience was more of a movement, more of a different kind of organizing. So it always gnawed at me, "Well, what's wrong with the cities? What's happening here?"

So a friend of mine called me from Cleveland and said, "We're organizing blacks and whites around issues like redlining and we got this guy who knew Saul Alinsky." And I said, "Wait a second, you're bringing together blacks and whites in a neighborhood?" He said, "Yeah, it's amazing. We're doing this thing and it's a lot different than the farm worker stuff. We're doing it based on people's self-interest." "How do you do that?" And he goes, "Well, it's working." So I left California and went to Cleveland.

Then when I came to Cleveland, the first person I met from this office was Trapp. Again, this guy he seemed like he was nuts. I was again scared shitless. I didn't know what I was doing or how to go about this or how to talk to people and ask basic questions that didn't seem stupid. Which is the amazing thing about both Gale and Trapp. You could ask the most ridiculous questions that they probably heard ten thousand times, but they'd not demean you or say, "You're stupid," which I was, and they'd give you an answer that made sense.

All the tensions I experienced in Cleveland where the whites didn't trust the blacks, all the white subgroups—like the Hungarians didn't like the Slovaks and the Slovaks... Everybody thought everybody else had it together. So you'd talk to the Italians and they'd say, "Yeah. Those Hungarians, they stick together. And they know how to go down to city hall and get what they want." And you'd talk to the Hungarians and they'd say, "Yeah. It's these blacks. They always do these protests and they're getting everything." You'd go talk to the Slovaks, they'd say, "It's these damn Italians. They've been running this neighborhood for years." So I'm thinking, "I'm going to get these people together?"

And it worked. I mean it really did. We created this umbrella organization called the Buckeye-Woodland Community Congress based on the NCO model here in Chicago. And out of that suddenly other people around the city wanted to get organized. So we housed a couple of organizers in our office to do a project in the Union-Miles neighborhood which was adjacent to where Inez's neighborhood is.

106 - GALE FORCE

At one point we said, "Okay. Here's the Buckeye-Woodland neighborhood right here. Why don't we do organizing here and annex that area too, the southeast side of Cleveland?" Well, truth be told the whites on the Buckeye-Woodland group looked at the demographics and said, "Well, we're going to be overwhelmed with blacks. We're not going to be able to control this Buckeye-Woodland Community Congress." They didn't say it out loud, but that was the message, "No! No!" Because actually the whites controlled Buckeye-Woodland in the very beginning, they were organized. Because the blacks didn't know one another, they were all moving in. Brand new. And all their institutions were still outside of the neighborhood, churches, mainly the churches.

So we had to do a separate project. The diocese was the catalyst for the organizing. This priest wanted to do something so he convinced Harry Fagan, who was then the director for the Catholic Commission for Community Action, the Cleveland-based diocesan agency, to put some bucks in here and hire two organizers. We helped train them.

That was the thing that sponsored Buckeye-Woodland. The priest that ran that agency wrote the grant. Then the Campaign for Human Development they gave the money to create that. So that's where Inez came in, through the door knocking by these organizers that were creating whatever it was called, Union-Miles project, around Epiphany parish.

One of their big first issues in Union-Miles was enforcing this new thing called the Community Reinvestment Act. They filed one of the first challenges on Society National Bank. So that was kind of the test for how this law was going to work or not work. Gale was involved in those early days.

Michael Westgate: So, aside from Chicago, would Cleveland be among the next tier of cities where Gale had the most impact?

Inez Killingsworth, founding board chairperson of Cleveland's Empowering and Strengthening Ohio's People (ESOP) and co-chairperson of National People's Action following Gale's passing: Yes. The NPA impacted Cleveland in so many ways. At one point in Cleveland, there were five or six community coalitions. It's like the whole city of Cleveland, each little section, each little neighborhood, had an organization. And they were all part of NPA. And we would come together in Cleveland as neighborhood people in action. So we had our own little mini Neighborhood People in Action instead of National People's Action. So all of the coalitions there would come together on a citywide issue and do some things.

We've done some things in Cleveland with deregulation of natural gas. That was one of the things that NPA and Gale in particular impacted because we were trying to get Sohio to do some things in terms of heating. The Home Energy Assistance in Cleveland was lacking the funds. People wasn't able to pay their heating bills. So the slogan then was "You have to make a choice whether to heat or to eat."

And Gale came in and gave us a real boost on it. Because NTIC was able to buy some stock that allowed us access into the annual meeting for Sohio. And Gale came. So we walked in and we just took over the meeting. They knew we were coming because they knew we had the stock. And they couldn't stop it because they had to have the annual meeting. So they were prepared and we were prepared also. But the thing that made the difference, they finally listened and they finally began to put money into weatherization. So lots of homes in Cleveland that were not able to be weatherized got weatherized from that action. So people had warmer homes because Sohio put so much money into the weatherization program. So it worked.

It was in 1977 that I met Gale, coming to a leadership meeting here in Chicago. I'd never heard of Gale. I didn't know anything about Gale.

Working in Cleveland, it was Union Miles Community Coalition is how I got really involved there. We had a problem in the community and people always laugh at me when I say we had a dog problem.

There were packs of dogs running all over the place. I couldn't get my children in school without having to watch them. Watch them get into the building and then, when it's time to come back, watch them get out. So organizers came through and said, "You know, you want to do something about that?" From there, they invited me to a meeting and I said, "Okay, I'll go." I didn't believe it because I didn't believe people had the power to change things or to make a difference. The status quo, the political leaders, made the decisions and you just abided by the rules.

But I found out differently once we had this little win. And then the organizers said, "Well, we have this national connection and we would like for you to go to Chicago for a leadership meeting." I'm like, "Leader? I'm not a leader. I just got involved in this issue."

So that's how I met Gale at this leadership meeting. And when I first saw her, just to listen to her talk with so much conviction, I said, "This is <u>something</u>. That lady is either crazy or she know what she's talking about." She kept saying to us, "You can do it. You can do it. You can do it. You can make a difference." And she always talked about, "You just got to keep organizing. You just got to keep organizing." So that was my first real meeting of Gale at that leadership meeting. It was in a basement of a church somewhere here in Chicago.

And when I left that meeting, listening at her being so convicted about, and so passionate about, an issue, it was in me that I can make a difference. "You can do it." So I decided to go back to Cleveland and try to implement what I heard.

We won the issue on the dogs. We discovered that there was only one dogcatcher for the entire city of Cleveland. And, after our first contact with the city officials, we got seven dogcatchers. And we had media attention. The dogs got cleaned up. It was like more and more people had the same self-interest that I had. And that was one thing that Gale talked about. "You'll find that there's a lot of other people that's hurting, that have the same self-interest. And you have to gather those people together and keep building and keep building." So we won that issue.

And that organization went from doing stray dogs to developing houses. So we went from a stray dog issue to a million dollar operation. And that was because of my first meeting of Gale. And I was president of that organization for about twenty years.

Ted Wysocki: The work you did, Michael, with Chelsea NHS, I think that was the other brilliance of Gale.

Michael Westgate: We were able, over a 12-year period, to rehab over 150 homes in the toughest part of Chelsea. We did get $10,000 for community organizing in Chelsea, funded as a subgrantee of NTIC, from the Department of Justice's "Weed & Seed Program", intended to weed out criminal activity and replace it with community-based activities. Chelsea's Police Department was also receiving funds from that program for Community Based Policing.

Ted Wysocki: Obviously the whole HUD battle was sort of a corollary to CRA. FHA was the predatory lender of the time, so it was the other, reverse side of government-sponsored redlining. Gale was willing to encourage her organizers and NPA to go into whatever issues were hurting people or were opportunities for people, and not to have the ego that she had to be the leader on all of this.

In my early organizing days, I read about this Community Development Block Grant (CDBG) program, and I said to her, "Well, we ought to do something on this. This is money that's going to be coming to the city halls, and we can guess what they're not going to do with it." She was very comfortable, "Fine. If you think it's an issue, go ahead. Go out and do it and organize it." So, in the Chicago organizing, I had the personal professional challenge and opportunity to basically go organize the first citywide issues that MAHA was doing, that Gale was not the leader of. I found my own leader and Gale was supportive.

As we heard from other cities, as that evolved, then she was totally supportive that there needed to be an NPA leadership team on CDBG. And that helped the formation of other NPA leaders, that they were comfortable that Gale was comfortable with them developing their leadership abilities, to be able to do multiple meetings at HUD, intentionally on the same day.

Because there were multiple issues and there were multiple leadership teams to tackle those.

Brenda LaBlanc, founding leader with the Des Moines chapter of Iowa Citizens for Community Improvement (CCI) and following Gale's death, a co-chairperson of NPA: My dad loved to go down to Hyde Park Corner, Speakers' Corner, in London, and listen. He was a union activist and an officer in the local Labour Party. He was an electrician, born in 1900, so he participated in unions when they truly were trying to get established. Not like they are now. They're fat. Then they were out in the streets. He liked to go down there and he was very good at heckling, so he would go to some Conservative guy and listen to him for a while. And he'd finally pick on something and start an argument. He only had an 8th grade education, but he read a lot of books. And he had a good vocabulary.

One of the things that annoys me the most about neighborhood organizing is that when you go down to city hall or a banker comes out or anything and you're from a poor neighborhood, they somehow expect you to be stupid. They talk to you like you're stupid. All the people I've known who live in my neighborhood and neighborhoods like mine, there's just so many variations. I mean some of them are highly intelligent. Not well educated, but that's not the same thing as being intelligent. And among the business types you meet, you meet some real dumbheads. They've had education, but they're still dumb.

Education doesn't just happen in schools. Education happens all the time. Children are learning all the time. They're sometimes learning the wrong things, but they're learning all the time. Because as they grow they're picking up things and they're processing it and thinking about it. They're learning.

My husband and I got involved with NPA after we saw a sign about a meeting about redlining. It took us six months and six banks to get a loan. We got turned down by five banks. And we'd both been in our jobs for quite a long time and we had by this point excellent credit. It was astonishing to me that we got turned down.

This was in the late sixties or early seventies because I joined Citizens for Community Improvement (CCI) in '78. We knew what redlining was and we knew we'd had an experience with it. Went to the meeting and they talked about CRA because HMDA was passed in '75. They told us how there was a law now that said that this was illegal, but that we needed to work with the banks in order to make it happen. And I thought, "Well, that seems like a very worthwhile thing to do."

I was almost 50 at the time. My kids were pretty well grown up and I had more free time now. They asked for volunteers to form a task force. I was very suspicious about CCI. "Well, who are these people? And what is their agenda?" Because I'd been to meetings before where some group was going to do something and you go and you find out they've got an agenda that you have to accept. Well, I don't necessarily accept other people's agendas. I have my own agenda.

I got up and told about our experiences, as did a lot of other people. They were all in the same boat. Most people didn't stay in and keep trying like we did, and never did get a loan. We talked about how bad that was and kind of stirred each other up. There were about a dozen people stepped forward and formed that first task force. And then we started working with CCI and I found out they don't have an agenda. Their agenda is our agenda. Isn't that nice!

There was no pressure to do this or that, but talk about it and work at it. We made the decisions. I really liked that and I enjoyed it. We started working with local banks. We didn't get very far in the beginning, but a lot of us stayed with it. In '78 the newspaper published figures from HMDA and they really showed that redlining did exist. And CRA was passed.

I got acquainted with NPA and Gale through Joe Fagan, who founded Citizens for Community Improvement (CCI) along with some other priests and religious groups in Waterloo. They moved to Des Moines in '78. They were working a lot on slum landlords, organizing tenants and such. But Joe Fagan got his training under Shel Trapp in Chicago. So did Paul Battle, an organizer in Des Moines. He trained under Shel too.

Cal Bradford: In Gale's mind nobody was ever evil. So you never backed someone into a corner they couldn't get out of. That was a real strategy. Trapp understood that too. You always have to give them an out. You can give them a chance to be a hero. Everybody can be a hero. Everybody can be one of us. Nobody is innately evil. It's like your kids. They do bad things, but they're not bad people.

But there was always room at the NPA conferences for everybody's issue. That was like another one of the rules. If there's more than one group, if there are several groups that are interested in something, they get a workshop. They get a session. "Because," Gale said, "you never know when that's gonna be an issue. You got to pay attention."

She was very proud of the pig farm issue. It hadn't developed as much till after she died, but it's because she respected those people. You also have organizations like CCI that have been around a long time and Joe Fagan and the leadership there. And when they tell you that pig farming is a big issue, you believe them because they didn't make it up out of their heads. They heard it from the farmers and the people.

Brenda LaBlanc: For "The Battle of New Orleans" we decided to take a car pool and drove from Des Moines down to New Orleans. That was my first experience with NPA, which was like nothing I'd ever experienced before. And a bit more bold than I had ever felt comfortable being. But I enjoyed it nevertheless. It was fun.

From *A Challenge For Change* (NTIC, 1976)
    Shel Trapp: My three major observations about organizing in the mid-1970s:

- There is a new growth in local community organizing, not only in major urban centers but, but also in smaller and middle sized cities and suburbs as they begin to face issues traditionally thought to be exclusively the problem of the large metropolitan centers. This growth in organizing will develop a whole new power base of community people who will be involved in their communities.
- Local community groups, through their experiences in NPA, will find it increasingly easier to coalesce regionally and nationally on a variety of issues. This coalescing will result in an ever-increasing constituency of people who recognize the untapped potential of community organizing.
- It will be out of this effort, locally and nationally, that a growing constituency of residents, leaders and organizers will be formed who will forge the next steps in the process of community organizing. (Introduction)

    George Knight: Gale, like many people, went from being a very astute local player to having a real grasp of the national systems and the interconnections. Although I think she struggled, like all of us have struggled, with an increasing setting-in of a mindset that says you can ignore the structural changes that are going on.
    She did have the ability to adapt to the changing universe. She could adapt right in a meeting. I mean if the person resisted, she would raise the temperature. If the individual was well briefed and was prepared to give way, she could turn it into a partnering and celebration just instantly.
    She had the ability to walk the streets. There was the chairman of Allstate, Wayne Hedien, great big guy, early chairman of Allstate. We walked the streets of Chicago talking about insurance, Gale and Bruce [Gottschall], Bill Whiteside [Director, Urban Reinvestment Task Force] and him. He turned out to be sympathetic to insurance issues. And Gale just turned it from a confrontation into a celebration. She had that ability to never sell past the close.

CHAPTER 5

"Take all that anger and energy and channel it constructively."

FIRST NATIONWIDE HOUSING CONFERENCE
St. Sylvester's Church, Chicago, March 18-20, 1972
FIRST ORGANIZING CONFERENCE,
Baltimore, May 1972

Michael Westgate: The conference held on March 18-20, 1972 at St. Sylvester's Church in the Palmer Square neighborhood of Chicago was the first major coming together of people nationally to share their stories of how public programs and private financial institutions were weakening and even destroying their neighborhoods. This was particularly true in the older cities of the Northeast and Midwest. Few had heard the term "redlining" before they came, but they recognized that what was happening in their cities was destroying them. As they listened, they became increasingly angry. FHA, the Federal Housing Administration, was high on the list of culprits.

Gale and Shel had gone from running the Organization for a Better Austin (OBA) representing a small number of neighborhoods to a coalition representing the entire West Side of Chicago (WSC) to the Chicago-wide Metropolitan Area Housing Alliance (MAHA). This expanded their leverage locally. Frustrated that they had gone as far as they could in Chicago with the issues, Gale and Shel realized they had to go national. To do this, they needed wider backing, hence a nationwide conference. What happened at St. Sylvester's Schwinn Hall was the first big step towards building a national coalition. People came not just as individuals. It was key to the future that they came representing the community groups to which they belonged. The dynamics and the tactics Gale employed nationally were ones she and Shel had developed over the years in Chicago.

Gale recognized that problems in her Austin neighborhood were not limited to Austin, or even to Chicago, but were shared by urban communities all over the country. The causes of the problems were equally broad. Federal housing policy was affecting neighborhoods as much as city agencies were. Although federal laws were passed in the late 1960s to make it easier for people of low and moderate income to own their own homes, the federal regulations tended to protect the banks and other lending institutions rather than the homebuyers. Some of the regulations actually encouraged fast foreclosures on mortgages. And some homes sold under federal housing programs were substandard. So Gale went from picketing slumlords to challenging federal agencies like the Department of Housing and Urban Development, especially the Federal Housing Administration and the Federal Home Loan Bank Board which regulated the savings and loan associations, the dominant mortgage lenders at the time.

The conference was successful beyond even the organizers' hopes. So many people came that the conference proceedings had to be broadcast on video monitors to rooms which held the overflow. An impressive roster of politicians attended, as well as press, the *New York Times* included. As one organizer put it, "The outside world probably realized better than we did what was happening. We just saw the conference as another step in fighting on the issues. But the outside world saw it as 'something new was happening.' That 'something new' was a new kind of unity."

From *We've Found the Enemy*:

At that conference we said, "We've found the enemy, and it's not us." Until then, all the organizing had played one group against another. White people were told the problem was blacks. Blacks were told the problem was whites. And Hispanics were pitted against both. Our object was to take all that anger and energy, and channel it constructively.

It was agreed at the conference that a national organization should be formed to work on neighborhood concerns. A month later a founding committee made up of delegates from two hundred local groups that had attended the Chicago conference met in Baltimore. Out of that meeting, National People's Action was formed, and Gale was the natural choice for chairperson. The name for the organization is appropriate. The organization is national, uniting neighborhood groups to allow them to work on nationwide problems. It is also very definitely about "people," ordinary people like Gale: whites, blacks, and Hispanics from working-class, mostly urban, communities. And it is certainly about "action." The night NPA was formed, in Baltimore, delegates attending the founding meeting learned that Secretary Romney of the federal Department of Housing and Urban Development was guest speaker at a dinner at the Washington, D.C. Hilton, so they boarded buses and traveled from Baltimore for an impromptu "meeting" with him to raise their own concerns about housing problems.

Since that night, Gale can often be found in similar scenes, characteristically at the head of a crowd, with a microphone in her hand, gesturing as she talks in her strong, enthusiastic voice to the crowd or to the official she is confronting. If she isn't leading a crowd, she is as likely to be running a planning session with representatives from some of the approximately three hundred local groups that have ties with NPA. Or, she can be speaking before a cheering audience of thousands at an NPA annual convention, engaged in negotiating in a small meeting with a federal official or a banking or an insurance company executive, or testifying before Congress.

Joe Mariano: The tradition of not letting anybody know where the buses were headed goes back to the original NPA. They wanted to get to Romney and they decided to rent a school bus or two or three and then go find him. But then it became the drill, "Okay. We're going to get on school buses and go to somebody's house." And then when they caught on, "Oh, well, NPA is in town," we started getting undercover police and all those kind. There's a lot of that that still goes on to this day. We began to realize as they say in football there's three strategies. You either overpower 'em if you have the strength to blow 'em off the line or use the end run. The surprise element is the trick play. It's that we can find out things, where people live, and if that gets out...

Like with General McCaffrey, the same thing. General Barry McCaffrey, the drug czar. We found out where he lived and we showed up at the house and he wasn't home. And later that night the Federal Marshals, the FBI and the Secret Service sent agents to talk with us. So they said, "Do you intend to do any bodily harm to the General?" "No. We're just trying to get a meeting with him and talk with him about his policies, this so-called 'war on drugs' and how he's changing it. He wants to advertise and etc, etc, etc." So they said, "Well, he's got high-level security. How did you find out where he lives?" I said, "Well, we have our ways."

You think about it. I mean this is before 9/11. From their point of view, "How'd they do this?" Earlier on, during big oil, I think there was a lot of fear too about terrorists. They viewed our people if we took over a meeting and stuff that we were kind of like terrorists. Gale would say, "No we're not. We're just neighborhood people."

Michael Westgate: The breadth and intensity of Chicago's community organizations was and is unlike any other city. Operating within those organizations and then organizing new ones gave Gale the base of knowledge and power to do what she did. Shel Trapp, the former United Methodist minister turned activist, was her indispensable partner and organizer of organizers nationally. Shel brought an anger against all the injustices he saw that complemented Gale's ability to see beyond her own anger and seek solutions.

The community organizations they invoked to deal with the major issues of the day in Chicago included the Organization for a Better Austin (OBA), Northwest Community Organization (NCO), West Side Coalition (WSC), and later the Metropolitan Area Housing Alliance (MAHA). These organizations, strengthened, expanded or founded by Gale and Shel, represented geographic growth as well as an expansion of tactics and solutions. They were set up to respond to issues. They moved on to find nascent groups in other cities that could join forces with them.

Shel Trapp: From fighting local lenders and realtors like Sky Realty with demonstrations of up to 1000 people, we went to start fighting FHA. We won several concessions from the regional office. At that time FHA had regional offices which did have some power. There was a big office here in Chicago on Wacker Drive and we hit that several times, usually a thousand people.

Michael Westgate: Press coverage was another critical ingredient in the success of Gale's operation and a major part of this was having good data. She knew, and taught others by example how to frame the issues and to develop relationships with the media.

Helen Murray: For a while there was a guy, Stan Ziemba, at the *Tribune* who did some stuff. It was cyclical. He carried our stories, including Fairfield Savings. Stan really respected us. He didn't do like real big, investigative things, but he was always reliable. He liked what we did. He knew what we were doing, "Call Stan. We're going to do this." And he would come. It wasn't just because he liked us. He really respected us. He grew up on the southwest side of Chicago. So it was different. He wasn't one of the pretty boys or the pretty girls. Boy, another annoyance, they wouldn't like to come out in the neighborhoods. "Well, are you going to do something on Michigan Avenue?" "Well, <u>no</u>!"

Remember Fairfield Savings? Well, there was a character there we went after, real local, hardheaded Chicago guy who was the head of Fairfield Savings. Oh, he'd bump heads with us. "We can't really move the savings and loan to Michigan Avenue for your convenience!" But Stan would come out, and Stan was a neighborhood guy.

There was John Herbers, this guy at the *New York Times* for a while, who did some very good coverage of Gale, very sensitive, smart man. Gale also met a couple of times with Bill Moyers. I was also on the radio with Gale and Studs. Honest to God.

Michael Westgate: In a March 20, 1972 article for *The New York Times* ("1,600 From Ethnic Groups Organize Protest Against Institutions They Say Are Destroying Central Cities") Herbers covered the first national conference and the rising anger because of "a significant increase in abandonment and decay of housing in recent months, disclosures of gross fraud and profiteering by real estate interests in large cities, and an increasing indifference of dwellers in the suburbs to the plight of central city residents."

Shel Trapp: We got a lot of local reforms out of John Waner. He was an old political hack. He ran for mayor on the Republican ballot.

Historically, the Republicans always put somebody up to save face and then they would get a political plum. Waner's plum was he got to be regional director of HUD.

At one demonstration, we'd gone in, taken over the lobby, and they'd shut the elevators down. I'm standing next to a cop and he's got one of those walkie-talkie things on his collar, "We're at a big demonstration over here; what should I do?" I heard back, "Well, how many people are there?" He said, "It's over a thousand 'cause they got the whole lobby filled and they're out in the street. Do you want me to start arresting?" Comes back, "Where you gonna put 'em, asshole? No." So right then I knew, "We're safe." Anyway that happened a couple times.

This fight had been going on probably a year with Waner, and he called Gale and me in and said, "Look. I agree with everything you're asking for, but I can't do anything more. You want anything more out of me, you got to go to Washington and change national policy. Look it, I'm telling you the truth; I am not lying. I have done everything I can do. You can demonstrate with ten thousand people! I can't give you any more. You've got to change policy in D.C." So Gale and I went back, "Holy shit! What are we going to do?"

Shortly after that, Jack Egan, who had been exiled [in 1966] by Cardinal Cody to Notre Dame, every once in a while he would hold an "organizers' conference" out there. Usually about a hundred and fifty folks from around the country would come. So Gale and I, we're at this thing and still stewing, "What the hell can we do with this thing, that FHA can't do any more for us?" We go up to one of our rooms. We were sitting there drinking and talking about this, and one of us said, "Well, let's have a national conference!" About four o'clock we go to bed.

I see Gale downstairs for breakfast and said, "You remember what we talked about last night?" "Yeah." "Still sound good to you?" She said, "Yeah. It sounds better." I said, "Me too. It's scaring me." "Naw. Nothing to worry about." So that's where the idea for the first national conference was born.

So we got a group of the leadership team that had really been in these fights. She talked to the OBA staff and I talked to the NCO staff and we started talking with them about holding this national conference. And they eventually bought into it and said, "Yeah. Let's go with it." And so, March of '72 we had the first national conference at St. Sylvester's.

The people that came were pretty much Midwest. But there had been two guys that I had trained at OBA, one had started an organization in Baltimore and one had started an organization in Providence. And they sent probably about thirty folks each. Then we had 'em from all across the country.

You're not gonna believe, nobody ever believes this story. I got a group of college kids and at that time in history at O'Hare Airport there was this big place on one corridor that had a big circle that had phonebooks. It was alphabetized around the circle. Albuquerque... They were set up on some kind of spindle so they flipped out. And there was the Albuquerque phone book. So I had all these kids go out there and I said, "Go to the yellow pages. Find anything with housing or community in it and copy it down." I think we gave 'em some parameters, the major cities. They'd come back with the lists. Anne-Marie, on the typewriter, would type up labels.

We were inviting people for a housing conference on FHA abuses. And we threw crime in there and insurance, lack of home mortgage insurance. Because we'd been fighting the insurance companies at the same time. I don't even think we had the word "reinvestment" then, probably just "banks not making loans in your neighborhood" or something like that.

It was also an election year. It was about a week before the Illinois convention or the Illinois primary. So most of the candidates were here campaigning and we got three or four Democratic candidates. I don't think we got any Republicans. As one of them signed on – "Presidential candidate McCarthy has agreed" – we were sending out updates. We're running this thing out of our NCO office, which was twenty-five foot in front and probably a hundred feet deep. And that meant we're stuffing all these envelopes and sealing them. That was till 4:00 AM. Then breakfast at our house. And Anne-Marie is typing labels.

Helen Murray: I called any organization from any neighborhood in the country asking: "Do you have this problem in your neighborhood? You ought to be here."

I described four problems (panic peddling and steering, insurance redlining, mortgage redlining, and FHA abuse).

Each organization invited was there to address action and Gale proved to be a real presence – wow! And the media were there, about 30 press organizations. The *Kansas City Star* really "got it", particularly about FHA. But other organizations didn't know how to report it. *Newsweek* had no category for who we were.

Michael Westgate: The *Newsweek* article (April 3, 1972) reporting on the conference, while referencing the participation of blacks, Puerto Ricans and Chicanos as well as whites, was titled "Here Come the Ethnics." It described the meeting as "an improbable alliance designed precisely to emphasize their similarities rather than their differences."

Helen Murray: I came back to Chicago from New Orleans in '72 because I wanted to get more training. Obviously I had some knack for the business, but I really felt like I wanted to work with some of the more seasoned people and get better skills and stuff. So I came back, and at that time people suggested that I go over to NCO and work with Shel. That was really where the action was and that's where I would get the best training.

But this was just like three or four weeks before the first national conference so all the energy was going to putting this conference together. And it really wasn't <u>the first</u> <u>national</u> conference it was <u>a conference</u>. There was no understanding that there was going to be a national organization out of this. I mean maybe Gale thought that.

But for the rest of us it was really focused on putting some national attention and pressure on these issues by bringing people together. I don't <u>think</u> any of the staff really believed that they were starting an organization. They were pushing the issues. That's not to say it didn't cross their minds, but that was not the driving force.

So I got involved in some of the national stuff, getting press people to cover. All the local organizers had a lot of local stuff to do. So I was filling in as best I could because I knew the Chicago scene, I knew the people.

Michael Westgate: The timing of the conference was brilliant. When presidential candidates George McGovern and Eugene McCarthy, LaDonna and Fred Harris plus Senator Percy said they were coming, Mayor Richard J. Daley came, particularly not wanting to be upstaged by Senator Percy. There was growing recognition that cities needed assistance and presidential candidates were offering to help. Of course the media came too.

This was a critical turning point in moving what had been a Chicago operation into one of national scope. The atmosphere at the conference was electric. Attendance surpassed expectations. Daley had not taken Gale seriously before this, so the national spotlight greatly increased Gale's stature locally. The conference proved to be the catalyst in turning a sense of powerlessness felt by individuals and local organizations towards a national focus, "Together we are going to do something about these problems."

Gale with George McGovern and Father Dodero at First NPA Housing Conference at St. Sylvester's Church, Chicago. Also attending were other presidential candidates Eugene McCarthy, LaDonna and Fred Harris, as were Eunice Kennedy, Senator Percy and Mayor Richard J. Daley. March 18-20, 1972.

Most importantly, this conference set the stage for the next 30 years and more. A group of leaders emerged who would plan the smaller follow-up working conference, to be held in Baltimore. In future years, an annual national conference, soon to be called the National People's Action, would be held in Washington. Public accountability would become a trademark.

Newspaper stories about scandals at FHA had appeared in individual cities, but there was little recognition that redlining was a national problem. People began to see that the FHA programs designed to bring private loans to underserved neighborhoods were often exacerbating the problems, not fixing them. FHA had been designed to help finance the growth of relatively uniform suburbs. Neither FHA's staff nor the system they employed of brokers, appraisers, lawyers, bankers and others had the background or the inclination to deal with inner city diversity, including racial.

Unscrupulous real estate brokers were the worst offenders in taking advantage of flaws in housing programs that rewarded the brokers and the lenders they partnered with. They were aided and abetted by an FHA whose administration was weak and whose officials were often ineffective and sometimes bribed.

From *Cities Destroyed For Cash: The FHA Scandal at HUD*
By Brian D. Boyer

Gail (*sic*) Cincotta may be the most unusual housing expert in the United States. She is a large, fast-moving woman with a kind of huge Wayne Cochran bleached blonde bouffant hairdo that is noticeable all by itself. But don't let that delude you about her achievements. With no advanced education, she not only taught herself the intricacies of housing, finance, and the FHA, but has taught thousands of others as well. Gail Cincotta created the National Peoples Action on Housing…she did this virtually alone, with no money and only a sense of the truth to guide her. (178-79)

I think the most interesting about the first conference was the working arrangements reached by ethnic whites, poor blacks, and Spanish Americans to fight the FHA to keep from ruining their neighborhoods. Their efforts may prove to be worthless as the low-income programs are killed, but their mutual understanding of each other's problems has been very rare in recent times. (179)

Michael Westgate: Gale was the most prominent person in leading the NPA but she was hardly alone. Shel Trapp and a host of others joined her in making this movement happen not just in Chicago but around the country. They started with virtually no money but depended first on the Catholic Church and later the Stern Family Foundation, the Ford Foundation and others to support their efforts.

Gale Cincotta (From *Cities Destroyed For Cash: The FHA Scandal at HUD*):

My name is Gale Cincotta. I'm 41 years old [actually 43]. I'm a housewife. I'm non-salaried. I've lived on the West Side of Chicago all my life. I live in Austin, a community that's undergoing racial change. I work on the real estate problems. I'm tackling them by understanding what the realtors do.

This past March [1972], we pulled together a conference in Chicago because of our frustrations with the FHA here. We had gone to Washington, and that only led to more frustrations. By reading the papers, we found out that the FHA was a national scandal and it was being covered up in every city. That's when we decided to have a conference.

When I first got into housing, I wanted to know who made the decision in areas like Austin that there would be a black or brown movement into. Originally, it appeared to me that it was made by realtors, blockbusters and panic peddlers. We thought that was the answer. But when we started digging into the problem we found the whole community was under FHA. The only mortgages that were being made were FHA. We discovered that the banks and the savings and loans were pulling out of the area and the FHA was coming in to fill up a vacuum. The realtors were coming in and using FHA to move people from old ghettos to the new ghetto. The whole problem became more complicated.

What we saw was a whole economic thing, almost like a conspiracy of people deciding that this area was going to go, or they were going to make it go, and some people were making a hell of a lot of money off the racial thing. [179-180]

I'm one of the few whites still living here. Only about 10 percent of the people here are still white. I stay because I don't like to be pushed around. I lived in Austin all my life. We've been working so hard here. Can we make a difference? Where the hell are we going to move? If somebody else has the power to decide where I'm going to live and when I'm going to move, it really turns me off. [185]

Of course, there are politics and money involved in the conversion of neighborhoods from one race to another. They just want to make money. So much of this is economic. If they can keep people hating each other and moving, everybody makes so damn much money. [186]

But the people feel that they have been taken. A lot of them are very angry. Minority groups have always been taken advantage of. It's such a pattern of always being taken by the "man". The minority groups have a feeling that a new community is a place to pass through. You go there for a couple of years, knowing somehow that you will not be able to stay, you don't know why, it's just part of the system to move. You move into a place, then urban renewal follows you out. It's just kind of a white, black and brown urban removal. [186-87]

The FHA scandal is national and it's so bad. I just don't know what else to say. It's sad that they're not listening to people. I think the hope is in the people finding answers for themselves. Nobody else knows them; they might as well give the people a chance to come up with some ideas. [187]

From *The Chicago Reader* (Dec. 21, 2001)
The Good Neighbor: Community activist Gale Cincotta's work was never done
By Christopher Hayes

For all of Cincotta's aggressiveness, she also had a sure grasp of the issues. Trapp remembers, "Gale had an ability to understand complex issues and talk to very 'sophisticated' people on levels that they could understand, and the next day be talking to neighborhood people on a level they could understand." That talent, he says, explains why Cincotta was eulogized by the same institutions – Harris Bank, Fannie Mae, *American Banker* – that she'd centered in her crosshairs: "The enemy realizes that we're not idiots. We're not just out there screaming, we're also gonna bring some answers to their problems that can make them look good."

Michael Westgate: Gale put the spotlight on the institutions, including city governments backed by federal urban renewal funding, and lenders backed by federal regulators and insurance who were responsible for the systematic destruction of whole sections of central cities.

She pointed out that urban renewal was a great source of profits for lawyers, developers, real estate brokers and others. Urban renewal caused great distress to owners and renters in the more depressed parts of most older cities, not just Chicago. Not until the 1980s did many cities recognize the value of solid older buildings and a neighborhood infrastructure which could be preserved and enhanced rather than torn down and replaced. In Boston, where I lived from 1975 until 2007, the contrasting approaches are the West End, torn down and replaced in the 1960s, and the North End, organized and revitalized from the 1970s on. By the 1990s, environmental issues started tipping the balance in favor of revitalizing cities. Roads and sidewalks, water and sewer, schools, churches, neighborhood stores were all in place. Why reinvent them, artificially in far-off suburbs, when they already existed where they had grown organically over decades, even centuries, in the cities?

FHA was not the only problem; city governments were colluding with real estate interests. The first conference demonstrated that there was a crisis in inner cities, nationwide. While it focused on the scandals at FHA which were being swept under the rug it was also, as Gale put it, "a warning to the 'money people' that their actions and inactions were coming under scrutiny."

FHA, paradoxically, had not even been a presence in the city, effectively redlining most urban areas entirely such was its focus on new construction in the suburbs, until President Johnson had changed its mandate.

Gale was one of the first to see that thousands of individual transactions were collectively ruining neighborhoods and that Chicago was not alone. She also saw that cities were partners in this conspiracy, whether by design or not, depriving changing neighborhoods of good schools and other basic services. But fighting City Hall was not enough. She wanted to find a way to precipitate changes in the national policies that fed the lending patterns behind changing neighborhoods. The cities were responding to these changes, not initiating them.

Who were initiating neighborhood changes? Before there can be in-migration of lower income people, there must be out-migration of usually slightly higher-income people. There are complex dynamics, including particularly in this era, race. But the availability and terms on which people could get home financing was and is one of the keys, and availability of financing is determined in large part by federal policies. Some of the problems of the 1970s were repeated on a more global scale in the declining housing markets of 2007-10.

Gale saw that to change national policy there had to be a spotlight shown on problems and people had to be mobilized in communities across the country. There had to be thousands of other people who could be organized to share the anger and frustration which Gale and Shel felt. If the problems of Chicago were beyond the ability of Chicagoans alone to solve that must be true elsewhere, and people must come together to take action.

From a radio interview by Studs Terkel on July 15, 1982

Gale Cincotta: So that going from the West Side Coalition, we had been meeting with HUD officials and bankers. Finally somebody [John Waner, Regional Director at HUD in Chicago] said, "We can't do anything more for you. You ought to go to Washington."

And our feeling was that what the politicians in Washington figured was, "Well, they're gonna go home, go back to their kitchen or wherever they ever came from and stop." Instead, what the people did was in 1972, in the spring, we decided that there had to be people like us all over the United States that liked their neighborhoods, wanted to stay there and wanted to deal with the problems. So we called together the first national conference of neighborhood organizations in the United States. And that was in March of 1972. And that's where National People's Action was born.

Helen Murray: *Der Spiegel* was there. I know because I was working with the pressroom. We had phones in the pressroom. We had the *Kansas City Star*. The *Kansas City Star* has this history of being a real adventurous and story-breaking kind of old-fashioned newspaper. I can still remember this guy, "Calling in for the *Kansas City Star* from St. Sylvester's Church." And it was like, "This is so cool! I can't believe this." And he'd be calling with all this passion. It was like an old movie. But the fellow who was there really had a sense of the bigger story of what going on and the money that was going down, particularly through some of the FHA stuff that was happening. And he really <u>got it.</u> And a lot of people, particularly people who are more shallow in their sense of media, including people from Chicago, they didn't get it.

The program was to identify the action that was to be taken by each and every organization. We knew what the problem was. What's the <u>action</u> to take on the problem? The four problems were the real estate practices – the panic peddling and steering, insurance redlining, mortgage redlining and FHA abuses.

At this point in history, FHA had been a suburban dream after World War II. And after the Johnson era, one of the solutions was "Let's put FHA in the city." And so it was just totally abused, I mean just left and right. And people were really taken in. Incredible things. I mean, people, it was life and death. This was really big bucks. People doing some really, really dirty stuff.

And we were experiencing that at the neighborhood level. I didn't work on FHA. I was always the redlining/reinvestment person. But I mean people were realizing, from anecdotal and cumulative anecdotal stories in the neighborhoods that this was not just by chance. This was not by chance.

From Case Study by Hallahan (11/7/91)

Kirk Hallahan: The anti-redlining movement began at a conference of neighborhood organizations held in March 1972 in a parish hall on the Northwest side of Chicago. Cincotta recalls that she had little idea beforehand that the event would be so successful or would be the catalyst for a major national movement. "We all recognized that even though we had made advances in our own cities, at a certain point we had to make an impact nationally. We touched a nerve." (2-3)

Michael Westgate: This conference was a conference of organizations—not a conference for individuals. Gale had learned from her Chicago experience that power had to be aggregated through groups and that power within each group had to be grown organically. She was never going to embark on building a national organization with chapters, from the top down. Hers was a chaotic [Dee Hock at VISA would later coin another term, "chaordic"] way of accepting as building blocks any organizations that recognized that there were problems and agreed to combine efforts to solve them. It led to a disparate group of churches, community organizations and others joining together, organized to later become the National People's Action.

G.C. Thelen Jr., reporting on the conference for the *Washington Post* ("Speculators, FHA Hit on Housing" – May 2, 1972), quoted Gale's charge to the participants, "What for so long have been considered natural phenomena – changing neighborhoods, deteriorating cities – are not natural. It's an outright plan and the government, the realtors and the big-money people are making a lot of money out of changing neighborhoods, out of the communities we call home."

Shel Trapp: We had asked Daley to come and it was touch and go. I mean if you had him you might as well have God. And so, maybe two weeks before, when he'd seen all these Democratic candidates starting to fall into place, and then when he saw [Illinois Senator Charles] Percy coming, he knew, "Oh, no. Percy's not going to upstage me. So I'm coming." So his office let us know he was coming.

Helen Murray: Mayor Daley had a real sense of the power that was there. He responded to power and there was a lot of power there. Yeah. And we could tell that by the newspapers. Daley walked in with at least some of the Democratic people, probably McGovern. And of course there was this whole trail of people that came in with him.

It was interesting. The Chicago press talked about the fact that Daley went to a meeting on the West Side of Chicago, but out of town press said these grassroots people have just exploded this whole thing. Then *Newsweek* didn't know how to peg Gale. And Gale of course was always the presence with her bouffant hair and the whole style and her size. When Gale walked in the room, even if she hadn't dressed the way she did, she had presence. But the combination was a wow!

So they didn't know how to peg her. Because in '72 people had learned about Black Power, right? But they hadn't learned about what we were doing because they didn't have a label for it. So *Newsweek* did this stupid article — calling it like *Laverne and Shirley*. I mean that was the best they could do, right? It's taking from TV. I think it was *Newsweek* that did that. A lot of them they had no category for who we were.

We had some organizations that came from neighborhoods in Chicago; the primary groups were from Chicago. Some of the organizations were from primarily Latino neighborhoods. Some of the organizations were from primarily African American neighborhoods. Some of them were white working class and some were mixed. And as these issues came up for a vote for action, they did it, not by numbers vote but by acclamation.

On FHA there were clearly differences based on the Latino neighborhoods or the African American neighborhoods as to which action to take. At the first national conference, the black neighborhoods, they weren't decided on which way they were going to go on something. The white working class neighborhoods were sort of decided on what they wanted to do. And Latino neighborhoods decided what they wanted to do and, physically, Latino people were standing on chairs with both hands up. And it was reported as the blacks because the press had learned about Black Power. I'm getting off on the media now!

This was always a problem with this organization. We weren't like the lefties and we weren't like the Black Power. We weren't the student activists. We were American people who were using democracy. Hello! And they just don't have a category for "democracy" in the press. They don't understand it. Or economics, excuse me, particularly economics.

Michael Westgate: Father Roger Coughlin who was at this first conference as a supporter, joined and stayed on the Board of NTIC long after Gale's death. Father John Ahern was the pastor at St. Sylvester's.

Roger Coughlin: Schwinn Hall at St. Sylvester's is a separate community hall. It was built by the Schwinn bike people. They were Germans. That was a German area. They were very successful and maybe that was their church. So they built this big building for them. That's where it was planned to have the first conference.

I just remember going up there. Nobody knew just what this was. Part of the strategy has to be using the tools of politics, including publicity. The City didn't know what to make of this, but they knew if you listened to the propaganda, thousands were going to be there. And so Mayor Daley came. Thousands <u>were</u> there. Thousands came and they couldn't believe it. From all over the country, people came to this first meeting at St. Sylvester's, the First National Housing Meeting. And the mayor of Chicago came. He's no fool. He wasn't going to take a chance that the community people would be there and him not showing up. So he showed up.

I was intrigued with everybody who was there. That's maybe the first time I really ever got to meet Gale. There were others. Looking across the room, I was wondering, "What is that pretty young woman doing with this bunch of roughnecks?" Helen Murray. She told us she got away with a lot because of [being] blond, blue-eyed. She could infiltrate all kinds of things. She sort of brought out the protective sense in me because I <u>knew</u> these guys. I knew them well. They were rough-edged.

Shel Trapp: At St. Sylvester's, the whole school auditorium was filled and we had chairs set up in the basement. Some college kids had figured out you'd video it upstairs and it would show downstairs. It ran wild, the first conference.

I don't think we had any enemies at the first one. So we didn't know what the hell we were doing. We didn't even know at that point who the enemies were. That is the fun of organizing—not to know what you're doing but do it. That's life.

At the end of it, one key line that Gale said. "We've been told by FHA, 'Oh, this is just a Chicago problem. We don't have that problem any place else.'" Well, Carmel McCrudden from Philadelphia was at that first conference. She was spinning tales that made us look like we were dealing with a Sunday school picnic about FHA abuses up there. And people from St. Louis were, "We got the same stuff down there." This was coming from all over. And at one of the very last sessions I remember Gale saying to the entire group, "We've found the enemy and it's not us!" That whole weekend is a daze 'cause I never went to bed for two nights straight.

From *The Grassroots Battle Against Redlining: From the Streets to the Halls of Congress* – An HTIC Publication (1975)

In March of 1972...in their final resolution, the delegates set the course for future actions which can and will continue to develop:

Whereas: We have come together to serve notice to the national leaders that decent housing is the right of all Americans.

Whereas: We have also come together to serve notice on the people in our communities that they need not accept poor housing and the abuse of a large and unresponsive industrial-financial-political housing complex.

BE IT RESOLVED: That we shall come together in our local communities and continue the work of this Conference at the grassroots level.

BE IT FURTHER RESOLVED: That we shall come together again in regional and national conferences to continue and improve upon the work of this conference.

BE IT FURTHER RESOLVED: That the federal, state, and local governments, the builders, and money people take warning. We will not permit this housing situation to continue. (4)

Helen Murray: I found myself going out to Baltimore to organize this [followup] conference. Finding a hotel, doing all that kind of stuff. Figuring out the logistics for the actions we'd have on Monday on the Senate Banking Committee. We had hearing testimony to be written and Gale testified. That was Senator Hart's committee. This was before Proxmire.

At least four hundred people came to Baltimore. We had a whole lot of organizational structure meetings about how we were going to work together in the future on Sunday. We had a dream team in the beginning there. We had a bunch of people who were so like-minded that one could start the sentence and the other could finish it, Ed Shurna, Ted Wysocki, Jim Caprero, people who all had a sense of where we were going. What Gale could do is work with all of us.

This was the first national hearing that we ever went to. Hart was receptive. We wanted HMDA. But people were very, in the old-fashioned sense, aghast at what we were saying. And the people were respected. What people were saying, I felt, was respected. There was the sense that we had entered a place of power that could make a difference. Here we were from the West Side of Chicago. I remember the bright blue and the stars on the rug in that hearing room.

Organizers never did the testimony. The leaders did. So mine was a dual role, to make sure the people that were there were there, and to be there for Gale, make sure she had her testimony, to be the glue. We had a lot of anecdotal stuff and Gale made great use of numbers. As we went on, we were recognized by more traditional people as really being on the cutting edge of something. John McKnight and his people up at the Northwestern Urban Center had a really smart sense that we were on the leading edge, and that this was what it was going to take. So they did a lot of stuff for us in a more sophisticated way, early on, that helped reinforce also, because it was also not just <u>us</u> saying it, it was Northwestern. So that was a real good piece.

There wasn't money! Gale and I used to sleep in the same bed at her son's house in Washington, her son Teddy. They'd have to kick a couple of the kids out of their room. We slept in the same bed in a lot of hotels too, because that was what you did.

Shel Trapp: At that conference we found out that Romney was at a fundraiser. He was Secretary of HUD. He has just come from being governor of Michigan. So we hit that. That set the style of NPA from then on. The Republican Party was having it. He was the guest speaker. He was in D.C. We were in Baltimore, so we just got some buses and went over there, hit it. Nothing happened out of the hit, but people were all juiced up. "Wow, whee! This is great!" So that was the birth of NTIC and NPA.

So we held it out there and we had four hundred folks at that conference. And at that conference, Anne-Marie and Gale and I had done some digging through and figured out we got to have two organizations, the way the tax laws were written. It's kind of interesting. They're more lenient now about what you can lobby for. And we thought, "Boy, we're gonna be fighting legislation all the time." Didn't realize it was gonna be such a small part of our agenda. So at that conference, we decided we needed to have two organizations, National People's Action on Housing (NPAH) and National Training and Information Center (NTIC), one that could lobby and the one that could do good works.

Helen Murray: So after Baltimore, we've got the institution organized and we've done the first testimony. Then we had to get all the paperwork done. Then we had to grow up and find out about how you file to be a non-profit organization. We had a wonderful young man who offered his services for us pro bono. Again we had no money. His name is Glover. Gale and I went on a lot of trips to his office downtown. He did the incorporation papers for NPAH and NTIC pro bono. NPA was National People's Action on Housing because the first founding causes were all housing. We dropped the H then very shortly thereafter because we finally realized that we didn't want to just be on housing.

Joe Mariano: NPA and NTIC are two separate organizations. NTIC is a legit 501(c)(3) and we have a board and all that stuff. NPA is a 501(c)(4). There's no structure to it. There's no board, no dues, no rules. No staff. It's a testament to imagination if you will. It works and it's low maintenance. You don't have to invest a lot. People said, "Well, we gotta have dues. We gotta have a constitution." It was, "Sounds like more work." Gale never wanted that, "Let's just keep it as simple as we can."

Michael Westgate: It was brilliant the way they ended up creating two complementary national organizations. Housing Training and Information Center (HTIC) was created in December 1972, hiring Gale as Executive Director at $12,000/year, Shel as Training Director at $10,000/year and Anne-Marie Douglas as secretary @$2.50/hour, according to HTIC board minutes of 12/30/73. National People's Action (NPA) would be the phantom organizing organization, a national network of community organizations. Over the years, it has included organizations from 39 states and at least 104 urban areas. HTIC, later renamed National Training and Information Center (NTIC), provided support and technical assistance to the organizations involved in NPA.

Helen Murray: But we were out there really to shake the trees and whatever name we could go by, we would do that. It was really fun, now looking back at it. Hard work, but a good time because it was a real labor of love. In the beginning there were so few of us, you did everything and probably not real well. But the funding increased. Gale was a genius at getting funding.

There's a wonderful picture of President Johnson. It's a series of pictures where he's doing the Johnson thing on somebody. It's a classic, where he gets closer and he gets closer, and he's like right in the guy's face, another member of the Congress. Have you seen that? I thought, "God, that's Gale."

I was gone for a year to finish my degree and then I came back. That was before CRA passed. I kicked off the statewide stuff on HMDA, but Gale and Shel were more involved in the national stuff, initially on HMDA.

One of the beauties about NTIC – I have to laugh – is that we didn't rest on our laurels. I have a sense of history; I was born with it. I'm a history teacher. When I was organizing, I was living in the present, and you have to. It's like the line about Broadway, that you're only as good as your show last night, or your next show. We had that attitude that this wasn't about who we were, it's what are you are doing now.

I left at the end of '84. It was my life for twelve years. It was a big, big personal decision to leave. I needed to change. It was hard. I gave myself a sabbatical, self-paid sabbatical.

Joe Mariano: Gale was very accessible, plainspoken. Almost like a genius. Here's this woman who doesn't fit the mold of what I thought was a leader. You know growing up in the sixties you had Martin Luther King, Jr., Cesar Chavez. Here was this woman who smoked, told it like it was and was a white ethnic, but right on the mark. I was just kind of, "Wow." This was like pretty amazing stuff. Just that she would do these kinds of things. Make demands. Ask the audience to come up. And then we were going to testify in Washington.

Those were the days when Geno Baroni was still around from the National Center for Urban Ethnic Affairs. He came and he was chatting with Gale, just a small circle. We had like a lounge area and we were all sitting around and just talking. It wasn't like a high-level strategy kind of thing, "Okay. We're going to do this tomorrow in Congress." It was like, "Where're you from? How're you doing it? What are you going to talk about?" People would interrupt with different stories. So it was pretty low key, informal. That was Gale's style. It wasn't a lot of pretense.

From The Ford Foundation Archives (January 12, 1976)
Program Action documents recommending a $125,000 grant over two years to HTIC:

Massive problems with HUD's insured portfolio and the economic and social wisdom of treating declining but still salvageable urban neighborhoods have been recurring themes in recent National Affairs grant requests. In scores of communities these issues merge with yet another ongoing National Affairs concern – working-class discontent.

Not until early 1972, when a loose coalition of Chicago community groups issued a call for a national conference on the problems of deteriorating older neighborhoods, was it possible to gauge the depth of grassroots feeling on these twin issues of HUD "abuses" and "red-lining."

John Herbers of the *New York Times* wrote of the gathering: "It was unusual in that it brought together in a display of harmony racial groups that traditionally have been antagonistic to each other in changing central city neighborhoods."

At a follow-up meeting held in Baltimore, 400 delegates identified the need for a new national non-profit organization to speak for and assist their beleaguered communities. Thus began the Housing Training and Information Center (HTIC). With assistance from the Center for Urban Ethnic Affairs and the Center for Community Change and initial funding from the Taconic and Stern Foundations, HTIC proceeded to develop and implement a three-tiered program strategy: neighborhood, city-wide and national.

Michael Westgate: Income of women of child-rearing age was discounted up to 100% until the 1960s. The US was not alone; in France, a married woman could not obtain a credit card without her husband's signature, until 1965. Women must work today because housing prices have escalated partly on the basis that there are two-income households. Partially as a result of that change, neighborhood movements on which NPA and NTIC depended for their strength are now deprived of the time women have to spend on housing and other issues.

Mary Volpe: People dismissed us at the beginning because someone said that there were these people on the West Side that were organizing a multiethnic group that was working on some issues, but everybody knows multiethnic groups don't work in Chicago! You know, we were just rabble. But, hell, wasn't this country founded on rabble?

CHAPTER 6

"You people wouldn't know what to do with disclosure if you had it."

INSTITUTIONAL FRAMEWORK FOR
MORTGAGE LENDING IN CHICAGO
Federal Home Loan Bank of Chicago (FHLB-C)
Federal Home Loan Bank Board, Washington (FHLBB)
Federal Housing Authority (FHA) Washington
U.S. League of Savings and Loan Associations, Chicago

Michael Westgate: I worked at the Federal Home Loan Bank Board (FHLBB) in Washington, DC from October 1971 through April 1975, after graduating from Harvard Business School. There was a lot of pressure, nationwide, to determine both the causes and the remedies for the wholesale disinvestment in cities across the United States.

The FHLBB and its subsidiary, the Federal Savings & Loan Insurance Corporation (FSLIC), regulated and insured the vast bulk of accounts at the nation's savings and loan associations. FHLBB and FSLIC were in key positions to address some of these issues. Since the 1930s the federal government has insured savings and loans, banks, cooperative banks, and credit unions, requiring review by federal examiners. During the period covered by this book, S&Ls were the predominant residential mortgage lenders in Chicago and throughout much of the U.S. They were all insured by my agency, FSLIC, funded by premiums charged to S&Ls. Reserves in 1971 totaled about $4 billion, with access to the U.S Treasury of an additional $10 billion. Losses were relatively small.

In Chicago, there were many ethnically based groups of businessmen who joined forces to create a small lending institution, taking in savings deposits at perhaps 3%, making loans to local homeowners at 6%, securing the properties with mortgages, and running the institution on the spread. Under Illinois' unitary banking law, each S&L (indeed every bank) was limited to a single branch. This had certain advantages in that they knew their customers well. Their primary source of capital, beyond their depositors, was the Federal Home Loan Bank of Chicago, part of the framework of Federal Home Loan Banks established in the 1930s.

S&Ls had run into problems in the Great Depression when many property values fell below loan balances and savers withdrew more funds than the S&L could provide. The federal Home Owners Loan Corporation (HOLC) was established in 1933 to step into the breach, initially making loans to individual homebuyers, thus recreating liquidity in the buying and selling of homes. HOLC's charter provided that it was to work with local lenders to "to meet the credit needs of their communities."

HOLC was unable to meet demand and evolved into the complex system of regional Federal Home Loan Banks, one of which was located in Chicago. The member savings and loan associations elected the president of the Federal Home Loan Bank (FHLB) in their region. The entire Federal Home Loan Bank System was governed by the three-member Federal Home Loan Bank Board (FHLBB) in Washington, appointed by the President with the consent of the Senate. The FHLBB also served as the governing board for FSLIC, insuring the accounts of depositors at S&Ls, serving the same function that FDIC did for commercial banks. The two have since merged.

During the 1970s, approximately 70% of all residential mortgage lending was done by savings and loan associations. The federal government had entered the picture through the Federal Housing Administration in the 1930s. FHA insured the loans of lenders, up to 90%. During most of its existence, FHA had confined itself largely to lending in the suburbs. The Farmers Home Administration (FmHA) served the same function in rural areas. FHA was correctly accused of turning its back on the inner city. It finally took on lending in Chicago and other cities during the Johnson administration, but without proper oversight.

Where uniform subdivisions made any deviation from the norm in lending conspicuous, the variety of structures and borrowers in older urban neighborhoods made simple rules hard to devise or enforce. Indeed, the laxness and fraud benefited those who were selling, more than those—often minorities—who were buying. Unfortunately certain lenders and the realtors and appraisers working with them took advantage of FHA. When the loans they made with FHA insurance became delinquent, they could simply foreclose the loans and bill FHA for the loan balance, plus accrued interest and fees. In some cases, property would be flipped: foreclosed, then sold again with another FHA loan. And sometimes it was flipped more than once.

From *Mother Jones* (November 1978)
Blackjacking the City Redliners
By John Conroy

The West Side Coalition's charges of corruption and fraud in the FHA housing market were eventually investigated by the Justice Department; and in 1971, the U.S. Attorney General handed down 70 federal indictments to real-estate agents, HUD officials and building inspectors.

Michael Westgate: In the 1970s the S&L business was pretty straightforward. The government limited interest rates paid on savings accounts under Regulation Q until 1977. If the S&L could lend money out at 2% above what it cost to borrow, the S&L could make money on the spread. S&Ls were restricted in lending in that 80% of their loan funds had to be lent to single family (1-4 unit) homes. If it was short on cash, an S&L could borrow from the district FHLB.

State examiners examine state-chartered banks and S&Ls. Federal examiners examine those that are federally-chartered and state institutions with federal insurance. FSLIC used to insure S&Ls while FDIC covered banks. Today FDIC insures both types. Federal insurance covering each account was raised to from $5000 to $20,000, then $100,000 and eventually $250,000.

Illinois had one of the most restrictive banking laws: "unitary banking." A bank could only have one branch: its main office. While S&Ls saw some of their depositors move to the suburbs, they still had substantial deposits from within their neighborhoods. But increasingly they made most of their loans in the suburbs, part of the national trend. Local applicants for loans were increasingly turned down as demographics changed. There was discrimination, both blatant and because of the practices of realtors, appraisers, lenders and government agencies. Some S&Ls actually moved out of their old neighborhoods into more affluent neighborhoods or downtown.

Until the 1980s, local lenders made most loans and continued to own and service the mortgages themselves. That gave them a long-term vested interest in the health of both the individual loans and the neighborhoods in which they were made. But it became increasingly lucrative to originate loans and sell both the loans and the servicing to large firms which used increasingly mechanized approaches to servicing. This was anathema to Gale, who had started her foray into housing by criticizing FHA and its abuses. She wanted local banks to own the success or failure of the loans made in each neighborhood.

George Behymer, retired savings & loan president from Cincinnati, was active in the US and American Savings & Loan Leagues, a founding member of NHS of Cincinnati, advisor to Urban Reinvestment Task Force and Treasurer of Neighborhood Housing Services of America (NHSA): I first met Gale when I went to Rutgers. George Sternlieb was a professor there and had a seminar on public policy and housing and integration. I had read his paper on abandonment. I said, "Here's somebody that knows the problem with abandoned buildings. And he has hit on it."

I thought, "Gee, I'd like to listen to this." This was on the company time. I flew down to Newark, rented a car and went over to Rutgers. Gale was there. It was almost like a classroom type of presentation with maybe 20 people. He would ask questions or encourage people to participate. Gale was in the front and he called on Gale several times to talk about the role of an activist. He quoted Alinsky quite a bit. I was real pleased with it.

They had a lunchtime, just a small group. I had sat at the same table that Gale was. Not deliberately. It just turned out that way. That's the first time I met her. Having already worked with Carl Westmoreland, an activist in Cincinnati, I thought, "Well, Carl must be of the same school as this woman." Because you could see that they were well prepared and they could articulate the positions. They had some attraction to the media because they were maybe rebels.

Michael Westgate: Gale was aware of the problem of lenders and borrowers entering into loan agreements where borrowers had little chance of repaying. It horrified her. The increasingly worldwide scope of lending problems, including predatory lending, was emerging at the time of her death in 2001.

There was clearly fraud as well as mismanagement both inside and outside the government. The old checks and balances where lenders lent their own clients' money with prudence (some would say too much prudence) were gone. Greed took its place. The beneficiaries were the brokers, lenders, lawyers and appraisers who participated in this scheme, both taking bribes and benefiting improperly from the actual transactions.

Those who suffered the most were the individual families taking out loans, losing their equity, their savings, and their credit-worthiness. Less educated borrowers lost the most. Many would have been better off continuing to rent. Blocks and entire neighborhoods suffered. Rampant foreclosures spelled doom for neighborhoods. Parts of Chicago suffered more during this period than any other city. As certain neighborhoods deteriorated, a self-fulfilling prophecy took place. It became unsafe for individual lenders to lend where no one else would lend. How would your homebuyers (and others like them) sell their properties when the time came?

In the early '70s there was growing recognition that a better-quantified, rational approach to lending might identify the risk factors in lending in inner cities. If the FHLBB and the S&Ls, which at the time made the majority of residential loans nationwide, could agree on what those factors were, perhaps the admittedly racial overtones in lending could be reduced. I volunteered and was commissioned to undertake a "Study of the Factors of Risk in Urban Mortgage Lending". The FHLBB committed $50,000 to the study.

There were thirteen responses from consulting firms, some of them quite thoughtful. We interviewed the two most responsive, RAND in California and the University of Pittsburgh in Pennsylvania. The University of Pittsburgh won and Dr. Alex Williams did a comprehensive sampling of the loans made by several of the S&Ls in Pittsburgh, a process which we facilitated. It was the first study of its kind in the country and it reached some interesting conclusions. Race was not a significant factor. Increasing family size correlated with loan delinquency but not with foreclosures. Logically, financial stress made people put food and medical emergencies ahead of mortgage payments but not to the extent they would lose their houses. Professors (perhaps absent minded) had high delinquency rates but few foreclosures. Highest risk for foreclosure was actually developers and other high-risk takers.

Simultaneous with completing the Study of Risk, I began working part-time with Bill Whiteside, founder and director of the Urban Reinvestment Task Force at the Federal Home Loan Bank Board. Whiteside could learn from my experience and the FSLIC study what happened when inner city loans and S&Ls went sour. I could learn from him what pro-active measures might be taken to involve lenders in seeking solutions to the disinvestment that led to the problems with which I had been dealing.

As the Study of Risk wound down, Bill asked me to become the third member of the staff of the Task Force, which he was putting together with the blessing of Preston Martin, chairman of the Board of FHLBB. The Task Force was not popular with the savings and loan associations who saw it as med-dling in their business-as-usual. At one point the regional Federal Home Loan Bank presidents, who are elected by the savings and loan associations of each district, voted no confidence in the program. They felt that responsibility for any government-sponsored programs belonged at HUD and were not particu-larly interested in hearing about the Neighborhood Housing Services program in Pittsburgh which had become the model for the Urban Reinvestment Task Force. Bill brought me on as Assistant Director for Administration but also with field responsibility for meeting with leaders among the lenders, city offi-cials and community in Kansas City, Missouri, and then the big one: Chicago.

Shel Trapp: The way the term "redlining" started was at a meeting with the president of the old Bell Federal Savings and Loan. There was a big map on the wall, a red line around basically the black and Hispanic community. We said, "What's that?" "Well, everything in the red line, inside the red, is our FHA area. Everything outside is the conventional." That's when we were in the midst of the FHA fight, too. When we first started, it was reinvestment agreements. Banks wanted to include the FHA loans as part of "This meets the agreement. We made an FHA loan." "No. It's got to be conventional." After that meeting, that's when we coined the term "redlining," meaning you'd only get an FHA mortgage inside that area.

Michael Westgate: FHA required (and still requires) appraisers to include in their forms whether neighborhoods are "stable" or "changing". At that time, "changing" was often a codeword, a cause for automatic rejection of loan applications.

While similar practices had undoubtedly been around for decades, redlining became infamous in mortgage lending nationwide beginning with the use of the term by Gale and others working with her in the early 1970s. Their publication entitled *REDLINING* was used before the Illinois legislature in 1975. While made illegal first by Illinois and then nationwide, redlining still persists in pockets, nationwide, many years later.

Use of the term "redlining" actually goes back to at least 1937 when the Home Owners Loan Corporation (HOLC) published a redlining map of Philadelphia.

The most persistent abuses were in the mortgage banking business. Virtually unregulated by the federal government and weakly regulated by the various states, mortgage brokers stepped in to take business away from traditional lenders. Paradoxically these mortgage lenders owe their existence, in large part, to the banks that own them, lend to them, or purchase loans from them. These relationships were aided and abetted by federal legislation that sought to modernize the financial market by removing barriers to the flow of capital. But in the process, much of the regulatory function intended to protect individual borrowers (and hence neighborhoods), financial institutions and the financial system as a whole was undone. Federal preemption of state legislation was particularly unfair to those states which had enacted protection for borrowers.

The Neighborhood Housing Services program, further addressed below, was a model for local banks and city government, led by local activists, to address these problems. It became strong in Chicago because of the strength of the participants. NHS of Chicago did not grow out of a vacuum. It was the result of a combination of forces. Gale represented the challenge. The Federal Home Loan Bank of Chicago represented the establishment. To give it credit, the FHLB-Chicago was trying harder than any of its counterparts in the Federal Home Loan Bank System or the Federal Reserve System. But it did not know the strength of Gale's forces.

Helen Murray: Mr. Bartell [president of the Federal Home Loan Bank of Chicago] said, "You people wouldn't know what to do with disclosure if you had it." Them's fighting words! We ruined his barbeque one time out on Golf Road. Gale was doing her Gale thing on him, in his driveway, and his steaks were burning in the back. "You people wouldn't know what to do with it!"

Anyway, FHLB-Chicago had done a voluntary disclosure, by zip code, disclosure, and they supplied us that data. But it wasn't by bank name. I mean it was just Bank A, Bank B, Bank C, Bank D. It was all secret as to who the banks were.

Now the other groups that had come to the first national conference, and been to Baltimore, were moving on similar fronts in their own states, some more than others. Boston particularly was doing some stuff. They were also pushing very hard on disclosure and a redlining law.

Michael Westgate: There had been considerable innovation under Pres Martin, who established the Federal Home Loan Mortgage Corporation (FHLMC, now known as Freddie Mac), raised the limit on interest rates S&Ls could pay, raised limits on insurance, and introduced variable rate mortgages. But Pres was an exceptional leader and he had left in 1973.

Pres Martin also sponsored the Center for Executive Development which became the Urban Reinvestment Task Force during his tenure. Congress later, in 1978, incorporated it as the Neighborhood Reinvestment Corporation (now known as NeighborWorks America). Bill Whiteside led it from its inception until 1990.

Bill Whiteside, Director of the Urban Reinvestment Task Force. He was successful in expanding it from under the Federal Home Loan Bank Board, obtaining a charter from Congress as Neighborhood Reinvestment Corporation. Chicago was one of the first NHSs and remains its best: As I said to Mary Lee Widener [who went on to found Neighborhood Housing Services of America, a non-profit secondary market for loans made by NHS and other members of the NeighborWorks network] when I interviewed her to join us on the Oakland program, "the Federal Home Loan Bank presidents don't like what we are doing and neither does the Federal Home Loan Bank Board. Leaving out the Chairman."

Ann Vick-Westgate: What about Neighborhood Housing Services of America and Neighborhood Reinvestment, was Proxmire involved?

Ken McLean, a Chicago native and Senator William Proxmire's chief banking committee staff member. He worked closely with Gale to write up the draft bill which would become the Home Mortgage Disclosure Act (HMDA). He also played a key role in drafting the Community Reinvestment Act (CRA): Yeah. He was the author of that legislation as well. Bill Whiteside came to us when it was sort of started up. It was started up by the Federal Home Loan Bank Board.

Preston Martin was Chairman of it and he wanted to see what the Bank Board could do to foster urban reinvestment and came up with this idea of the neighborhood reinvestment group. So it was all done regulatorily; there was no legislation filed. He [together with Mary Lee Widener] just somehow created it and got it started.

So then in '76 Carter was elected President and Pat Harris became Secretary of HUD. So the issue came up what's to be done with this little nascent group that the Federal Home Loan Bank Board had started up. And the bureaucrats at HUD reached out with their long fingers and said, "Hey, you know, this is urban investment. This is our business! You know, we should have control of it."

They wanted to grab it. Whiteside and company came to us to see what we could do about it and so we got the idea, why not, let's have a permanent sort of corporation, a Neighborhood Reinvestment Corporation. Call it a corporation because it sounds conservative and Republican. And keep it out of HUD.

So that's what we did. We drafted it and, again, put it in a housing bill. It wasn't quite that close for some reason. There was more of an inside baseball fight. The bankers didn't care too much one way or the other, whether it was in HUD or whether it was in the Bank Board. So we didn't have the banking lobby to contend with. We basically had the HUD bureaucrat lobby. They weren't as powerful.

Proxmire was taken with Whiteside because we had a hearing on his program and he described what they did: two or three guys go into a city and try to get the banks organized and the local groups and the local city hall bureaucrats, as part of a concerted effort to bring money back into the community. And Proxmire was taken by that because, again, there was no big HUD program, a lot of massive spending. But it was organized on a very small scale.

So Proxmire asked him at the hearing, "What's your budget?" And Whiteside said five million or some really ridiculously low amount. So Proxmire said, "Well, that's pretty small. Couldn't you use some more money?" And Whiteside said, "Not really, Senator, if we had more money we wouldn't spend it effectively." And Proxmire turned to me and said (whispering), "That's my guy."

So from then on for years afterwards he was a big booster of Whiteside. In fact, that's what convinced him to take Whiteside's side on the argument about preserving the independence of the neighborhood reinvestment group and keeping it out of HUD. Because he was convinced if it became part of HUD, they would pour a lot of money into it. You know, the HUD bureaucrats that's what they do. And it would degenerate into an ineffective program.

Michael Westgate: We heard that a couple of senators voted for it because they said, "If HUD's against it, it can't be all bad!" I was actually working for the Federal Home Loan Bank Board. My first job after business school was Assistant to the Director of FSLIC. So I knew Bob Bartell [President FHLB of Chicago].

Helen Murray: I'll be darned. Well, we were a thorn in his side that poor man. But he dealt with us.

Michael Westgate: We got $30,000 from him. And Al Fenderson was his general counsel. Fenderson was my regular liaison. I came out to Chicago from Washington probably twice a month for three or four days each time. It was my job to make the rounds of every bank and get as high as I could. You know, senior vice president if I couldn't get to the president. And say, "We're going to have a meeting in a few months and we're going to try to set up an NHS. Who's the most senior person we can get from your bank to come to it?" It was useful to be coming from the Federal Home Loan Bank Board because they couldn't lock me out. They had to see me because I could go back and, through Whiteside, talk to Preston Martin, the chairman of the Bank Board, and say, "X in Chicago isn't responding." But I got a good response, particularly from the S&Ls. I met with the redevelopment czar for the city, Lew Hill, to get the city's support. That's also when I got to know Gale.

Helen Murray: Yeah. Lew Hill. I took a class with him at Roosevelt when I went back to school. Maybe I helped to shape this, because I'd already had some stuff. I'd had organizing already so I was interested in taking economic classes and political science classes. He had these wonderful color maps that showed the ethnic progression by neighborhood of different groups as they came into the city.

You'd see the Italians and then you'd see them 20 years later and it was like they all got on the Grand Avenue bus and went that way. And all the Germans took the Lincoln Avenue bus and then out to the suburbs here. Right? And he'd have these progressions of different colorful ethnic maps. And of course the blacks always stayed right <u>here</u>. Then they got to be <u>here</u>. And then they got to be <u>here</u>. And it was just all this compressed stuff.

Michael Westgate: My being transferred to Bill's operation, still retaining my job title as Assistant to the Director of FSLIC, was in part to defuse the contention that Bill had no support from within the FHLBB. He had faced a devastating meeting of the presidents of the Federal Home Loan Banks where almost all of them had voiced lack of support for Whiteside's operation, then named the Center for Executive Development.

In the meantime, heat was being generated by a public wanting to know why center cities were declining. There was increasing focus on discrimination in lending. Women of childbearing age were asked by loan officers what their plans were for having children, even what kind of birth control they were using. Their income was discounted in part or wholly, based upon their answers. S&Ls, together with bankers, were defensive and pressured their regulators not to make further demands on them. It was not until much later that the FHLBB issued regulations outlawing discrimination, although there was Fair Housing legislation through HUD, which allowed those individuals who felt they had been discriminated against on the basis of race, ethnicity or national origin to seek redress after the fact.

Gale was fearless. She volunteered to assist the FHLBB education drive by speaking or running a workshop at the next S&L industry convention. Noting that she did not mind the odds of being the only neighborhood spokesperson in a room of lenders, Gale pointed out that lending officials needed to meet more regularly with the people who were their customers.

Cal Bradford: It was wonderful to hear Bob Bartell say, "Gale's absolutely right. You need to listen to her. She's going to do the right thing. Pay attention to her now, and do what she says now rather than later." Here was this guy who wasn't going to speak to her. She was this annoying person. Didn't want to have anything to do with her. He was an expert; he'd done research on banking and everything. He was a well-qualified academic as well. And he ended up standing up to these other executives in the financial world, saying that they should pay attention. That to me was a classic because [Gale and company] were throwing streamers back there at his house.

They all went out in buses, because he wouldn't meet with them, to his house at night and he's having company. So Bartell is having a barbecue out in back and they're throwing red streamers over the back fence of his house. He lives up in Winnetka or Barrington, way up. Screaming and yelling, demonstrating and passing out leaflets to his neighbors, they're saying, "Oh, yeah. The guy who just moved here from Detroit, we don't know much about him. Is this what he's doing?" "Oh, yeah. He's screwing the neighborhoods."

Then, of course, all these people came on school buses with their kids. The kids had to go to the bathroom. So while Gale has got her megaphone and they're yelling at him out in the back with his company, Mrs. Bartell is opening the front door and letting the kids come in one by one to use the bathroom. Yes, it's the confrontation, but there's something so incredibly human about it at a more basic level that makes it both humorous and powerful. And then he agrees to meet with them. And he brings doughnuts to this meeting.

Roger Coughlin: Now we're up talking to Bob Bartell. "What do you want?" They told him what they wanted. They wanted him to do this research in this area. So it was all done and he thought it was... Oh, you know the story! It was all done. Fool those community people. Get your scissors out. He cut the names off, the names of the savings and loan industry.

Now what do we want? They had heard about this Neighborhood Housing program in Pittsburgh. So they said, "That's what we're gonna have here in Chicago!" It was a good negotiating point. So Bartell says he will get the commercial banks and the savings and loans. "And we'll sit down and we'll meet and we'll come up with some plans." So, okay, I get invited because, I guess, if nothing else, I had the workers on the payroll.

Michael Westgate: This was the meeting for which Bartell provided funding from the $30,000 we needed for the year's work leading up to an NHS for Chicago and which I was orchestrating under Bill Whiteside. There had been some approaches taken to the problems of lending in inner city Chicago by my agency, FSLIC, including merging fourteen failing savings and loans into stronger ones. Some of these had not gone well. Informed people knew there had to be some new approaches.

Roger Coughlin: So it was over here in the Hyatt Hotel in the West Building. I was talking with the President of Talman Federal Savings and Loan because he was one of the good guys. Talman was maybe one of the biggest savings and loans, certainly in the Chicago area. Wonderful! A very substantial [S&L] and the federal government, FSLIC, made them link themselves with a failed savings and loan out in Arlington or someplace and it destroyed them. It really, really, really took the heart out of them and their funds.

All of a sudden, they're talking to me and they're looking at the end of the stairs. They look over my shoulder and one of them says, "Oh, my God, look who's coming down the stairs!" So I turned around. Who was coming down the stairs? It was Gale! Now Gale was a substantial personality. Of course, she was also a substantial person.

So she comes down the stairs. "Oh, my God!" Like "My lunch is going to be ruined!" they're saying to themselves. So, any rate, we have lunch and they decide that we will now go out to a place in Wisconsin. There's a big resort out there. We're going to go out there for this meeting and doing this planning. What they wanted was the Neighborhood Housing Services. They were going to put the plan together for the Neighborhood Housing Services.

So out we go. We're out here at this meeting and Bill Plechaty [one of the bank presidents] is chosen as the chairman of it, so he's running these meetings. So [a couple of days] after this meeting over there at the Hyatt, we got on a bus and we went out there to the big resort at Williams Bay on Lake Geneva. Within a day somebody shook Plechaty up, and he'd say – and there would be all the rest of us geniuses – "Gale, what about that? What's the facts on this and what do you think about it?" The only person who mattered to Bill Plechaty as having anything really to contribute as far as he was concerned was Gale Cincotta – after one day, after one day!

He saw it because Gale was a simple, brilliant, honest person. She never lost any of those virtues. Behind it, of course, she was tough. But Gale could take the most complicated matter and explain that. She could have explained negative matter. She'd be able to explain that to me and I'd say, "Oh. That's what a black hole is. Okay. Fine."

Gale could take any of those things and make them very simple and that's why she was respected, I understand now, when she'd go down before Congress. She was able to wade through all the frills and get right down to what this is about and explain it. She was always brilliant, never lost her sense of humor, never lost her interest in food and never lost her interest in her friends.

You'd have a meeting with all the people and there'd be some community people there. This is not like a committed missionary who goes over and does what is morally right. No! Gale would go over and sit with her friends, poor black people from the West Side. These were her women friends. That's just the way she was. Her simplicity. She was brilliant and she was afraid of nothing. But she was simple in terms of her relationships. She never thought herself as being more important or somebody who she wasn't.

At the NHS Initiative first meeting at Lake Geneva, the resort in Wisconsin, the President of Talman and Bill Plechaty were particularly "good guys."

Michael Westgate: The trade associations of the savings and loan industry were not supportive of what Gale was trying to do, or of the efforts of Pres Martin, Bill Whiteside and myself at the Federal Home Loan Bank Board, or of what Mary Lee Widener was doing to form Neighborhood Housing Services of America (NHSA). They felt threatened by change.

George Behymer from Cincinnati was one of the few savings and loan presidents who understood from the beginning what the issues were and had an instinct for what some of the solutions might be. He and I co-chaired the lenders' session at the small first national conference of the Urban Reinvestment Task Force in November 1974 in Boulder, Colorado.

George Behymer: When I was on the urban lending committees at both the savings and loan leagues [U.S. and National Leagues], Barry Tate called me. He was an officer with the U.S. Savings and Loan League in Chicago. He said very nervously on the phone, "You got to get here to Chicago. You got to be up here as soon as you can get here. We got a meeting demanded by Gale Cincotta for 9:30 tomorrow morning. We got to get our preparations. We want you up here. Norman Strunk, the Executive Director, wants you up here as soon as you can get here."

I got on a flight from Cincinnati that afternoon. They began to lay out all the precautionary steps they had taken because they were anticipating Gale to have a bunch of protestors jamming the lobby and jamming the elevators and certainly jamming all the office space at the U.S. League's headquarters. He had alerted the U.S. Marshals. And reviewed the communications systems that they had with the security people within the bank building and what emergency areas that we as staff could escape to. It was unbelievable the emotion and fear actually.

They wanted me to get there early. They were going to go through again the rehearsal for this big protest that was going to take place. I got there and of course Barry was there. Bill McConnell was there. Norman Strunk was there. They nervously waited. They had a huge tape machine, two foot wide and at least three feet high with reels all over. They had microphones placed at the table in front of the officers of the U.S. League. They kept saying, "Well, you've got a chair here, George." And I said, "No. I'll sit around the corner here on this other side."

They were waiting for some kind of signal from the ground level up to them as to when Gale was coming and how many thousands of people were going to be with them and all that. Finally, right on schedule, it was announced that Gale and her entourage were coming. They had this beautiful boardroom for this meeting. It was a huge room. It was all wood paneled, big over-stuffed office chairs, the whole nine yards.

The doors open and here comes Gale and Paul Brophy. He probably had a legal background. Then slowly and very deliberately came these ten or twelve white-haired ladies with walking sticks, walkers, crutches and seated themselves, all well dressed, very, very proper. Took several seconds to pull those overstuffed chairs back and then get seated and then try to pull them up to the table.

Meantime I kept looking at the door because the doors were double doors and I was seated on the opposite wall so I could see out to the lobby and almost to the elevator. And I kept thinking, "Well, is this it?" And they all seated. Norman, somewhat relieved, but still skeptical, said, "Well, Gale. We've talked to our attorney and I would like to read a prepared statement." And she said, "Norman, be my guest."

So Norman Strunk reads this prepared statement about what was the policy of the U.S. League and its mission and how many members and all the other pertinent data. He finishes and there was sort of a pause, like, is Bill McConnell going to say something or anyone else? And then Norman Strunk said, "Gale, whatever you'd like to say."

Gale looked around. She was extremely polite. She said, "Well, thank you, Mr. Strunk. I think we here understand the mission of the savings and loans in Chicago and nationwide. I do have some questions though. Norman, you live in Evanston... Norman, do you currently have a mortgage?" "Well, yes." "Norman, did you apply for a loan to a savings and loan?" "Well, yes. My mortgage is with X savings and loan." "Did you have any difficulty in getting your loan there?" "Well, no. I didn't."

Then she turned to Bill McConnell and asked Bill the same things. She would read off the jurisdiction they were in. Obviously she'd already researched all the mortgage records and deed records of all the U.S. League members. Then she'd say, "Did you get a mortgage loan on your property, Mr. McConnell?" Very polite and very slow, very deliberate. He said, "Yes." "And did you get less than you wanted to borrow? Or did you get more than you needed?" "No. What I asked for they approved." "That's very good. I'm happy for you."

Then she'd turn to Barry Tate. She said, "Well, Barry, do you own a home?" "I don't have to answer that." "Well, do you have a mortgage on your home, Barry?" "I don't have to answer that. I'm not going to answer." "Well," she said. "Let me read off if my information is correct and maybe you could say 'yes' or 'no.'" So she proceeded to name the mortgagee, the amount of mortgage that Tate had on the record. She said, "I don't have the unpaid balance, but I don't think it's germane to this conversation."

Then there was a pause and she turned and she says to the little white-haired lady next to her, "This is May Brown. She lives at such and such a place in Cicero. How many times, May, have you gone to your savings and loan there and requested a mortgage loan?" The response from May would be, "Well, I went several times." "What did you experience?" "They said since my husband was only drawing so much income that I didn't qualify. And the house wasn't appraised for what we had to borrow." So Gale said, "So your request was rejected?"

Then she said, "Now Peggy Smith." She went all the way round the table with the same type of questions to them. They obviously were retirees. She'd say, "Now when did you first start applying for these loans in your neighborhood?" or "When did you find that you couldn't get a loan from your local savings and loan?" "Well, when my husband was actively employed and that was 22 years ago. We only wanted to borrow for ten years. We felt that it was a modest house, but it fit our needs. The children were grown, but he was still gainfully employed." "What kind of response did you get?" "Well, there was a reluctance because they said ours was a 'changing neighborhood.' I really didn't have an explanation of what a changing neighborhood was." "Did they make the loan?" "No. They didn't."

She went right around the table one by one. There were about three people attending from the press, but one that was particularly interested. She didn't interrupt. She sat quiet and took notes as to what was transpiring. So after maybe 45 minutes when all the presenters and so forth had finished and everything else, Gale said, "Norman, these are white people in nice neighborhoods, not as luxurious or as affluent as you live in. However they could meet the same income test and had the same ability to repay their debt and probably would honor the debt with the same loyalty that you would have. Doesn't it seem strange that all of them were turned down because they were in 'changing neighborhoods?' What is the definition of a changing neighborhood, Norman?" And Norman made a half-hearted attempt to respond.

Anyhow, they adjourned. The reporter came up and asked me some questions and they yanked me out and said, "Don't give away the store, George." That was when Gale said, "George, you're fine. I'm not worried about you. This is just between Norman and I." Then Gale left.

CHAPTER 7

"They came up with a codename: MAHA."

METROPOLITAN AREA HOUSING ALLIANCE (MAHA)
NATIONAL PEOPLE'S ACTION (NPA)
NATIONAL TRAINING AND INFORMATION CENTER (NTIC)
CHICAGO HOUSING COURT
NATIONAL HOUSING CONFERENCES OF 1973-1974

Joe Mariano: The National Housing Conference in 1973 was a raucous convening of national neighborhood chieftains which won a "payback program" for minority buyers of "defective" homes sold under the aegis of the Federal Housing Administration (FHA).

This was officially known as the HUD 518b payback program for homes sold with major structural programs.

Shel Trapp: MAHA started after that organizing conference in Baltimore. Gale and I get back, "Okay, we did that. What now?" We didn't know what the hell. You wouldn't call it a coalition then. It was a bunch of folks that had gotten together. So we started trying to get some money. We learned about the Stern Family Fund, a very interesting fund, basically run by this family.

At that time, it was very avant-garde to have a woman executive director. You were really on the cutting edge. So Gale and I decided she would be executive director, and I don't know if I even had a title. I didn't care about titles. But anyway, she was the head honcho. So she and Ray Bailey from Detroit, who was a black guy, they flew out to San Francisco.

Basically it was a family reunion when the board of the Stern Family Fund met. She and Ray went up, and I didn't want to go along because it looked white male. Much better with a black guy, white woman. Don't get me in the mix. So we role-played, the three of us, what they were gonna say, and the pitch they were gonna give, and all that. And they go out there and, lo and behold, they come back with a commitment for $40,000, passed through the Center for Community Change. So here we had $40,000, this twenty-five foot storefront on Division Street, Gale and I, Anne-Marie one day a week, and a German volunteer. Gale's salary would be $12,000; mine would be $10,000.

This was to form a national alliance. The $40,000 was for Gale and me to do this nationally. Then we just started this while sitting around, looking at each other in the office, trying to figure out what the hell does this mean… Obviously we were pushing some of our issues. It came to mind, why don't we form a citywide coalition? We had South Side, West Side, Southwest Side, North Side. So we did it and that became Metropolitan Area Housing Alliance. NTIC came just slightly before MAHA, which never was incorporated, just an ad hoc group. I stole some support out of the West Side Coalition budget.

Father Coughlin called me and said, "Look. I got this Area Service program." He was in a very powerful position at that point in Catholic Charities. "I can get you twenty organizers. I'll pay 'em all. Would you supervise them?" He said, "By the way, I'll pay you too." Hey, that sounded like a pretty good deal to me. I said, "Sure." So they were my staff. Well, that happened also at NCO. I had German organizers there. They were all free. You had to pay their housing; that was it. I had them.

Ed Bailey: MAHA was a very strong group. She had white groups. She had groups all over. She had Chicago, some north and west and everywhere. Well, after a while, some of them felt that MAHA was a little too much authority. And a lot of them just split – broke away. She lost some like that. That's all in the game. And one time two or three people came to me and asked me if I would break away and join another. I said, "No. No way." I wouldn't even talk with 'em about it. Gale and we were just too much, the relationship too strong.

Shel Trapp: MAHA fought groundbreaking battles in Chicago, one of them over the collection of data on loans and deposits at savings and loan associations in Chicago. This was to become a precursor to the HMDA law providing data on which the Community Reinvestment Act could be acted upon.

MAHA targeted the Federal Home Loan Bank because they were the weak link. Beat them up to disclose savings and loans—which they did, collectively. Woodlawn was, except for University of Chicago, the poorest neighborhood in Chicago, $50 million in deposits and $24,000 in mortgages.

The first time that Gale testified we used some of that data, but then we also did title searches. This was before anything was computerized. We had students title-searching the neighborhoods, street by street by street. You had to go look through a file card. All by hand. And we'd track FHA mortgages. The first time she testified in Congress it was FHA data that she used – one whole neighborhood, not one conventional loan. All FHA!

From the Ford Foundation Archives
HTIC Technical Assistance Proposal **(March 5, 1975):**

At the end of 1973, HTIC developed the concept of the "Chicago Laboratory", based on the theory that one could not truly be of assistance to other cities unless there was an ongoing dealing with issues and training of staff in Chicago. Thus, in December 1973, twenty-three community groups throughout the city of Chicago were pulled together to form the Metropolitan Area Housing Alliance (MAHA). Using MAHA as a model, specific issues were approached, specific victories were won, and new skills in coalition forming were learned.

Michael Westgate: One of the victories of the Mortgage Coalition that evolved into MAHA was forcing the Federal Home Loan Bank of Chicago (FHLB-Chicago) to conduct a survey of its member savings and loan associations. On June 10, 1973, they met with Richard Platt of the Federal Home Loan Bank Board (FHLBB) in Washington and Al Fenderson, General Counsel of the FHLB-Chicago. A month later they had no response from the FHLBB or the other regulators with whom they had tried to engage. July 10, they met with John Stipp, President of the FHLB-Chicago, at his home and he apologized for no progress. On August 8, at a meeting with the FHLB, for the first time the FHLB admitted, "redlining occurs but we don't know what to do about it". On September 4, the FHLB called a surprise meeting to review a survey document they had prepared, which was unsatisfactory to the Mortgage Coalition.

On September 7, they met to approve a revised survey form, to include data on loans made, covering the period 6/30/71-6/30/73. The FHLB would aggregate all the data and provide total savings accounts by zip code as well as the number and amount of loans – conventional, FHA/VA, construction and home improvement – by zip code. The survey was to be voluntary and anonymous so no enforcement would be possible against any S&L, according to the NTIC publication *Grassroots Battle against Redlining* (GBR) which reported that 127 local savings and loans provided the data requested at the end of the 1973.

On December 1, 1973 the 13 groups involved formed MAHA.

This was a milestone. No similar targeted gathering of data had taken place around the country other than the study by the FSLIC, *Factors of Risk in Urban Mortgage Lending,* which I supervised that included a study of all the loans made by First Federal Savings and Loan Association in Pittsburgh. Those results were published by Dr. Alex O. Williams and cited in a study by George M. Furstenberg.

There was also a California law passed in 1964 requiring state-chartered S&Ls to submit certain data to the Commissioner of Savings & Loans but I am not aware of any efforts to utilize that data prior to the movement begun in Chicago by Gale and others gathering data to buttress their campaign for HMDA and CRA.

From Ford Foundation Program Action documents (January 12, 1976) recommending a $125,000 grant over two years to HTIC:
A 1973 Federal Home Loan Bank of Chicago survey of its member savings and loans to disclose mortgage-lending patterns was the direct result of highly publicized MAHA negotiations. Sixty-five percent of the city's savings and loans completed the voluntary survey. The information acquired supported HTIC disinvestment claims and led to both city and state laws requiring disclosure of mortgage placements on one hand and the development of the nation's largest Neighborhood Housing Services program on the other.

Michael Westgate: In his November 1978 article for *Mother Jones,* "Blackjacking the City Redliners," John Conroy reported that several groups had left MAHA "dissatisfied with the coalition's administrative framework and with the amount of input that member organizations are allowed." Cincotta shrugged off the deflections as "natural growing pains" and said she expected some of the groups to return. Many of those departing still praised Cincotta's accomplishments and courage.

From Case Study by Hallahan (11/7/91)
Kirk Hallahan: Apart from protest actions, NPA and its HTIC affiliate recognized that being able to document instances of neighborhood deterioration was going to be critical for obtaining reforms. In instances of discrimination, such as refusal to sell a house to a minority purchaser, proof was generally not necessary.
Neighborhood disinvestment was different. Banks consistently denied that redlining took place and argued that neighborhood decay was due to many factors. The unit of analysis was whole neighborhoods, and in order to establish that disinvestment occurred as a result of loan practices, NPA had to have proof. (4)
Beginning in 1972, MAHA, as the NPA local affiliate, began studying housing patterns in Chicago. The group would select particular neighborhoods to determine demographics, the kind of housing stock, costs and family income figures based on census data. Then using property records available on microfilm in the basement of Chicago City Hall, they would

compare lender data. Cincotta recalls, "One neighborhood would have all conventional financing; and the other was all FHA. The only difference was that one was in the suburbs and all white, and the other was inner-city and black." (5)

Jimmy Cincotta: By the time I finished high school, Gale had moved on to housing. The other thing that made her a leader is she brought people together and that's how MAHA started, because she eventually became the president of OBA. It was a volunteer position. And then you start doing the work – OBA, Organization for a Better Austin – how you make Austin better. Then as you start talking and you're hearing from other people, "Oh, Woodlawn. The same things are happening there." Or Wicker Park or wherever, the same things are happening. So then you start talking to those people and that's how MAHA started, Metropolitan Area Housing Alliance. So then it moved to housing. So looking at who were the enemies. So overcrowded schools…the redlining…so why can't you get a loan? "I could get a loan last year when the neighborhood was white. Why can't I get a loan this year now that it's half black? What's going on?"

And that's how CRA came in. MAHA did that. So it became Metropolitan Housing. And then bringing those communities together, and then you start looking and you're saying, "Well, now it's been happening in these communities in Chicago, but it's also happening in the communities in Boston, in Cleveland, Toledo, Denver…" So then you start connecting to them. And that's how it went to NTIC.

Helen Murray: MAHA was our local organization. After the West Side Coalition, some pieces of that went by the wayside. So we needed a new coalition of community organizations which was Metropolitan Area Housing Alliance. So we're on Division Street. Those of us who were the redlining/reinvestment staff for NPA were also the redlining/reinvestment staff for MAHA because we were the link.

MAHA was never formalized. We were fine with that. I used to say to the guys, "We aren't one organization. We're an action machine. Have gun, will travel. We know how to get people together, make a name, and go and do something." We didn't worry about spending two years formalizing another organization. That was our strength that we were so mobile, that we didn't get bogged down in worrying on about those details. Now there comes a time when you have to worry. When you've been with NHS, that's a different kind of thing. You <u>have</u> to worry about the details.

Michael Westgate: MAHA was great experience to get under their belts locally while founding NPA nationally. Both could be freewheeling organizations responding to crises and opportunities to build coalitions. But on the staffing issue, the relationship between Gale and Shel was very special. That would have made it very difficult to bring in a number two, a future leader.

Cal Bradford: Well, you would have had to change everything. Shel would have had to work with other people, and they'd have to bring in another organizer. In a way, it ran on personality. It had an advantage of not having a structure, but it also had this tremendous disadvantage. There was no one planning for that disadvantage. They were just sort of pretending it didn't exist.

As long as Gale and Shel were there and had energy and they had resources, it worked great. It didn't shortchange issues much because Gale and Shel both had this commitment. They had that notion that the leadership brings the issues. Whoever shows up to the leadership training, if you pay your dues, you get to be a leader. It was the most simplistic and in many ways sort of naïve notion of advancement. And it worked so well.

As Trapp said, and as Gale said too, but mostly Shel, "There's no reward for being a leader here. You got to pay your own way to every meeting. Every once in a while we get somebody to pay. But you pay your own way to meetings. You got to sit on the bus for a long time. If you show up, we figure you care because there's no other reason to do this." It doesn't make any sense. That's not a meritocracy or anything. It's all self-defining. And yet it worked. So it makes you have to rethink what's really going on in the world because it worked so well.

Roger Coughlin: Before all this, they had come up with a codename called MAHA. MAHA was before NTIC. You're not supposed to understand MAHA because it wasn't an organization at all. Naw. It was a codename under which people organized different issues. It's MAHA on this, MAHA on that. And the newspapers knew it, so the newspapers would give it coverage. You got coverage. It was through this codename called MAHA, Metropolitan Area Housing Alliance. They were part of it.

From *DISCLOSURE #1* (August 1974)

MAHA's other major success was in housing courts where they got the Housing Court to set aside one day a month for MAHA cases, so that they could focus their staff time and bring all their witnesses—and their landlords— on a specific scheduled date. Ted Wysocki was successful in bringing in date-stamped video footage showing all the horrific conditions some tenants were enduring. MAHA reduced a backlog of five years, back to 1968, up to current cases in 1973. Every community group submits complaints to Corporation Council (*sic*). Two hearing rooms are reserved the 2nd Tuesday of every month: one for code violations, one for demolition cases. The State's Attorney performed the service of conciliator in the "People's

Court," and that led to 25 landlords repairing buildings. Backlog is reduced from 5 years to 1 year.

Ted Wysocki: Between the time I first met Shel and when I really first met Gale, that particular winter quarter I went to study up at the University of Toronto, with a political theorist that I wanted to study as part of graduate school. While I was there, I was living with a group of people that were into videotapes. So I got exposed to video in that situation, came back, found out that as a student at the University of Chicago I had rights to pull this equipment out.

So I started doing that and we were actually going out and videotaping slum buildings that were used in Housing Court. I had to be sworn in – that this videotape was unedited and was taken within the last twenty-four hours. The whole citywide Metropolitan Area Housing Alliance (MAHA) was being organized at the time as a citywide coalition of different groups in different neighborhoods. The commonality of this issue was the fact that slumlords kept getting continuances, and the Housing Court never was enforcing it.

So as a graduate student, one of my early memories was actually seeing the video images being etched by a court artist on the news, because the local news was enthralled. There was this "Wow! Wow! Revolutionary! Gee, I wonder why TV stations couldn't go in and videotape slum holdings?"

Michael Westgate: At their third annual conference in April 1974, Mayor Daley surprised everyone by declaring his own version of CRA, requiring banks and S&Ls doing business with the City of Chicago to disclose deposit and loan information on the basis initially of zip codes and then of census tracts.

Daley's proposing the city ordinance restricting the deposit of city funds was a combination of hard work and good luck. Gale regarded FHA-insured loans as an abdication of lenders' responsibility. For years, she had had college students, working through professors at Northwestern University, poring through deeds, street by street, to show patterns where conventional loans were being made or not made.

Combined with the data from the Federal Home Loan Bank of Chicago, she would finally have, on a composite basis, both deposit data and loan data. Along with anecdotal knowledge, this was enough to demonstrate to Mayor Daley that there were real wrongs to be righted. It was fortuitous that Daley's own speechwriter had been denied a loan in Hyde Park but steered towards a loan elsewhere shortly before Daley had to give a speech to the Annual Housing Conference in April 1974. The Chicago City Council passed the Chicago Disclosure Ordinance in June 1974.

Shel Trapp: Daley was not really as supportive as he came across in that speech at that conference. I liked old man Daley. He recognized power. If you could demonstrate power out in the neighborhood, and if you would go through his chain of command, you could get a meeting with him. When you got a meeting with him, you knew you were going to get something. I never came out of a meeting with Daley where we didn't get something, enough that we could claim a big victory.

From *Urban Disinvestment: New Implications For Community Organization, Research and Public Policy* by Arthur J. Naparstek and Gale Cincotta (Joint Publication of The National Center for Urban Ethnic Affairs and NTIC, 1976)

Negotiations with municipal officials led to Mayor Daley's strong stand against redlining, and to the City Council's passage of the municipal anti-redlining ordinance. More significantly, the Chicago City Council adopted an innovative city depository program which requires that all financial institutions receiving deposits of city funds pledge not to practice redlining and to disclose deposit and lending information by census tracts (zip codes during the first year). The first of its kind in the country, the ordinance also authorizes savings and loan associations to be city depositories for the first time. Its passage was a primary result of the documentation of redlining in the city by the Federal Home Loan Bank Survey and the continued efforts of community groups to raise the issue of redlining. (25-26)

Shel Trapp: Two days after we got that notice that Daley had accepted our invitation, this guy calls us and says, "Look. I'm writing Daley's speech. Could I meet with whoever's the right person so they could tell me what kind of conference this is, so I get something that would make sense the Mayor saying?" So we're sitting there talking about all our issues and we're talking about banks not making loans.

Anyway, the speechwriter was talking about the banking issue. "Now wait a minute. You mean banks will make a loan in one neighborhood but not in another?" "Yeah." "Damn. That happened to me when I came to Chicago. Six months ago. I wanted to move into Hyde Park and they wouldn't give me a mortgage. I ended up buying in Lincoln Park 'cause I couldn't get a mortgage in Hyde Park. My God! Talk some more about that." So we talked more about that. "Well, geeze, if he gets a little bit of that in the speech, Daley's speech ought to be really good, about how banks are bad people."

So Daley's up giving his usual "Welcome to Chicago dees and dats" talk and he said, "And this one thing about banks not making loans in certain neighborhoods. That has got to stop! And I can tell you right now, that next Tuesday there will be an ordinance introduced into City Council which will require any bank that holds city funds to disclose where they have their deposits come from, and where they make their loans."

How the fuck did this happen? I hadn't suggested it to the speechwriter. The speechwriter had gone back, transferred his anger to Daley. And, well, old man Daley when he said, "It's introduced into City Council" you might as well say, "It's one of the Ten Commandments. It's done."

From Case Study by Hallahan (11/7/91)

Kirk Hallahan: When Daley attended NPA's third annual conference in April 1974, the controversial politician was greeted by a combination of boos and applause. However he received rave applause when he announced support for disclosure of loan and deposit data by local banks.

Chicago soon thereafter passed the first municipal disclosure ordinance in the country – a pivotal event in the movement. By getting a major city to agree to require disclosure, the group could prove that a legislative remedy worked. They also had a tool that they could use to generate the important most commodity in their fight: facts.

A month earlier, MAHA had persuaded Alderman Dick Simpson to introduce an ordinance specifying that any bank wanting to serve as city depository had to prove observance of an anti-redlining pledge by providing detailed annual reports. When considered by the Council's Finance Committee in early June, the bill was actually strengthened to include business loans, to make reporting by census tract versus zip code, and to include savings institutions. The ordinance passed in late June after industry opposition dissipated; major institutions said they could live with the ordinance. (7)

Ted Wysocki: So I got exposed to the video and actually the first conference that I taped was 1974. I remember watching Gale tear apart a federal bureaucrat who had been totally non-responsive to those issues. This was a guy from the Federal Home Loan Bank Board, Dick Platt. This was in like the Third National Housing Conference so they were in the school gym – the gym held a thousand people – and reading him his rights as a government bureaucrat.

We did do an edited videotape of what would have been the Third National People's Action Conference because the big theme for that year's conference was Gale dismissing Dick Platt – which is relevant today –saying, "If the bank regulators won't do this, we will go to Congress." That was what she was vowing to the people in attendance, and this was '74. So that moment of the Third Annual NPA Conference in the spring of '74 was what then led to the whole organizing and researching, of getting Proxmire to hold hearings basically a year later. So there were obviously meetings or strategy sessions at different times in D.C., but in terms of any formal, public thing, it would be those Proxmire hearings in'75. Then, as you know, NPA started doing the annual thing in D.C. So we would then end up putting the video equipment in the back of my Volvo station wagon, and driving off here.

From *Urban Disinvestment: New Implications For Community Organization, Research and Public Policy* by Arthur J. Naparstek and Gale Cincotta (Joint Publication of The National Center for Urban Ethnic Affairs and NTIC, 1976):

One of the most successful conferences was the Third National Housing Conference held in Chicago in April 1974. Attended by some 1,000 delegates from across the country, it resulted in:

> (1) A commitment from the Urban Reinvestment Task Force of the FHLBB to establish the Neighborhood Housing Services Program in Chicago;
> (2) The Governor's establishment of his Commission on Mortgage Practices, formed to study the problems of redlining in Illinois;
> (3) Mayor Daley's strong stand against redlining, which led to the City Council's passage of the municipal "anti-redlining ordinance." (28)

The National Training and Information Center's major accomplishments then reflect the use of neighborhood street organizing, research, confrontation, negotiation and policy formation, and include:

- Establishing the annual National Housing Conferences – conventions attended by an average of more than 1,000 delegates from across the country, and noted for their significant reform recommendations;
- Continuing the NTIC as a clearinghouse for disinvestment/redlining information, and a center for policy and program development both in Chicago and nationally, through publication of its monthly newsletter, *DISCLOSURE*;
- Securing, through the efforts of MAHA, the creation of the Governor's Commission on Mortgage Lending Practices, in the state of Illinois, and prompting reforms in the housing/mortgage/lending policies of the state of Illinois;
- Securing the Neighborhood Housing Services Program – a reinvestment incentive program jointly sponsored by the Department of Housing and Urban Development (*sic*) and the Federal Home Loan Bank Board – for Chicago;
- Winning numerous reinvestment commitments from Chicago area depository institutions; and,

◆   Establishing, through collaboration with state and local officials, the
        Loan-to-Lender Program for reinvestment, a novel program using
        public bond monies for establishing a mortgage pool for formerly
        redlined inner-city areas." (28)

From Case Study by Hallahan (11/7/91)

Kirk Hallahan: NPA's use of extensive research might be its most
distinguishing characteristic. (22) People's Right to Know formed the basis
of NPA's primary conclusion in the claims-making process: the only way the
community would know whether redlining existed was through disclosure.
This theme was repeated throughout the initiative to circumvent objections:
all the bill did was to give the community (or Congress) the facts so they could
decide for themselves." (24)

The fourth and final symbol was plain folks. [The others being
neighborhood, equality and people's right to know.] In keeping with their
origins, NPA effectively positioned itself as made up of truly working class
people: the group's very name underscored this emphasis. Cincotta expressed
the importance of their approach this way: "Not knowing the rules – and
being really grassroots – we came in as citizens. Maybe the Congressmen were
tired of hearing from trade associations and groups in Washington. If you
think of Congress never seeing real people, and remember we were operating
nationally, we came in as Hispanics, and blacks and whites. We weren't talking
about overthrowing the government, but how we needed banks. We weren't
asking to nationalize the banks. We said we needed them – and their brains –
to stabilize our cities." (24)

Two objectivist authors concerned with the economic reality of
redlining summed up the effect as follows: "In having their way in the halls of
Congress and in many state legislatures, these upstart Davids with very meager
resources have routed the Goliaths of a major industry. How that would
happen is a major puzzle…but one factor has clearly been their ability to place
financial institutions on the ethical defensive." [Quoted from Gittenberg and
Wachter, *Redlining and Public Policy,* 49-50] (25)

Joe Mariano: The demand for disclosure of bank loans was raised at
this conference. As a result, anti-redlining laws were passed in cities and states
around the country. In Cleveland, Ohio in 1975, the Buckeye-Woodland
Community Congress convinced one of the local city councilmen, Basil
Russo, to sponsor a disclosure ordinance, modeled on the City of Chicago law,
and when it passed the Council, it was the only other municipal government
besides Chicago to have a disclosure law on its books.

Cal Bradford: Gale's early years, probably until the time Ted Wysocki left, you had pretty much the same people from the beginning. You had Anne-Marie and you had Helen Murray. You had Ted Wysocki. You had Ed Shurna. This was the same bunch of people. And Shel, of course. So you had this incredible institutional memory. And the leadership was pretty much very stable too. From Chicago and from the Bronx and from Boston, you had a certain core of leadership that was pretty much the same.

The turnover was in the government. So it was interesting. The neighborhood people would go to a meeting and the government people would say, "Well, we can't do that." And the neighborhood people would say, "No, you <u>did</u> that seven years ago when we were sitting around this table and you took it away from us. So don't tell us you can't do it because we know you did it before." They'd screw you off and come back home. "Wow. We did do that, you know." So the institutional memory was all on that one side.

Gale didn't believe she was all that unique. She thought there were other people like that. You can see it sometimes. You see it sometimes in Brenda La Blanc when she's got to handle something. She has a lot of the same senses that Gale had about when to push, when not to push, when to stop what you're doing and worry about the fact there are kids there. There's a lot going on, particularly at the demonstrations that you have to be aware of. Most of the men leaders can't do that, quite frankly. Women are aware both of the personal things that are happening and the issue things. They're much better at that.

They're all good leaders but I've always thought if Brenda had started out younger, for example, she probably could have done pretty much the same thing, given the same chances. Once Gale was there, there was no replacing her. It wasn't so much that she fought it, but no one ever considered it. Early on there were some battles about trying to vote for someone, to have elections and have officers.

That's another thing I think is the brilliant part of it. Not just not moving to Washington. But NTIC is this legal entity and it's a nonprofit and it does its education/training thing. But NPA—NPA is like a political Brigadoon. It comes out of the mist whenever people all get together. John McKnight described NPA as like a VISA company. It's a conduit that everybody works through and it's very powerful, but it actually doesn't exist. The banks and everybody are actually the ones doing the transactions, but there's a shell. They allow other people to be powerful. He says NPA is like that shell. So everybody goes to Washington and to NPA conferences. But the magical thing is, when they go home, they're their own group with their own name, with their own identity. It isn't like they're a chapter of somebody in Washington.

Ted Wysocki: The most famous HUD Secretary escapade while I was there was the takeover of Pat Harris' office when she was HUD Secretary. Our lead HUD organizer, Tom Fox, had his hardcore contingent that never was intending to take their appointments and went right to the Secretary's floor on the elevators. The rest of us – I was staffing Community Development Block Grants policies at this time with another delegation – actually took our appointments. The intentionality was to have troops in reserve. We actually had walkie-talkies. I had one leader in my group who knew that when I gave her the sign, it was time to end the meeting. In the meantime we were continuing to probe all of the substantive Community Development Block Grant issues with that Assistant Secretary. Similarly some other meeting was happening on another floor.

The strategy was, when necessary, the extra troops would know where they were going and would move up. It played out perfectly fine because, just as the security thought they had the initial watch group under control and this was winding down, you now had all these other people out of the elevators and totally swamping what was going on.

So at that point Pat Harris was actually in a Cabinet meeting at the White House, and lower-level people were saying, "Well, the Secretary would be pleased to meet with you tomorrow morning at 9:00 a.m." And everybody goes, "Okay. Great. So where are you putting us up?" And they go, "Well, what are you talking about?" "We all checked out of our hotel this morning. We don't have hotel rooms. Where are we staying?" "Ohhhh."

Long story short, they landed up calling her and she left the Cabinet meeting to come over and meet with us. Obviously it was not the time or moment to do substantive meetings, but coming over out of the Cabinet meeting, she promised a meeting that happened six weeks later, and HUD paid for twelve leaders from around the country to come back for the day-long meeting! Gale might have missed that one. She might have been sick and had to turn over the negotiations to some other NPA leaders.

There was an African American woman from Roseland who became the one who dealt with it. Actually it turned out she was a very effective leader because Pat Harris was the first African American woman HUD Secretary. At some point this woman took Harris on, on just issues of respect, "I don't care who you are, you have to respect that we're living with your agency's mistakes." It was very effective.

A year later HUD invested like $150,000 in security for the Secretary's floor. Then the next year when we came, they did not book one meeting in their building; the meeting was in a church hall two blocks away from the HUD building in terms of making sure that that didn't happen again.

Joe Mariano: The black woman from Roseland was Lenore Rodgers. She was a close collaborator with Gale on FHA issues.

Gale, when she was doing a lot more speaking, she would put her speaking fees into NPA. So it had an income stream but it was minimal. It was under $3000 a year. It's never been a lot.

There are no officers. I mean maybe on the papers there might be names, but I haven't even looked at that in a long time. I have no idea who's on it. I might be on it as one of the signatures at this point.

We always have to explain the relationship between NPA and NTIC. Like last night [at NTIC's party celebrating their 30th year of organizing and the 25th anniversary of CRA] one of the bankers came up to me and said, "This is good." I said, "Well, what do you mean? Why is this good?" She said, "Because our experience with you has been NPA."

Basically her message was they see the yellow school buses and they think these crazy people are coming. And it's just the rabble. And these unwashed masses come through the doors of these executives and it's like, "Who are these people?" "Protestors." "So find out what they want and get rid of 'em."

She said to me, "This is good for my bosses to see because they see you one way and this [party] shows…" She couldn't find the right words and finally she said, "More sophistication, that you know how to eat with a knife and fork, in my mind. You're not crass. You know how to put on a good show and that kind of thing."

Cal Bradford: They kept saying, "We don't want you to pay dues. We don't want to have officers. Because then there are going to be political battles inside NPA about who runs it." And there were some. Off and on there were groups who wanted to run it and fight about it. But Gale and Shel's view was if you want to be a leader, you show up. And if you show up often enough and you say things and people respect it, you're going to be a leader. And if you don't like it, you just go home. You can't join. You can't quit.

Ann Vick-Westgate: The issues have to come from the community. And then does the staff come up with ideas for how to deal with those issues?

Marilyn Evans started as a local public housing leader from Cincinnati's Communities United For Action and moved to the national level, working closely with Gale on the reinvestment issue. Marilyn became President of the NTIC Board of Directors and continues her organizing work in Cincinnati, Ohio: They help us simplify the issues and how to break it down so that we'll be able to break it down to our leadership when we get back into the community.

Gale was a master at it. And Trapp was too. It was interesting how they could take the issue and break it down to where you could understand it. Understand it to a point to where you could communicate it back to someone else in your leadership. They may not have been into the trenches that you'd been in when you got to the national level or to the next level. But they are able to understand the communication so that they can become creative and give out suggestions and ideas too.

Ann Vick-Westgate: Cal Bradford told us about going into a meeting at the Federal Reserve and Volcker had staff there, all these economists and whatever. And Gale started to talk and soon enough the economists were taking notes. I think she had the ability to break things down, put them in a way that people could really see the picture. He said it was most impressive. These economists came in to educate these people and ended up getting educated by them.

Marilyn Evans: That's another acrobatic move on Gale's part. We came in with anger because we had no place to air it. We was passive because the injustice has been going on for quite some time. That's another thing they told us when we were young: we didn't have power, and anger was bad too.

Particularly if you're a woman... You're supposed to suffer and wait until the "here and after" to get your rewards. But Gale had the knack of saying, "Okay – and this is when I got further up in knowledge and training – we don't want to kill them. We just want them to come to the table to begin to talk about what we have in the neighborhood, where we want to go and make them a partner. We want to give them some saving grace." I said, "They're my enemy. Why you want to save them? They don't need no grace."

But you hear how she turns it around in one of those sessions to where, "This is America. This is what democracy promises us. And if you want to win as well as we do, we have to have a win-win situation here. You want to make money. We want you to make money. But we want you to change that policy that is affecting us and our community in order for you to make money. We'll support you. That's the American way, isn't it?"

So she would be able to turn that, and do that, and them people would just be... I mean they come in all huffy and puffy in their three-piece suit and briefcase and slamming things down. But by the time that meeting was over with, we had everything we went in there for. And they walked out like they was our best friends, or they were Gale's sons and daughters.

She knew how to take confrontation and turn it into negotiation and when to make that transition in a meeting. And to go from being angry to saying, "Okay. We're in this together. Now how are we going to work this out?"

Took me a long time to learn that skill. It's a real hard skill, especially when you personally is involved with the issues. You know, the anger. And do you still kick their butts when they're in the meeting, when you finally get them to the table? No, you got to set that aside. What is your purpose of coming to this meeting? You can be angry all the time, but what is your purpose? "I want this." "Well, then that's what we need to go after." And then the second rule is that you're not going to get everything you want. So set your scope up higher than what you expect to get, and go with that, and negotiate that.

It's hard to translate that into your leadership because you understand where they're at. They're angry. They done lost a house. They have to go to welfare. They lost a member because of an incident. It's like so many issues that they come in with. You have to give them time to deal with it.

One family, their utility got cut off and they froze to death. How do you go in, sit down at a table, with someone who caused your relative to freeze to death and get past that anger? So it's a learning lesson. It's a skill that is very, very, very hard to do. But Gale showed us. Gale taught us – by action. By watching her do it.

Because I know many a days when we came out of a meeting, I said, "Why you taking that?" And she would explain to me. But she showed me more these things. Sometimes she'd just smile.

Michael Westgate: The origins of both Gale and of Shel had to do with religious organizations, with the Catholic Church in Chicago and so forth. To what extent was religion there in terms of the NPA groups or in terms of NTIC?

Marilyn Evans: Well, as our leader, Gale, she didn't push religion. The only thing that she ever said was. "Just trust in the God. Just trust in the Lord." She used to fool like that. Not organized religion, but a basic morality. And the only religion that I think she had that she really pushed was to stop injustice.

Cal Bradford: Gale said, "The power is not in the organization; the power's in the lack of the structure. The power's that the organizing structure is in each community. And there is structure beyond that."

You go to Washington. You beat up on the members of Congress. The members of Congress knew that when they went home someone was going to beat up on them at home. They're not afraid of the National Community Reinvestment Coalition or even the National Fair Housing Alliance that I love and work with. They know, when they go home, those groups aren't there. That's a thing you do in Washington. NPA was different. NPA was, "No. This is something that's going to terrorize all of you at home."

Ann Vick-Westgate: How would you describe the relationship between NTIC and NPA? How do you distinguish between the two organizations?

Inez Killingsworth: NPA is made up of coalitions across the country and it serves as an entity that allows <u>local</u> community groups to have access to the national level. You couldn't do it alone. Well, you could but it would take you longer and harder to just take your local issues straight into a national setting. But, if you're under the umbrella of a national organization that already has that link, it allows you to take your issue to where it needs to go.

Cleveland got started on the predatory lending issue and none of us knew what it really was. But we knew people were hurting because people were telling us stories. So we contacted NTIC to say, "Look. This thing is bigger than Cleveland." And NTIC began to do this study. They can take things and move it to the next level where the local people can't. So we rely on NTIC to do the research for us. So then once they did the research, okay, here it is. So it's under the umbrella of National People's Action and we was able to carry that national.

One of the first groups that we were working on was Citi Financial. So we have a written agreement and that was something that was started with Gale that unfortunately she didn't see the end result. But she gave us a mandate just before she passed, "to get the crooks". We started on the predatory lending in 1999 and the agreement was reached in 2003. There was the ceremony at NPA.

Michael Westgate: Is there any formal agreement between NTIC or NPA and the member organizations?

Inez Killingsworth: No. There is no agreement. You don't have to. It's open. NPA is open for any and every organization to come participate or to share. So it's up to that group how much they want to participate. Lots of groups come. A lot of them don't get up-front leadership positions but they attend the workshops and they may get something there. But a lot of people come just mainly for the networking, to be able to learn this is what I can do and take it back to my community. A lot of people get a lot of energy out of it. If you're kind of burnt out, you think, "Okay. It's time to stop. We can slow down." You just get refueled.

Michael Westgate: Get your annual fix.

Ann Vick-Westgate: So have the agenda and the hits been set for the next NPA conference yet or is that part of what goes on later?

Inez Killingsworth: That's part of what goes on at the leadership meeting that's coming up in January. At the leadership meeting you evaluate based on what happened last year—did we get results? The strategizing goes on in January.

Ann Vick-Westgate: The people that come to the leadership meetings are invited. How do they get chosen? How did you? Did someone approach you and say, "Do you want to come?" to your first leadership meeting?

Inez Killingsworth: Well, the local organization does. They asked me, the organizers. We were in a planning meeting locally and we were discussing the leadership meeting that would happen. So they said, "Who would like to go?"

Ann Vick-Westgate: Were there any arrests from the actions at NPA this year in Washington?

Inez Killingsworth: None that I know about. There's three sets of police in that area. And the Capitol Police is probably the roughest police. They're mean. And maybe I shouldn't say mean. They're doing, basically, their job. Sometime I think they get overzealous in it. And then you have to look at it from another standpoint. They don't <u>know</u> what to expect so they're prepared. But they know we come every year and usually they know when we're coming before we get there because I'm quite sure that we're being bugged and taped somewhere along the line. So we don't have anything to hide. But we can take care of our site visits in a way that keeps them thinking.

But, basically, the police are nice and, when they come, we just involve the police in what we're doing. The police need a raise and this kind of makes them... "We're not the violent ones so we're your friends." And people start to chanting that. And then we train people when the police come you don't try to stop them from getting up front. Just open up, part the way and let 'em come through. The police come in and we just lead 'em straight to the leaders. And when they get up, then we tell 'em why we are there. And if we're having a problem, we'll engage the police. "If you will just ask this person to meet with us or to take this letter or to just whatever, we'll leave." And sometime they become the negotiators for us.

Then we keep our word, we say we're leaving. And we leave. That's what basically happened at Mel Martinez' [Secretary of HUD] house. It was just one or two policemen that came. And when the policeman came to me, he said, "Did you get your meeting?" He just came straight to me because he knowed that they know the routine.

And I said, "Not yet, but we'll get 'em." He said, "Well, I'm gonna go out and I'm just gonna clear the streets. I can't have the street jammed up." I said, "No problem. Go ahead because my people are getting on the bus, but they're not leaving. They're not leaving until I leave." So I think we have trained most of 'em. But the Capitol Police is probably the little exception...

So a lot of times the strategies that we came up with, it was just almost like pulling it out of the sky somewhere. You get together and people start to strategize. But one of the most effective things that we do, we play the "what if" game. We try to look at what if this happen, what if that happen. What if they say this, what are you gonna say and that type of thing. Role-playing is a very important factor.

Ann Vick-Westgate: You weren't surprised when they did something because you'd already talked about what if.

Inez Killingsworth: Right. And when it comes out, it's amazing if you do that role-play. And when you hear it back, it's like, damn, how did you know they were going to say that?

Ann Vick-Westgate: The other thing that's really impressive is that the leadership is women.

Inez Killingsworth: Yes, sure. She was very, very high on that, women being in leadership positions. In the organizations you will find a lot of men that take the leadership role, but overall you're gonna find the women doing that, a trait that Gale liked. She liked the women to have power. But we don't exclude the men…

Ann Vick-Westgate: How do new groups get involved with NPA? You don't fill out a membership form. You don't pay a membership fee. How do new groups get drawn in?

Marilyn Evans: Maybe there's another group in the city that may be having some problems, and they know that this group over here go every year to NPA and come back, and that's all they boast about is that. So they may tell them, "If you want to get in and join, that's the time to do it." But issues are what we operate on in NPA.

Michael Westgate: So the proliferation of issues on the agenda does that strengthen the group, weaken the group? Is it too diffuse?

Marilyn Evans: No, I don't think it has weakened the group. It has made it much, much stronger, because there is a multitude of issues that we all face at different times in our community, and in our own personal lives. It gives us a resource to reach out to begin to fight pieces of this that we need to fight.

Michael Westgate: What's the process of deciding who the hit is going to be on this year?

Marilyn Evans: Well, it's always a secret. We don't tell that to everybody. It was sort of like a secret through the whole thing. Only key leaders who was in that action and would be up front knew whose house we were going to. That had to be kept secret.

Ann Vick-Westgate: My mother raised me that you don't show up at people's houses uninvited, much less bringing several hundred people who are shouting behind you. So how did you get comfortable with the hits?

Marilyn Evans: Well, at first I was like you. That's not nice. You know, that's not mannerly and I wasn't raised this way. But somebody said, "No, you wasn't raised that way and that's probably the reason why we got these problems!"

Ann Vick-Westgate: Taking the toilet paper and stringing it through the trees...

Marilyn Evans: Yeah, taking it to the trees and then delivering a toilet to the front door or whatever... "That's not good, Gale." She says, "What's not good is in your neighborhood you got people starving to death. You got children who's dying for the lack of insurance, healthcare. You've got crime, drugs on the corner where your seniors are not safe. That's not good. And the reason why we're here – we only got one or two days to do it in – is to take that message to them. So whether we got to walk across their lawn or in their face, we got to get that message to them. Get them to the table so they can set down and begin to help us solve some of these problems we have in our neighborhoods. So we can have a lawn to walk on just like that lawn."

So that made sense because I had to go back to my community and see all the injustice and it isn't right. I have to stop thinking about being nice, being mannerly. Which is more "not nice," walking across their lawn or living the kind of life we have to live?

CHAPTER 8

"I'm not going anywhere Gale Cincotta's going... Stop the bus ...I'm getting off." "Gale is like a heat-seeking missile."

NEIGHBORHOOD HOUSING SERVICES (NHS) OF CHICAGO

Ed Williams was a senior banker at Chicago's Harris Bank. He served as a credit reference for Gale on banking matters: The NHS, after NTIC, was an organization that Gale loved and supported the most. That's where she spent her time and her energy. She was a drum major for that organization as much as she was for any organization. People could easily confuse her between the two.

Michael Westgate: Lew Hill, head of Chicago's Redevelopment Authority and Richard Daley Senior's czar of housing, was the person I dealt with when we planned the original formative NHS conferences out at Lake Geneva. Without Hill, we would not have gotten the Mayor's blessing.

There were real battles with some of the bankers. We had three busloads of people going out to our first workshop. I was on the lead bus and giving directions to the bus driver. We were a couple miles underway and in one of Chicago's tougher neighborhoods when one of the bankers came up to me screaming, "Do you know who's in the back of the bus?" I said, "Who?" "Gale Cincotta!" "You're right." "Well, I'm not going anywhere Gale Cincotta's going! Stop the bus. I'm getting off." I told the bus driver to keep going.

That evening we almost had fistfights between bankers and neighborhood activists, but that banker on the bus turned out to be one of the more supportive people, and joined the board. Real skeptics like Bill Plechaty were there from the beginning and became strong advocates. Strong emotions led to strong commitments which were at the core of Chicago's NHS and remain to this day. Chicago was not the only city where this dynamic worked. But it was the first time the Urban Reinvestment Task Force used it so successfully. Gale's anger and the anger of many others there found a creative outlet for their energy in NHS.

Bill Whiteside: There was an excitement that we got out of seeing people change overnight. We used to talk about "born again bankers." And they really were! They really were! They would come to us uptight and close-lipped and unwilling to sit too close to someone different, you know. And they'd end up going round.

George Knight: I'd been an organizer at NCO and started at Bickerdike [Redevelopment Corporation]. Bruce Gottschall worked at Bickerdike. Bruce called and said, "I'm working for the Federal Home Loan Bank of Chicago." And of course I ribbed him. I said, "Oh, you've sold out." And he said, "Yeah. Just like you." It went back and forth. Then he said, "You're not going to believe it. We're trying to bring together Gale and the thrifts and if possible the City to try and figure out how we can work cooperatively to set up a loan fund."

Ed Williams: Bruce was coming out of a stint with the Peace Corps. NHS in Chicago is just a huge success story. We find that New York and San Francisco and others come to Chicago to look at what NHS of Chicago is doing. It's part of our being able to work together. Bruce and I have spent many hours in the building here where Bruce learned many years ago you can't design [bank] products in a vacuum. You can't assume that I know what you need, so therefore I'm going to go off and make it and come back and tell you, "This is what it's going to cost you."

He is successful because we've done product design together where he's coming and saying, "What we're seeing in our ten neighborhood offices are these kinds of needs. And here's how things have changed since we developed our product three years ago." You know you meet with the banks and say, "Okay. How can we put this together so it's something that meets the needs of communities as we now see them?" It's something that the banks can fund, they can buy, they can lend into. So we will sit down and do product development, literally, meeting after meeting.

Michael Westgate: There was Bill Whiteside, Jim McNeirney, myself, and a secretary when I started in 1973. We had grown to about ten when I left in March of '75.

Getting Chicago started was my mission. I was commuting out there almost on a weekly basis until I met Bruce. Actually I'd been going out there about six months by the time I met Bruce and hired him basically to help identify the neighborhood players, to follow up on my visits to all the bankers, and then act as coordinator for the workshops which we hoped would result in an NHS for Chicago.

The bankers were all pushing me very hard to hire another guy who had a strong real estate background, but I knew he didn't have at all what we were looking for. And Gale, thankfully, solved the problem when I was running out of time with these guys. Because any time I came to Chicago, they asked, "When are you going to hire him, when are you going to hire him?" And Gale said, "I know this guy that I think you ought to interview." So she was the source of Bruce getting the job.

George Knight: Well, Gale always had the rare ability in any set of circles to see both the bigger picture and the small or critical steps or details that really would influence the long term. And not get hung up on a lot of other stuff. She always had that unique, incredible ability. When we were starting to build coalitions between the different community organizations in Chicago, Gale would almost always end up as the spokesperson because she could negotiate for the heart of the matter.

Michael Westgate: There were several secrets to NHS of Chicago becoming the strongest in the country. Behind the scene were Bill Whiteside and Mary Lee Widener who guided the whole NHS movement in adapting the original Pittsburgh NHS model nationwide. They complemented each other, founding respectively the Neighborhood Reinvestment Corporation chartered by Congress in 1978 (NRC, subsequently renamed NeighborWorks America) and its companion non-profit secondary market, Neighborhood Housing Services of America (NHSA). NHSA was chartered earlier, in 1975, as a non-profit 501(c)(3) organization in California and is specifically referenced in the legislation establishing NeighborWorks America, through which it received very substantial funding over the years.

Behind the scenes was Preston Martin, the charismatic chairman of the Federal Home Loan Bank Board. A former Commissioner of Savings and Loans in California, he had the clout to single-handedly allow Whiteside to begin operations and sustained him despite strong opposition from the Bank Board and the whole system. Without Pres's support, none of this would have been possible.

Mary Lee and Gale shared a room at the formative first meeting of what became NHS of Chicago, talked long into the night, and forged a relationship that endured for almost three decades.

Mary Lee Widener: Let me just say that Gale's reputation had preceded her of course. The activity at which I met her was the formation of Chicago Neighborhood Housing Services, the "Workshop I." The reason there was a workshop is that Gale had been a part of the activities in Chicago. Some of which involved pretty aggressive demonstrations against the banks. And the Federal Home Loan Bank of Chicago leadership got quite concerned and people in Washington got quite concerned. So they tried to get Gale in and some of her folks and talk to them.

When I got there the rooms had been assigned. And at that point Workshop I housing accommodations were double occupancy so there were always two people to a room. Obviously I didn't know her, just only had heard of her. Didn't know what I'd run into. But fortunately I don't judge people by what I hear. I wait and see what they communicate to me.

We went into the workshop and had a day of activities before she and I ended up rooming because you come in early in the day and you go through the communication workshop, then the logistical stuff. We had done all of that. So I'd gotten some sense of her before we got there. But nothing substantively happens on the first day. It's just a get to know you with a communications specialist. So with that I knew what we needed to do the next day. That we needed to get to a partnership formed by the end of the day and that she would be key to whether or not that could happen. So I knew what my assignment was for that night. But I didn't have any idea of how she was going to respond to that.

So when it was time to close the evening and she and I went to our room, we sort of cordially got to know each other. Then we both started probing each other to see where our value systems were, see what each value system was about. In the kind of personal exploration, Gale and I figured out that we were in the same place in terms of what we were trying to do. We just had different styles of getting there.

She shared with me then, as she did many times after, that she did not like the style that she felt pushed into. But she just hadn't found any other way to make people pay attention. That what was going on was wrong, it had to stop. If you couldn't talk sense into people rationally, you had to be irrational. And you just had to make pain.

Ann Vick-Westgate: Make pain?

Mary Lee Widener: Yes. Make pain. And nobody was going to pay attention until they also were in pain. So she shared her remorse about that. Which gave me an opening to talk about this other approach that there was a possibility of creating a partnership where everybody won. Nobody had to give up who they were and what they believed in. We all could work toward that goal together. Explained to her how the workshop partnership day worked and how she could influence that. I let her know where the decision points were, how the whole thing would play out, what the objectives were in the agenda. Which you can't see as a workshop participant, all you see is an agenda.

The agenda just basically said – and they were standard all the way through the doing of workshops – in the morning of that partnership day, they would be hearing from another group presenting their experience as partners. But that's all it said. So you heard from the residents, you heard from the lenders, you heard from the city, you heard from the executive director. Then after that, in the afternoon, the group went into workshops – each group separately, the residents, the city, the lenders – to ask themselves what they would need from each other in order to have a true partnership.

I let Gale know that that was her opportunity to go in and put on the table everything she was demonstrating for. If this partnership formation workshop went the way the others had gone, the other groups would put on the table what they wanted and hopefully by the end of the evening everybody could agree to give everybody what they wanted. Then you had a partnership and you didn't have to fight.

She bought into that strategy completely. She was happy, and I mean happy, to have an option that was not the normal style that she felt pushed into. She confided in me the strategy that she felt she needed to employ to get there. I made sure that I did the things that I needed to do to support her having the room to get there. Her challenge was that she could not afford to lose credibility and appear to be co-opted. She had to have time for the solutions to be organic and come out of the group. She couldn't just walk in there and lay down some things.

So there was all of that. If I recall we ended up needing more time. But as a result of all of that, there were some bumps in the road in getting through the day. But she was working on her strategy all day. By the time the workshop was over she had achieved it. Gale unequivocally is the reason that partnership workshop came together.

Michael Westgate: There were a number of decisions I made as project manager for the process leading to the formation of NHS of Chicago. I was determined to make my mark personally, and to show I could build a better NHS than anyone else could. Former efforts in Boston, Plainfield, NJ, and Washington DC were limping along.

My attitude was shaped in part by my recent success in liquidating Republic Savings & Loan, a bankrupt savings and loan in Washington, working myself out of a job projected to take 3-4 years in less than two. Harvard Business School, from which I was a 1971 graduate, also shaped my attitude, for better and for worse. I felt I could quantify and present alternatives more clearly than others and apply business approaches in the interface between staid federal and city bureaucracies, community activists and banks. My presentation to the Federal Home Loan Bank Board on the value of Republic S&L's portfolio under their merger with Home Federal S&L in Washington was based on the Net Present Value of all assets (performing loans, non-performing loans and real estate owned). It was accepted by the FHLBB and utilized for workouts with other S&Ls in Chicago and elsewhere around the country. I was able to talk the language of the lenders and had first-hand experience of the problems that faced Chicago lenders. They knew and I knew what would happen if we could not find a solution to their growing problems.

I had worked on the waterfront in New York, as Assistant Commissioner of Ports & Terminals, 1967-69, and in the process was able to help South Street Seaport Museum get started. John Lindsay was not a Mayor Daley, but I was not a stranger to big city politics.

I found Gale Cincotta on one of my early visits and benefited from her visionary view of Chicago, its neighborhoods, who the leaders were and what might or might not work with the lenders and with the city government. I insisted that Gale Cincotta had to be in the process from the beginning. She was anathema to some of the lenders who had been subjected to the tactics of Organization for a Better Austin (OBA), with sit-ins and green-ins in their lobbies. A member of OBA had been arrested, charged with setting fire to Sky Realty's office. Although there was never a conviction or connection proved with OBA, the perception was that this group would be difficult to work with.

Gale had a reputation as a troublemaker and was feared by some as much as she was revered by others. Many people in Austin still regard her as a saint. But I convinced Al Fenderson, General Counsel at the FHLB of Chicago, and he convinced Bob Bartell, its President, that we had no choice but to invite Gale to be part of the process.

Full participation of the FHLB of Chicago involved backing our program with $30,000 up front, and pushing its member savings & loan associations, reluctantly at first, to support it. Gale's reputation, which combined threatening behavior and then working out solutions, actually made my work infinitely easier.

Chicago needed Gale Cincotta and Shel Trapp to inseminate the process correctly from the beginning. There was an anger and an impatience to find and implement a solution that all sides wanted. My job was to help catalyze and capitalize that energy. Some people make the analogy between organizing a community and making an omelette that once the eggs have been broken and started to cook it's very difficult to start over. I would take the analogy back further. Organizing NHS of Chicago was a very organic process. It took a lot of well-formed organic eggs and a hot skillet to maximize its potential.

Gale was a strong leader with a long-term vested interest in having a successful program and a willingness to participate in the often-painful birthing process. She would improve the chances of making it work. She was also the one person in Chicago with the citywide reputation who could help us in the contentious process of selecting neighborhoods if, in fact, the lenders and the city were willing to proceed. This would be a shared experience between Gale and Bruce Gottschall and all the lenders, community leaders and city officials, upon which he, if selected as the executive director, would be able to build.

We provided a model solution, patterned after the original NHS of Pittsburgh, PA. The Urban Reinvestment Task Force had few resources of its own but showed people in each city how they might combine public and private resources in a flexible manner. I was one of the few federal employees who encouraged people like Gale to call me collect. When the FHLBB stopped me from doing that, I had Gale call me person-to-person, had my secretary tell her I wasn't in, and called her right back. Telephone calls were relatively expensive in those days and struggling nonprofits like Gale's literally could not afford to call Washington often.

One decision I made was great for Chicago but not, in retrospect, for the larger long-term interest of the Urban Reinvestment Task Force for which I worked—or for me. Bruce, with Gale's encouragement, I suspect, asked me while he was still on our payroll if he could seek funding from Chicago-based insurance companies. I encouraged him to go ahead. This dismayed Bill Whiteside when he heard about it. More than previous NHSs, Chicago was host to a number of national banks and insurance companies. Bill could not have the NHS of Chicago and the URTF competing in fundraising among the same Chicago companies simultaneously.

My motivation was to make Chicago shine. In retrospect, I was too proactive for my own good because in promoting Chicago's success, I helped put it far ahead of other NHSs in the process of being formed. I should have checked with Whiteside first and he would have made it clear that he was the one who should approach the national insurance companies on behalf of all NHSs across the country, including Chicago. This, together with Gale's public roasting of Dick Platt, Bill's boss at the FHLBB, played a part in Whiteside and me parting company.

Gale was a fantastic resource in bringing in the right mix of community activists from around Chicago's neighborhoods. There was strong representation of whites, blacks and Hispanics. When it evolved that there were five neighborhoods demanding to be the first target areas for NHS but the banks were only prepared to fund three, the three selected represented a good racial balance; the other two negotiated that they would come on board in the ensuing two years.

I was the first one to explain to Gale, as we toured her neighborhood in Austin, how the original NHS had worked in Pittsburgh and how we were hoping to expand it in other cities. Those where we had first tried (Boston, Plainfield, NJ and the Anacostia neighborhood in Washington, DC) had not yet panned out. Indeed they never would. But learning from the inside what was missing from those first ventures, I had high hopes for Chicago, which Gale and I shared.

Gale was recognized for seeing the big picture, certainly for Chicago, in 1974, and was developing a national reputation. She always had a strong organizational platform from which to speak beginning with the Organization for a Better Austin (OBA), then city and statewide through Metropolitan Area Housing Alliance (MAHA), and nationally through Housing Training and Information Center, subsequently renamed National Training and Information Center (HTIC/NTIC). She was the one who could transcend neighborhood politics. She could speak to the bankers and to Daley and the city machine in a way that would make people listen and, quite often, make things happen. She had developed the ability to be brashly confrontational on the picket line in the morning and then sit down in boardrooms the same afternoon with the chief executives she had just picketed to make a deal. She became chairperson of the NHS Site Selection Committee, critical to the organization's success.

From *DISCLOSURE* #4 (December 1974)
Neighborhood Housing Service: New Reinvestment Strategy

Gale Cincotta, director of HTIC, regards the establishment of the NHS program in Chicago as a "breakthrough in our efforts to preserve Chicago's communities. It represents the type of positive contribution to the solution to the problems of redlining and disinvestment that must be forthcoming from the financial community in an even greater amount if we are to reverse the tide of disinvestment in our communities and, consequently, save one of our most valuable resources—viable neighborhoods and sturdy housing stock."

Michael Westgate: In liquidating the assets of the failed Republic Savings & Loan in Washington, DC, it was clear it took a combination of adverse market conditions and bad management to suffer the kinds of losses they had. Their concentrated heavy investments in the 14th Street Corridor and in Anacostia, at high loan-to-value ratios, together with the actions of a notorious loan officer nicknamed "10 point Pete," had led to the S&L's collapse. For a fee of 10%, Pete would reportedly see that you got your loan. Under standard procedures of the FHLBB and FSLIC, who were governed by the same three-member board headed at the time by Pres Martin, Republic had been merged with Home Federal S&L with FSLIC guaranteeing most of the losses.

Every month Home Federal would present us with a list of delinquent properties being foreclosed. At foreclosure FSLIC would write Home Federal a check for the balance of the loan, including accrued interest, legal fees, etc. and the property became ours to manage and sell. There was little motivation for Home Federal, or other S&Ls serving similar roles, to seek other solutions.

Many of the properties were multi-family, mostly occupied and poorly managed. Given that these were foreclosed properties from a bankrupt savings and loan, they were not the best properties in Washington. They were virtually all multi-family buildings of four to 50 units. A staff person working for me said we were inheriting "the cream of the crap" in Washington real estate. There were over 1000 people living in the buildings which ended up in our portfolio. My job was to bring on better management companies, order whatever repairs were needed, and prepare the properties for sale.

I consolidated management with the best firm in the area: Frank Emmet Real Estate. In one case, 1412 Chapin Street, N.W., the local HUD office expressed an interest in making the property a model for how quickly HUD could operate. They claimed that the biggest single obstacle was getting the property vacant so that construction could begin. We accommodated them by starting to move everybody into other properties of ours nearby. That precipitated a rent strike and a visit from a newly formed Chapin Street Tenants' Association to Chairman Martin's office. The building's guards, also black residents of the District of Columbia, said they had misheard the reason for the visit as being to "leave a present from the Chapin Street Tennis Association". It turned out to be a large bag of garbage. Fortunately Pres Martin took it in stride.

We did vacate Chapin Street in 60 days but, despite repeated pleas to HUD to expedite the process, the best we ever got from them, over a year later, was "we haven't turned it down yet." We sold the building, as we did the others, to private developers. There were not at that time community development organizations in DC to whom we could have sold them. That incident demonstrated the failures of HUD, made us sensitive to the problems of Chicago, and shaped the future dealings of the Task Force with HUD.

Our formula for sale of our properties was a simple one, 10% down with a purchase money mortgage, whereby we wrote a mortgage for 90% of the purchase price, secured by the property, at just below the prevailing rate at the time on multifamily buildings of 8% interest. For the sales price, I used "net present value," calculating projected income for the property, less expenses and capital improvements needed, for the next 20 years. On average, this required a discount from the book value at foreclosure of about 30%. Given that book value was for an originally inflated loan and included accrued interest, fees, etc. this did not seem too high a discount to pay. I got Board approval for the approach. For smaller projects, my boss could sign the approval; for properties over $50,000, I needed Board approval. This basic approach was adopted by the Board and recommended to the Chicago office of FSLIC which was dealing with fourteen failed S&Ls. With $4 billion in reserves from insurance premiums collected from the S&L industry and an additional call on the U.S. Treasury, we were in a position to take risks. But none of the mortgages we wrote in Washington defaulted.

It seemed foolish to keep myself and two other staff working in a reactive mode on properties as they were foreclosed. Why not calculate the value of the whole portfolio, ranging from strong well-secured loans to delinquent, based in one case on a building with loan disbursements for a completed building but only the basement dug? With Board consent, I hired a team of four appraisers, appraised all properties with loans over $500,000, all loans that were delinquent, and a sampling of all others. Each day I had all four appraisers place a value on one property, as a control sample.

It was an eye-opener one day when three of the four placed a value of $25-27,000 on an 8-unit apartment building in Anacostia where the fourth placed a value of $50,000. His explanation was "I thought financing was available there." When he discovered it was not, he changed his appraisal to conform with the others. This drove home to me how critical financing was to determining value. It is a fiction to say fair market value is what a willing buyer is willing to pay a willing seller. It is the <u>bank</u> or other source of financing, relying on appraisers who have to take into account where and on what basis financing is available, which is the primary determinant of value. We discounted each loan to bring its yield to current market rate, sold the whole portfolio to Home Federal Savings & Loan and disbanded my office. What was programmed as a three- to four-year workout we finished in about 18 months.

It was a good introduction and a good foundation for dealing with the lenders in Chicago who were experiencing similar problems on a larger scale.

Ed Williams: Gale and I met during our affiliation with Neighborhood Housing Services. We really got to know each other in '84 and that's when, I would say, we began to have a relationship, when the Bank of Montreal was in the process of acquiring the Harris Bank, and the CRA Coalition at that time asked the Federal Reserve for a delay in reviewing the application for the acquisitions.

Gale herself, I think, benefited personally from those meetings. She developed different aspects of her approach and style as a result of those meetings because now she was meeting on a regular basis in the banks with bankers. She began to get a feel for bankers just as people rather than bankers as adversaries, redliners, whatever it was that was on their minds at the time.

Then even over a longer period of time she began to realize that there can be people who work downtown, and dress up and go into these big buildings, that can have the same objectives, same goals, as we do. They may go about it differently. Their approach might not be the way we would do things, but nonetheless they want to achieve some of the same things that we do. Therefore we need to adopt a different style to work with people that we feel have that motivation.

But, even though she began to think like people do when they enter a regular business transaction, she never ever left her activist training or feelings because she could just as easily pick up the bullhorn as she could the telephone. Everyone knew that about Gale. She learned an awful lot from those meetings. That the way to get someone's attention that you want to work with is not to surround their building with 500 people and then ask for a meeting, but ask for a meeting and if it's granted then fine. But if you're not getting someone's attention, then you surround the building with the 500 people. Her methods changed to appropriately meet the situation that she was dealing with.

There was another situation where perhaps she put herself at risk even more. It showed me the kind of person that she was and how fair she could be. Although many people thought that she never had a fair bone in her body. Which is quite untrue.

We had a problem with one of our CRA exams in 1991. We took issue with the rating that we received because at that time there was a lot of confusion about what qualifies as acceptable CRA performance. It's clarified quite a bit since then. But, anyway, we got this less than satisfactory rating. I called Gale to let her know about it, give her a heads up. "It's coming out and it is what it is and we don't agree with it, but there's not much we can do." She said, "Well, I think you ought to have a press conference and I want to be there." And we did have one and she was there. And she issued a press release.

I don't know if she had ever done this before, where she said that a bank had been rated unfairly. She essentially said that if Harris Bank cannot get a passing grade on CRA ratings then there's no bank in the country that should. For an activist, and someone who helped get CRA passed probably more than any other individual, to come out and do this was remarkable. There is a page from the *Consumer Bankers Association Newsletter* which says, "In Twist, Community Group Defends CRA Record". It wasn't lost on anyone that this was quite an unusual situation for this courageous woman to take:

Gale said, "My conclusion is that if the Federal Reserve Board can get Harris, they can get anyone. Judgment standards are ambiguous, the criteria for compliance unclear. Are you using Harris to kill CRA and therefore kill our neighborhoods?"

Gale had something that she hosted in her office called the Lenders Group where we would get together in this little room where she smoked. She wouldn't quit smoking so she spent I don't know how much money retrofitting the ceiling with all these suction devices, which still didn't work. But she hosted these meetings to which the bankers were invited when she needed to talk about something.

Anyway, there were any number of these groups meeting, of the same people, same organizations, maybe different levels from the respective organizations, at Gale's office. It was mostly the more senior people from the City or from the banks that were meeting. But then there were like the lending officers themselves, meeting amongst themselves. So we had any number of these different groups meeting, working at the various levels on similar or identical issues.

Gale was really able to understand issues and problems before they became clear to others. She had a real knack for that. She could see two or three examples of something and connect the dots. More often than not she was right. And then once she was locked onto something, she had a focus where she would want to see it through. "This is an issue. This is a problem. And we've going to do something about it." And then she would just stay with that issue. Even though there were a lot of other things she might be working on, she would stay focused on this issue that she has picked up as a priority. And do whatever it took whether it was calling on bank CEOs, or going to the mayor's office, or off to Washington. She would just stay on it like a heat-seeking missile. If it took coming to sit down and have Cokes in your boardroom to talk about it or getting the yellow bus out, she'd do what it took to get it done.

Once it was done then she would have a nice soiree to say, "Let's celebrate. We'll hold hands and we can look back and say we accomplished something and feel good about it." Then she'd put that aside and go about her business. Before you knew it, she was onto something else. It was always something and just never, never downtime for her. She always had an issue she could pick up.

She learned that there are many different ways to accomplish what you're after and there's not just my way. But look at what might work best. So she was adaptive, to her credit. There are activists today that haven't learned that lesson.

Michael Westgate: Cincotta and Gottschall were able to use each other then and over the years. NHS was Cincotta's urban workshop, the opportunity to test her theories. She chaired the critical NHS Site Selection Committee, on whose decisions the whole process could have foundered. Gottschall could call on Cincotta to rally the troops. She could say and do what he needed to say but could not say to his partners at NHS, particularly the City and the lenders, without his being associated with it. Some people may feel it inconsistent to demonstrate against someone and simultaneously bargain with or actually receive benefits from the object of your demonstrations. Gale showed few such qualms. She changed hats frequently and effectively.

Bruce could even call on Gale in a way that she might feel she had to threaten to demonstrate or actually demonstrate against institutions which were providing financial support to NHS. It would have been counterproductive for Bruce to do that in his role. Yet Gale through one of her own or related community organizations could very legitimately do so. They were great allies.

Bruce Gottschall, Executive Director of Neighborhood Housing Services of Chicago 1975-2009: I've been on NTIC's board for maybe fifteen years, Gale was on my board from the very beginning. And she was head of our Operations Committee for years, which was the program committee, and also the Site Selection Committee.

Michael Westgate: I remember that battle. When five neighborhoods said, "This isn't going forward unless it's here." And the bankers said, "Well, we've got funding for three." And then we hashed it out that these three would start the first year, to be followed by this one in the fourth and that one in the fifth."

Bruce Gottschall: Right. We had the three and then West Inglewood was in the wings as the fourth one. And so it was North Side, South Side and West Side, the three sides. You've got to have a neighborhood in each part of the city. We don't need one on the Lake, that's okay. Northwest, it was mostly black but it was also Hispanic, increasingly Puerto Rican. And then Austin would have been African American. And Pilsen or Heart of Chicago was mostly Mexican.

So she really had a critical role in choosing the neighborhoods. Well, it's Austin for one! And Near Northwest was another one, NCO territory – Shel Trapp's organization. And then actually the one on the South Side, the Heart of Chicago, was really the City's initiative. They wanted it there. So that was the three that got NHSs.

We've now done a total of nineteen neighborhoods, including some that we started and moved out. Like the Northwest, we were there seven, eight years. Then we were gone. Austin, we no longer have an office. So there are places that we were in that we don't have a neighborhood office anymore. Some we expanded and said, "Well, this is not a new neighborhood." We wanted to get to twenty by the year 2000. We never quite made it, but close.

Bob Bartell was the president of the Federal Home Loan Bank of Chicago. Two weeks before our NHS workshop he got a list of who was going to be at the meeting. Bartell reviewed the list and he saw Gale's name on there and he said, "I'm not going to be in the same room with her." Then I said, "Hey. How are we going to have a meeting around NHS and neighborhoods and neighborhood involvement without Gale being there? It's just impossible." And so he said, "Okay. Well, it's your responsibility. I don't want to be embarrassed." She had just gone out to his house—leading a demonstration on a Sunday afternoon—a few weeks before so he was pretty sensitive.

Gale, the way she always talked about it, wore two hats. I mean, "We wear different hats at different times." And that was the classic, to be able to picket one time or visit people's neighbors and cause all kinds of commotion, and the next week be in the same room and just talk normally. "Let's work something out here." "What do you mean? You just embarrassed the hell out of me. You went to my neighbors and said I was an asshole. And now you want to sit across the table from me and talk about something? What do you…?" But she did it. Why not? It's always something that she was able to do, and people accepted it.

Brenda LaBlanc: It's a different way to make friends.

Bruce Gottschall: When you can't go to the cocktail parties, I guess you've got to figure out some other way to meet people! Gale was never embarrassed about anything and <u>really believed</u> what she believed, and knew it was right. So she just would not care what anybody thought. Most of us were going, "Well, I don't know if this is right. This is a little complex here. It's got all these sides to it." She'd say, "Nope. This is the way it is."

She had a certainty about things. She knew what was right and she just had the instinct. And she was right. There's only one side to the story, and this is it. So somebody would be, "Holy cow. How can we ask for that? How can we do that? That's going so far off the end." She just was not embarrassed and she would just charge ahead. But once she got to a point where there was some capacity to talk, then she could sit down and talk and figure out, "Okay. What can we get out of this?" Rather than, "Let's just keep beating. Let's just keep going to the nth degree." "Well, okay. I think it's at a point now where, let's get something. And then let's figure out what the next step is."

That was her classic line with the NHS. She'd say, "Well, okay. We'll take three of those. But we're still going to beat the shit out of you! Three of those NHS things... We'll take three of those. Those are nice. Yeah. Those are good. They'll help some people. But we're still going to go after you on these other things." So that was the switching hats capacity. Three of those nice little things!

After Austin, then it was the West Side Coalition piece, getting those three organizations together which were African-American, Italian, Hispanic, Eastern European. And people had the same issues so to speak. You had, then, the insurance redlining thing. So it was then figuring out how to coalesce those groups together. Gale was the natural person who just emerged as the people followed, who spoke for and who enunciated most vehemently and clearly.

I never did go to any of the NPA actions. I kept my separate hat. We had people, Emily Dunn, for example, who went. She was a board member in West Inglewood and then people from Roseland, Grace and people like that would have been involved before with Gale. But there are actually a number of people from NHS who got into meetings with Gale, and then got into these other pieces. But I kept my separateness.

There are stories here about police who were "with" Gale and people. They had to do their job but they also knew that what Gale had to say made a lot of sense because they'd run into the same issues themselves.

Ann Vick-Westgate: So how did Gale function as a board member here? She's a natural leader. But how was she in a collaborative situation where she was a peer?

Bruce Gottschall: Gale became chairman of the Operations Committee. She was that for a long time. Finally, a couple of years before she died we got a co-chairman. "Hey, Gale, if you're not here, what are we going to do?" So we did get somebody to be the co-chair with her. She would in a sense dominate the meeting. But she also got things out of people by asking questions, and just going after things and asking, "Why is this one...?" She was always forcing people to describe things: why I was working here, why we aren't doing this, and always the whole thing of setting the bar way up here.

Bruce Gotschall, second from left, founding Executive Director of NHS of Chicago, with Gale, center. Gale was instrumental in selecting the almost twenty neighborhoods which NHS of Chicago tackled during her lifetime. West Humboldt Park was one of them.

As soon as you achieved one thing, or you haven't even achieved it, it looks like you might achieve it, then she'd say, "Okay. Now we've got to do these three things over here." "Gale, can't we rest for a minute? This is a great victory. Look what we did." "Oh, yeah, but…" She wouldn't even pay attention. That was great, because it kept you focused on the future along with the present. But it was sometimes pretty hard for me, hard for other people too, because they didn't realize what was happening in terms of what her style was. And why that was so important, to not rest on your laurels.

It was great to just talk through strategy with her on what's happening in this neighborhood both on the personal, individual front—who's working with who or not—and how that's working. And what we've got to do there, as well as the strategic in terms of what needs to be accomplished. So she was a great sounding board and would have great instincts about who you've got to involve or how you've got to do it, or what you've got to worry about or how to think about it.

Gale actually would not tell you how to do it or, in our conversation, wouldn't tell you what the answer was. It was just kind of the conversation and the questions and so then out of that you developed the strategy. So she didn't jump to conclusions, although she did. But she was able to ask enough questions to then be able to fit it into some schema that was in her mind about that she'd seen this before or that kind of thing. So then she would jump into it. I suppose it would depend on the people too, because sometimes she would tell people what to do. But if you went to her with questions, you'd get analysis and a thought process. It wouldn't be long, but it would be long enough to get some direction or clarity. So that was not unique, but it was special.

Bill Plechaty was the first president of NHS of Chicago. Gale always liked Plechaty because he was pretty straight and she could deal with him. He was not a liberal; he was a conservative. But he was in this, trying to figure out some things to do. She always liked people who were clear and straight shooters, rather than wishy-washy liberals as she would think of them. I don't know how she perceived me. So it was interesting because she would almost be more comfortable allying with someone who was conservative because she knew where they stood, then you could figure out how to get them to a position where they were supporting your direction.

Mike Moskow was Assistant Secretary of HUD, in charge of Policy Development and Research. He made HUD's first grant in support of the Urban Reinvestment Task Force and its NHS Program. Moskow went on to become President of the Federal Reserve Bank of Chicago: I went to HUD in 1973. I was there two-and-one-half years. I left in the middle of '75. The first six months I was doing a major study on housing policy because

Nixon had suspended the 235 homeownership program, the 236 rental program and the public housing program. I met Bill Whiteside after that six months because we were so busy with that study that I didn't have much time for other things. He started telling us about the NHS program and we sent a couple of key people out to Pittsburgh to see. I remember the stories that they came back with were just legendary about what was going on. What they were doing in Pittsburgh was very similar to what's being done now in NHS here in Chicago.

There was a story that the people in Pittsburgh told us that what really motivated the formation of the Pittsburgh NHS was that someone put up a sign saying, "This is going to be an urban renewal area." As soon as people saw that sign they said, "Whoa, this is not what we want." Because urban renewal, of course, has this history of coming in and ripping down homes and really destroying neighborhoods.

So they formed a community group which worked on preservation of the homes, preservation of the neighborhood and getting the group to work together which of course is the basic principle of Neighborhood Housing Services. And it's a very powerful thing. You go beyond just housing. There's a key counseling component to it. There's the renovation, there's the neighborhood safety, there's schools and jobs that come together on the neighborhood level. And it requires strong leadership at the neighborhood level but also close working relationships.

We talked with Bill about it and he explained the basic principle of neighborhood preservation. It was just so logical to us that we said, "Hey, this is a fantastic idea." This is of course quite different from where housing policy and community development policy were prior to that. It was always the emphasis on new construction and also urban renewal. And our policy shift was toward what we called the "direct cash assistance" in those days which was the enlarged Section 8 program to try to give people funds so that they could move into areas that would best suit their needs. We weren't building new buildings or building new homes, they could fit into neighborhoods, fit into existing structures.

The neighborhood piece of this, the neighborhood preservation piece, fit right in. It was just a logical component of this thrust to let people decide where they can live. The government wasn't smart enough, wasn't wise enough, to make decisions on where people should live, but let people make that choice themselves. And if they were in neighborhoods already, let's do everything we could to preserve that neighborhood, to improve that neighborhood, rather than destroy that neighborhood.

Of course as I learned in Chicago, Chicago has a history. When they built all the public housing here, much of the public housing destroyed neighborhoods. Now we're ripping down these buildings, of course, and making great progress now. So the whole concept just sort of fit together. And then Bill must have suggested to us this idea for a secondary market, NHSA, and that too seemed very logical.

My first dealing with Gale was on the fifth floor here at the Federal Reserve Bank of Chicago. In my first six months here [in early 1995] she came in and demonstrated in the lobby. She had somehow gotten past security. We didn't have as tight security as we have now since 9/11, but, with eight billion dollars in the vault, we have pretty tight security here! So she got a group in and had a toilet, I remember. And they were banging drums or pans or something.

Alicia Williams, Vice president for consumer and community affairs at the Federal Reserve Bank of Chicago: Gale threw the CRA regs, regulations, in the toilet!

Mike Moskow: That's right. And when we heard this banging we looked out and I said to my staff, "Figure out what to do about it!" So Gale started to talk. They wanted to meet with me and we said, "We'd be happy to meet with you, but you've got to schedule an appointment like everyone else does." I refused to meet with them that day. Eventually they left. Then they did set up a meeting several weeks later. She was here and who was the other fellow, the British guy—Malcolm Bush. He was with her from Woodstock [Institute] and a few others. And they said to us that there were new regs being issued and Larry Lindsay was heavily involved, as a member of the Board of Governors.

There was an issue about what you would disclose, what information would be disclosed. And Lindsay took this position, that because of confidentiality you couldn't disclose some business loans, something to do with the City. Gale and Malcolm told us – and they were absolutely correct – we were disclosing them in Chicago already. Remember the City had a rule that if you got money from the City you had to disclose by census tract both deposits and loans?

And these were business loans as opposed to housing loans. That was the issue. The housing loans you could disclose because they were individuals, but Lindsay took this view you can't disclose the business loans because of competitive situations. You'd put that business firm at a competitive disadvantage if you disclosed the loan.

Larry took a very strong position on this. They came in and said, "Contrary to what your policy may be, the City of Chicago requires you to do this. And they are disclosed. They're put in the library; anyone can go look at them there." And we, as a result of this, checked into it. Gale was absolutely correct. We then wrote a letter to Lindsay explaining this that this was already being done in Chicago and therefore we felt there was no problem on competitive disadvantage for those firms here. It didn't discourage any firms from doing it. And we supported the idea that they should disclose these, which they still do.

But that was the first time I met Gale. Of course, I'd heard about her, but that was the first time we'd really met. Then over the years I saw her at various events and she came to see us a couple of times. She was very worried about predatory lending. And FHA.

Well, when Lindsay was touring here he made some comment about FHA, "It's the reason these neighborhoods have deteriorated so much." All the abandonment, the foreclosures were FHA and if it's FHA, it's HUD's fault. The local head of HUD called me and we had a meeting with them. And we got NHS here involved and that really started the work we were doing in the foreclosure area.

From "The Next Move", *DISCLOSURE* #4 (December 1974)

Gale Cincotta: The past year has seen substantial gains. Through our Annual Chicago Housing Conference and our series of regional conferences, more community groups are joining the national network of people working together on redlining, disinvestment and reinvestment.

Because of these efforts, the Federal Home Loan Bank Board (FHLBB) has picked up a community idea and developed the Neighborhood Housing Service into a national program. This is a good program and we support it. But in the FHLBB' s own words, "it is not a panacea for the problem of disinvestment." Because it is limited to smaller impact areas within cities, we still must continue our battle against the national problem of redlining and our fight for national mandatory full public disclosure. The "housing crisis" may seem lost among our other economic woes. But when the full effects of the new Community Development Act are felt, we're going to find that more federal funds were wasted with little decent low and moderate income housing to be seen as a result.

Federal anti-redlining regulations and national mandatory full public disclosure of the lending industry must be our top priority in 1975. Other low-interest rehab loan and mortgage programs may move us along. But the next move must be one—that brings us all the way home –– to beautiful neighborhoods. Cries of "FULL DISCLOSURE" must ring throughout the country.

Michael Westgate: Gale continued to play a supportive role for expanding NHS programs nationwide. She testified in favor of establishing Neighborhood Reinvestment Corporation, successor to the Urban

Reinvestment Task Force where I had worked, and where she had played such a critical role in the success of the Chicago program.

From *DISCLOSURE* #31, (Sept. 1977)
NHS Expansion Wins Senate Support

NPA won a victory in August when the Senate Banking, Housing and Urban Affairs Committee voted out a proposal that would make the Urban Reinvestment Task Force and its programs, such as Neighborhood Housing Services, permanent and independent with increased funding. In testifying at July 25 hearings, NPA Chairperson Gale Cincotta said:

"The task force has proven its ability. National People's Action has asked previously of this Congress that the NHS program be expanded. We are strongly in support of S. 1724. NHS should be recognized as a separate entity and, as such, will gain status as a concrete commitment to the ever-increasing need for a national neighborhood reinvestment policy.

The bill sets up the Neighborhood Reinvestment Corporation as a Congressionally chartered non-profit independent entity. The Senate committee approved an appropriation of $15 million for fiscal year 1979, $20 million for fiscal year 1980, and $30 million in fiscal 1981. The committee also agreed to back a $10 million supplemental budget request for fiscal year 1978.

The Neighborhood Reinvestment Corporation has so far gained many supporters, including the new Federal Home Loan Bank Board chief, Robert McKinney. The only strong opposition came from HUD, who wanted the bill put off for a year for more study… It's a good sign when the Senate recognizes the ill effects of leaving a good program under HUD's supervision.

Under the proposed change, the present Task Force's members' participation would be maintained by appointing the Secretary of HUD, the Chairman of the Federal Home Loan Bank Board, a Governor of the Federal Reserve System, the Chairman of the Federal Deposit Insurance Corporation and the Comptroller of the Currency to the new Board of Directors. Sen. Garn introduced an amendment which was accepted that the committee designate the Federal Home Loan Bank Board Chairman as permanent corporation chairman. He explained that the change is to keep the HUD Secretary, even 20 years from now, from taking over. The Neighborhood Reinvestment Corporation bill will be voted on by the full Senate after Labor Day."

George Knight: Bill Whiteside wasn't always the easiest person to work for. He later worked closely with Gale. As Chicago NHS had success and really became a model, that also helped reinforce Gale's national role too. She then had another avenue to play a national role and was very constructive in that. And Gale had, of course, a huge impact on the Task Force with her testimony.

Michael Westgate: Whiteside told us that when Gale gave testimony, she said, "I want the Urban Reinvestment Task Force budget raised from $2 million to $100 million. And I want it done this year." It took you a while to get up there, George.

George Knight: Twenty years.

Kathy Desmond: Thank you, Gale.

George Knight: It would have been a catastrophe.

Michael Westgate: That's what Bill said in the hearing. He said, "No thank you." And that got Proxmire interested.

Bill Whiteside: I was invited to a seminar in another state. Two of the people there were Robert Kuttner and Ken McLean, two of Proxmire's assistants. We hit it up pretty well. It was a group of about 10-15 people. All of us were interested in housing and things like that. And so we spent a lot of time together.

In fact, when we came back – I had a Jaguar then – and got into the airport, my battery was run down. So I persuaded them to give me a push. And so they pushed it, the two of them pushing behind, me sitting inside waiting to throw it into gear, until we came to a hill and they let go and it started. And as I drove away I thought, "Well, that's a great way to get acquainted with a couple of staffers of a Senator."

But not long after that, this action took place in Washington and Gale was on a panel to speak on a recommended Neighborhood Commission. And I was on it. Gale came first.

Proxmire didn't have any other members with him; he was solely in charge of the hearing. And he came to Gale and she had eighteen demands, which she went through. And one of them was that Bill Whiteside's operation, his group "which are the only people in Washington who know anything about neighborhoods," should have $100 million.

Proxmire said, "W-e-l-l-l, Mr. Whiteside, what will you do with this $100 million?" I was terrified because the General Counsel and several other people from the Bank Board were sitting behind me and he obviously thought Gale and I had rigged this. I didn't wet my pants but everything.... I said, "I believe our work should expand; I'd like to see it expand. But $100 million would destroy it because we couldn't have the same quality of staff. If we had to spend that kind of money in a hurry, all of our quality would be diminished. But I can reaffirm that we could use more money."

And it went on. I got my only, in my whole life, national news article. It was an AP story. And the headline was "Bureaucrat Turns Down $100 million." A couple of days later Ken Mclean and Bob Kuttner show up in my office. They said, "OK. How much can you use? And what kind of an organization should it be?" I said, "Well, the Tennessee Valley Authority has always appealed to me." It has public money and it operates like a private operation.

They said, "Actually, we were thinking of something like that too, a government corporation." And they handed me a one-page double-spaced outline of a Neighborhood Reinvestment Corporation Act. Well. It didn't have that name yet. And they asked me to make changes in it, to improve it, add to it, cut anything out I didn't like. And get it back to them.

So I headed to Oakland. Mary and Warren Widener [an attorney and mayor of Berkeley at the time] and I sat down around their kitchen table. Warren brought some law books. By about ten or eleven o'clock that night, we had drafted the bill. It was several pages long by then. Because I knew the end run would be the way government works and that there would be all kinds of compromises and so on. So we put in everything we could possibly want.

The next day I headed back in Washington and took it over to them. And things started happening pretty fast. The very next day the Senate unanimously passed it by voice vote. Because Utah's Senator Garn had come on and so you had Proxmire and Garn, the two top people in housing and urban finance. Garn was a former mayor of Salt Lake City, who understood housing as a mayor. And I never met him. He was the ranking Republican while Proxmire was the Chairman of the Housing, Banking and Urban Affairs Committee. They wanted it and they got it. They passed it verbatim with our whole laundry list on it. Everything we could possibly want.

I didn't know how conservative Proxmire was financially. So this turning down the hundred million dollars really appealed to him. And I was his hero for that. He wrote some stuff, crazy stuff, in the *Congressional Record*. One was headed something like "Whiteside Wrestles Urban Problems to the Ground." I was the first man he'd ever heard who was doing something social and wasn't trying to spend all the money in the world.

The next thing happened was a member of the Federal Home Loan Bank Board General Counsel's office dropped in on me and said, "Oh-h-h, since <u>when</u> have we been entering legislation?" I knew I was going to have to tell him. And a brand new guy, Garth Marston, had been Chairman for a few days. I got worse threats. Well, the Senate passed it in '76. Then it hit the House in the next legislative year, in '77.

The Chairman, Garth Marston was his name, he was very standoffish with me. And I was told he was constantly debating whether to fire me or not. We'd all attended a hearing and we were walking back. And he and I were walking side by side. The Carter administration has just come in. And he said, "Well, how do the other agencies on the Task Force feel about this legislation? I said, " Well. The FDIC is in favor of it. The Comptroller is against it. The Fed hasn't taken a position on it. And HUD is in violent opposition to it." He said, "Wow. Well, if HUD's against it, it can't be all bad!"

So that got rid of that anxiety of momentarily being fired. Then, in a few months there were hearings.

At a hearing of the House Committee on Housing and Urban Affairs it came up to a vote. And there were 20 odd members of the committee. It was like 4 to 1 in our favor. HUD lost. It was Goliath… HUD's opposition was because it wasn't their show.

Someone had told the HUD Secretary Carla Hills that she would take over the Urban Reinvestment Task Force and that it would become part of HUD. I didn't know this at the time, but part of the interest on the part of our supporters, in both the Senate and the House, was never to let it get into HUD's hands. And the fact that HUD might take it over they knew would destroy the spontaneity and the flexibility.

Michael Westgate: This backing of Neighborhood Reinvestment was symptomatic of Gale's ability to switch hats. Having raked Richard Platt over the coals a few years earlier, she became a vocal supporter of this initiative of the Federal Home Loan Bank Board. Her sense of timing, as always, was impeccable.

Did Gale come across as satisfied with what was being accomplished at NTIC or NHS or in Chicago generally? Or was she frustrated?

Bruce Gottschall: Well, that's interesting, because she clearly got a charge out of the legislative successes, getting that stuff done, and seeing change. Just the fight and winning something was a charge. She really liked the NHS piece, because she could see people getting their house fixed. So she needed both. She was interesting. That's why the whole two hats thing worked. The way that she was, she needed both of those things. She needed to see people getting some immediate benefits right now, as well as looking at the longer term, and seeing these larger pieces accomplished and done. So that was an important thing to her to see that.

That's probably what endeared her to people too. Because people were fighting, then saw some benefits, so they enjoyed the fight, but also then saw the particular impacts. So that's the kind of people in a sense that were attracted to the activity. People really had the excitement of getting to battle and doing that, but were very grounded and seeing the results.

Other organizations emulated her tactics and got inspired by what she did. She had an impact greater than the organizations she worked with directly. She set the high standard. So even those people who either the tactics weren't quite right, either they were too much or they were not enough

– because there were people on all sides of it – my sense is that they measured themselves by whether they did as much or better than Gale. Because she was the person, or the embodiment, of getting some of this stuff done. So what she did pushed the field, pushed everybody to do as much or more. So whatever tactics they were using, they had to demonstrate that those tactics were at least as effective as Gale's, because that was the measure.

Some might have said she sold out to the lenders too quick. Others would have said that those tactics really don't create the long-term results. But she was working on several different fronts. She could use her confrontational tactics and then sit down and negotiate a big agreement with Fannie Mae. Tying the research to the direct-action type things, some would say, "Well, the research wasn't good enough." So you got into all those kinds of pieces. But it did set the standard, and so it pushed everybody here locally to use research. Use research and then accomplish results that were significant. Set the standard high enough for other places to say, "In Chicago, they're doing this and Gale's doing...." So that created, to a degree, a cult of personality.

I don't know if there were particular places where maybe there was some impact on the "election side of it". There might have been, but that really wasn't important to Gale. "Once they get in, they're all bad anyway. It doesn't make any difference who gets elected. Once they get in, you know what..." She would not trust anybody who got elected. This was one of the reasons she wouldn't run for office herself. Either because the system is such that she knew that someone really couldn't do it from inside, or felt they couldn't do it from inside – or the process of getting elected compromised them.

When Jane Byrne got elected, we said, "Now we got someone..." She said, "Bull shit." She was right. Byrne was just like anybody else. So she had to beat her up and do the whole thing. Now with Harold Washington it was maybe a little different in terms of how she would proceed then.

But an alderman or anybody else, "You seemed like a good guy, and then

Gale on panel with Mayor Harold Washington, Chicago's first African-American Mayor. He appointed her chairperson of his Commission on Women. ca. 1985.

you got elected. Well, now you're a bad guy. So what do we got to do to keep you honest or make you do something that you couldn't do otherwise?" Understanding that, "Hey. We've got to be here to beat the shit out of them, because someone over there is giving them money. And they've got to tell them, 'Here's why I got to do it—because they're beating the shit out of me.'" Whatever. So she could understand and use that.

Cal Bradford: Gale didn't have to know everything. She would trust Bruce Gottschall, or anybody that she was working with that she trusted. She would call me or she would ask Bud Kanitz in Washington. She didn't want to know all the technical stuff, but she did want someone that she could trust to tell her what she thought would be the truth. They'd be honest, at least make an honest mistake if they made a mistake. So she'd say, "Well, someone's got this idea and the mortgage bankers want to do this." So she'd call up, "What do you think about this?" She didn't have a need to know it; she knew she could learn it from others. So you just develop trust like anybody else would.

Bruce Gottschall: Even within the lending pieces, that was some of the same thing. The allies within the bank needed her to say, "We're getting the shit beat out of us." So tell the executive vice-president or the president, "Hey. We got to do this, because look what's going on." And so they needed that kind of outside stuff and Gale understood it and provided it.

She always kept her word. People knew that she hadn't compromised her integrity anywhere along the line. She got a lot of support from the churches, especially the Catholic Church in the early days. But then the Cardinal changed and that cut back on a lot of the church's involvement.

Gale would be great because she had a sense of people and we had a lot of different neighborhood people involved. She would know the good ones from the ones that weren't and she would create a shield. She could read them. She might have known their histories too. But she could read right away where someone was coming from, and whether they were coming from some agenda or self-interest. Self-interest is a critical organizing piece, but a personal self-interest that was distorting what they were going after, or some personality, she could read that pretty quick. She would be willing to front, to solve a problem, by neutralizing somebody who would have been a pain in the ass, or a group that would have been a pain in the ass. And who wouldn't have allowed us to do what we needed to do, because we would have been trying to bail that whole thing.

To neutralize them she would just confront them and say, "Hell, no!" She would just know that they were trying to put something on, and she'd say, "We're going to do this." Then she would take responsibility for saying she'd decided it, even though it might have been me saying, "Gale, I need help on this thing and I can't say this." So she would not be at all reluctant, because she knew what we were trying to do in terms of getting the real people together. She didn't want to be sidelined by people bullshitting. So she would just decide to do something and say, "We're going to do it." Say, "It was decided this way and, if you don't like it, too bad because we're going to do it this way." And that would be what she would do, and you can go do your work.

So it was community involvement in the process and getting everybody involved to a point. But at some point you'd say, "Wait a minute. Let's not just play around here. Let's do something."

Michael Westgate: What was her relationship with the mayor?

Bruce Gottschall: With Daley, Senior, Gale developed some mutual respect. I was never in a meeting with the Mayor and Gale. But my sense was clearly, from what was done, there was some simpatico and there were some of the same agenda pieces so that worked. I think she always hated Byrne. She thought she was full of shit. I think that was her basic sense. Probably right.

She wouldn't buy into the fact that she was "some reformer" and was going to do good things. She was just more of the same.

With Washington, there was some mutual respect there, and he was on some of the same agenda that Gale was on, all kinds of neighborhood pieces.

Gale with Mayor Richard M. Daley celebrating the 25th anniversary of NTIC at The Como Inn, Chicago, 1997.

So I think that was good.

With Rich Daley now, I think he really respected her too. That was a pretty good working relationship. They would have been on some of the same agendas too.

When there was more equal rights type stuff, she sensed that, and then really agreed with it and bought into it. But it wasn't a push at the outset. She figured if she could do it, others could do it. But that wasn't an overt agenda most of the time, to find women as leaders.

Other women said, "Well, gee, if Gale can do this, maybe I could do it!" It's hard when you try to explain to staff who didn't experience it or experienced a little bit of Gale, how you create the understanding of what the importance or the different pieces of Gale were. We try to do that from time to time. Even when Gale was around, to try to get people at meetings and that kind of thing, because there was an aura there and an importance of understanding the history.

Bill Whiteside: Gale and I had an interesting relationship, really two relationships, one real and one in the mind of the public. I've seen her in enough of her actions… She saw me as part of the Establishment even though I was the only one in Washington who "understood neighborhoods". So we were always a little cautious around one another.

Gale and I would joke, though, about how she was always doing promotional work for us. She was getting the neighborhoods stirred up so they were ready for us. And it kind of happened—neither of us planned it—that often we'd get an invitation to develop an NHS where she'd done organizing before.

She was an immensely, as you know, powerful force in the Chicago program. And having her as a born-again organizer made a world of difference. I am equating that to the born-again lenders. Well, she had this thing she talked about as "changing hats." So you picket a banker all day, then you take off your organizer hat and you sit down in the NHS meeting and you put on your NHS hat and you work together to solve the neighborhood problems. Sitting at that table with the same guy you've picketed all day. The bankers found it harder than she did! They even got it eventually. That was the born-again part.

Ed Williams: She had an amazing capacity to participate. Even with her health problems when she had to have a wheelchair waiting for her, she made the meetings. She had to be there. Like with our neighborhood lending meetings that we were doing quarterly, we had developed somewhat of a schedule like on the third Tuesdays and so people could come report, and you wouldn't have to guess when it's going to be. If it was on a time when she was going to be in Washington for something, she'd say, "Well, can you change the meeting to the next week? I'm going to be away." So she would ask for that to know if we could do that. She wanted to be there. She wasn't doing it by proxy. She wasn't sending her assistant. She was there every meeting.

NHS, I think, more than any other organization in Chicago, can get support of substantial amounts of money much quicker than any other organization. They can get $100 million literally and in a very short period of time. We've done it. We know we can do it because of the reputation that NHS has for integrity as well as delivery on what they say they're going to do. They produce the results. And people like being with a winner and with a leader. And they like if they're innovative and they lead, they're creative and so forth. So you want to be with them. You want to be around them. And Gale of course was a big part of helping them to achieve that credibility.

CHAPTER 9

"Redlining is destroying the backbone of our country."
"Redlining is now illegal in the State of Illinois."

NATIONAL CONFERENCE OF 1975
ILLINOIS CRA REGULATIONS AND LEGISLATION

Bud Kanitz: In terms of redlining, the interesting thing about that terminology is that most people assume that it's a banker's terminology. But it really comes out of the insurance industry. In the initial hearings in Springfield there was an independent insurance agent named Hank Schwab who testified about redlining. He said, "I have two maps here. One is an insurance map. And you see it has a red line. I can write insurance outside the red line, but I can't inside the red line. Now here is another map of Chicago and I have drawn a red line to denote where the Latino and black populations are. You will notice that the lines are practically the same."

So that's from whence redlining came. I recently ran into an insurance agent who has been in the insurance business long enough who corroborated this story. He said, "That's right. It was an actuarial thing. We got maps from our actuarials that said you can write insurance here, but you can't over there."

From "The Next Move," *DISCLOSURE* #6 (March 1975)
Gale Cincotta: It's Annual National Housing Conference time! We have made a lot of progress in this past year. When we had our FIRST National Conference in the spring of 1972, everyone was talking about the crisis in American cities; but no one had ever heard of redlining then and the FHA scandals were still being swept under the rug. The SECOND Annual Conference resulted in the 235 victory and the voluntary FHLBB lending survey conducted in Chicago. Last year's THIRD Housing Conference rang with chants of "Full Disclosure" and resulted in legislation being passed or presently pending in many cities and states.

This year's FOURTH Annual National Housing Conference will finalize several victories in the making. Senator Proxmire has been invited to speak about the Congressional hearings in May on national disclosure and federal anti-redlining legislation. HUD Secretary Carla Hills has been invited to announce her department's plans for ending the FHA scandal of fast-foreclosure.

The whole housing situation remains critical. The new Community Development Act [including the new Block Grant program to be administered by HUD] is unlikely to bring us any closer to the national goal of a "decent home" for every American. More rather than less federal intervention is necessary to save our cities. The government cannot pass the blame or buy its way out of the housing crisis. We have come a long way since March of 1972: we know now that many of our urban problems are a direct result of federal policies or non-policies.

The past three years have proven that neighborhood organizing is alive and well in America. Victories have been the result of all our efforts in city after city. The challenge now is to think ahead and develop a PEOPLE'S PLATFORM for 1976 so that we can hold our governmental officials accountable for our common needs. Our next move is to strategize at this year's Annual Conference how we can better coordinate our local activities into a national grass-roots network.

Michael Westgate: *New York Times* writer William E. Farrell reported in his April 21, 1975 article "Urban Parley Acts To Halt 'Redlining' and 'Blockbusting'" that 500 people from 40 cities came together at the Fourth Annual National Housing Conference as "a coalition of blacks, Latinos and whites who have been told in the past that the problem was each other."

Ted Wysocki: So my exposure [as a volunteer at NTIC/NPA] was right when they were beating the drums about needing HMDA. The first step, literally, was volunteers going in and looking through the title searches and seeing at what point did conventional lending stop. Austin and Englewood and Roseland would have been the communities that would have changed to African Americans. Then there were others, communities that had not experienced racial change yet, that were looked at, and they still were all getting conventional loans. The research came out of conversations between Cal Bradford and Gale.

Bill Greider, the reporter at the Senate Banking Committee hearing, said that those hearings were very impactful because, seriously, there was like shock. Like, nobody had known. In the conversations about civil rights that had obviously gone on for a decade ahead of 1975, none of that had really specifically come out, documented, in that kind of way. I want to say it was in May of '75. I literally remember we were up drawing these handmade posters (talking about high tech graphics!) for Gale's testimony. We did do an edited videotape of what would have been the 3rd National People's Action Conference because the big theme for that year's conference in 1974 was Gale dismissing Dick Platt – which is relevant today – and basically saying, "If the bank regulators won't do this, we will go to Congress."

From *DISCLOSURE* #7 (April 1975)
People's Platform For 1976

In 1976, we'll look back to this conference as the birthplace of the People's Platform.

FULL DISCLOSURE NOW!

Bold new advances down the long road to forcing full disclosure data from all lending institutions were made by delegates from people's coalitions gathered together at the Fourth Annual National Housing Conference in Chicago.

Delegates from cities across the country directly confronted Robert Bartell, president of the Chicago Federal Home Loan Bank, in Saturday's afternoon panel on the disclosure issue. Bartell, in his infamous "twinkie-toes" act, after trying unsuccessfully to hedge completely around the issue and lying bold-facedly about his past unwillingness to deal intelligently and responsively with some of the community groups, was finally forced into laying bare his unwillingness to support the disclosure bill pending before the U.S. Senate Banking and Currency Committee. Bartell, whose office regulates federally chartered savings and loan associations, finally refused to sign a letter of support for the bill. Inappropriately, he likened action on disclosure to the concept of "private citizens enforcing laws against murder."

Bartell's whole act of being "buddy-buddy" with the people, while refusing to deal with their demands was not appreciated. For example, his casual mention of "Gale's been to my house", in reference to Gale Cincotta, chairperson of NPAH, gave the impression that he was accustomed to inviting community leaders over for Sunday tea. In reality, Gale was at his house with 60 people from Chicago's Metropolitan Area Housing Alliance (MAHA) who were holding him accountable for his non-action on the disclosure issue while his steaks burned on the grill. Bartell's never forgotten or forgiven Gale for this inconvenience.

Bartell's unresponsiveness at the Conference personifies the disinterested negligence of professional bureaucrats in government at all levels. The panel ended with delegates coming to the stage handing Bartell copies of the supporting letter for the Disclosure bill that Bartell refused to sign.

Appearing before Bartell on the panel, Robert Kuttner, chief staff of the Senate Banking and Currency Committee, discussed the details of Senator Proxmire's mandatory disclosure bill. Kuttner praised the past efforts of NPAH, telling the crowd that Proxmire's "Home Mortgage Disclosure Act" exists "largely through the efforts of this group and Gale Cincotta." He urged delegates to testify in favor of this legislation, Senate Bill 1281, at the Committee's hearings in Washington during the week of May 5th, warning of strong opposition to the bill from the lending industry. Kuttner informed the delegates that he has been told in private by lobbyists from the industry: "You know, this is going to make us look just terrible."

Kuttner cited the lending industry as a textbook example of capitalism, seeking to maximize profits and minimize risk, "which has many times in the past meant the redlining of city neighborhoods." He urged the delegates and the other community panel members from Boston, Cleveland, Rochester, Baltimore and Chicago to "light a fire under those other legislators so we can get this bill passed."

GALE CINCOTTA IN "The Next Move" (same issue)

We're on the move – to Washington, D.C. and in cities across the country. A national grass-roots network has grown out of our common experiences. Neighborhood organizing is alive and well and operating at a national level to boot. And at the other end of that boot are the politicians, speculators and bankers who have been kicking us around for so long. The boys are being called home and then to account for their continued neglect of the neighborhoods.

This year's 4th Annual National Conference proved that last year's chants of "Full Disclosure" are finally being heard. Mr. Bartell may still give lectures on good lending practices, but he may soon find himself on the college campuses instead of in the FHLB's Chicago office. The reason is that Congress is realizing that redlining is destroying the backbone of our country – viable neighborhoods.

Our May activities in Washington will highlight redlining, FHA and C.D. [community disinvestment] as the issues most vital to our neighborhoods. From these national actions, regional conferences and our continued local efforts, our People's Platform for 1976 will grow to bring our neighborhood needs the national attention they deserve.

The next move is our Washington trip, but for reinforcement this must be followed up with strong local efforts. Before the end of May communities should hold public meetings, inviting their city and state officials as well as their Congressional representatives to take action on the issues vital to the rebuilding of our neighborhoods

Keep Organizing -- We're on the Move!

From Ford Foundation Program Action documents (January 12, 1976) Recommending a $125,000 grant over two years to HTIC

By 1974, with 10,000 HUD-insured buildings in default or foreclosure in Chicago, HTIC retained a researcher to analyze HUD's computer reports. This information permitted HTIC to first identify and then negotiate with those mortgage companies engaging in over-speedy foreclosures and to convince HUD of the need to issue new regulations to insure forbearance on the part of all mortgagees nationally.

Cal Bradford: NPA is a wonderful lesson. It's like CSI-type stuff, except it's indirect. How do you know things? They would get into buildings because they knew the secretarial staff for the whole building, and they could figure out where the entrances were and what was open at certain times of the day and how people normally got in, stuff like that, to get into buildings. They'd know the policemen. They went through these other routes that no one ever thought of. It's pretty obvious if you think about it.

Ted Wysocki: I worked with NPA for about eleven years, so from '74 to '84. One of the first things I actually did for Gale, when I went on paid staff at the end of my year of graduate school in the summer of '74, was to start *DISCLOSURE,* which obviously still continues. And the way they started that – this is Shel and Gale – they said, "Oh, we're going out to this meeting with Monsignor Baroni. There's going to be all these other groups there. How about if you drive out there, and we'll tell you where to stop on the way, and we'll tell you where to stop on the way back, and then what you could do is you could write up what these groups are doing in their cities." And that was basically the first issue of *DISCLOSURE* off the infamous mimeograph machine in the back room.

Gale wasn't a writer. I would interview her. We would sit down. I would find out what it is she wanted to write, what did she want to talk about this time, write it, give it back to her, make the changes she wanted. And obviously developing that relationship with Gale, you did learn how she would say things. If you were to review the columns, you could see where it more captured writing in her vocabulary. All you had to do was sit down with Gale and then get it back to her.

Cal Bradford: She actually said she could work more easily with Republicans. She said they disagreed with you more, but that was all right. You can negotiate with someone as long as you understand where they are.

Ann Vick-Westgate: You worked with her a long time. What made her effective?

Ted Wysocki: I always found that first she really was nonpartisan. This is a tribute to her style, that she could develop a better relationship with a Jack Kemp, as a HUD Secretary, than she could with an Andrew Cuomo. Now those are two different sorts of personalities and egos. She really didn't care if you were the Republican governor of Illinois, if you were going to be responsive to the issues, that didn't matter. What made her effective is there wasn't any of that kind of partisanship. She was also obviously very articulate on what the issues were, and very persistent in terms in handing something out.

Michael Westgate: The problems of redlining in Chicago came to the attention of Illinois Governor Daniel Walker, who had been elected in 1973. While not unique to Chicago, Chicago was clearly the most dramatic example in the state. The governor established a Legislative Investigating Commission, which held hearings to study mortgage practices in Chicago in 1974.

One of those working with that commission, Patrick Quinn, went on to become Lieutenant Governor in 2002 and Governor in 2009. Gale and her people worked with Quinn and others, resulting in the 1974 Illinois Anti-Redlining Regulation, the first of such state regulations. It and subsequent Illinois legislation passed in 1975 were precursors to the national Home Mortgage Disclosure Act (HMDA) and Community Reinvestment Act (CRA).

From *Urban Disinvestment: New Implications For Community Organization, Research and Public Policy* by Arthur J. Naparstek and Gale Cincotta (Joint Publication of The National Center for Urban Ethnic Affairs and NTIC, 1976):

Chicago-based efforts to confront the redlining issue resulted in the creation or enabling of two reviewing and negotiating bodies: a Governor's Commission to review and formulate recommendations concerning disinvestment and redlining, and the existing State Legislative Investigating Committee was empowered to study redlining. (24)

Bud Kanitz: They did pass CRA in Illinois before Washington. There was a Chicago city ordinance and then there was a disclosure law in Illinois. That brings me to my interesting story about one of my first real involvements with Gale. Because I was working at the Industrial Council of Northwest Chicago as the executive director, I had a lot of contacts in the Governor's Office. Dan Walker was the governor at that time and I knew a lot of his staff assistants. One of them used to be an organizer at NCO. So that was how I hooked into that.

— Gale called me up once and said, "I gotta go to Springfield to testify and, since you know more about politics in Springfield than I do, will you go down with me?" Now in retrospect I find that somewhat ironic that anybody would know more about politics in Springfield than Gale Cincotta. But I remember driving her down to Springfield and it probably was the first time she testified before a state legislative committee on redlining. The chairman of the committee, George Ryan, was grandstanding big time because there was a reporter in the room from his hometown, and he wasn't paying any attention to the issue of the hearing. Ryan later became the governor. So even the first time she testified, Gale was already training future governors of Illinois.

What Governor Walker did was name a blue ribbon panel to look into redlining, and appointed Gale to it. Luis Davila was on it from NCO. It was a blue ribbon commission. They held hearings; they looked into redlining.

Walker was critical, his administration coming in and opening a lot of doors. He was probably the first politician that Gale got his ear and, as a result, the rest is history, literally. He was a populist kind of a guy. He had never run for political office before, but he took his name Walker and he walked around the state. It was a very populist kind of a thing and he got a lot of support as a result of that.

My main contact that I used to help Gale was Pat Quinn who was one of Walker's major operatives when Walker became Governor in 1973. So it was Pat Quinn's behind-the-scenes help with the Governor's Office that created this blue ribbon commission on redlining. Pat Quinn went on to become Governor of Illinois himself in 2009.

Then Gale got the Chicago ordinance passed which required that if the City of Chicago deposits money in your bank, you can't redline.

Joe Mariano: They got the Illinois legislation too. That was always Gale's pattern. It would be to get something in the city, something in the state and then, of course, go national. That's what was going on in predatory lending too, the same pattern when she died. It was get the city to do something, go after the state and then some kind of national strategy.

We'd sit in staff meetings and talk about what she was going to do at NPA. And Gale goes, "Fine. You can make your suggestions. I'm still going to do what I'm going to do. You're not going to script me."

From Case Study by Hallahan (11/7/91)

Kirk Hallahan: Not to be outdone by Mayor Daley, Peter Kasaros, an aide to Governor Dan Walker, told conference attendees that his boss would appoint a 27-member Blue Ribbon Panel Commission on Mortgage Practices and announced the state would issue a regulation barring state-chartered banks from redlining. The panel was appointed in early May of 1974. Illinois' 350 state-chartered savings institutions had been prohibited from redlining by a regulation that had gone into effect in January of 1974. Cincotta and her group had met with S&L regulators on several occasions before adoption of the new regulations, which were the first in the U.S to define redlining. (7)

Illinois already had a policy, dating from the tenure of State Treasurer Adlai Stevenson III in the mid-1960s, to allocate deposits of state funds to banks according to their record in making "social investments" – loans for housing rehabilitation, minority businesses, and businesses in high unemployment areas." (footnote, 8)

The state legislature also got into the act by creating a 12-member Illinois Legislative Investigating Commission, also in 1974. The Commission, which heard testimony from Cincotta and others, issued a 409-page report that called for annual disclosure of each institution's savings and mortgage activity (including figures for their primary service area), five-year reviews of performance, public hearings about the relocation of facilities (which would give consumer groups opportunities to testify) and public hearings on redlining complaints. The ultimate results of these dual efforts were two bills requiring disclosure and barring geographic discrimination. They were signed by Walker in September 1975. (7-8)

Michael Westgate: Fortunately for Gale, John McKnight at Northwestern University was willing and able to commit a significant number of students to help do the number crunching to prove redlining among state-chartered savings and loans around Illinois, in addition to that already proven at the city level in Chicago.

Helen Murray: As we went on, more traditional people recognized us as really on the cutting edge of something. John McKnight and his people up at Northwestern – they had a really smart sense that we were on the leading edge, and that this is what it was going to take. So they did a lot of stuff for us in a more sophisticated way, early on, that helped reinforce also, because it was not just us saying it, it was Northwestern. So that was a real good piece.

From *The Grassroots Battle Against Redlining: From the Streets to the Halls of Congress* (HTIC 1975):
The MAHA Mortgage Coalition grew to include 13 community groups. The 1973 voluntary survey of savings and loans in the greater Chicago area by the Federal Home Loan Bank Board showed significant disinvestment and redlining. When this survey data became public, community pressure intensified, eventually resulting in a meeting between Illinois Governor Dan Walker and Chicago neighborhood residents. This session led directly to the major victory of the Office of the Commission of Savings and Loan Associations for Illinois amending its rules and regulations in January of 1974 to include the first official definition of redlining as "the practice of arbitrarily varying the terms of application procedures or refusing to grant a loan within a specific geographic area on the grounds that the specific parcel of real estate proposed as collateral for the loan is located within said geographical area."

This new regulation was not only the first anti-redlining regulation in the country but it also specifically referred to geographical discrimination. While community people remain dissatisfied with its enforcement, the regulation served as a model in other states. (6)

In Chicago, the MAHA FHA Coalition focused their pressure on the new regional FHLB president, Robert Bartell. Appearing before the Governor's Blue Ribbon Commission on Mortgage Practices on September 24, 1974, Mr. Bartell repeated his refusal to conduct another survey to the commissioners stating that he believed that his predecessor, Mr. Stipp, had submitted to the original voluntary survey under duress. When asked by Commission member, Gale Cincotta, whether he would at least advocate a federal anti-redlining regulation to Mr. Bomar, chairman of the FHLBB in Washington, Mr. Bartell refused to do so on the grounds that the FHLBB doesn't have the authority to establish such a regulation against discrimination on a geographical basis. In addition, Bartell informed the Commission that the FHLBB had determined that disclosure was not an effective way of discovering discrimination. "Community people wouldn't know what to do with disclosure." (10)

Michael Westgate: These comments by Bartell were to prove a rallying cry for Gale since she and her community-based allies actually knew better than anyone what to do with disclosure. She continued to rally people behind the MAHA coalition. It was during 1975 that HTIC changed its name to NTIC, symbolic of the organization's becoming more inclusive, although its primary mission continued to be housing. All this activity in Chicago and in Illinois was both the result of Gale's work and an incubating environment in which her work could continue to take root. The dynamics were self-reinforcing.

Bud Kanitz: As a result, Governor Walker put out an executive order. Because at that point Illinois had unit banking, banks had only one branch. That was headquarters. They couldn't branch around in the neighborhood or in the suburbs. Well, this was the start of being able to branch in Illinois.

There was a savings and loan in my neighborhood, smack in the middle of NCO, called Fairfield Savings and Loan. They wanted to branch into the suburbs and Governor Walker required that they disclose where their deposits came from and where their loans went. Fairfield Savings and Loan, located at North Avenue and Damen Avenue and Milwaukee Avenue, straddled two zip codes. So in their disclosure they showed that like 95% of their deposits came from zip codes 60622 and 60647 and about 4% of their loans went into those same zip codes. So that was the first actual proof of what Gale was alleging in terms of redlining.

Michael Westgate: This test case of Fairfield Savings & Loan wishing to establish a suburban branch proved the need for CRA. Figures quoted in *DISCLOSURE* #6 (MARCH 1975) also confirmed what Gale and others suspected:

202 - GALE FORCE

Bank Practices In Chicago's West Side Red-Lined Communities, based on year end '74 figures, with home loans in zip codes 60612-22-23-24-44-47-51:

Bank	Savings	Home Loans
First National	$121,453,000	$292,000
American National	5,116,000	0
National Security	43,250,956	744,000

Helen Murray: Disclosure was a pretty lefty kind of concept for the Illinois legislature. A lot of them are really hooked in with the real estate industry and everything else. But, anyway, we had fresh air people who were new to the legislature. Mike Holowinski is the guy who at that time sponsored the bills. But we had this whole network of people that were willing to work. And we worked our buns off. We went back and forth down to Springfield on buses. We would call people we knew, anybody that knew a pastor or an activist in Peoria or anywhere else. We were trying to get a statewide bill passed. You know you have to have a statewide base. And we got it.

The anti-redlining law wasn't a real strong law, but it was a symbol. Then we got the state disclosure law. Shortly after, we got the national disclosure law. So we were willing to let the state one go because the national HMDA covered more and did more. The anti-redlining law that we wanted at a national level evolved into the CRA. Because we weren't even sure how we wanted to see a law effecting lending at that point. You know, how do you make an anti-redlining law work?

By the time we were doing this in 1975, Proxmire had the job as chairman of the Senate Banking Committee. But Hart was there the first time in '72. '75 is when we got HMDA and that was Proxmire.

Our efforts at the state and national levels were simultaneous. We were pushing at both doors at the same time. On the disclosure we pretty much knew what we wanted. First of all, we wanted it by zip code: all the money they took in, and all the money that went back to that zip code. And we were like real straight. We knew exactly what we wanted. Now the minutiae when you have to work with Washington or Springfield, that was a different story.

Mary Volpe: The state passed it first. And the only reason the state passed it first was that Dick Daley had given the o.k.

Walker was the type of governor that would send buses to pick up our seniors and take 'em down state. If you were down there and he knew you were fighting something, he would send people down and say, "You're invited up for lemonade and cookies." He had parties. He knew to wine and dine.

So the sequence on CRA was first there was a commission at the state level. I mean we got that legislation passed. In fact we had phone lines in my basement. That night that they were passing it, it was going through in the evening hours. We had people from most of the groups. It wasn't just our group. We were negotiating. They would come to the telephone. That's what made it bad because they were making pap out of the original redlining law. If it had passed, how it was supposed to go in…. But you made concessions to people.

We knew it was going to pass because Phil Rock, who was President of the Senate, was Daley's man. Phil was from this area, he was the hardest person to sway. All of a sudden Rock is the sponsor. So we knew that that word came from Daley to John Casey, who was his mentor and alderman and committeeman here. And Phil was told to put his name on it. To this day he tells everybody he did this, the redlining bill.

And it was a much stronger law. We sat there and we had to concede certain things. It's like when we did the regs for the mortgage bankers. We should not have done regulations because they're iffy. But we were all very naïve. Remember none of us had attorneys working with us. Which is amazing. How crazy can you be? A bunch of crazy people writing legislation and demanding things…

Michael Westgate: It is remarkable that people like Gale Cincotta and Mary Volpe could accomplish what they did. Too often, and increasingly, groups including nonprofits and municipalities resort to hired lobbyists and law firms to articulate and press their cases in state capitols and in Washington. This group did it on their own. Of course it helped immensely that Mayor Daley endorsed their effort. But the actual language of the laws and the twisting of arms in the Legislature, that was the work of Gale and company.

The sequencing of their successes at different levels also turned out to be brilliant. Banks seeking deposits from the City of Chicago complied voluntarily with its requirement that they disclose lending data. That made it impossible for the banks in Illinois to prove that it would be too expensive to comply. Passage of state legislation applying to all lenders in Illinois similarly weakened the opposition at the national level. The explosiveness of the data which Gale amassed through Northwestern put bankers on the defensive. The politicians realized that they were dealing with a powerful force.

Mary Volpe: It really got me because it was being watered down. When people said something, I said, "You know, the problem is that maybe if we had been smarter and more sophisticated in our technique we might have been able to hold off for certain things." But we just wanted that law to get _ passed. We had enough power. We had enough people. Oh, God, we had people! It was just rabble. Of course our country was founded on rabble! We did it the same way!

I'll tell you, old man Daley had to be convinced that it was right. I think, up to that time that he said "No," he truthfully believed that there was no such thing as redlining. I think all of a sudden he got convinced that this was not doing his city any good. You got to understand his feelings. He loved Chicago. His blood was in Chicago. I truthfully believe that he thought that his city was being ruined. And it was proven to him that the areas were being hurt, the older areas, especially the ethnic areas where they put in the savings and loans, where they didn't have banks. A lot of the savings and loans wanted to be banks later but they served a thing that people could get homes.

We'd drive back to Chicago and go back the next morning. None of us were smart enough to take sleeping bags and sleep in the park somewhere or anything or share a room. We'd come all the way home and then go all the way back. Four of us in this little car with our legs up to our... It's a miracle we had any legs left!

But it was bad. We could not go in. And then all of a sudden, when Walker came in, it was open and we started to come in like human beings. And we could do lobbying and everything. It was very accessible. Lots of people don't remember that. They weren't around.

It was just like their own little world down there in Springfield. I used to love to take people down – voters, older voters who swore by the system – and let them sit in a session when they're playing baseball in back, and one woman's nursing a baby, and they're eating their lunch, and nobody's paying any attention to what's going on. I've had people yell, "I'm paying for this?" But the deal is that I liked to have people see what went on downstate. Lots of people, they'd die without seeing it or what happens at City Hall.

Illinois CRA would not have passed if Walker or Daley had opposed it. Truthfully, it would not have passed. Phil Rock retired some years back. When he was President of the Senate for many years he controlled it. He'd work both sides of the aisle. It wasn't just one against the other. So he would have drawn all the Democrat votes off of this automatically. And drawn some of the Republican votes. The Republican votes were against it 'cause of the banking institutions.

Michael Westgate: Shel Trapp has a more jaundiced take on the Illinois regulations and legislation. Yet even he admits that they were of more than symbolic importance. He also saw the ways in which community groups could play vested interests off against each other to accomplish community ends.

Shel Trapp: Governor Walker set up a redlining commission. Gale was on it. Yeah, that was a fun commission even though I don't know that we won anything. It was made up of bankers, realtors, insurance and neighborhoods, pretty evenly divided. The redlining problem was in Chicago.

It was funny 'cause whenever the issues came in, it always seemed that it would be of specific interest to either the realtors, the insurance companies or the banks. But they wouldn't align with each other. So we'd come in and align with the insurance or – I don't think we ever aligned with the realtors, 'cause Gale just couldn't. When we'd align with the insurance companies, we'd be betting against the banks. Next time there'd be some insurance thing and we'd align with the banks. And these guys, they could never get together. And they could never understand that we're hopping back and forth from one side of the fence to the other as powerbrokers. So we got all kinds of different resolutions or whatever that damn thing did. We were power brokers. Which didn't amount to a hill of beans, but we had a lot of fun doing it.

    George Knight: Gale was going from local and state to national, and broadening her scope. They took a busload of people down to Springfield a couple of times to get it passed. With Chicago's backing, it passed pretty quickly. It was a pretty simple enumeration kind of thing. It certainly became more complex as it moved to the federal level and then more institutions were wrapped up in it. But it started off as a fairly simple thing. You just had to report where you had made your loans.

    The bankers all learned. With the Woodstock Institute, graduate students doing research, it was <u>lethal</u> data the way they were preparing it. So the bankers became much more sophisticated about when did you actually apply for the loan versus when you had inquired. And all this kind of game playing that went on certainly expanded enormously after the federal legislation.

From *DISCLOSURE* #9 (July 1975)
Illinois Passes State Disclosure.

    It was a good day in the State's Capitol for Chicago residents and community groups.

    The continued efforts of MAHA leadership to inform the Springfield Legislature about redlining, FHA foreclosures and abandonment problems were rewarded. The General Assembly passed three pieces of anti-redlining legislation which are presently awaiting the Governor's signature.

    Disclosure Legislation requires that banks, savings and loans and mortgage bankers disclose semi-annually the dollar amount of home mortgages and home improvement loans made by zip code and by census tract. The type of loan, either mortgage or home improvement, must be specified.

    With the Governor's signature, the Fairness in Lending Bill makes redlining illegal in the State of Illinois.

    In addition, because of an amendment to the Savings and Loan Act, the Commissioner of Savings and Loans will have the authority to refuse relocation applications if that relocation would leave the area without adequate credit availability.

MAHA leaders also fought long and hard to keep two bills relating to FHA fast foreclosure and abandonments alive. These new bills were passed by the House as Committee Bills to be voted on by the Senate in the fall when they next convene.

According to Gale Cincotta, co-chairperson of the MAHA Mortgage Coalition, "community groups from throughout the Chicago area, Peoria and Rockford are to be lauded for making the State respond to the people's needs."

From *The Grass-Roots Battle Against Redlining: From the Streets to the Halls of Congress* (NTIC, 1975)

Results of initial disclosure data obtained through Chicago's city ordinance for 1973 — A comparison of the total housing investment in 1973 was only 1.5% of banks' savings deposits from Chicago neighborhoods. The study further shows that even when the Chicago banks do invest in housing, most of the money goes to the Northside Lake Shore and suburban developments. 83% of the investments by the reporting banks went out to these areas, while only 17% of the housing loans were made in the communities between the lakeshore and the suburbs.

All across the country, the bankers are crying that disclosure is too expensive for them to do. Yet in Chicago, we find that at least 41 banks found the incentive of holding city funds strong enough to compensate for any additional costs of disclosure. (12)

This battle started at the roots: the neighborhoods of our cities. To be won successfully the war must be waged at the national level by a network of community leaders. Locally we have hassled individual lending institutions at the peak hours of business; we have threatened to withdraw our savings; we have visited lending and regulatory officials at their homes; we have pursued municipal and state legislation. All these tactics have drawn local attention to the problem of redlining. In some cases, these individual fights have resulted in a few neighborhoods receiving home loans and mortgages. But we cannot rely on individual lending institutions to save our neighborhoods. We cannot monitor every financial institution to see if they honor commitments they made when the controversy was the hottest. We must coordinate all these local efforts and focus on national legislation and regulation. (14)

Helen Murray: Then, of course, there was HMDA. That was one of our agendas right away; we wanted disclosure. We had the first anti-redlining law in the country, in Illinois, but it's off the books now, preempted by the federal. We got the city ordinance but then we wanted the state. See there were quite a few state-chartered banks in Illinois. So we were organizing for disclosure in Illinois and an anti-redlining law in Illinois. We were organizing for a redlining law nationally and a disclosure law nationally. We wanted it all! When we were organizing in Illinois, we had a governor, Dan Walker, who brought in a lot of progressive people with him -- a lot of new people to the legislature, which was a blessing because we have some people in Illinois politics. A lot of the people that came in with Walker are still around 30 years later.

CHAPTER 10

"You gotta have an outcome."

THE FORD FOUNDATION AND OTHER SUPPORTERS

Anita Miller was the "adventurous philanthropist" Program Officer at The Ford Foundation responsible for funding Gale's operation at NTIC. She subsequently directed the South Bronx program for Local Initiatives Support Corp (LISC) and also became Acting Chairman of the Federal Home Loan Bank Board: I really loved what I saw at the NHS in Pittsburgh. They had a couple of bankers out there who were incredible guys who were true believers, largely [Harold] Tweedy. I came back and I said to Lou Winnick, "I think we should fund this." But also I said, "There are this many bank districts in this country. What we want to do over time is have one NHS in each of the 12 bank districts. Because all of these lenders are going to say, "Oh, this was a unique situation. It can't happen here!" So he said, "Well, let's get started and we'll see."

Mike Sviridoff was then a vice president at Ford. He was Lou's boss and my boss. He started LISC [Local Initiatives Support Corporation]. Sviridoff said to me, "Go do an NHS in Washington and in Baltimore." I convinced Bill Whiteside that it was a good thing to do because you could get the Congressional leadership on the bus and get them to Baltimore in very quick time. It was the best one in the country outside of Chicago.

Oh, of course, Chicago. Bruce Gottschall. But Chicago always did everything great in housing. They still do, to this day, the best work in the country. We couldn't take people to Chicago—but to Baltimore we could take them. It really turned out to be a very, very, very good program.

Michael Westgate: The Ford Foundation played a key role in NTIC being able to expand beyond Chicago, similar to that of the Catholic Church and the Stern Family Fund in the early years. At the request of Lou Winnick, the Ford Foundation allowed us complete access to their archives for the purpose of writing this book. The Ford Foundation files were fascinating because they included not only the proposals and the letters back and forth, but also the internal discussions at Ford and in-house evaluations by staff and consultants of the effectiveness of NTIC – what they're doing well, what they're not doing well, whether or not we should fund them for another year. We got several thousand pages from Ford. Ford's initial grant to HTIC on Feb 5, 1976 was $125,000, slightly more than HTIC had requested.

The Ford Foundation also played a major role in the formation of the Urban Reinvestment Task Force, chartered by Congress in 1978 as the Neighborhood Reinvestment Corporation, now operating as NeighborWorks America. The Task Force was progenitor of the NHS programs in Chicago and elsewhere. By 2000, more than 240 NeighborWorks organizations were operating in all 50 states.

But in 1975, Whiteside was under fire from within the Federal Home Loan Bank System for pushing the envelope too far.

Bill Whiteside: This memo had been sent out saying that we were going to phase down at the end of starting up these programs. But Preston Martin was still there when three Ford Foundation program officers—Lou Winnick, who was their top U.S. guy, Anita Miller and Bob Chandler—came in and talked to Preston Martin and the other two board members and said, "You guys really have something here. Don't lose the NHS program. We're supporting it. We think you're really breaking new ground for government and urban problems. You can't just drop it."

And Pres called me in and said, "I talked to them and they're certainly right. But we can't do it by ourselves. We've got to have some company." I said, "Well, I'm working in Dallas and it would certainly help to get the banks in there. Could we maybe try to get the Federal Reserve in?" He said, "Yeah. And the Comptroller of the Currency and the FDIC." And I said, "Well, it would help a lot." And he said, "Well, write a letter. I'll sign it." So he wrote to Arthur Burns, Chairman of the Fed, also to the Chairman of the FDIC and the Comptroller of the Currency. They all agreed to come in and so that's when the Urban Reinvestment Task Force was born.

It was because, as a Nixon official, Pres was taking too much heat for being out in front.

The others did not provide any funding. The most important thing they did was that every new program we started began with a luncheon hosted by the regional Federal Home Loan Bank, the regional office of the FDIC, the regional office of the Comptroller of the Currency and the regional Federal Reserve Bank. Bank presidents respond to invitations like that! They're either chartered by those institutions or they're regulated by them. So that was magic in terms of getting the financial institutions involved. You could not overrate that.

A kind of mystique evolved. Pres Martin said it was all right. Arthur Burns told me when I called on him in followup to the letter, "I know about your work. I was on a plane coming to Washington that stopped in Pittsburgh and a young man [Tom Jones] sat next to me with mud on his shoes. He told me that he was Director of Neighborhood Housing Services in Pittsburgh and that he was coming to a meeting with you. He had to crawl under a house and inspect the foundation on his way to the airport. I told the President, President Nixon, about this and about the man with mud on his shoes. And how real and practical and meaningful this program was."

Once, I was on the phone in Dallas and the operator interrupted me. We were stuck in Dallas for not having the banks involved. I was talking to someone locally. And a voice said, "This is the Government of the United States. I'm so and so at the Federal Reserve. I'm calling at the direction of Arthur Burns, Chairman Arthur Burns. And we have made appointments for you with the three largest banks in Dallas. Would you please call and confirm these appointments." ... Glory days!

Anita Miller: Just about the time I was joining the Ford Foundation there was a big meeting in Chicago about FHA. Gale and others had called this meeting and had invited groups from across the country. They did not know how many were going to come. Obviously a thousand people came.

The first big meeting was when they sent out the word: "It ain't us, it's the FHA and we're being blamed for what the federal policies are. Once you put FHA only into a neighborhood that means it's going downhill. There's no place for private money, private people pull out."

I was not yet on at the Ford Foundation as the housing person. So they sent out somebody else, a consultant, who came back and said, "This is a rowdy mob. The Ford Foundation can't do anything with this group. These are not our kind of people." Meantime I thought it was great! Which is why the consultant was no longer in the job and I was brought into the job. Because I had been working with a group in East Harlem and I really understood what was going on in the real world.

NTIC came to Ford for money and I got their request. I went to Lou Winnick and I said, "You know, they're doing good stuff." And he said, "We can't touch them in a million years. It's one thing to confront. We only fund people who have solutions and who are willing to work with others to bring about solutions." And this was perfectly legitimate. I mean nobody from any of the big legitimate foundations would just fund confrontation. They are always looking for outcome.

So on my own, I was the Ford Foundation, I said to Lou, "I'm going out to meet with her." And I met with Gale and Shel over breakfast. They both told me that neither one of them had any life insurance for their families. They were not even drawing down a salary, or much of a salary. And they had no money and they wanted to continue the work. So I said to them, "You gotta have an outcome!" I had then begun to fund the Neighborhood Housing Services programs in Baltimore. Brought another foundation in to do Cincinnati. We were doing Oakland, Washington, D.C.

So I said, "You know, the logical thing is that you confront and the banks and the federal system then go forward with Neighborhood Housing Services. And what you've done is you've then accomplished what you set out to do. You're bringing mortgage credit into your neighborhood." So that was the beginning.

Then the proposals come in to me and they were the worst proposals I ever saw. But they didn't care about writing proposals. So I said to Gale, "How would you feel if I edited your proposals?" She said, "Go ahead. Do it." I turned around, rewrote her proposal, sent it back to her. And I said, "You are free to change anything and everything that's in this proposal. But I think this is really what you want to say. And, if it isn't, it's okay. Make it what you want to say." She never changed a word.

From the Ford Foundation Archives
HTIC Technical Assistance Proposal (March 5, 1975)

The technical assistance aspect of HTIC has increasing demands placed upon it as many cities move beyond the surface aspect of urban decay to the strategies needed for creative workable programs, not only to stem the tide of blight and deterioration, but to reverse the process to the point of urban reclamation. The expertise of the HTIC staff has moved beyond the point of merely raising the issue; HTIC now deals in the area of practical solutions. This can best be documented by the direct involvement of HTIC with the Urban Reinvestment Task Force in establishing the Neighborhood Housing Services (NHS) program in Chicago... REQUEST TO FORD: $119,000 over two years.

From HTIC proposal to the Ford Foundation (September 18, 1975) [Proposal rewritten with assistance from Ford Foundation staff and resubmitted on November 13, 1975.]

The time has come when the community can no longer merely assume a negative position on issues. It must now have the research and technical assistance which will result in a positive role for the community in correcting the problem. A new type of organizing is called for which goes beyond the stage of confrontation to the stage of negotiation. We visualize the next step as being the state of partnership in which the private and public sectors will sit down with communities to jointly assume responsibility for the development of workable programs. As more community leaders and organizers are trained in this approach, neighborhood preservation and revitalization will accelerate significantly. (13-14)

To date, much of the work of HTIC has been crisis-oriented and this factor has lessened our effectiveness. It is hoped that a new influx of resources will serve to alleviate this problem by providing sufficient staff to prepare for and deal with relevant issues. (16)

Anita Miller: Back came the proposal. I had a proposal then. It went into the file and I was able to fund her and fund her and fund her. And that really gave them the credibility to raise more money.

From Ford Foundation Program Action documents (January 12, 1976) Recommending a $125,000 grant over two years to HTIC:
As an agency which has been both nurtured and funded by the National Center for Urban Ethnic Affairs ($50,000 over two years), HTIC was included in a recent National Affairs evaluation of the NCUEA by Lewis Feldstein. The evaluator points out the centrality of Gale Cincotta to the work of HTIC, her effectiveness in raising lessons learned in Chicago to a national level, and her ability to work with other cities and other local groups – particularly ethnic communities that have had only limited and recent experience in translating concern into community action. He reports further that HTIC's success with these groups has not involved exacerbation of racial issues; to the contrary, the organization continues to maintain a heavily multi-racial makeup both in Chicago and nationally.

Feldstein also interviewed lenders in both Chicago and Washington – initially HTIC adversaries in the difficult Chicago disclosure controversy, but now active partners in the Neighborhood Housing Services effort. The words used for how bankers view Mrs. Cincotta is "respected." They see her as someone "capable of understanding the needs and limits of her opposition, of compromising and shifting tactics when necessary."

Weaknesses pointed out by Feldstein are largely in the HTIC technical assistance and training program and are attributed to a shortage of funds and the resultant need to stretch an overly thin staff. Similarly, in the area of research – while quality is deemed high – in-house capacity had remained limited – again due to insufficient funding. It is in the interest of meeting these needs that a grant to HTIC is proposed.

In just three years HTIC has become a significant voice on behalf of fraying inner city neighborhoods. Its leadership has proved equally credible to minority groups, white working-class homeowners and financial institutions and legislative bodies.

Foundation staff have monitored the growth of HTIC carefully with two inter-related questions in mind: 1. Would HTIC move responsibly into hard programmatic activities? 2. Would HTIC – under the tutelage of the Foundation-funded NCUEA – continue to play an important bridging role between white ethnic urban dwellers and their new minority neighbors? Both questions have been answered affirmatively.

A two-year grant in the amount of $125,000 would permit the organization to enhance its research and technical assistance capacity and to mount a structured training program for personnel from conservation-minded, urban working-class neighborhoods across the country.

Anita Miller: The sad thing was – this does not have a happy ending – when I went off to Washington to become a member of the Federal Home Loan Bank Board, Franklin Thomas took over the Ford Foundation. The work that I was doing was assigned to someone named Bernie McDonald. And it was just at the point in time when Gale wanted to take on the insurance companies in the same way that they had taken on the banks and the savings and loans.

Of course the insurance companies were buying all of these mortgages that were being originated from all over the country. Freddie and Fanny were really not big players then, but the insurance companies were huge. And Bernie never got it. He never really got it that what they had done with the banks and the savings and loans, they had to do with the insurance companies. The thing about the insurance companies was they were scared out of their minds that they would be regulated by the federal government. They were only regulated by state agencies. So the leverage that Gale had would have been enormous, but it never happened.

Michael Westgate: Gale may have missed an opportunity to bring the insurance companies under a CRA umbrella—but would they have been a more formidable opponent in Congress than the banking industry? Forewarned about CRA, were they preparing a greater defense?

Anita Miller: I don't know what other sources she got money from to do the insurance companies and if they ever did them, but it's a question. It's a shame. I would have kept funding her. I just felt that there was nobody else who had done what she had done. And my portfolio at Ford at that time was saving the existing housing stock. That meant public housing. That meant existing neighborhoods. And it meant the management of publicly assisted housing. It really was pretty wide open. You know at Ford when you don't have a general subject area, you have to write a program paper about how you're going to spend money in a particular area. And it changes every five or six or seven years.

So I had the existing housing stock, securing the future of the existing housing stock – which meant all these neighborhoods that were being mobilized by NTIC. So that's the story of how Gale began to sit-in or picket the homes of the presidents of the Federal Home Loan Banks in the morning and negotiate with their members in the afternoon – because she had to have an outcome.

So when I left Ford that was the end of funding for NTIC. But, you know, sometimes I think if I hadn't done that, they would have gotten the insurance companies. But I figure they would have gotten them anyway. I didn't know that was going to happen.

Michael Westgate: In pushing Gale towards outcomes, Ford had a positive influence, both on NTIC and on NHS. Gale was fortunate to have Anita advocating for her, but Anita's enthusiasm for Gale was not shared by Lou Winnick, her boss at Ford. When asked for comments for this book about Gale, all Lou had to say was that she was a "flaming liberal and not on the same political wavelength" as him, at all.

Anita Miller: I'll tell you how Neighborhood Reinvestment Corporation was created. That was the Urban Reinvestment Task Force. That was the beginning of whatever it is now [since renamed NeighborWorks America].

I get a call from Bill Whiteside that they want to have federal money and Proxmire's going to hold hearings. So I go to Lou Winnick and I said, "Should we testify? They want me to testify." He said, "Absolutely. They're a grantee. You're familiar with the program. You can testify."

If it had not been for Gale having sensitized Proxmire, and Proxmire understanding what the Urban Reinvestment Task Force was all about, I'm not sure he would have been out there, to create and fund the Neighborhood Reinvestment Corporation. Bill may have gotten to Proxmire, but I think that Gale intervened and educated him, and Proxmire could see the value.

Then I was on the Neighborhood Housing Services of America board for a while, before I went to the Bank Board.

Michael Westgate: It's interesting that Ford was funding the protagonist, Gale, at the same time that you were funding the solution through Mary Lee Widener at NHSA.

Anita Miller: Yeah. Of course, that's exactly what I was doing! And that was what I <u>intended</u> to do. But I could never say that. I can remember once saying to Winnick, "Gee, isn't this a great strategy?" He said, "We're not supposed to have strategies like that." I said, "Okay." But that was what it was all about.

Ann Vick-Westgate: I would hope Ford <u>did</u> have strategies like that.

Anita Miller: Not really. You did when you were supporting civil rights groups for them to carry on their work. But here we were supporting two groups to be in conflict with one another and through the conflict resolution come up with a good program for the country. It was different.

That is exactly what I did, because without Gale, Bill Whiteside would not have been as successful. Without him, she would have had nowhere to go. She really contributed enormously to the success of Neighborhood Housing

Services because she put all those lenders, all those Federal Home Loan Banks, on notice that they <u>had</u> to pay attention.

Michael Westgate: Well, that's how I got to go to Chicago. There had been demonstrations and a recognition that something had to be done.

What made Gale such a special person? Why was she so successful? And why have there not been many Gales out there? What does it take to help another Gale rise from the next generation?

Anita Miller: Well, Gale was a genuine leader. She had every leadership quality you'd ever want to see in anybody. She was gutsy. She was not afraid to confront power and she had the ability to rally people around her. She was very incisive. She could see through a whole lot of "stuff" and call and see who could deal with the core issues. When she saw it, she wasn't afraid to go after it. Name it and go after it. She was very selfless. She was truly passionate about the neighborhoods. She was colorblind at a time when not everybody was colorblind. She was working with African Americans, Latinos and it didn't matter to her. Am I right?

When Gale called that first National Housing Conference at St. Sylvester's, Chicago, in March 1972, it was incredible. "It's not us. It's them!" That was what she said that resonated with everybody. And they didn't know her. She was an unknown at the time. She was a wonderful woman.

Gale accepting *Ms. Magazine's* national award as one of the top ten women in the USA in 1985.

She got some award in Washington [as one of *Ms. Magazine's* "Women of the Year" in 1985] and I was invited to the dinner. I was never so honored in my life that she would think to invite me. Here I am, this Ford Foundation program officer, the Member and Acting Chairman of the Federal Home Loan Bank Board, and I was truly honored that she invited me. It was a way of her saying, "I recognize all that you did for our movement." But I did it for the movement because I believed in it. I believed that that was the only way.

But when I got to New York I saw the implications of it all. And I had an anger in me, like Gale did. Although you can't display that when you're a Ford Foundation program officer, I had firsthand been involved in trying to make sure we addressed the injustices of the society.

Then along come this woman with all of this energy and so direct and right on! I just admired her and I admired the organization that she led. And Shel, my God, what a lieutenant he was! You can't leave out Shel. He was a very good tactician. Am I right?

I think people respected him a lot. He's the one who got his hands the most dirty. He was like the operating guy; she was the visionary. She was out front and he was the operating guy. I'm not sure she would have been the great Gale without him. I just thought she was wonderful.

How she felt inside I don't know. But on the outside, she was absolutely fearless. If she were not as self-confident, she could not have gotten other people to do the things they did, like picketing on a weekend the house of the president of the Federal Home Loan Bank of Chicago. I mean getting people on a bus to go out there. She was their leader. If she wasn't so confident, they would have never done it.

Michael Westgate: Andy Shaw interviewed Gale for the *Sunday Chicago Sun-Times* ("She smiles, shouts for neighborhoods" – July 11, 1976). In the article Gale maintained, regardless of her increasing national prominence, that she still was just a mother and daughter with responsibilities at home. When Shaw questioned her on her hardnosed tactics, Gale replied, "What we've always used is good data, good research and confrontation. If it means losing rather than get angry, I get angry."

Gale carried no baggage, which was a big advantage. She took no federal funding for anything in those early years. She was free to engage targets of opportunity where most of us are constrained by whatever context we're working in. I was Executive Director of a Neighborhood Housing Services (NHS) program in the Boston area for twelve years as well as having the experience of working years earlier with Anita, Gale and others at the beginning of NHSA. But Gale would just see an opportunity with much more clarity than I did. She could identify where the power was and go after it.

She would always state the problem clearly in a way that other people, whether they were sophisticated or not, could understand. She might not have a solution, but she damn well knew what the problem was. And she thought she knew who should solve it, and she'd say it.

Anita Miller: Gale Cincotta from Chicago had more to do with the rescue of urban neighborhoods in this country over the last decades than any other single human being. Thanks to her confrontational style, the Congress was forced to pass the Community Reinvestment Act which held financial intermediaries – banks and Fannie Mae and Freddie Mac and the whole savings world and the people who regulated it – accountable for the fact that they were withholding the flow of mortgage credit to distressed and working-class neighborhoods thereby crippling them or crippling their opportunities.

To lead picketing at the home of bank regulators showed a passion for the accountability of everyone involved in destroying neighborhoods. She was absolutely incisive. She saw the world as it truly was and made other people see it that way. She was an outstanding human being.

I told you I loved her. There was just nobody else like her. I did good things. Before I even went to the Ford Foundation, I worked with a group in East Harlem that turned out to be a big disappointment. We did a lot of redevelopment on some key blocks and I learned a lot in the process. But this woman was very, very special. I was able to confront—but not like her.

To be able to confront she needed to organize the minions, people by the thousands who could be called upon. And she did that. Now she had other people who worked, but she led this whole movement. And without her inspiration, it wouldn't have happened. I nominated Gale for a MacArthur fellowship. She should have gotten it but didn't.

I had a perfect rational for funding Gale's work. There was no problem at all. It went forward. I talked about them as being an organization of neighborhoods in Chicago that were working to bring in mortgage credit. They had developed a modus operandi with the Neighborhood Reinvestment Corporation, at that time the Urban Reinvestment Task Force. And we already were funding the NHSs. If she could focus on outcome – go beyond confrontation and focus on outcome – she would get funding from us and everybody else in the world. And that's what happened.

When I sat at the breakfast with Gale and Shel, I can remember sitting in this cruddy diner-restaurant in Chicago. I must have been out there on other business and tucked this breakfast in. They told me they didn't have any health insurance for their families. And Shel was supporting a family. She at least had her husband's income. Here was all this devotion and all this energy and all this commitment and his family was paying a very big price for it. In most nonprofits there's somebody with some support, a spouse or another. They don't go on the breadline.

Anyway, it was a very good breakfast. It really was. The thing is they took it to heart. They realized that I was a friend and that what I was telling them was to help them. Then, of course, I followed through on every commitment I ever made. Which is very important

Ann Vick-Westgate: And you provided sustaining support. It wasn't the "We'll be right with you for three years and then you're on your own."

Anita Miller: This breakfast was probably in '72. I went to Washington in '78. I hung in as long as I could and I would have kept hanging in.

From the Ford Foundation Archives
A Monitoring Report: The National Training and Information Center by
**Robert Kolodny prepared at the request of the National Affairs Division of
the Ford Foundation (June, 1977)**

There is no simple analog for NTIC, no equivalent organizational
type to which it can be compared.

NTIC is closely identified and indeed shares home office and key
staff with two other organizations: The Metropolitan Area Housing Alliance
(MAHA) and National People's Action (NPA). It is often important to
emphasize the interrelatedness and inter-dependence of the three entities.

The formal training program is new with the Ford grant, but
apparently it has roots in a three times a year training program that Catholic
Charities used to run in Chicago for organizers. These were operated under
the aegis of the Chicago Mid-America Institute, primarily drawing people
from the Midwest in the Catholic Charities network. Their program phased
out at the same time NTIC began to run its school.

The only basic criteria is interest in community work. But the
general principal seems to be, in this part of NTIC's work as in much of
the rest, "not to say no." Various members of the staff point with pride to
a number of occasions where saying "yes" to people without credentials or
any sign of special qualifications has resulted in substantial breakthroughs on
neighborhood and housing issues in other cities. They argue that there is no
real way to know ahead of time what is going to pay off and what is not; so
except for screening out obvious "crazies" and people who totally misconceive
the purpose of the program, all comers are welcome.

This is an organizer's program; there is no mistaking that.
Neighborhood problems and how to deal with them are discussed, and the
uses and abuses of public programs as well as techniques of local program
development are reviewed, but the real appeal is to people who are interested
in careers as organizers, and the subject matter is the theory and practice
of community organization. One respondent who is well acquainted with
the training program commented that it is the very essence of community
organization work to be flexible, to be able to roll with the punches, and this
flexibility, he feels, appropriately characterizes the training sessions.

But strategies for program development and dealing with specific
issues are emphasized at an increasing number of leadership training and
special issue conferences NTIC has mounted in the last year. The most recent
and perhaps most successful example is the "State Strategies for Housing"
conference held in Chicago in February of 1977. This two-day event was
cosponsored by the Committee on Illinois Government. State legislators from
15 states and the Virgin Islands made up the bulk of those who attended,

along with staff members from regulatory bodies and housing agencies in 11 states. The program focused on the issue of redlining and disinvestment and was intended to inform participants on mortgage disclosure and the role of regulatory agencies. The NTIC staff itself was astonished at how little information state legislators and regulators had on the issues discussed. A similar but smaller three-day conference on mortgage disclosure was held in November 1976 primarily for city officials. In January 1977 the Catholic Charities National Staff was brought to Chicago for a program on the same general themes. NTIC has also run several one-day seminars for university faculty, which are essentially an attempt to introduce them to NTIC as a resource.

Their ability to continually tailor their basic formats to suit varying audiences and their willingness to constantly adapt and make it available in modes appropriate to the needs of different groups is noteworthy. My own and I think my fellow participants' reaction to the quarterly training programs is perhaps best summed up by a comment in one of the written evaluations: "a good course, which could be a great course." The events and material that come through as having most impact and value to participants are those involving a direct experiential sort of learning, as distinguished from didactic elements.

The second element that comes through most powerfully is the role model that the staff itself presents. They come across, in my experience and as best can be judged from the written evaluations, as authentic and committed people who know what they are doing and how to do it, and do it for the most part with integrity and élan. There is no one among them so self-important or full of themselves that they are not accessible to the trainees and willing to talk honestly and directly with them. The absence of posturing and noblesse oblige is, it seems to me, a substantial virtue.

NTIC had no real model for their training program when they started it, except for what may have been provided by the Catholic Charities precedent and the personal educational experiences of the training staff themselves. Most if not all of them learned community work through apprenticing to a senior organizer in a Chicago community, a venerable type of schooling which has produced a cadre of organizers that no other city can match. This tradition is extremely strong, and is a source of pride – in my judgment, rightfully so.

NTIC's research program is issue and action oriented and only distantly related to what would be considered research at an academic institution, or a research department in a government agency. In line with its objective, however, it produces an extremely high caliber of work. Much of the work the research staff does never gets published, nor was it intended to.

Their main function is to provide briefing and information backup to others, particularly to the lead organizers operating on behalf of NTIC, MAHA and NPA, as well as to generate studies and reports of general usefulness to the NTIC network around the country. Perhaps what is most notable about the research activity is the fact that it is taken seriously by the overall NTIC operation and plays so important a role in its work.

A good part of the consultation to other community groups continues to be free, piggybacked onto trips being made to paying clients or for other reasons, and often involves sleeping in some host's home and generally accepting potluck as a substitute for daily maintenance. Indeed Gale claims that she agrees to sit on many organization's boards as a means of getting around the country. Since fare to attend board meetings is paid, she is able to tag on visits with members of the network and sometimes to potential funding sources for NTIC.

According to NTIC's own records, the staff had 42 separate speaking engagements in 1976, ranging from lectures at universities to being the featured speaker at a neighborhood congress held in another city. Beyond that, NTIC was requested to testify at seven House or Senate committee hearings in Washington, five legislative or regulatory agency hearings at the city and state level, a hearing sponsored by the Federal Reserve System, and three separate HUD hearings. In addition, throughout the spring the staff testified at both Democratic and Republican platform hearings around the country.

A simple, and I dare say undisputed, observation to be made about NTIC is that it accepts and indeed creates for itself a staggering workload. Even if one discounts by fifty per cent what one sees and hears at the NTIC office and the staff's own report of its activity, it would still be an enormous undertaking. What is more, NTIC continues to expand what it does at a rapid rate, this despite the fact that it has no promise of support for the additional staff it needs to pursue at a human pace what it has outlined for itself.

NTIC believes in the local mass organization of citizens and in the development of a cadre of people who have organizing skills as pre-requisites to the resolution of the housing and neighborhood issues that it has taken on. Indeed, for NTIC, organization precedes program development as a philosophical principle.

NTIC is in the admirable if highly pressured situation of being the supplier of what its own activities create a demand for. Thus NTIC's work is self-reinforcing, which as it is successful keeps on generating more demand for each of its products: viable organizations and coalitions, organizers, informed leadership, research, information, and above all creating tactics and strategies for generating short term improvements and fundamental reforms in the long term.

Chicago is unlike any city in the United States that I know of, in the number and size of mass-membership, neighborhood organizations capable of sustaining themselves over time.

In fact it is very difficult to get firm titles for people. It appears that they vary according to the particular task that is being undertaken or the particular audience that is being spoken to. NTIC has no compartments serving to separate key individuals from each other. The staff members relate to each other primarily in network fashion, direct contact being made between those people who are most concerned with a task, with no particular piece of business necessarily going through any one individual. That is to say the acknowledged leadership, Gale and Shel, are kept informed, but much work goes on without their "clearing" it. Much of this defies the usual rules of organizational life. What is more, salary is not necessarily commensurate with role.

Two individuals with whom I spoke and who are privy to the internal deliberations of the organization confirmed my own general impressions. No one doubts that the leadership of the organization rests with Gale Cincotta, but that is a reflection of her acknowledged competence and creativity, and is not simply a matter of title or status.

Most of my informants are full of admiration for the amount of work that gets done by NTIC. Indeed, the comment of one is that a large number of people across the nation overestimate its power and strength. His view is that it is consistently at the very margin of doing all that it can possibly do with the manpower that it has. In effect, it is attempting to keep a national network of organizations alive essentially on the staff work of half-a-dozen people.

It is my strong sense that NTIC has made some fundamental conceptual and organizational breakthroughs towards dealing with urban housing and neighborhood problems in the U.S. They have had a number of practical successes in terms of dealing with FHA abuses and other problems created or abetted by federal programs in older neighborhoods. They have also had surprising initial success in putting red-lining on the national agenda and getting legislation passed which, while weak in itself, symbolizes a substantial breakthrough in terms of popularly identifying credit and credit allocation as central to the urban crisis. But these achievements are fairly well known and have been fairly well documented (although NTIC has perhaps not been given as much credit as it may deserve – according to fairly neutral observers NTIC did much of the hard research and organizing work, only to have credit go to other groups). What may be less obvious and less well understood, is the extent to which they may have refashioned the Chicago model of community mobilization to deal with neighborhood issues as they are manifested in the

1970s. Their major contribution appears to be linking of organization with community development, and the shattering of the "turf rule" in C. O. work

While Trapp was not directly trained by Alinsky or at the Industrial Areas Foundation (IAF), he was tutored by Alinsky-trained workers. Trapp and all of the younger staff in the office, most of whom he trained, acknowledge Alinsky as the original source. Nevertheless, in two important respects NTIC has transcended what is understood to be the classic IAF approach. They deliberately attempt to link community organization with community development program activity and program delivery. This linking is a violation of what is thought to be the pure Alinsky approach to community organization, which rejects programs and service delivery and concentrates entirely on political organization and the mobilization of neighborhood power.

Alinsky's original rule is to organize strictly on a neighborhood basis, focusing solely on neighborhood issues. Thus there is within some of the traditional groups in Chicago, a great resistance to coalition building. The "turf principle" is supreme. Gale, however, apparently learned from her own early PTA and neighborhood experience what you cannot do, operating only at the neighborhood level. Indeed, the early Alinsky approach made some sense when neighborhoods still had viable institutions and the resources of these institutions could be captured or mobilized toward neighborhood improvement. However, the increasing centralization of power and resources, both on a metropolitan scale and in society at large, along with the decline of neighborhood institutions in older urban areas, have left the parochial Alinsky-style organizer bereft. However, staff at NTIC also understand, and this seems to be essential, that without an organized local base and local accountability, the reach for authority and resources at the city, state or national level is likely to become increasingly alienated from the felt needs of the locality.

What distinguishes Gale's and Shel's work, according to just about everyone I have spoken to save their few sharp critics, is their ability to operate vertically. They begin with neighborhood-based organizations (and the way issues are experienced and understood by local leadership) but they have somehow welded these organizations into MAHA, a metropolitan coalition that is hardly perfect but that is able to act on common issues and negotiate on a citywide basis. MAHA, with NTIC support, also organizes at the state level on issues of mutual concern. But perhaps their most remarkable achievement has been NPA, the national coalition of neighborhood and citywide groups, and their ability to affect federal policy in Washington through the mobilization of this network.

The judgment of a staff member of the Proxmire committee is that the Mortgage Disclosure Act of 1975, HMDA, which is conceded even by critics of NPA to be their victory, was one of the few major pieces of legislation in recent memory passed by consumer action that derived primarily from the local level.

NTIC's special promise, it seems to me, is the ability to bridge wide divisions, both spatially and conceptually.

Of NTIC's total income, some $30,000, or 10%, is raised directly through its own activities. It is not clear how much direct income from NTIC activities can be augmented, particularly in view of the inability of many of those it serves to pay more than the nominal fees.

Gale and Shel attribute some of their money problems to their tendency to do what circumstances call for, and to look for funding afterwards. They contrast themselves with groups which do not move until they are fully funded. Obviously they feel virtuous, if poor, in this regard. There is evidence that this is in fact one source of their chronic underfunded and understaffed condition. But the other source of the problem is their apparently limited success at fundraising, which they also acknowledge.

There is truth to the statement that they will often do something first and never get around to raise the funds for it; indeed they complain that other people often take credit for their work and sometimes get funds to continue it. But it is also apparent to me that as a group they are not very good at analyzing their own organization and communicating its achievements. They were able to communicate with me, but only in fragments, and while I was, as is evident, impressed with their operation and with the individuals involved, I had to pick up much of this by indirection. Their record keeping is extremely poor, partly because they regard follow-up as too costly (secretaries are at the bottom of their staff priority list). They argue that if you keep full records of everything you have done, and everyone you have seen, and how many people came in and out, this inevitably means you are not doing something else. Indeed, in terms of their budget and staffing pattern, it seems to me that both the quality and quantity of their work is high.

NTIC has a Board of Directors, but it does not meet or function as a group. Apparently the board members function as individual advisors to Gale and to a lesser degree Shel. That an augmented and more active board would be a significant contribution to NTIC is not certain. The organization functions adequately as it is, and is already held accountable by its grassroots constituency. Moreover, staff freedom is important in an organization like this which, after all, is not in a routine or very predictable line of work. Nevertheless, a somewhat larger board composed of outside supporters with national reputations and institutional credibility, could offer some protection against financial crisis and other threats to the organizations and might play a constructive role if issues of succession to leadership ever arise.

That there are tensions and strong competitive currents among the major elements in the neighborhood network becomes evident even to the uninitiated observer. NTIC has its critics among other activists, and some of them feel that the Chicago group has not been as ecumenical and mutually supportive as it could.

As NTIC has developed rather rapidly from a small Chicago-oriented group to one with a national constituency and a national press, it has required more financial support and felt itself entitled to more credit. Some feel it had achieved this at the expense of other groups and, especially in the case of the National Center for Urban Ethnic Affairs which acted as a mentor and conduit of resources in the early days, by biting the hands that fed it. Given the generally thin public and philanthropic support for this kind of activity, characterized as it is by militancy, the sense that they are in competition is probably realistic. My view, however, is that it is the vying for leadership that is the most important factor.

Some reduce the problem to strong personalities, rubbing against each other and preventing collaboration. Most agree there is no profit in or possibility of getting to the bottom of such mutual grievances. The matter of group identity may be slightly more accessible, since there is a fairly widespread feeling that there is a "Chicago style" which gives rise to a "Chicago clique." The fact that some of this resentment may be compounded of envy simply complicates the problem. But, whatever the sources, it presents a real issue in "foreign relations" for NTIC. If they aspire to be a Center for a national movement, as they clearly ought, it seems to me that they must attend to this appearance and/or reality of exclusivity and cliquishness and confront it seriously.

In terms of philosophy and approach the critics' most serious complaint is that NTIC is too confrontational in style and that it never really gets into program development. There is the feeling that the objective is sometimes to keep the pot boiling rather than to make progress and that more negotiations and less "mau-mauing" of public and private sector officials might lead to more real gains.

Cal Bradford: But Gale always liked to see what was going on and she could hear. She'd listen. It was just like being in a room with a family and they're all talking. And she would hear all those things. She's the original multi-tasker. All the stuff would filter through. She refused to ever let them restructure those offices. Every one they had – the two on Washington Avenue and the first one they had over by Catholic Charities – they were all those big open rooms. She just insisted that it be that way. She wanted people to bump into each other, to have to go by each other, to talk to each other.

Gale responded to people and she didn't really care. She knew that her neighborhoods were diverse, but she didn't care where the staff people came from. This is an organization that started in the early 1970s after the race riots in the cities. It started in organizing in racially changing neighborhoods.

One of the interesting things about this disclosure of information is Gale believed people could use it. Once more, she believed that it was important because neighborhood people needed to know because they were the only ones who really cared about their neighborhoods and, if they got it wrong, they suffered. "All these other liberals," she said, "who are trying to help us, it doesn't make any difference to them. 'It's not your neighborhood, it's not your ideas, to you it's just an abstract ideal. It's about feeling good, helping poor people. It doesn't make any difference to you personally whether our neighborhood survives or not.'" So she was right that, in the context of the way they tried to organize, they really did care more about the truth behind the facts, about whether they were true facts or not true facts because it was your life.

That's the thing that's so interesting is the information. Too bad our CIA doesn't work this way. Information really did flow to the top. And then with all those organizers, you'd look at the office structure. If you looked at the architecture of the way Gale insisted things be, it's interesting. They're all open spaces. She didn't want the cubicles when they had cubicles and all that stuff. Every office they've been in, her desk was in a place where she could see everybody else like a teacher. In their new office they can sneak off into the computer room. She didn't like that so much.

Michael Westgate: With Shel it was clear that, for an organizer, it was a priority for him to keep the pot boiling. How do you keep organizing people if the major problems have been solved? For Gale as a leader, it was important to point to accomplishments. She was more ready than he to move to the resolution stage. The tension between them was a constructive one, differing sometimes on timing and strategy but not on the ultimate goals which they shared. She could articulate problems and get to solutions, relying on Shel to rally the troops and make sure they got there.

From the Ford Foundation Archives
A Monitoring Report: The National Training and Information Center, **prepared at the request of the National Affairs Division of the Ford Foundation**

Robert Kolodny: My own view is that NTIC and the people that compose it are in fact more confrontational in style. But it seems to be a somewhat out-of-date view of where they are now to claim that they reject programs and community development. In many ways, the critics focus on Shel Trapp's influence in the organization, and in my view misinterpret it. Persons in Chicago who are probably most familiar with NTIC confirm that it is the strength of the partnership between Trapp and Cincotta that has made it work. Internal to the organization Trapp appears to enjoy equal status and have equal authority in most respects. Indeed, in some ways, Shel can take responsibility for Gale's emerging as a community leader and activist, since it was during the period he organized in Austin that she first came onto the public scene. Nevertheless, in terms of overall approach and philosophy and the perception of the world, Gale is the charismatic and dominant figure. Shel's own understanding of their teamwork is that it is Gale's function to know what the issues are. Like a good organizer, he sees her as the leadership in identifying what is moving people at the street level. One observer described Shel as coming back to Gale repeatedly, as if to an oracle, to get her version of what the emerging issues are. Only when she has sufficiently articulated them and made them concrete will he begin to think strategically and tactically, which is his forte.

One astute Washington observer of the Chicago group's activities points out that the key to understanding NTIC's success is that their militance is essentially tactical and not ideological. The substance of their demands can be seen as quite conservative at heart – safe neighborhoods, home ownership, civic responsibility. Their only real doctrines are democratic participation of those affected and accountability to them by elected officials and privately controlled institutions. Thus their pragmatic aims keep them in the mainstream, confusing and somewhat disarming the reaction to their very direct tactics and rhetoric.

The final issue with NTIC is one of process: the reported tendency toward staff domination of the organizations they help develop and the manipulation of other organizations and leaderships to achieve their national goals. My sense is that NTIC is manipulative in the sense that it tries to develop a larger strategy and stay ahead in planning terms of what is developing locally, but never to get so far ahead that the organizers take over from the leaders.

NTIC's command of organizing practice and of the issues, plus their tactical skill, are denied by virtually no one, not even their competitors and critics.

A final piece of evidence on NTIC is the regard with which it is held by a number of people who operate in other realms – in government, in the academic world, in research, in legal services, and in finance, banking, and development. It is regarded as an organization which can be worked with, which can be trusted, and which has a clear sense of its own mission.

From NTIC Response to Evaluation (October '77 letter to Anita Miller):
    Shel Trapp: The evaluation was helpful in that it gave us an opportunity to look at ourselves through someone else's eyes. We feel that Bob's analysis of our operation will be helpful not only in the immediate future but over the long haul as well.

    Bob is correct that we have a problem in this area (finances and fundraising) and we are attempting to correct it. We do not, however, see this as a "lovable weakness"; rather it is a matter of time and resources. It appears to me that a good part of fundraising consists of building and cultivating relationships with potential funding sources. We will meet with any funding source, but we simply do not have the time and resources to spend in developing relationships in the hope that some day it may become a new source of funding. [He includes a list of funding sources they have met with in September.] If some of these come through, we may be able to deal with the problem of record keeping.

    Regarding the Board, we are wrestling with the various suggestions which Bob raises. Because of our uniqueness, it is difficult to determine a workable solution. We must be able to maintain our flexibility to respond immediately to issues as they come up. We will be approaching John McKnight to see if he is willing to serve on the board. We have frequent conversations with Ron Grzywinski, but have never thought of him in the position of board member. I guess our basic problem is that our current structure has got us to this point, and we are nervous about doing anything that might jeopardize the effectiveness of the Center.

From the Ford Foundation Archives
Letter from Ford Foundation Program Officer Basil Whiting, Division of National Affairs at Ford, to Richard O. Ristine, Vice President and Secretary of the Lilly Endowment (January 8, 1976):
    Our discussions with Gale Cincotta were successfully concluded and we have this date made a two-year grant of $125,000 to HTIC. With our budgets being cut in half, this is about as much as we can do – in fact, it is $25,000 more than we intended, but her city and national operations look so good, her proposal is so solid, and the demands on her so great that we scraped up the extra amount.

    Pablo Eisenberg: At one point, during the end of Gale's tenure on our board at the Center for Community Change, we had a sharp disagreement. The Center and I were eminently successful in raising money at the same time that we attacked the foundations. I had just started the National Committee for Responsive Philanthropy. So while we took money on the one hand, we attacked foundations on the other.

There was always a lingering feeling in Gale that it was unfair. That here she was, on the firing lines, and we were sort of an intermediary. She couldn't get money and we did. I remember at one point going out to Allstate where Gale had held them up for a big chunk of money through intimidation and persuasion.

At the meeting, the program officer, a mid-level executive, said, "I talked about the Center for Community Change with Gale Cincotta and she said we shouldn't fund you." All I could say was, "Well, why don't you talk to some other people." I didn't say anything about Gale. I ended up going over her head and we got money. You know, a board member, for God's sake. "What the hell are you killing us or trying to kill us? And we're supporting you!"

I went to MacArthur on NTIC's behalf. I went to several other Chicago foundations on their behalf. I came back and told her, "Look. MacArthur has a legitimate point. MacArthur said you don't have a board of directors and they insist on nonprofit accountability." They originally convened a paper board of which my colleague Andy Mott was a founding member, but their board never met. It was clear neither Shel nor Gale wanted a board. I said, "You're not going to get any money from any of these foundations unless you have a board of directors. Now you don't have to have an intruding board but you have to have a board."

Well, Gale didn't like that. Then I got secondhand word that she was accusing us of undermining her at MacArthur. So I called her up and said, "Look. I mean we don't want to go to war with you. But if we have to go to war with you over foundations, we'll do it and we'll win. So why don't we meet in Chicago." So she and Shel and I had this long dinner, at her favorite Italian restaurant. We had a long, hard talk and the issue was resolved. But she always had that thing about "the money should go to me, not to anybody else." That was a little side of her that some people didn't see, but I think we still loved her. That was just part of her tough, fighting nature, the thing that made her so good.

We did work it through. The collaboration was mostly between Allen Fishbein and Gale and NTIC on the community reinvestment stuff, and the banking and lending. After that there was a little edge to our personal relationship. I took it as part of Gale. I'm not sure that she forgot entirely. But she was an important force and we supported her wherever we could.

Ann Vick-Westgate: What were the characteristics that made her effective?

Pablo Eisenberg: Well, Gale had guts. Very few in the nonprofit world have that. I mean you look around today nonprofit leadership is totally gutless and mostly ineffective. She also had a vision. She knew what she wanted to accomplish and set out organizing strategies to do that. But, interestingly enough, she could compromise with the powers that be when it was necessary. So she had a good sense of strategy. And, in a sense, people always thought of her as shooting from the hip but that wasn't the case. She and her cohorts did their homework. So they had the facts and they knew which banks were putting money where, and what the statistics were.

Ann Vick-Westgate: So was it her force that got CRA to a national agenda and to the Congress?

Pablo Eisenberg: I think so. NPA was the driving force for that and organized enough grassroots organizations that reached enough Congressmen that it made a pull. My sense is that the whole Home Mortgage Disclosure Act paved the way, and that was also largely Gale and her troops. So I think she deserves that "Mother of CRA" title. I mean she is the mother. It wasn't the only issue that she was on but that remained the sort of "leitmotif" of her NTIC push, other than Shel's doing organizing work trying to create new organizing groups and supporting them, mostly with Mott Foundation money.

Ann Vick-Westgate: Were the politics of confrontation a large part of what made her effective?

Pablo Eisenberg: Oh, absolutely. I think that's the only reason. The potential of confrontation is the reason Allstate's been in it. Aetna was a real different situation. I knew John Filer and folks at Aetna well. It was a combination that she was edgy and they didn't want to fool around with her. But the fact is that the philosophic folks at Aetna believed in it. Ironically enough, at one point they were our largest funder at the Center for Community Change.

We bought our building which is the oldest extant building in Washington, which is right at the foot of K Street and Wisconsin, dating back to 1751 only because Aetna was willing to give us within three weeks a $700,000 below-market mortgage, a loan. At the time the interest rate was fourteen and a half percent. And they gave it to us for nine and said, "Pay it back when you can." It was unparalleled and we haven't seen that in the corporate community since John Filer died. He died after he left Aetna. He chaired the most effective and well-known commission on philanthropy and public needs called the Filer Commission back in 1975.

So they funded her because both they didn't want to mess with Gale – and that was important. It was always "I don't want to mess with her" – and because they really believed. In fact they took out a half-page ad in several newspapers bragging that they were supporting Gale Cincotta. It was extraordinary.

So confrontation was absolutely essential. But that certainly was Shel Trapp's style of organizing. He came out of the quasi-Industrial Areas Foundation movement.

Ann Vick-Westgate: Shel's anger was initially more out of his own circumstances. Gale's anger was more at "them."

Pablo Eisenberg: Anger at the society. Yes, and that's why she kept it in rein. In a sense, yes, it was personal and she had had a hard life. But it was anger at the society and therefore it was a sort of seething anger that didn't blind her to good strategies and patience. For her, it was a long fight and she knew it.

Michael Westgate: What gave her the self-confidence in the early days?

Pablo Eisenberg: Gale started out as sort of a neighborhood mother, and rose up the ranks, and slowly felt her confidence coming. That sort of learning period, growing period, made a difference. Then it sort of built up, and success built on success. There was conviction that she was right, that her mission was honorable. That lends a lot of strength.

But the other thing was, she never had to rely on charm with anyone. She didn't have to pretend to play the cagey female come-on role, and all that. She was direct, and charm was not her attribute, and I think that made her stronger. So I think she conveyed to people that what they saw was the real thing, that she wasn't putting on any airs. She never put on airs. She was confident in herself and where she'd come from. She wasn't pretending to be fancy upper middle class.

Ann Vick-Westgate: What were Gale's weaknesses? What were the things that perhaps made her less effective?

Pablo Eisenberg: The one experience that Andy and I and others at the Center had about her accusing us of taking money away from NTIC. Despite the fact that at least I had gone to other foundations to try to raise money for her. It's not personal envy. It was sort of an annoyance that somehow this middle class guy had friends in the foundation world. I'm now the most reviled guy in fact. That somehow we couldn't take our CCC money over to her. And she knew what our finances were because she sat on the board. Sometimes she was annoyed that other folks would get publicity, be in the newspapers and headlines and stuff.

She was not a team player. And she was not a very good coalition player on issues that did not directly affect her particular issue or issues. We tried to get her involved in other coalitions. The Center for Community Change pulled together most of the major national coalitions related to poverty and race, issues like that.

The issue of race was an interesting one. Diversity was not the nature of her staff. She was criticized for sort of being partial to white organizers and white neighborhoods and so on. I don't think she saw it that way.

Cal Bradford: That goes back to an issue not of diversity of staff, but about how you get interracial groups. Because I was always fascinated about how is it they could organize in racially changing neighborhoods and it worked and people didn't hate each other. Shel would probably kill me for saying this: I asked Shel one time about how you set up the meetings. "Well," he said, "in a really tough neighborhood like Marquette Park in Chicago when you call a meeting, when you're going through the neighborhood, you tell the blacks that the meeting starts a half-hour before it starts. So they're already there. Then when the white people come, if they don't want to work with black people, they'll just go home because they'll see that they're already there. And the people who come are willing to work with black people." That's one of the first things.

Ann Vick-Westgate: Why wasn't the NTIC staff more diverse? She had a diverse constituency, through NPA, in the communities and leaders that they were working with, but the NTIC staff is pretty much white.

George Knight: As the '70s came on, the opportunities for talented black and Hispanic staff exploded beyond exponential. So that you would sign on for NTIC for incredibly low wages with your spouse supporting you. That model just, with Shel's temperament, interest but lack of assistance, taking the easy way, it just doesn't happen now. We certainly struggle. I mean you certainly know the early history of the Urban Reinvestment Task Force. The turnover among the minority staff was very high, particularly the talented. I can remember more than one occasion someone coming in there in tears and telling me about this wonderful job offer and saying, "George, what can I do? They're offering me double my salary." I said, "The only thing you can say is 'thank you' and congratulations."

Ann Vick-Westgate: She was the leader, but many of her troops at that point were black. Daley initially dismissed her saying, "It's a multiracial coalition, and a multiracial group has never worked in Chicago. We don't have to worry about these people."

Pablo Eisenberg: She certainly was more comfortable. I mean she was as abrupt with blacks as she was with whites.

Ann Vick-Westgate: According to Jimmy Cincotta, her youngest son, the house was filled at all times. He had friends of all colors. He dated a black girl. And those just weren't issues with Gale.

Pablo Eisenberg: Somehow she never could get a diverse staff. Now at the time it may have been that there wasn't a huge amount of interest on the issue for black organizers. Although at NPA they got them from outside of Chicago. But it was an issue that people raised. Certainly some of her critics, who could have been really accused of being discriminatory, raised it for their own purposes.

Good organizers always think it's their way and their method and their organizing, and their turf is the best and the most important, and so they have a grudging, if that, admiration for fellow organizers. She had a little of that. Not as bad as some of them. They're just terrible. The Alinskyites don't talk with the Gamaliel folks and so on. It's pretty strange.

Ann Vick-Westgate: Gale was a combination of organizer and leader. She learned what she could from Trapp and kept her leader role.

Pablo Eisenberg: Yeah. That was anti-the conventional way. You couldn't be both organizer and leader. By virtue of her personality and drive and energy, even if she wanted to separate it, she could not have. And it would have been a disaster if she had. See that's where Shel was so important.

Shel did take the organizer's role and step back. He always did. I've seen his book; he sent it to me; I read it; I like it. I think it's a good book. Shel was a much more difficult guy. Gale was much more open. What you saw, you got. Right? I mean in a funny way. There was no deception about it. Shel you just never knew what he felt.

The leadership problem is the major one and when you look around nonprofits, foundations are the worst. There's not one leader in the whole 70,000 foundations. Where are the John Gardners, and the Bill Bondurants at Babcock, and John Filers and all those? There's nothing. And in the nonprofit sector, there are very few.

Cal Bradford: This is going to come out of left field, but I predominantly blame the foundations for the organizing base in Washington being gone. The foundations' job was to be the dependent link. The whole purpose of having these foundations is that those people who are out of the mainstream, who didn't have the main access to things, would have some source of support. The things they're doing maybe make the foundation people feel good but they don't show any courage or any creativity anymore. They used to show more.

CHAPTER 11

"Gale Cincotta had more to do with the rescue of urban neighborhoods over the past 30 years than any other human being."

HOME MORTGATE DISCLOSURE ACT (HMDA)
(passed by Congress in Dec. 1975,
signed by President Ford Jan. 2, 1976)

From her first monthly column, "The Next Move" in *DISCLOSURE* **#1 (Aug. 1974)**

Gale Cincotta: Full mandatory national public disclosure is our primary demand today. Our target is Mr. Thomas Bomar, Chairman of the Federal Home Loan Bank Board in Washington. Disclosure will not solve the problem of redlining. The industry weeps over how tight money is. But the fact remains that whatever money is available is not going to our communities. Disclosure will support the claims we have been making for years.

Demands for disclosure are sweeping the country. The list of cities fighting redlining is growing. This newsletter includes only some of the cities investigating the problem. At some point, Mr. Bomar will no longer be able to turn deaf ears to our cries. He will have to return to Congress to obtain approval for his proposals. We have to be ready so that when he appears he answers our proposals as well. Now that the national docket is clear of impeachment, our chances for a full congressional investigation are better. But it will only happen if we insist. This issue requires us working together nationally. We've visited presidents of savings and loans and officials in regional FHLBB's offices. It's time we visited Mr. Bomar himself. If he won't come to us, we'll have to go to Washington.

From Case Study by Hallahan (11/7/91)

Kirk Hallahan: In particular, the groups targeted the now-defunct Federal Home Loan Bank Board [FHLBB was replaced in 1989 by the Office of Thrift Supervision] because the savings and loans they regulated were organized as specialized mortgage finance institutions and originated half of all mortgage loan volume.

A *Wall Street Journal* story summed up the regulators' attitudes this way: "Thomas R. Bomar, chairman of the Federal Home Loan Bank, says his agency 'probably has the authority to require full disclosure' from the more

234 - GALE FORCE

234 - GALE FORCE

than 2,000 federal savings and loans it regulates nationally but 'we're not sure this is an appropriate function for us to get into.'" He adds: "We're set up to regulate primarily the solvency of these institutions. To make a major jump into this new field would require at least $100 million addition to our budget and a 50% increase in our 850-member examining staff. We're not sure it's worth it."

In the same article, Cincotta replied: "We think the industry and the regulatory agencies should be able to come up with some ideas for ways to stop redlining. So far we're only getting a lot of stopgap measures and bureaucratic runaround while our neighborhoods are going down the drain. I'm not sure we need new laws and regulations, but something has to be done. If we don't get responsible action from more savings and loan executives soon, a lot of them are going to get tired of seeing us on their front yards and in their offices." [Source: Brown, "Critic Says Lenders Hasten Urban Decay" 23] (6)

Michael Westgate: A *Washington Post* editorial entitled "Truth in Savings" (May 9, 1975) responded to the banking industry argument that redlining did not exist saying that, if true, the information disclosed under the proposed legislation would prove the industry correct. However if redlining did exist, "we see nothing unfair in letting depositors know where their money is being invested. You might call it 'truth in savings.'" (13)

Anita Miller: Gale was the most dynamic, important woman on the whole urban scene of the last decades. Without her there would be no accountability on the part of financial institutions and financial regulators for what they were not doing in these neighborhoods that was crippling them. She organized the nation. She organized across the United States of America bringing groups to Chicago in the early '70s and stood before them and said, "It's not us. It's them!"

Michael Westgate:: Gale and Shel had realized early on that they needed to have two sister organizations.

One was to lobby Washington in an unfettered manner, responding to changing needs and changing constituencies, an organization of organizations. Having no office, no staff, no funding, NPA was very difficult for those in control of our society to try to control. At the same time, they needed another organization, NTIC, with a hardworking year-round staff to provide technical assistance and training to neighborhood organizations throughout the country, at all stages of development. NTIC also provided the logistical staffing needed to pull off NPA and its annual conference – some would call it an assault on Washington.

This duality of agencies is the model they developed to successfully take on national issues.

When they set out to hold regulators responsible for the problems in home mortgage lending, beginning with the President of the Federal Home Loan Bank of Chicago, their goals were not radical. They were seeking enforcement of a series of laws and programs enacted since the 1930s, designed to make home loans available to those willing and able to borrow, on a fair and equitable basis. To achieve these goals, at times their tactics were seen as radical. But as Gale taught others to say, "Which is more not-nice? To have rats nibbling at the feet of your children as they sleep, or to have people on your lawn protesting because you won't meet with them?"

Just as Gale had documented the effects of redlining in Chicago with a study of lending patterns of each savings and loan association, they recognized the need for national data to prove their case against redlining nationally. With the regulators refusing to respond satisfactorily to their demands to collect this data, Gale and Shel organized through NPA to get Congress to enact the Home Mortgage Disclosure Act (HMDA) in 1975.

From Case Study by Hallahan (11/7/91)

Kirk Hallahan: Cincotta had already appeared before four Congressional hearings. The first two occurred just after the creation of NPA. In testimony before Senator Philip Hart's Subcommittee on Antitrust and Monopoly, Cincotta had first raised the issue of redlining and voiced their frequently made claim that the enemy was "the real estate companies, the insurance companies, the savings and loans and banks and the big powers. And to our amazement, it was the Federal Government, the FHA and HUD that is destroying our communities." [May 1, 1972] (8)

Shel Trapp: The next step then was the national fight. Proxmire entered because he was on the Senate Banking Committee and became its chairman. He was the logical person to go to, an ally, a good guy and very progressive.

We never had much contact with him in Wisconsin. We did have some folks from Milwaukee. Through my work with Father Coughlin, he flipped me into the national network with Catholic Charities. He would let us do workshops at their national convention, on all these issues. They had a meeting of about thirty folks from Catholic Charities across the county and a few other of our folks at a retreat center up north here. We wrote the Home Mortgage Disclosure Act on the floor of a rectory, from about eight o'clock at night until four o'clock Sunday morning. And it was a beautiful law. I mean banks couldn't have bought a roll of toilet paper without us having them disclose it. It was how much banking inside the city, how much banking inside the state, how much banking outside the state, where your deposits came from. It had everything. The people writing it were people from across the country. It was brought together through the Catholic Church essentially. And there were some of our leadership in there too.

Wrote this beautiful thing and that was the original thing that we took to Proxmire. It had farm loans in, everything, business loans. He pared it down before he even submitted it. He said, "Look. This thing ain't going no where." So he submitted a fairly decent piece and then it got chopped to shit as it went through the Congressional process.

I'd say maybe 10% percent of what we wrote on the rectory floor came out at the other end of the sausage making. It went in maybe at 40%. By the time it went through the Congressional process it got hacked up some more.

Ann Vick-Westgate: So is the original document findable in any way?

Shel Trapp: Are you kidding? I'm sure all these drawers here at NTIC are empty, just empty. I never saved anything. When I retired three years ago, I took my clipboard home and one plaque that NPA had given me and that's all I carried out of the office. Oh, and my training book. It's all my training designs for the training sessions I do. And Gale? She saved things as a stack here, a stack there, a drawer, not with file folders.

Ken McLean: The first time I met Gale was before CRA. It involved the Home Mortgage Disclosure Act, HMDA. She was an activist in Chicago and she had persuaded the Chicago city council to enact a mini local version of HMDA. She was active in an anti-redlining movement in Chicago and that was her focus. Her goal was to try to shed the light of day on where local banks were putting their money. She took that victory and sort of went nationwide with it and came to the Congress.

So this would have been '74. I do remember she came to my office and was pushing the HMDA, Home Mortgage Disclosure Act. She talked about what she'd done in Chicago. I'm from Chicago myself and I knew some of the neighborhoods pretty well that she was talking about. And then she talked to Senator Proxmire. She was big. She was feisty.

From Case Study by Hallahan (11/7/91)

Gale Cincotta: We were in [Proxmire's] office – he was one of many lawmakers we had visited that day. He was especially interested in our concerns, and was familiar with the progress of our Milwaukee affiliate in fighting redlining in his home state. He said if we wrote a bill calling for disclosure, similar to what we had proposed in Chicago, he would introduce it. (Hallahan personal interview – 9)

Ken McLean: She came in when CRA was not even on the horizon. She was HMDA and she was basically the only one who was pushing it. The neighborhoods, the neighborhood movement, the community reinvestment movement was pretty much non-existent. They really didn't have very much political influence at all. And were it not for someone like Proxmire who was pretty much independent, it never would have seen the light of day. There was no particular political capital in it for him because he didn't really have a lot of groups in Milwaukee that were pushing for it. This was the first time the issue came up.

The first time we met with Gale, the Senator was not yet Chairman of the Banking Committee; he was the ranking Democrat, the number two guy. The number one guy was John Sparkman from Alabama. He was clearly conservative and wasn't really big on the anti-redlining issues. But then in '64 he moved on to the Committee on Foreign Relations and Senator Proxmire moved up to become the Chairman of the Banking Committee.

From Case Study by Hallahan (11/7/91)

Kirk Hallahan: Proxmire, then a fourth-term Democrat from Wisconsin, was an exceptional ally. He was sympathetic to consumer issues and to housing and had been instrumental in passage of truth-in-lending legislation. Proxmire's involvement was also fortuitous. As the second-ranking Democrat on the Senate Banking Committee, he was in line to become chairman in the event that Chairman John Sparkman moved to the more prestigious Foreign Relations Committee – which is exactly what occurred the following January. Proxmire, a former journalist and publishing executive, also was adroit in capturing media attention.

Upon Proxmire's ascent to the chairmanship of the Banking Committee, McLean became committee staff director and hired several investigators. Bob Kuttner, a journalist by training and a self-professed "progressive type," was given the project and served as the principal liaison with NPA and its affiliates.

The Wisconsin senator's bill was read for the first time on the floor of the Senate on March 21. In his remarks, he cited specifically the work of Cincotta and HTIC in Chicago. Proxmire vigorously worked the bill by scheduling four days of hearings in early May; the proceedings would eventually fill 1,633 pages. (9)

The power of having facts was suggested at the Senate vote, where Proxmire told his aides that Cincotta and her group's studies were chiefly responsible for the Senate's favorable action. [Proxmire statements to Hallahan, also in contemporary newspaper coverage] (23)

While NPA's tactics in Chicago combined high levels of conflict with a relatively low-key approach to publicity, these components were reversed when the issue was tackled in Washington. In the capital, a high-powered (and contrived) publicity campaign was combined with intensive, but routine lobbying. Proxmire and his staff recognized that redlining simply did not have sufficient visibility to capture the serious attention of Congress. If they were to be successful, they needed to stir up awareness and interest. As Kuttner recalled, the story of a multi-racial neighborhood group going up against the rich and the powerful was "good copy." (28)

By winning approval of the Chicago ordinance, NPA could use the Chicago experience to win state support. Chicago also served as an example for other cities. The experience in Illinois, in turn, provided powerful evidence that national action was necessary. It was not coincidental that Governor Dan Walker was a major witness in both the Senate and House hearings." (30)

Michael Westgate: Actually, Gale was a master at using successes at each level of government to bolster her arguments at others. It was, after all, on the urging of FHA Regional Director Waner that she had gone to Washington to seek relief on FHA issues.

She went to Washington, had some victories, especially HMDA with its requirements for financial disclosure, and later CRA, which she parlayed into further victories in Chicago and in Illinois.

Gale sitting behind Richard J. Daley. Both are testifying at a hearing on redlining, 1975.

Joe Mariano: Tom Gaudette believed we shouldn't go national, that we should do local organizing. So I think there was a split early on with Gaudette over going national.

So there was that tension. Not that Gale wanted to go national but they couldn't keep winning locally anymore. That was the problem. They'd won all they could win in Chicago, and they kept getting told, "You have to go to Washington." On FHA and CRA, all of those kinds of issues that they had won here in Chicago, the officials kept telling them, "We've gone as far as we can go. You've got to go to Washington."

From Case Study by Hallahan (11/7/91)

Kirk Hallahan: HMDA is a case of special interest legislation that managed to circumvent normal channels and become law without a groundswell of public opinion or support – and certainly not from the perspective of the press as an institution that ferrets out problems and brings them to the attention of the public or policy makers. Rather, Proxmire's manipulation of the media agenda is an insightful example of the press agenda-setting function reflecting – not leading – to public policy agenda-setting. The passage of HMDA reflects the intertwined relationship between the press and politicians – and how the media can be used unwittingly by lawmakers to advance particular agendas, and thus convert particular social constructions into political realities." (31)

Ken McLean: All of a sudden you had lost a very conservative Southern chairman and moved to a Midwestern activist-populist chairman. So that was a whole new ballgame. Proxmire took the HMDA ball and ran with it and got it enacted that very first year of his chairmanship in 1975.

When Proxmire first came to Washington, he was elected in 1957 to fill McCarthy's unexpired term. It was a big switch. He had run for governor three times in Wisconsin and lost. So when McCarthy died, they had a special election and the Democrats had to come up quickly with a candidate. They didn't really have a solid candidate so they figured, well, let's put in Proxmire again. He'll lose but by then in '58 the regular election will occur and by that time we can find a stronger candidate. And then you get the seat back.

So Proxmire ran and his opponent went around the state accusing Proxmire of being a three-time loser. So Proxmire, in his inimitable style, turned that to his advantage. He would go into a local Rotarian or Chamber of Commerce group and he'd say, "Now my opponent has accused me of being a three-time loser and that's right. I ran for governor three times and I lost, so I know what it feels like to lose. And if you've never lost anything in love, in business, in your life, then you ought to vote for my opponent. But, if you have lost, you ought to vote for me because I know what it's like to lose." So it made him a human being, a regular guy. It made his opponent kind of a phony or hypocrite.

So, lo and behold, he won the election and it preserved it, kept the Senate Democratic. At that time there was a danger that the Democrats only had a one-seat margin because they'd lost another seat in the meantime. If Proxmire lost, Lyndon Johnson would have lost his job as Majority Leader.

When Proxmire won, Lyndon Johnson called him up at three in the morning, 'Congratulations, Bill." Proxmire had never met Johnson and his wife. And Johnson said, "I'm sending a plane for you. I want you to come right to Washington." He sent a plane out. Proxmire and Helen arrive in Washington and Johnson meets them at the plane, slaps him on the back. And he says, "Well now, what committee would you like to be on?" And Proxmire says, "Oh, I'd like to be on Finance." Johnson kind of looks at him. Of course Finance was the guardian of the oil depletion allowance and Proxmire was a northern liberal in the Paul Douglas frame that was against it.

And Johnson says, "Well, I don't know if we can do that. Tell me a little bit about your background." So Proxmire says, "Well, when I was out of college I worked for J. P. Morgan." And Johnson said, "Oh, well, we've got just the job for you. We can get you on the Banking Committee." And Proxmire didn't know any better, he thought that was a coveted committee assignment. It actually was kind of a backwater then. And it didn't really become an activist committee until he became chairman. But were it not for Johnson, he never would have been. He would have been on some other committee; he never would have been at Banking.

Michael Westgate: But what a difference Proxmire made – billions of dollars in additional lending in communities that needed it.

Ken McLean: But Proxmire played the game as a loyal freshman. He was quiet and deferential to his elders; he didn't speak up. And he did that for about a year and a half. Finally he just got fed up. He'd been in the Senate for about a year and in '58 on Washington's Birthday... The Senate traditionally closes down on Washington's Birthday and somebody gets up to read the Washington Farewell Address and then they adjourn. So Proxmire takes the occasion to get up on the floor and deliver a speech against Johnson.

He gets up and talks for 30 or 40 minutes saying what a tyrant Johnson is and who is he to tell other Senators how to vote. And he goes on and on about what a dictatorial leader Johnson is, at some length. At the Press Office they said, "Well there were two farewell speeches today in the Senate, Washington's and Proxmire's." So Johnson had it in for him. Used to call him "Senator Pissmire." Never liked him after that.

There was a lot of opposition to HMDA and the only way we could get the bill through was to put a five-year sunset on it. That was unfortunate because then every five years it came up for renewal and the bankers would oppose the renewal. So the neighborhood movement had to use up a lot of personal capital just to get the Act renewed. Which meant that they couldn't use their political clout to get other stuff enacted. They were playing a kind of defense and wanting to try to preserve what they had. It wasn't until 1988 that it became a permanent law.

From *DISCLOSURE* #8 (May 1975)
THE PEOPLE GO TO WASHINGTON
May 5 event showed Washington grass roots national agenda

The People's Platform for 1976 is built on the strength of neighborhoods and regards Neighborhood Preservation as the key to the survival of cities. The basic planks in the platform that is being presented to leaders of both parties are:

> Full mandatory disclosure by all financial institutions
> Reinvestment programs by the private sector for urban centers
> Stopping of FHA abandonment and fast-foreclosures
> More and better senior citizen housing

Landmark Victory on National Disclosure

"Redlining involves something as basic as the survival of America's great cities," noted Senator William Proxmire (D-WI) as he opened the hearings of the Committee of Banking, Housing and Urban Affairs on the Home Mortgage Disclosure Act of 1975 (S. 1281). Armed with documentation, homeowners—young, old, black and white, from neighborhoods as far east as Providence and as far west as Oakland – crowded into a Senate hearing room to speak in favor of the Disclosure Bill that they have worked on for the past year.

Gale Cincotta, chairperson of NPAH, began the community people's testimony. Referring to NPAH's three-year grassroots battle against redlining, she asserted that "Neighborhood Preservation is the top priority of NPAH's growing national grassroots network." Ms. Cincotta presented research which Senator Proxmire was later to call "an excellent job" and "fine documentation" that "certainly provides the facts."

One of her exhibits documented the mortgage patterns in three Chicago neighborhoods over the past twenty-five years. The study showed a severe withdrawal of conventional funds and an influx of FHA-insured loans during the racial transitions of Roseland and West Englewood. This change in financing occurred despite the fact that new black residents of these neighborhoods are of substantially the same income and occupational level as the former white homeowners. Meanwhile, the third neighborhood in the study, Jefferson Park, has not undergone a racial transition and has not been victimized by the dual financing system. The patterns and practice of lending made evident in this study demonstrate a destructive and discriminating misallocation of credit.

Total blame was not placed solely on lending institutions; rather governmental regulatory agencies such as the FLHBB received much criticism. Senator Adlai Stevenson (D-IL), a co-sponsor of the bill, remarked during the hearings that the situation is "more shocking because of the acquiescence of government agencies. In some cases policies of government agencies have accelerated this process."

When Mr. Bomar testified late that week during the four-day hearings, Senator Proxmire asked where his data was to support his claims that the institutions do not redline. Bomar admitted he had none. Proxmire then asked him whether disclosure wouldn't provide him, as a head federal regulator, with such data to determine redlining practices. Bomar became speechless and only nodded his head in the affirmative.

From Case Study by Hallahan (11/7/91)

Kirk Hallahan: On Thursday, May 8, 1975, the *Post's* business section reported that representatives of lending groups voiced "vigorous objection" and told the committee "the bill is unnecessary and economically unsound, would put the information into the hands of 'pressure groups' and would be costly." Interestingly, the two major banking executives who testified were from Chicago where the redlining issue had first festered. Grover J. Hansen, president of First Federal Savings and Loan Association of Chicago, called the plan unworkable and unnecessary because there was still no proof that redlining existed. Underscoring the power that the activists had exhibited, he said that the bill would lead to "private enforcement of public policy by special interest pressure groups." John Perkins, president of Continental Illinois National Bank, said "surely the Congress would not desire that sound lending policy be abandoned in favor of an equal dispersion of mortgage loans in each area of a given city so as to avoid any appearance of unfair discrimination on the basis of property allocation." (12)

Michael Westgate: Reporter Nicholas von Hoffman of the *Chicago Tribune* called the bankers' testimonies "many, wondrous, contradictory." ("Hemming, Hawing and Redlining" – May 13, 1975)

From *DISCLOSURE* #8 (May 1975)

After the bankers and other lenders finished their testimony, Mr. Proxmire characterized it as a "series of generalized impressions." In contrast, he reasserted that the community people who testified presented "strong documentation" on the effects of redlining. Before adjourning the hearing, Senator Proxmire told the bankers "I don't understand the objection to getting the facts out."

The Disclosure Bill (S 1281) also received the support of Senator Edward Brooke (R-MA) after he met with several NPAH delegates on the day of the hearing. The bill has now passed the committee by an 8 to 1 vote and is awaiting action on the Senate floor. One major compromise was made, supposedly to avoid a Presidential veto, that does not require disclosure of savings data. Lending data, however, which has always been the main objective of the disclosure fight, is required by census tract.

While in Washington, NPAH delegates also met with several House representatives. As a result, Rep. John J. Moakley (D-MA) has introduced HR 6596, "Mortgage Disclosure Act of 1975." This bill has been co-sponsored by twenty other Representatives, including Rep. Morgan Murphy (D-IL). The House Bill provides for disclosure of savings data and lending data by postal zip code, and adds mortgage bankers to the list of financial institutions resurveyed (*sic*) to disclose. Thus, the House Bill offers the opportunity to still have disclosure of savings data made mandatory when the Senate and House bills go to Conference Committee.

The House is now awaiting the Senate's action and has not yet sent the bill to a House sub-committee. However, NPAH urges concerned citizens to write supporting letters to Rep. Reuss (D-WI), chairman of the House

Gale testifying before U.S. Congressional committee in Washington, D.C., on redlining. Gale was able to gather statistics, thanks to work of John McKnight, Cal Bradford and students at Northwestern University. Gale presented data in ways that were very clear and difficult to refute.

Banking, Currency and Housing Committee; Rep. Barrett (D-PA); Rep. Annunzio (D-IL) and Rep. St. Germain (D-RI) who are all key subcommittee chairpersons.

As Gale Cincotta concluded her testimony on the Senate Bill, "the regulatory agencies needs national full disclosure to analyze our national housing crisis and develop positive reinvestment programs to encourage the private market to preserve our neighborhoods. The people need national mandatory full public disclosure in order to continue their grassroots battle for the survival of our neighborhoods."

The Mortgage Disclosure Act will be passed. And it should be hailed as a landmark victory in American politics and as a tribute to the grassroot efforts of neighborhood people throughout the country."

Michael Westgate: Gale was masterful in attracting national as well as Chicago press. Senator Proxmire was also interested in making his mark as the new Chairman of the Senate Banking Committee. He was adept, for example, at building momentum through the hearings by having the first day, May 5, reserved for community groups to testify. The bankers were allowed to testify on May 6 and the federal officials on May 7. Together Gale and Senator Proxmire got maximum media coverage.

In a May 5, 1975 *New York Times* article ("Homeowners Ask 'Redlining' Curb"), William E. Farrell stated that more than 150 representatives from 20 cities, many of them carrying the results of research in their communities, appeared at the hearing and voiced strong support for the proposed legislation. In a follow-up article on May 26, Farrell reported Proxmire's statement that "perfectly sound neighborhoods in every major city in America are dying premature deaths for lack of mortgage credit". There was also the response by the U.S. League of Savings Association's representative that "zoning policies, the strict enforcement of housing and health codes, the attitudes of property owners and their neighborhoods, good housekeeping by city agencies, equitable property tax systems and many other factors" had to be taken into consideration.

In the same article, Senator Jake Garn, a conservative, was quoted as saying that denying the existence of redlining was an insult to his intelligence. Unfortunately, under pressure from financial institutions, Senator Garn later switched from being an ardent ally to supporting the bankers' position.

From *DISCLOSURE #10* (August 1975)

Sen. Tower of Texas and Garn of Utah introduced a bill to make disclosure a three-year pilot study in twenty cities selected by the FHLBB. Sen. Garn would accept an amendment by Sen. Stone of FL to restrict the study to zip codes and prohibit the use of census tracts.

The lending industry is fully behind these amendments since they would effectively take the wind out of the grass-roots movement for national disclosure during the next three years, limiting the extent to which redlining could be made a national campaign issue in the 1976 election.

Close to thirty senators may be wavering on the question of the Tower/Garn amendment. As of the Congressional recess, this industry-supported amendment was five votes away from being defeated.

From *DISCLOSURE* #11 (September 1975)
Disclosure Passes Senate
After months of deliberation and a heated floor debate, the U. S. Senate on September 4th 1975, defeated the Tower-Garn amendment by a vote of 41 to 40 and passed S.1281, the disclosure bill that community groups across the country have been supporting by a vote of 45 to 37.

As reported previously, the amendment introduced by Senator Garn from Utah would have limited disclosure to a pilot study in 20 cities. As Senator Proxmire, who introduced S. 1281, pointed out in the floor debate, "make no mistake about it, if the Senators accept the Garn amendment, they vote to cut the legislation. That would be the end of this legislation."

The disclosure legislation as passed defines "depository institutions" as commercial banks, savings banks, savings and loan associations, and credit unions which make federally related mortgage loans. Such depository institutions which have a home office or branch office located within a standard metropolitan statistical area (SMSA) shall disclose the number and dollar amount of mortgage loans and home improvement loans which were originated or purchased during each fiscal year (beginning with the last full fiscal year of that institution which immediately preceded the effective date of this Home Mortgage Disclosure Act of 1975). The effective date of this legislation is 90 days after its enactment and its authority shall expire three years after the date of enactment...

The Board of Governors of the Federal Reserve System is charged with prescribing such regulations as may be necessary to carry out the purposes of this Act. Compliance with requirements shall be enforced by the Comptroller of the Currency for national banks; by the Federal Reserve Board for member banks of the Federal Reserve Board; for member banks of the Federal Reserve System that are not national banks, by the Federal Deposit Insurance Corporation, also non-Reserve banks insured by the FDIC; by the Federal Home Loan Bank Board for institutions regulated by them; by the National Credit Union Administration for any Federal credit union; and by the Federal Trade Commission for requirements not committed to any other government agency.

The final bill passed by the Senate does allow the Federal Reserve Board to exempt from national disclosure any depository institution within any state or subdivision that the Board determines to have similar disclosure requirements and enforcement.

Finally, S. 1281 calls for a feasibility study of requiring depository institutions to disclose by geographical location the source of savings deposits. Other studies include an impact analysis to determine whether lending patterns have changed as a result of disclosure and a sample study of how disclosure was used by local governmental agencies and community groups.

Michael Westgate: Thus HMDA passed its most important test in the Senate by a single vote.

The legislation did not provide for information on the sources of lenders' funds. Nor did it include mortgage bankers, both of which were in the original versions Gale and Shel drafted on the rectory floor. Those omissions were to bear bitter fruit thirty years later. Risky lending practices were allowed to take place after zealous deregulation. The American and indeed world financial systems came close to collapse. While application of HMDA requirements to mortgage lenders might not have prevented all excesses, it would have highlighted the information that might have permitted regulators, Congress and private watchdogs like NTIC/NPA to see and publicize some of the coming problems.

From Case Study by Hallahan (11/7/91)

Kirk Hallahan: The Republican minority, in its dissenting commentary, complained "most of the supporters of S.1281 who testified see it as a tool to give community groups leverage over the financial institutions to achieve their ends". [Senate Banking Committee Report] They chided the hearings for being stacked in favor of the community groups, listed several urbanologists who should have been invited to testify, and raised industry-originated concerns related to the costs and complexity of compliance. Most significantly, they complained about the "misleading" data that had been originated by the Library of Congress in its D.C. Redlining Study, and used by Proxmire to fuel the issue. They responded with their own study using data obtained from the Metropolitan Washington Savings and Loan League. (17)

S. 1281 was originally introduced in the House as H.R. 8024, with several comparable versions also introduced, notably H.R. 6595 by Rep. Moakley. Later Proxmire shrewdly would arrange for the bill to be attached as Title III to H.R. 10024, a piece of priority legislation that extended the flexible ceilings on deposit interest rates and extended a moratorium on electronic funds transfers. This move helped assure speedy House consideration since the other matters were considered essential – and veto-proof. (18 – Footnote)

From *DISCLOSURE* #12 (October 1975)

National mandatory disclosure moved another step closer to reality on October 7th as the full House Committee on Banking, Currency and Housing passed a disclosure bill by a vote of 25 to 12. Although disclosure of loans by census tracts remained in the final draft, disclosure of savings data was deleted from this House bill as it was in the Senate's version.

One major change from the H.R. 802 that was the result of National People's Action on Housing's grassroots lobbying was to amend H.R. 10024 to designate the Reserve Board with the authority to prescribe necessary regulations to carryout the purposes of this act. The House bill originally had the Secretary of HUD prescribing regulations, which was unacceptable to the many people who have dealt with HUD's deregulating, industry-favoring guidelines. In the current version of the House bill, HUD is responsible for securing disclosure data and furnishing summaries to appropriate governmental officials and committees.

H.R. 10024 also shows more sensitivity to people's reported concern that financial institutions would be exempt from a strong federal disclosure law through weaker state ones. While still authorizing the Board to determine inconsistencies and to exempt institutions, the bill notes that "this title does not annul, alter, affect or exempt any person subject to the provisions of this title when complying with the laws of any state or subdivision thereof." The bill goes on to note that if such state laws differ in requiring greater geographic or more detail than the federal law, the Board cannot rule the state law inconsistent. Although specific state laws and individual institutions will have to be discussed, Section 306 of this act now seems to be written to insure that the stricter law will take precedence. The House bill takes effect ninety days after enactment except in the case of depository institutions with assets of $25 million or less, who must report fifteen months after the date of enactment. H.R. 10024 now appears to be written to only require disclosure of loans made after the effective date. This will undoubtedly be the major point of contention when the Senate and House bills go to conference, since S. 1281 includes loans during the last full fiscal year...

On October 31, 1975, the landmark "Home Mortgage Disclosure Act of 1975" passes the U.S. House of Representatives by a vote of 177-147. The passage of the Disclosure Act, which is Title III of housing bill HR 10024, is a major victory for the National People's Action on Housing, which lobbied extensively on its behalf.

A similar disclosure bill, numbered S 1281, passed earlier in the Senate. While the House and Senate bills are basically the same, several important differences exist between them.

- Under the House bill, disclosure is by census tract, when this can be done at a reasonable cost as determined by the Federal Reserve Board. In other cases disclosure is by zip code area. Under the Senate bill all disclosure is by zip code area.
- The House bill mandates disclosure for 4 years, while the Senate version covers only 3 years.
- Under the House bill, the Federal Reserve Board regulates disclosure, while HUD is required to collect data and submit it annually to Congress and other officials. HUD is not involved with the disclosure process in the Senate version.
- The House bill originally provided that the Federal Reserve Board could (and it implied it should) bow to the state law if it is stronger. It was amended on the floor to exempt federally chartered institutions from this dual responsibility. The Senate bill does not contain this weakening provision.
- While both bills mandate disclosure for the last full fiscal year, the Senate version requires this information within 90 days after enactment, a full 3 months sooner than the House's 180 day requirement.

Disclosure backers, led by Sen. Proxmire of Wisconsin, are hard at work determining the best way to reconcile the discrepancies between the two bills. Two courses of action appear open. The first is to introduce the House bill into the Senate. If it passes, the bill moves to President Ford's desk for his signature. The second course is to send both bills to a joint House-Senate conference committee to work out the differences between them.

Whichever method is chosen, it now appears certain a national mandatory disclosure law will soon be a reality.

From *DISCLOSURE* #14 (December 1975)
Next Step – Ford

The resolved version of the national disclosure bill retained most of the provisions set forth in HR 10024:

- Disclosure will be by census tract.
- The bill mandates disclosure for 4 years.
- The Federal Reserve Board regulates disclosure, while HUD is required to collect data and submit it annually to Congress and other officials.

- ◆ Where a stronger state disclosure law exists, state-chartered institutions will comply with state law
- ◆ Disclosure will become effective 180 days after the bill is enacted

President Ford is now in a position to make mortgage disclosure national law. He'd be hard pressed to veto a bill that has no negative national effect nor requires appropriation of monies. Communities across the country will be watching and waiting to see this final step taken.

From his Foreword to *Urban Disinvestment: New Implications For Community Organization, Research and Public Policy* **by Arthur J. Naparstek and Gale Cincotta (Joint Publication of The National Center for Urban Ethnic Affairs and NTIC, 1976)**

Senator William Proxmire: The documentation on redlining was collected in hearings last May before the Senate Banking Committee. It is hard to recall an issue where the impetus for reform came so directly and persuasively from grass roots organizations. So compelling was the testimony we heard that within several months Congress enacted and President Ford signed into law the anti-redlining bill which I sponsored, the "Home Mortgage Disclosure Act". The legislation was passed despite a strong backlash during this session of Congress against new regulatory legislation of any kind.

In many ways, the Home Mortgage Disclosure Act is the best kind of reform legislation because it merely provides community groups and local officials with information, and leaves the precise remedy to the locality. It is also fair to say that the disclosure bill would never have become law but for the research and local organizing activity undertaken by the National Training and Information Center under Ms. Gale Cincotta's leadership. The very idea that mortgage investment disclosure would be helpful in the fight to save cities from arbitrary disinvestment came directly from the community groups.

Michael Westgate: Gale's enthusiastic reaction to the signing of HMDA was reported by Stanley Ziemba in the *Chicago Tribune* ("Redlining battle: Major victory for activist here"—Jan. 3, 1976): "It's like having a baby, or at least a kidney stone removed. Few people may realize it yet, but this legislation represents an awfully big victory for the neighborhoods of Chicago and other cities across the country. It could guarantee their survival."

From *DISCLOSURE* **#15 (Jan. 1976)**

On January 2, 1976, the "Home Mortgage Disclosure Act of 1975" was signed into law. A tribute to the grass-roots efforts of community people across the country, this disclosure law represents the raising of "redlining" to a national issue. Community leaders who led this fight from the streets to the halls of Congress are now gearing up for the even more important fight over implementation…

Areas of the law which need clarification are:

- The definition of "depository institution" as an institution which makes "federally related mortgage loans"
- The need for disclosure information to be made available to the public at a central location within an SMSA
- Disclosure "by census tract, where readily available at a reasonable cost, as determined by the Board" should be ruled across the board for all SMSA's
- The need for other federal regulatory agencies to adopt anti-redlining regs similar to the Federal Home Loan Bank Board's
- Exemption by the Board of State chartered depository institutions, if it determines that state disclosure laws are similar to the Act, should be ruled in favor of the strongest law.

More important is the question of when will disclosure be available to the public. The Federal Reserve Board officials assigned to draw up the regulations are Janet Hart and Robert Plotken, Department of Saver and Consumer Affairs, Board of Governors of the Federal Reserve System, Washington, DC…

Disclosure is on the books. But we still need the data in our hands.

Michael Westgate: HMDA was largely of Gale's making. Its provisions allowing for greater stringency at the state or even local level were clearly hers.

George Knight: Absolutely and so incredibly critical. It was so classic Gale that you get the data and with the data you can end the argument. HMDA wasn't a very complex statute as I recall. It was a pretty simple statute.

Michael Westgate: The timeframe in Washington was remarkably short. HMDA was the primary focus of National Peoples Action in May 1975. Proxmire had hearings in June. They had it through the Senate in October, through the House in November, through conference committee in December. And Ford signed it on January 2, 1976.

Gale, in typical fashion, did not rest on her laurels after the passage of HMDA. An August 12, 1976 *Chicago Tribune* article ("Protest leader calls for U.S. help in anti-redline battle" by Alan Merridew) quotes her saying "quietly", "The next step is a federal anti-redlining regulation…I think one would be a natural followup to the disclosure regulation, which can be used as a monitoring tool."

Bud Kanitz: Gale never joined coalitions. As a matter of fact, I could never even get her to join the National Neighborhood Coalition officially when I was the executive director—even though we probably talked at least once a week during my entire fifteen years at the Neighborhood Coalition. But Gale's idea of a coalition was something she led! And others coalesced with Gale. She was the mountaintop…

Larry Lindsay would be the antithesis to Gale. In a NeighborWorks publication last year, he wrote an op-ed piece that organizing is passé… that protests like Gale Cincotta led to get CRA passed, that that's all passé, and the way you have to do things now is you work in collaboration.

Well, that's essentially what happened because the paradigm that Gale always used, whether it was on CRA or going after an insurance company, it was essentially confrontation, then after the confrontation there would be collaboration and then there would be cooperation.

Michael Westgate: Gale saw confrontation as a necessary step. Collaboration and finding a workable solution was the end goal. Gale was also a great adaptor. She learned quickly what worked on a local scale and adapted it to the national scene (and vice versa). She studied her audience and knew how to appeal to those in power. The first test of HMDA in the courts was in Cincinatti, just three months after President Ford had signed the bill into law.

From *DISCLOSURE* #16 (March 1976)
U.S Court in Cincinnati Declares Redlining Illegal

It has finally happened. The practice of redlining certain communities as undesirable for conventional mortgage loans, which community groups have recognized as illegal for many years, has been officially declared illegal by Judge David Porter in the United States Court for the Southern District of Ohio.

The redlining case, Robert Laufman vs. Oakley Building and Loan Co., which is the first of its kind to be tried, involves a white couple who attempted to get a mortgage loan in a racially changing neighborhood in Cincinnati. The couple filed suit charging that a loan company denied them money to purchase a home because of the racial characteristics of the neighborhood. The loan company originally advised them that loans were available but after the application was made the loan company rejected them on the alleged basis of racial composition of the neighborhood. In Judge Porter's opinion, on a procedural motion by the defendant, he stated that redlining was prohibited by the Fair Housing Act of 1968, the Civil Rights Act of 1964, and anti-discrimination regulations approved by HUD and the Federal Home Loan Bank Board. The Judge also analyzed the Home Mortgage Disclosure Act of 1975 and found it consistent with the court's interpretation of Title VIII of the Civil Rights Act of 1968. This interpretation noted that building and loans companies were prohibited from denying a loan on the basis of race "where the purpose of the loan was to finance the purchase of a home in an integrated neighborhood." With this opinion established, the case can now proceed to trial.

Pearl Buckwalter of Cincinnati's Coalition of Neighborhoods concludes: "This decision will have tremendous impact for our neighborhoods. It will set a legal precedent and issue a warning to the financial industry that citizens will use litigation to stop redlining."

Michael Westgate: NTIC's publicizing of such victories from around the country in *DISCLOSURE* encouraged others to utilize all the weapons at their disposal – passage of legislation, victories in court, identification of "enemies" among bureaucrats, demonstrations and sit-ins. All this made good copy in the major media.

In a July 6, 1976 *New York Times* article, Carl Holman, president of the National Urban Coalition, called the emerging community groups "really a new breed of cat... They are effective because they use property owners, shopkeepers and others in their coalition and they do their homework. They let you know that they can use your technical help, but they insist on calling the shots." ("Neighborhoods Turn to Self-Help For Preserving and Improving" by Ernest Holsendolph)

Cal Bradford: All the things that I learned in graduate school about sociology— Gale defied all those things. She defied all the rules of business about the way you learn things. It's all wrong. If someone looked at it, it's all wrong. And it's what? Thirty something years of an organization that shouldn't have worked ever in the first place and it's gone on for thirty years. It's made some really big changes.

Michael Westgate: But the battle did not end with passage of the HMDA legislation. It was up to the regulators to enforce the law and Gale foresaw the problems that lay ahead.

From "The Next Move," *DISCLOSURE* #21 (August 1976)

Gale Cincotta: After all this time, after all the letters, after all the testimony, after all the meetings—national mandatory public disclosure is due at midnight on September 30th. The law of the land is now awaiting compliance by our financial institutions. A couple of forms and the compiling of data that the banks and S&L's should have on hand anyway will fulfill the public's right to know where their hard-earned savings have been invested and set the stage for reinvestment in their neighborhoods.

However, our four-year fight is not over. The word that is coming in from around the nation is that most of the larger redliners are already using every, and any, excuse imaginable not to comply on September 30th. But this time when they try to thwart our right to know, they will be breaking the law.

Actions are already being planned in several cities for a "bank-in" on October 1st at the largest institution in town that fails to comply. Individual institutions must be confronted directly with their failure and the attention of federal regulators must be drawn to the illegality of their non-compliance.

Again the task has fallen to community people to insure that the laws of Congress and the will of the people are fulfilled. We have fought hard and long for disclosure. Midnight, September 30th is our moment of victory. But we must be prepared to hold our financial institutions accountable to our disclosure law on October 1st.

The Next Move: Visit your local bank or S&L on October 1st and say – "Disclosure Now!"

Michael Westgate: The American Bankers Association continued to be Gale's top adversary nationally. The ABA had lost the battle in Congress but was responding to the demands of their membership to continue the fight on the regulatory front. ABA staff tried to back out of a meeting scheduled with representatives of MAHA and NPA. They didn't realize that TV crews would show up.

From *DISCLOSURE* #22 (Sept. 1976):
Hide & Seek With the ABA

The American Bankers Association fresh from a confrontation with MAHA and NPA during the bankers' annual meeting last June 14 in Washington, DC were again treated to a healthy dose of tried and true citizen action Sunday, September 19 in Chicago.

Seven MAHA organizations from the north, south and west of the Chicago area converged on the O'Hare Marriott Motel to attend a meeting scheduled by ABA representatives with MAHA. But, alas, the ABA turned chicken again and, at the sight of real community people accompanied by major newspaper and TV reporters, fled the meeting room. At that point, the hide and seek began with ABA hiding and MAHA seeking. MAHA leaders followed Thomas Ahart, Urban Affairs Director, and his six flunkies out to the motel lobby where a one-act play was given to motel management and guests on what citizen action is all about. Jeannie Pillar, SCC, Camille Conrick, NAC, Perry Hamilton, POPCO, with other MAHA leaders and TV cameras rolling demanded to know why ABA, which had agreed to the meeting, now refused to meet. Mr. Ahart: no comment.

Next, ABA escaped to an elevator with MAHA in hot pursuit. Finding ABA reps hiding in Mr. Ahart's sleeping room, MAHA demanded that ABA come out.

Shouts of "Come out, come out!" and "We want our meeting!" soon brought hotel management and security police who agreed to try to mediate. But it was only after a long distance phone call to the Lucas, Kansas, home of ABA president Rex Duwe, that Mr. Ahart was persuaded that it would be easier to meet with MAHA than lose his motel room or perhaps his job!

As a result of the meeting, Mr. Ahart has agreed to present our demands to his Urban Committee and to his governing board which meets October 1 in Washington, DC. The demands MAHA made are that (1) ABA condemn the practice of redlining, (2) support a national anti-redlining law, (3) start an affirmative marketing program, and (4) start reinvestment programs that will preserve our neighborhoods instead of destroying them.

Will we win those demands? Well, as one MAHA leader was heard to remark, "It's not if we will win our demands, only when we will win our demands. The ABA has to learn that when MAHA says there's a meeting, there's a meeting. The next lesson we'll teach them is when MAHA makes demands, ABA complies."

Postscript: As all of you know by now, it takes everyone in the NPA network to make things like this work. Demand a meeting with the ABA in your community. For an organization claiming a membership of 97% of the country's banks, a budget of over $13,000,000 and a staff of over 300, it's about time they do more than lobby the Congress for special favors. It's about time they do something in your community now!

Ken McLean: Did you ever get into the issue of Gale attacking the American Bankers' Convention at McCormick Place? You know that story? You know, Gale sort of specialized in invading meetings and conventions of bankers and hooting and hollering and embarrassing them and blowing horns and stuff like that. And the bankers just hated it and they just expected it.

So one year they had their annual convention at McCormick Place in Chicago. They were afraid that Gale and her troops were going to come in and parade and make a lot of ruckus. So they set up these elaborate barriers that would prevent any unauthorized person from getting into the building. Except Gale figured, well, McCormick Place is right on the lake. You know if not by land then by sea.

So she hired some kind of a boat. She was going to land right outside the convention and then sneak in the back way. I don't know how many people she had in the boat. But it was overloaded and the boat almost capsized and they had to call the Coast Guard to rescue her. She almost lost it. The bankers were quite amused about Gale's aborted efforts, how she'd attacked them by boat. The boat was almost capsized and they had to be rescued. But it made the news.

Michael Westgate: Gale, with strong support from Northwestern University in particular, had collected, analyzed and presented enough evidence to convince Congress to pass HMDA. But there was no way this voluntary effort could be sustained nationally. It had to be the banks and S&Ls which provided the data and they would do so only if the regulatory agencies required it. Then, on an as-needed basis, neighborhood groups could analyze it and take corrective actions if necessary.

From "The Next Move," *DISCLOSURE* #22 (Sept. 1976):

Gale Cincotta: Neighborhood People across the country are presently visiting their financial institutions—in order to collect the disclosure data necessary to nationally analyze the effect of lending policies on their neighborhoods. And what is Congress doing? After those lengthy hearings, after countless letters from their constituents back home, after intensive opposition lobbying by the industry, after debates on the floor of the House and Senate, Congress deemed the legislation crucial enough to pass. And yet, that same Congress has not mandated any federal agency to collect, publicly distribute and analyze this all important data.

Again, the burden has been left to us the people of the neighborhoods. And as we face a new Congress after the election, we must be prepared to pick up a hammer to nail down money for our neighborhoods. The disclosure data is the nails for building reinvestment strategy. The hammer required is the national anti-redlining law preventing geographical discrimination.

Nationally we are following up the commitments made by the FDIC and the FHLBB to collect and analyze the disclosure data, investigate lending practices and develop reinvestment recommendations. Ideally, after collecting and analyzing the data, we should be meeting with local and state governmental officials and lending representatives to implement reinvestment programs in our neighborhoods.

No matter who wins the presidential election or what shifts occur in Congress, our next move is to push for national legislation prohibiting geographical discrimination. Not until redlining is clearly against the law will we find our money flowing freely to our neighborhoods.

We got the nails to rebuild our neighborhoods. Now we want the hammer to nail them home. It's our money.

Michael Westgate:: Gale also realized that the premise that housing prices are set by equally willing and informed buyers and sellers is a fiction.

It is the financial institutions, based on the appraisals that they commission, which sets the prices—or at least 70-95% of the prices, depending on the level of financing which they provide. The buyers control 5-30% of the price, depending on their down payments. Sellers play a relatively passive role. They can accept or reject the combined offers made by the buyers and lenders.

Sellers usually employ real estate agents to act on their behalf. Unfortunately, particularly in a "changing neighborhood," there are too often unscrupulous agents who act illegally in individual cases to profit at the expense of both the buyer and the seller. Or, less obviously, they may encourage changeover since agents, who are paid on a commission basis, have greater chances to profit from a neighborhood's changing hands rapidly. The faster the changeover, the greater the opportunity for profits.

From *DISCLOSURE* #24 (Dec. 1976)
Appraisal – The Concealed Weapon

Appraisal is the method used to determine the value of a home. In a normal situation the mortgage lender wants an appraisal of the property so that it can be determined how much money should be lent on the home. However, behind this simple definition is a concealed subjective process that results in life and death decisions for a neighborhood. Biased perceptions and subjective evaluation are prominent in the appraisal process just as they have been in mortgage lending. In many city and inner ring suburban neighborhoods, the proximity of a home to minority populations and/or the projected "economic life" of the neighborhood becomes a more important consideration in appraisal than the age or quality of the property.

A recent survey of realtors in Chicago showed drastic variances in the price of similar type property from one neighborhood to another. The price range for a brick six-room two-flat from 50 to 70 years old varied from $28,000 to $70,000. The only explanation for this variance was the geographic location of the property...

How do these variances develop? When a neighborhood is initially targeted for decline, appraisal is used as a form of redlining. When someone wishes to sell their home and finds a buyer who agrees to a certain price, the deal is dependent on the buyer getting a mortgage. If the parties agree to a price of $25,000 and the buyer has a $5000 down payment, the buyer needs a $20,000 mortgage. But because the appraiser and the lending institution perceive that the area may decline, they may value the property at $22,500 and only offer a $17,500 mortgage. This lowballing of the market price means one of two things, either the buyer will have to come up with an additional $2500 or the seller will have to accept $22,500. If either balks, the deal is off and redlining through a low appraisal has taken place.

If the seller agrees to accept $22,500, it is the beginning of declining property values in a neighborhood. These initial transactions are then used as comparables which appraisers use in making future decisions about the value of property in the neighborhood. A declining trend is established which eventually drops the bottom out of the market. The lenders' and appraisers' perceptions of decline are fulfilled through their own standard operating procedures.

Michael Westgate: It is the self-fulfilling nature of appraisers' reliance on each others' figures that is particularly difficult to tackle. Appraisers are required to arrive at their determinations of value by three supposedly different methods. The first is replacement cost; the second is an income approach (what is its value based on rental income projections); the third is comparables. The last is the one most commonly given the most weight. In my opinion, all three should be given equal weight. The other change I would advocate is not giving the appraiser the amount of the offer. He/she should make their appraisal independent of that information.

From *Urban Disinvestment: New Implications For Community Organization, Research and Public Policy by Arthur J. Naparstek and Gale Cincotta* (Joint Publication of The National Center for Urban Ethnic Affairs and NTIC, 1976):
A report entitled "Home Mortgage Financing and Racial and Economic Integration," prepared by the U.S. Commission on Civil Rights contains among its findings that "a professional appraisal form used until the early 1970s inquired whether a neighborhood's ethnic composition was changing. If such a shift was occurring, the value of the property would be lowered for appraisal purposes." (13)

***DISCLOSURE* (in the same issue):**
One encouraging aspect is that the United States Attorney's office is presently suing the Society of Real Estate Appraisers, the Federal Home Loan Bank Board, the American Institute of Real Estate Appraisers, and the U.S. Savings and Loan League to remove from the textbooks references to "changing", "transitional" and "homogeneous" neighborhoods. The appraisal manuals emphasize the term homogeneous, meaning all white, as describing the ideal neighborhood for investment.

Community people cannot wait for the government to place controls on appraisals. This concealed arbitrary process of appraisers and lenders which categorizes and destroys neighborhoods must be openly challenged by the organized community.

Michael Westgate: Less than a year after President Ford had signed HMDA, Gale and others were back before Congress taking the regulators to task. It was to prove an uphill battle which consumed much of NPA and Gale's energies over the coming years. They did ultimately prevail, but this was a taste of the long fight yet to come.

DISCLOSURE (in the same issue):
Oversight Hearings on Disclosure

On Tuesday, Nov. 23, 1976, the Senate Committee on Banking, Housing and Urban Affairs held hearings on the implementation of the Home Mortgage Disclosure Act. The principal witness, Gale Cincotta, Chairperson of NPA, recommended additions to the regulations governing the Disclosure Act and called for three critical legislative amendments. Ms. Cincotta pointed out that the Federal Reserve Board to date has failed to exercise its authority to make the many necessary regulatory additions.

The first regulatory recommendation presented by NPA was for a standardized reporting format. At present, financial institutions are allowed to report in a variety of "homemade" formats. A uniform reporting format will reduce confusion and inaccuracy in collection and analysis of the data. "Homemade is fine when you're talking about soup," stated Cincotta, "but when federal data is concerned we ought to be more professional."

Another regulatory recommendation was that federal regulatory bodies collect the data from all institutions immediately. As astounding as it may seem, no federal agency is now charged with that responsibility.

Finally, there must be established by regulation a tight time schedule by which the Federal government checks for compliance with the law. The FDIC's and FHLBB's existing schedule is to check for compliance as part of their regular examining process. At that rate the compliance check would run well into the second year's reporting.

Ms. Cincotta also noted that her recommendations were proposed to the Federal Reserve Board by NPA during the time that the regulations were being written. The Fed, however, chose to ignore them.

Michael Westgate: In a move which proved prescient for the future, Gale asked that mortgage bankers be included in reporting mortgage data and that all financial institutions disclose the composition of their entire portfolios. Had these been in place, and published on a computerized basis, as she also demanded, the foes of deregulation would have had data to fight harder against deregulation in the coming decades. The regulators might have seen the sources of the real estate bubble of 2002-10 in time to at least slow the growth of the bubble and, conceivably, to prevent the world-wide recession which followed.

DISCLOSURE (in the same issue):

In the second part of her testimony, Ms. Cincotta proposed three [additional] specific legislative amendments to the Disclosure Act for Congress to consider:

1) The Act must be amended to include disclosure by mortgage bankers.
2) A federal agency must be appointed the task of compiling, computerizing, analyzing and publicizing the disclosure data.
3) The act must be amended to include full investment portfolio disclosure.

Terming the amendments "critical to the future of our country and the first step towards a national audit," Ms. Cincotta went on to say: "Last year's Congress, with considerations of such proposals as the Financial Institutions Act and the FINE study, considered radical changes in the financial institutions' structure of this country. These discussions can be expected to continue next year. How can any changes in banking and savings and loan structure, including inter-state branching, be intelligently considered without full knowledge of past lending patterns and national pictures of redlining?"

As a final note, Ms Cincotta pointed out the need for a national anti-redlining law: "This country needs legislation that outlaws geographic discrimination in lending. The practice of denying a loan to any individual solely on the basis of the geographic location of the property is the most insidious form of redlining and must be stopped! Such a law should contain strict enforcement provisions and penalties."

Michael Westgate: It was Gale's dream to have "a national audit" by which she meant a balance sheet showing all the sources and uses of funds in the national real estate economy. It was a remarkable vision for a woman with a tenth-grade education. But it was one to which the chairman of the Federal Reserve and others with whom she had working sessions should have paid more heed.

The FINE Study to which she refers, was the "Financial Institutions and the Nation's Economy" report, a very wide-ranging study done by the House Banking Committee.

Completed in 1973, it recommended, among many other controversial measures, consolidating the regulators while expanding the role of S&Ls to include checking accounts.

HMDA was "sunsetted," requiring renewal every five years. The lending industry immediately began fighting against its renewal in 1980. It finally attained permanent status in 1988.

From *DISCLOSURE* #41 (Oct. 1978)
Lending Industry Opens Drive To Kill Disclosure Acts

The industry's main argument to date is that nobody is using HMDA reports, so they are a needless expense. Soon they will argue that redlining no longer exists—so why report lending patterns?

A survey done by a lending industry trade association, the U.S. League of Savings Associations, supposedly documents HMDA's uselessness. According to this survey, 71% of the 1,943 S&Ls responding had not received a single request for their 1977 HMDA report. But the survey covers fewer than half of the over 4,000 S&L s in this country. And since the survey was done in July while the S&Ls only started reporting 1977 loans in April 1978, the league's sample is both hurried as well as incomplete. Despite this, Rollie Barnard of the League admitted in August testimony before the House Financial Institutions Subcommittee that one S&L in Illinois had received 741 HMDA requests!

In testimony before the same subcommittee in late July, the federal lending regulators gave their opinions on HMDA. While not explicitly negative about HMDA, the regulators left themselves plenty of room to eventually oppose extension of HMDA.

Cantwell Muckenfuss III, Deputy Comptroller of the Currency, had the most positive comments about HMDA. He admitted that the Comptroller's office has used HMDA in Fair Housing examinations and he also cited an NTIC study showing use of HMDA in 39 of the nations' 50 largest cities. But these comments were blunted when he added: "It appears that, in the regular Fair Housing examinations, use of HMDA data is too time consuming when analyzed meticulously, and that the time costs do not justify the inconclusive results obtained."

Another regulator, Federal Deposit and Insurance Corporation Chairman George LeMaistre, said that "if it is deemed appropriate to continue some form of mandatory disclosure after the expiration of HMDA a more useful system of disclosure should be designed". LeMaistre also testified that "given the conceptual problems associated with HMDA (lack of data on mortgage market demand and the exclusion of some lenders), the federal supervisory agencies have been reluctant to commit the resources and absorb the costs that centralized collection and processing of HMDA would entail."

The regulators seem to be saying that HMDA must be greatly expanded before they will take the responsibility to do anything meaningful with it. Neighborhood groups must continue pushing regulators to use what is already available. NPA would like wider disclosure under HMDA and mandatory central collection. For now, regulators must be pushed to use or at least collect the data that does exist.

Regulators can never be expected to push for a tougher HMDA. One reason for this is that they compete with each other. They must try to keep lenders from transferring to the jurisdiction of another regulator with fewer controls. This competitive atmosphere makes it very unlikely that any of the regulators will propose expanded HMDA. In other words, the regulators are saying they will only act on HMDA if it is expanded, but that they won't support expansion. That support of double-talk calls for pressure.

CHAPTER 12

"The mental constructs we used in writing CRA were like a Kafka novel in which the banks would be perennially accused of some crime but we would never quite define what the crime was."

PASSAGE OF COMMUNITY REINVESTMENT ACT (CRA) (1976 - October 12, 1977)

Michael Westgate: As soon as HMDA passed, Gale and Shel moved on to get enforcement powers and pass the Community Reinvestment Act (CRA) in 1977. These twin pieces of legislation would shape how regulated lenders responded to individual needs for financing housing, on a neighborhood and community level, for decades to come. Had they brought the insurance companies and the mortgage companies under comparable national legislation, the mistakes made in mortgage lending which led to the national housing crisis of 2007, spreading globally in 2008, would not have happened or would at least have been mitigated. It is the unregulated lenders, not those regulated and subject to CRA, which were responsible.

HMDA was in many ways the brainchild of Gale Cincotta. It embodied in federal law the concepts Gale had been advocating in person, in actions, and through the *DISCLOSURE* newsletter. HMDA metamorphosed many times between the piece of paper described by Shel Trapp and the final product of Congressional committee hearings and the political process. CRA was the implementation of policy, based on the data collected under HMDA. One was of little use without the other.

From "The Next Move", *DISCLOSURE #15* (Jan. 1976)
Gale Cincotta: For too long, bankers and bureaucrats have tried to sell us the concept of a "throw away" society. Older neighborhoods, older homes, and older people have been considered expendable, yet they are the backbone of this country, our cities are made up of older neighborhoods. And the mentality that classifies them as disposable which has created the crisis which we must now confront.

We need a National Neighborhood Reinvestment Policy. Even though we have raised the issues, legislation still is proposed that ignores our needs. Although the ink has not even dried on HMDA, the DISCLOSURE bill, the industry has tried to slip major financial changes and further disinvestment policies by us.

It is no longer enough to react to bad legislation. We need a national decision that neighborhood reinvestment is a top priority. In 1947, when Europe was in crisis after World War II, a decision was made by our government that saving Europe was the top priority. A Policy Planning Staff was established within the State Department to develop short-term and long-term strategies for what was later to be called "The Marshall Plan". The dollars were allocated to make it work. The older cities, the older neighborhoods and the older people of Europe were not considered disposable.

Now in 1976, it is time for our government to realize that America's neighborhoods are in crisis. The decision has to be made, just as it was made for Europe. A plan to save our neighborhoods has to be developed and the dollars found to make it work. We are not disposable.

A National Neighborhood Reinvestment Policy is essential to the future of this country. The need is there. The demand is there. Our agenda of NEIGHBORHOODS FIRST is there. But Congress is not there. The private sector is not there. Where are they?

Michael Westgate: Gale continued to battle on several fronts, not just with Congressional testimony, but through trying to make her agenda part of the national Democratic Party agenda. She also worked hard to get the Federal Home Loan Bank Board as well as the other regulators to pay more attention.

From *DISCLOSURE #16* (March 1976)
FHLBB Moves on Reinvestment

During the past months many of us have been pursuing the concept—Reinvestment. As usual the community has been ahead of the regulatory agencies. The Federal Home Loan Bank Board is starting to take their direction from us.

On Dec. 4, 1975, the FHLBB took action to establish an Office of Neighborhood Reinvestment by approving FHLBB resolution #75-1088. The reason given for this office is "to provide better and more efficient assistance to savings and loan associations in neighborhood reinvestment efforts." Specifically, the Office of Neighborhood Reinvestment will:

- assist the Board, the Banks, the members of the Federal Home Loan Bank System and other financial institutions in the development of programs and strategies to increase and stabilize urban residential lending;
- provide assistance in the organization, development, and continued operations of "Neighborhood Housing Services" programs;

- provide assistance to other public or private urban preservation or improvement programs;
- and collect and disseminate information regarding urban preservation or improvement programs.

It took the FHLBB two years to admit that redlining exists and write an anti-redlining regulation. It has taken them only a year to learn that reinvestment is needed in the urban centers. They are learning much faster these days.

When local groups now meet with local institutions on reinvestment strategies and meet the same old rhetoric, a good demand might be to have the Office of Neighborhood Reinvestment come out and teach the local institutions about reinvestment. If they say they don't know what that is, tell them to look up: The amendment relating to the creation of the Office of Neighborhood Reinvestment/Title 12 – Banks and Banking / Chapter V – FHLBB / Subchapter B – Federal Home Loan Bank System / Part 522 – Organization of the Banks. Throw their own regulations back at them.

From "The Next Move" (from the same issue)

GALE CINCOTTA: On to Washington. The date is set. On June 13th and 14th, 1976, grass-roots people from around the country will be attending National People's Action's Fifth Annual Conference in Washington, DC. The banking regulators, the HUD bureaucrats, and the Congressional representatives are all in Washington. It's time for us to be in Washington.

This is a party platform. We cannot let the election politics and the bicentennial hoopla keep us from our goal of a National Neighborhood Reinvestment Policy. The People's Platform: Neighborhoods First has to be dealt with. Our neighborhoods cannot afford headlines about pretty politicians and petty scandals while our cities continue to be sold down the drain.

From Neighborhoods First meetings that have already been held throughout the country, people have raised the issues of a neighborhood reinvestment by the private sector, a cleanup of the FHA scandals, more CD funds for rehab and better senior programs. During the next three months, we have to continue to build the People's Platform: Neighborhoods First at the grass-roots level...

As the seniors have said, "Don't Agonize—Organize!" Organize your Neighborhoods First meetings. Organize your groups for our next move on Washington, DC.

Michael Westgate: An article in the April 23, 1976 *Kansas City Star* ("'Saving Neighborhoods' Vital, Demo Committee to Be Told") reported on the arrival of NPA representatives to testify before the Democratic National Committee's regional platform hearing. "Everyone is complaining about the lack of focus in this presidential campaign," said NPA chairman Paul Bloyd. "Well we're talking about specific issues, things people are concerned about."

Bud Kanitz: Gale's "kitchen cabinet" on policy issues in those days included Tommy FitzGibbon and me and Cal Bradford. I was talking to a banker and he was bitching about Gale: "All that Gale wants is more programs and funds from the federal government." So he and I got into a big argument because I said, "The only reason Gale wants funds from the federal government such as HUD is because funds from the private sector, as in banks, dried up in low and moderate income neighborhoods. And that's why she pushed to get CRA passed."

From "The Next Move", *DISCLOSURE* #18 (May 1976)

Gale Cincotta: The next move is to Washington, DC. As we have been saying, we have only seen the tip of the disinvestment iceberg that continues to sink neighborhood after neighborhood.

- While Community Development funds continue to pad administrative salaries, Chicago still has over 3,000 abandonments in need of rehab, Atlanta over 4,000 and Detroit over 8,000.
- 75% of all applicants for HUD Section 518(b) payback continue to be rejected for unstated reasons.

Government officials are beginning to send out the icebreakers.

- On April 16th, the Justice Department filed suit against the nation's savings and loan associations, mortgage bankers and real estate appraisers for allegedly under-appraising homes in racially changing areas.
- A federal judge in Cincinnati has sent to trial a suit against a lender for denying a mortgage to a credit worthy family in an integrated neighborhood.
- Congress is holding Senate hearings on how governmental regulators supervise the country's financial institutions.
- Senator Humphrey has picked up our challenge of establishing a Marshall Plan for the cities and neighborhoods.
- The Democratic Party Platform is hearing the planks of our People's Platform: Neighborhoods First.

But we can't lose the momentum. We need a National Neighborhood Reinvestment Policy that includes a federal law against redlining on the basis of geographical discrimination. We need a policy that provides programs and incentives to reinvest in our neighborhoods. We cannot afford to have our proposals lost. We need to be in Washington for National People's Action's Fifth National conference on June 13th and 14th to see these proposals through.

Now's the time for USS NEIGHBORHOODS to steer through the icebergs before the call of "abandon ship" is sounded. On June 13th, the call is "All hands on deck!" Take your battle stations in Washington.

Bud Kanitz: Gale's interactions with Congress primarily were with the banking committees because they have jurisdiction over things like CRA and HMDA. But they also have jurisdiction over the HUD budget. There were two people in Washington that Gale would talk to, me and Allen Fishbein. Allen was "Mr. CRA" at the Center for Community Change, until he left CCC in 2003. But he had started at CCC in 1978, the year that CRA went into effect. So he has the absolute best archival knowledge of CRA from a legislative point of view of anybody in the world.

But when it came to getting Gale involved in policy matters in Washington, Allen served as the secretariat of something called the Save CRA Coalition, which brought organizations like NPA and ACORN together with the National Community Reinvestment Coalition. And Fishbein was the glue that held it all together to be able to do national advocacy.

Allen Fishbein was chief reinvestment strategist at the Center for Community Change. Gale often sought his counsel on the workings of FHA and on banking regulations: She knew that was her strength – speaking truth to power, and looking at it from the neighborhood lens. You could say it was her personality, or her need to be the center of attention, or to get things her way. The other way to look at it is that she just had this clear sense that she knew what was right.

From "The Next Move", *DISCLOSURE #19* (June 1976)
NPA's Fifth Annual National Conference, June 13-14, 1976, Washington, DC

Gale Cincotta: At our First National Conference in 1972, we called ourselves "city survivors." We identified the economic "profit-motivated" reasons why our neighborhoods were being destroyed and decided to be more than survivors by organizing nationally. Now in 1976, we find ourselves together again, but this time as participants in the decision-making that affects our neighborhoods.

We have brought our People's Platform: Neighborhoods First to the Democratic and Republican parties. On Monday, June 14th, the Senate Committee on Banking, Housing and Urban Affairs will be holding precedent setting hearings on the needs of America's neighborhoods. We have moved our issues from the streets to the halls of Congress as we did last year in our successful legislative battle for national disclosure. This time we're coming to DC with a wish list of issues we want Congress to deal with.

But Congress won't be the only one hearing our demands. June 14th will also be the date of the unveiling of the People's Bicentennial Monument to HUD—debris from abandoned homes throughout the country as a reminder that HUD's policies must be subjected to continuous vigilance. When the American Bankers Association meets on June 14th, they will find us there asking where their assets of $1,397,264,810,0000 are being loaned.

Michael Westgate: In a June 2, 1976 column in the *Washington Post,* "Beating The Drum On The Blue Collar Blues," Nicholas von Hoffman stated that in that bicentennial year 2,000 delegates to the NPA conference "apparently are intending to put their firecrackers under elected officials." Referring to Real Estate Investment Trusts he opined, "would that a modest fraction of the billions [bankers] have wasted on unwanted oil tankers and unsold condominiums had been dropped into some of our good, older neighborhoods."

From *DISCLOSURE #20* (July 1976)
When in the Course of Human Events...

On June 13-14, approximately 2,000 neighborhood leaders from 60 American cities and towns found it necessary to journey to our nation's capital to declare that the public policies of our federal government are denying them the decent and suitable living environment to which the laws of nature and of the government itself entitle them.

Redlining/Disclosure: In a meeting with the FDIC, they agreed to analyze data nationally and provide the information to community groups.

Reinvestment: NPA leaders testified before Senator Proxmire's committee on the need for a National Neighborhood Policy Act which he has co-sponsored with Senator Garn of Utah.

NPA Urges Neighborhood Policy: Amid the tumult of NPA's June convention in Washington, DC many community leaders found time to spotlight the widespread failure by HUD, CD and FHA experts and to praise the success of many community based programs working for neighborhood preservation...

The Senate committee was considering passage of a National Neighborhood Policy Act (S. 3554) which calls for a Presidential Commission which would, in Proxmire' s opinion, "make it a matter of Congressional intent that neighborhoods should be conserved and revitalized, and that policy should support that objective."

The Commission is to include five community group leaders among its twenty members and is authorized to evaluate current public policy and private investment, and to make recommendations to promote private reinvestment and to adapt public policy to neighborhood preservation.

Ms. Cincotta urged Congress and the proposed Commission to implement sixteen recommendations including double dollars for Community Development rehab funds, expansion of the Urban Reinvestment Task Force from $2 million to $100 million, rehabbing all HUD abandonments, passing national anti-redlining legislation, and overhaul of HUD, a restructuring of FHA, regulation of all mortgagors, expansion of the payback program, forebearance requirements, vast expansion of senior housing and senior subsidies, generic drug laws, LEAA grants directly to community groups, a war on hard drugs, and a national utility lifeline legislation.

American Bankers Association DC Meeting
Attended By 500 Community People:

On Monday afternoon, Redlining/Reinvestment groups paid a visit to the Washington Hilton where representatives of banks across the country were meeting. While "redlining" the meeting (and the Hilton) with red streamers and ribbons, leaders requested a meeting with conference officials. The wait was long and the bankers were reluctant. Four messengers took the NPA message to the ABA officials: (1) a hotel security guard, (2) a DC police officer, (3) a sympathetic banker delegate from New Jersey, and (4) a federal police officer. But the bankers stayed locked up in their conference rooms, guarded by a cordon of policemen.

Finally, after two hours of protest and chanting, former ABA president, Rex Morthland, agreed to meet outside the Hilton with the group. Alas, the ABA, he said, is "unfamiliar" with redlining. When pushed further, Mr. Morthland rejected the idea of another meeting with NPA representatives to clarify the issues and the demands. The ABA confrontation served to reinforce the need for a strong national anti-redlining law. The ABA is not going to take the initiative to end redlining by American banks.

FDIC Agrees To NPA Demand: At the close of Sunday morning's panel, Redlining/Reinvestment leaders put the demand for a disclosure report to Dr. Paul Horvitz, Director of Research for FDIC. In a signed statement, Dr. Horvitz agreed to compile a report and make it public. (It would seem that Dr. Horvitz' decision to deal with the facts of redlining and community pressure were profitable for him. He was promoted within the FDIC one week after the conference.)

Michael Westgate: During the 1976 conference, delegates boarded a bus, a van and twelve cars to "hit" the Capitol Hill home of Garth Marston, acting chairman of the Federal Home Loan Bank Board. Banging on his front door and calling for him, Gale and delegates handed out leaflets attacking Marston to neighbors attracted by the noise.

George Knight: Garth Marston got very upset. That bounced back on the Urban Reinvestment Task Force. The Bank Board knew that Gale was involved and close to Bill Whiteside who was perceived to be a shadow presence in the organization.

From "The Next Move," *DISCLOSURE #20* (July 1976)

Gale Cincotta: We won in Washington on June 13 & 14:

- HUD investigations of CD allocations
- FDIC collection and analysis of the national disclosure data
- National community hearings on crime

And most importantly, National People's Action moved the U.S. Senate to hold the first Congressional hearings on neighborhood policy. Senator Proxmire's proposed National Neighborhood Policy Act acknowledges that we all live in neighborhoods and this is the year of Neighborhoods First...

However, we raised our issues so much that President Ford has now jumped on the People's Neighborhoods First bandwagon. The President has appointed a cabinet level committee on neighborhood policy. This "star-studded committee" includes Sec. Simon (Treasury), Sec. Richardson (Commerce), Sec. Butz (Agriculture), Sec. Matthews (HEW), and is chaired by none other than HUD Sec. Carla Hills. This is Ford's response to our problems—appoint a committee of top bureaucrats led by the number one neighborhood offender Carla Hills with no provisions for participation by community activists.

Ford's committee and Proxmire's committee are ours. We raised the issues. We know what the problems are. The Ford-Hills committee must hold community hearings in all our cities. We cannot afford someone making political hay without making political commitments.

The next move is to follow-up our Washington victories with increased activities in all our cities and a joint attack on any Presidential commission on neighborhoods that doesn't include us. In short, Keep Organizing!

Michael Westgate: During the fight for HMDA and CRA, NTIC sent out a number of publications to get the message to the troops. They were reasonably priced. In addition to *DISCLOSURE*, which appeared every month or two, other publications in 1975-76 included:

- *The American Nightmare: Federal Housing Administration*, NTIC, 1975, $1.50
- *Dynamics of Organizing*, Shel Trapp, 1976, $2
- *Lending Policies Exposed: Prime Factor in Neighborhood Decay*, NTIC, 1976, $2
- *Urban Disinvestment: New Implications for Community Organization, Research and Public Policy*, Gale Cincotta and Art Naperstak, NTIC and National Center for Urban Ethnic Affairs, 1976, $2

From *DISCLOSURE #25* (Jan. 1977)
State of the Neighborhoods

Gale Cincotta: Neighborhood people have been cheated, lied to and systematically denied their right to control the decisions that affect their lives and communities. With each passing year and each new administration, the game remains the same.

Legislators, regulators and lenders, in their pursuit of profit and political position, have abandoned their responsibilities to the American public for efficient government and sound financial security. Every day officials in the public and private sectors make their far-reaching decisions without concern for people or knowledge of their needs:

- Decisions which provide tax shelters for the rich rather than incentives to build decent housing for the poor;
- Decisions which extend credit for foreign oil tankers that sink to the neglect of mortgages for the American home buyer;
- Decisions which give downtown development priority over neighborhood reinvestment;
- Decisions which encourage housing starts that most Americans will never be able to afford while vacant homes capable of rehab await the bulldozer.

New dealers may shuffle; but they still stack the cards. Legislators fail to legislate. Regulators refuse to regulate. They don't care whether neighborhoods live or die. It's time we put an end to this game.

It's our money. Our tax dollars, our spending dollars and our savings dollars, that keep this economy flowing but none of it flows back to us. We're angry and we have every right to be. They're our neighborhoods. Our lives and our children's futures are at stake.

It's time we exercise our rights of "first claim" on the resources of financial institutions and governmental agencies at every level:

- Our right to mortgage credit based on our financial standing, not the geographical location of the home;
- Our right to the revitalization of our neighborhoods by city governments;
- Our right to preserve and rehab existing housing stock;
- Our right to feel secure from crime;
- Our right to equitable utility rates as small consumers;
- Our right to have access to the decision-making process.

But rights are not granted. Rights are won...

Michael Westgate: Gale did not lessen her pressure on Washington when the Carter administration succeeded Ford's. Glen Elasseer of the *Chicago Tribune* quoted her on February 1, 1977 in a meeting with officials of the neighborhood coalition, "There's no honeymoon for neighborhoods... There is not going to be any honeymoon for Jimmy Carter... We're tired of being treated as bastard children." ("No Honeymoon for neighborhoods – Cincotta in capital to raise Cain at HUD")

Ann Vick-Westgate: How did HMDA grow into CRA?

Ken McLean: HMDA passed in '75 so then in the next Congress, starting from '76-78, Senator Proxmire wanted to follow up on it. With the victory over HMDA, he got interested in the neighborhood movement and the problem of neighborhood disinvestments, urban disinvestments. There was a guy from Minnesota who did a lot of work on it, Cal Bradford. He had written some interesting scholarly articles about the whole neighborhood disinvestment process. So we started holding hearings on it and gradually the idea of CRA evolved from those hearings. It wasn't really pushed by Gale. Senator Proxmire really invented CRA in pretty much the form it took.

Michael Westgate: CRA was not authored by Gale in the way that HMDA was, but Proxmire himself referred to her as the "Mother of CRA." Without the push from Gale and NPA, CRA is unlikely to have passed. For both laws, Proxmire was indispensable. Without his being in the right place at the right time, neither would have seen the light of day.

Ken McLean: The other thing about Proxmire is that he was a populist when it came to economic issues. He was very active in getting the pro-consumer legislation through; he was pretty much anti-big business. But he was very much a conservative when it came to federal funds. He was very skeptical especially of the HUD massive spending programs like urban renewal, model cities, UDAG, community development action block grants. He felt that a lot of the spending was wasteful and unproductive.

So he was looking for ways to make cities and neighborhoods more livable without spending a huge amount of the taxpayers' money. So in some ways the HMDA and CRA were natural issues for him. Here's a way to get private sector money back into our cities and neighborhoods without a massive HUD bureaucracy and the like and without massive federal spending.

So CRA evolved from his experience as chairman of the banking committee. As it turns out, back then in order to get a new bank charter, or even a new branch in a neighborhood, you had to come to the bank regulators in Washington. And you had to prove that the neighborhood needed a new bank. So if there were already some branches there and you felt you could do a better job in competing, they would say, "Well, no, sorry. We don't need a new branch." So it was almost like getting a radio station or a TV station.

It was a limited scarce resource that was allocated by the federal government. They had a monopoly on charters or branch locations and they gave them out. But they didn't really exact any quid pro quo. They gave them out if they felt that there was enough business for a new bank – they wouldn't muscle in too much on other people's business.

So from that we got the idea, well, if radio stations and TV stations can exact a public interest requirement… If you want to get a new TV channel you've got to devote a certain percentage of your broadcasting time to public programming. So [Senator Proxmire] said, "Why can't we apply that to banking?" And I said, "There's no reason why not. It's entirely logical". So that's where the idea of CRA came from. We drafted it, got something down on paper.

For a while we toyed around with percentages – that a bank would have to invest a certain percentage of the money that it took in. If a bank took in $100 million locally in deposits, then they would have to invest x percentage of that locally in loans. We shied away from that because he just didn't think it would work. It smelled too much of credit allocation.

So he kept the wording of it fairly loose. That banks have an obligation, not a requirement, but an obligation or a responsibility to meet the credit needs of their local communities. Their record in doing that would be taken into account by the regulators when they were issuing new charters and branch applications.

It was kind of a political process that we set up and the neighborhood groups would be able to come in and challenge a new branch application on the grounds that that particular bank didn't have a very good lending record. The regulators would have to listen to that and weigh it with all the other factors and make a decision.

Our idea was essentially to empower the neighborhood movement politically with some clout. Get them in the door. Back in those days the bankers wouldn't even talk to them. Didn't have to. So after CRA they had to talk to them. And it eventually grew and neighborhood groups became very adept at convincing banks to spend more money in the local neighborhoods.

Ann Vick-Westgate: So that's where Gale entered in, taking that legislation and that opening and using it in her neighborhoods.

Ken McLean: Yeah. That's right. Gale and then all the others – a lot of other neighborhood groups from around the country – began looking at the law and realizing the potential to extract the commitments from local banks. So that was the basic idea. It got through by a fluke.

Ann Vick-Westgate: How much of a fight was it to get it through?

Ken McLean: It was a terrible fight. The one advantage we had was Proxmire was chairman of the committee. Being the chairman of the committee, whenever a bill was before the committee the chairman would draft the bill and that became the document that the committee was working on. So if you put something in the bill and somebody wanted to knock it out, they needed a majority. If it was a tie, the tie goes to the runner, in this case being the chairman. So it saved the bill and that's exactly what happened.

There was a housing bill up in '77—a bill that had to be reauthorized. And he realized that CRA could never get through as a stand-alone measure. The banks had too much political power to be able to keep it bottled up. So he said, "Well, let's stick it on the housing bill. Maybe we can get it through if it's part of a much bigger housing bill."

So we did that; we could put it in the housing bill. And we were still down by two votes. We didn't have enough votes to get it passed on the committee. And then the S&L lobby were playing their hands. One day when we were meeting on the housing bill they got a senator to introduce some special amendments that favored the S&L industry. It sort of broadened their lending powers. So they were playing the same game. They were trying to stick it in the housing bill expecting that, well, the banks can't oppose it if it's part of the housing bill.

The only problem was there were two senators on the committee that were very much interested in banking reform, Ed Brooke [R-MA, 1967-79] and Thomas McIntyre [D-NH, 1962-79]. So they had this bill, sort of this general banking deregulation bill, that would broaden the lending powers of not just for the S&Ls but for banks and credit unions and everybody. They had this package they wanted to get through. And here came the S&Ls end-running the banking bill and sticking their stuff on the housing bill.

So they were just livid because the S &Ls succeeded. They got it added to the housing bill. Brooke and McIntyre were very much upset with them. And so their staff people said to me, "Well, my bosses are going to vote for CRA if you'd make a few little changes in the bill." So we said, "Okay, we'll make a few little changes." So that got us up to a tie vote. Somebody on the committee moved to knock it out and it failed on a tie vote. That means it stayed in the bill.

So then a few weeks later we took it up on the floor. And it came up on a Monday and there were about twenty absentees. The banking/S&L lobby got a senator to move to strike it from the bill. And on the Senate floor the motion to strike failed by about four or five votes.

But if you look at the absentees, about fifteen of the absentees would have voted against CRA and only five would have voted for it. So if they'd waited another day, they could have knocked it out. They just had poor timing. We couldn't tell when they would offer the amendment to strike. So it was pretty much their ineptness that allowed it to get through the Senate.

It never got through the House. So we went to conference with the House and the chairman of the Housing Subcommittee, Lud Ashton [D-OH, 1955-81], was very much against CRA. He didn't think it belonged in the bill, that it was kind of a stupid thing. And he just fought us tooth and toenail and wouldn't give in.

But he was for massive HUD spending programs. That's what he wanted. So you can see the deal that finally emerged. Senator Proxmire had to swallow his fiscal principles and agree to some extra spending that he really didn't want to agree to and Lud actually said, "OK, I'll take CRA." So that's how it got through.

There's one interesting issue on CRA about credit allocations. The bankers were saying this was credit allocation— next thing the U.S. will be a socialist country, government bureaucrats will be allocating debt. That was the big argument then. And it was fairly effective. Not only that but the bank regulators chimed in. The head of the FDIC and then the chairman of the Federal Reserve Board, Arthur Burns, said, "This is really bad." He talked in a W.C. Fields kind of pace. "This is the road to serfdom!"

So when it came up on the floor in the debate, I dug up a letter a few years before that Arthur Burns had sent to all the banks around the country. For some reason the Federal Reserve was worried about the financial plight of feedlot operators. They had overextended themselves and they had all these cattle and it was kind of a dip in the market and they were threatened with bankruptcy unless they can get credit. So Burns writes a letter to all the big banks in the country urging them to do the patriotic thing and loan money to these beleaguered feedlot operators. Well, you know, if that isn't credit allocation, what is?

So we trotted it out when the issue came up on the floor and somebody on the Republican side talked about credit allocation. We trotted out the Burns letter and said, "Well look at this! Here's Arthur Burns advocating credit allocations so what's with that about it?"

Michael Westgate: Who else in the Senate was involved either pro or con?

Ken McLean: Well, I know who con was. The people against it were Cranston [D-CA 1969-93] from California, and the Senator from North Carolina, Morgan [D-NC 1975-81]. We didn't really have any real strong allies. Some of the Democrats tolerated it. "Well, this is Proxmire's baby, you know. If he wants to get this through, we're not going to stand in his way."

It was really Proxmire. Were it not for Proxmire, HMDA would never have been passed. It would never have seen the light of day. And CRA would never have seen the light of day.

This was the Carter White House so they were mildly supportive, but they didn't spend a lot on time and muscle to get it through. The White House lobbyist at the time was Orrin Kramer. I think he runs some kind of a hedge fund now.

Bob Kuttner was on our staff. He did the staff work on CRA and maybe HMDA too. Kuttner has become a big political guru now; he runs the magazine *American Prospect.*

CRA was tailor-made for a group like Gale's to first of all be able to embarrass bankers, but then, secondly, know when to cut a deal. You raise hell and cut a deal…

John Hyman was then Comptroller of the Currency. Of the three banking agencies Hyman was probably the most helpful. He didn't exactly stick his neck out, but he didn't try to shoot a lot of arrows in it like Arthur Burns did. Then he spearheaded the regulations that surprised us. Our concept of CRA was to have a fairly small statute on the books in which the banks would have an obligation to do something but we never quite precisely defined what it is they had to do. So, no matter what they did, there was always some argument about you really ought to do more. We never wanted to put down on paper "if you do this exactly then you're ok." We didn't want to have that dividing line.

The mental constructs we used in writing the CRA act were sort of like a Kafka novel in which the banks would be perennially accused of some crime but we would never quite define what the crime was.

Ann Vick-Westgate: Was there anything in writing the legislation that you didn't get in but you wanted in, that you had to compromise and leave out?

Ken McLean: The big fear of the conservatives was credit allocation so we put in the law, especially in the legislative history, no, this is not credit allocation, there is nothing in this legislation that makes the banks make any one particular loan. We were not in favor of banks making bad loans. We were not in favor of any percentage requirements. So that became part of the legislative history and influenced the floor debate and the committee reports and when they write the regs.

And it is the regs that are so detailed that it scared the "bejesus" out of the smaller banks. The big banks were pretty much active in opposing it. The small banks from smaller towns didn't really have an urban disinvestment issue anyway so they were kind of on the sidelines. But then when the regulators came out with these detailed regs about CRA, the smaller banks were just terrorized. They said, "Oh my God, we're gonna get sued. We're gonna get our knuckles rapped. We're gonna be pilloried. Why can't we get exempt?"

So for years and years the small banks from Wisconsin would come into Proxmire and complain about CRA and say, "Why can't we get an exemption? We don't do anything bad." For about ten years after CRA. Finally they realized they could live with it. But for about ten years every year they would visit Proxmire and push for an exemption from CRA. And he would waltz 'em around and say, "Well, you make some good points, you know, and we'll have to think about it."

Michael Westgate: How about the unregulated mortgage industry? Was there any discussion of how to deal with mortgage bankers and others?

Ken McLean: Very little then. Over the years that became an issue but back then you were primarily focused on the depository lenders, the S&Ls and banks. It's hard to apply the concept to a mortgage banker because they don't have any actual money themselves. They act as the middleman between the lender and the borrower.

Back in the '70s mortgage bankers weren't quite the force that they are now so most lending was done by primary lenders that paid the loan from their own portfolio and held the loan.

There used to be a saying back then in the S&L business. This is probably a little before the '70s but in the '60s when things were kind of settled down, they used to call the S&L business the "4-6-3 business." You take money in at 4%, you loan it out at six, and you hit the golf course at 3:00.

Michael Westgate: What kind of a legacy did Gale Cincotta leave and what's the unfinished business? Obviously predatory lending is one of the big issues today.

Ken McLean: Right. Back then it wasn't even on the horizon. Redlining was the big issue. If you go back and search the newspapers, you'll find that there were a lot of stories in the papers about redlining. There was a pretty interesting series of articles in Washington about the D.C. banks who took money in, in the low-income minority neighborhoods in Washington, but most of the mortgage loans they made were out in the suburbs.

Michael Westgate: Did insurance redlining come under Proxmire's committee?

Ken McLean: Well, we tried to get it and we never quite successfully grabbed off the insurance jurisdiction. We had some competitors over that, the Commerce Committee and to some extent the Judiciary Committee because they had jurisdiction over anti-trust. So we were never really able to get a handle on the insurance redlining.

Michael Westgate: Were the problems concentrated in the cities?

Ken McLean: Pretty much urban, pretty much in the cities. Cal Bradford just wrote some interesting articles about the dynamics that drive the disinvestment process. You know bankers are not totally irrational in not wanting to loan money in a declining community. When a community is perceived to be declining, property values are going to go down because a lot of people leave and it's hard to sell. And the lower income people come up to replace them and then more people leave. Pretty soon property values plummet and the security for the loan is jeopardized.

So it's almost like a self-fulfilling prophecy. Bankers become a little nervous, and then their own nervousness leads to the fruition of their fears. So you need some kind of a counter-dynamic to reverse the process. You know, get money and people and activities, and energy and vitality coming back into the community.

Michael Westgate: At the other end of the spectrum you get the gentrification, which again becomes a self-fulfilling prophecy. It was not on the agenda in those days.

Ken McLean: That's right. It's sort of dawning as an issue. There were a lot of issues with FHA which Gale specialized in scoring. A lot of the block-busting tactics in Chicago were put together by an unholy alliance of mortgage bankers and FHA. Mortgage bankers could always get FHA insurance. So the mortgage banker would go into a lily-white neighborhood in Chicago, an urban ethnic one like where I grew up on the Southwest Side, blue collar, lower middle class, working-class neighborhood.

They'd go into a neighborhood like that and warn all the white people, "The blacks are coming, the blacks are coming. You've got to sell out, you've got to sell out." Well, everybody would get scared and sell out. And the FHA would come in and make mortgage loans to black people who really weren't up to snuff as far as homeownership was concerned. They lived in apartments and didn't have the income to support the mortgage.

The mortgage banker didn't care because it was all insured by the Federal government. So they'd have a lot of unqualified black families moving in who maybe had the house for a year or two, then they had to foreclose on them. And it became boarded up. The whole neighborhood was decimated by this unholy alliance.

So, oddly enough, even though the S&Ls and the banks opposed CRA, Proxmire was really on the side of the primary lender. He was always a little bit skeptical of the FHA and mortgage bankers because they had no real local stake. They made a loan and they sold it off into the secondary market or to some other distant funder. So they didn't really care whether the neighborhood went downhill or not. Whereas a local lender has got a stake in the community; he does care about the dynamics and the prosperity of the local neighborhood and wants to see it grow and prosper. So he's got a stake in the community.

Michael Westgate: How about the role of Fannie Mae, of Freddie Mac back then?

Ken McLean: Well, again this goes back to the mortgage bankers. They talk a pretty good game but, again, they don't have this stake that a local primary lender has. The only thing different about Fannie Mae and Freddie Mac is they do have some private capital involved, probably not enough. But there are some investors who would lose money if Fannie and Freddie were to go under, so that makes them a little more conservative than mortgage bankers who deal strictly with FHA, and FHA is a government program. All they would lose would be their jobs. They wouldn't even lose their jobs, would they? There's less counter pressure in the FHA segment of the market.

Ann Vick-Westgate: What happened with the subsequent reauthorizations?

Ken McLean: Well, fortunately CRA had learned their lessons in HMDA. CRA is permanent law.

Michael Westgate: Did Gale and others lobby other Senators from around the country on CRA?

Ken McLean: Well, they did but you have to say they really weren't as strong as they are now. And Senator Proxmire really got it through pretty much by smoke and mirrors. It was one of those flukes of history that everything just fell into place about the right time.

Nobody paid much attention back then to the neighborhood movement. Now, you know, Phil Gramm became chairman of the banking committee a few years ago, the Republicans always hated CRA, they want to repeal it. But they realized they wouldn't have the votes to repeal it; they'd be hearing from the neighborhoods. CRA and other factors helped the neighborhood groups gain political power so they finally had some clout. So the best the Republicans could do would be just to "reform it" and even then they didn't have the votes although Phil Gramm certainly tried.

**From *Credit to the Community: Community Reinvestment and Fair Lending Policy in the United States*
By Dan Immergluck (Armonk, NY: M.E. Sharpe, Inc., 2004)**

Supporters of federal anti-redlining policies did not begin with CRA. The notion of pushing through a statute that obligated banks to serve their local communities, and to penalize those that did not, was seen as a politically unfeasible first step... It certainly helped that MacLean had grown up on Chicago's southwest side, a part of town threatened with decline. He had discussed issues of neighborhood decay with Proxmire in the past and arranged a meeting with the senator for NPA. [143]

Michael Westgate: McLean being from Chicago, understanding first-hand the problems Gale was fighting, was indispensable, as was Proxmire's moving up to chair the Senate Banking Committee.

Cal Bradford: John McKnight saw the need for the Woodstock Institute as did Ron Grzywinski, who was operating the South Shore Bank in Chicago for investment. Early on, we had these conferences. Gale would come out, as did Bob Kuttner from Proxmire's staff. And McKnight and Grzywinski. All these people would come out for two or three days. That's one of the times where we talked about the Community Reinvestment Act. Gale had this idea. Kuttner had met with Ron Grzywinski and Ron had written on the back of an envelope what he thought banks should do, literally, and gave it back to Kuttner. Then they had this meeting out there.

In the midst of all of the discussions about reinvestment, and how neighborhood economies worked, Kuttner kept saying, "Well, what can we do in Washington?" And that's sort of what came out of it because Kuttner had already worked with Gale on the Home Mortgage Disclosure Act. That was clear to her – the first thing you had to have was disclosure. You had to know what people were doing. That's because she felt strongly. You know, it's an interesting, conservative, democratic notion even for economists. It's like if you have information, then you can act. And you don't need the government. You don't need too much, but you need some protection from too much power from corporations and stuff. It's a very conservative philosophy really.

People can take care of themselves if the information is there, if everybody has information. If we don't know what the banks and the insurance companies are doing, then they're not to be trusted. "Because in a real economy, everybody has knowledge," Gale said. "That's what economists always tell me about. Everybody has knowledge and makes informed decisions." She was just saying, "Well, we just want to make informed decisions. And you're not treating us all the same. Wealthy people have access to stuff we don't have access to. So we're going to make you tell us where you make your loans."

Disclosure was a big issue in insurance redlining. "Find out where you have your policies and then the neighborhoods can analyze all this." And she really believed in that. That's why they named the newsletter that. It had been called *The National Peoples Action on Housing Newsletter*. Right away it became *DISCLOSURE* because that was the key issue. And always, in the early years, the solution to most problems was disclosure. The liberals would have said the solution's got to be some government program. "Just give us the facts and we'll deal. We'll take it from there."

Michael Westgate: Gale had a powerful argument: "Just level the playing field."

Cal Bradford: It's part of a whole sense of building leadership and confidence. Gale really understood what Ivan Illich was about, even though I don't think she ever read him. It was, "Well, you can't then create a bunch of professionals to run it for them. You either trust people or you don't trust people. All those other people are running their own lives in the suburbs. It's because they don't have to figure out how to make their own loans. People are willing to make loans to them and make investments in them. So if you just treated us the same way and made investments in our education, in our physical structure, then we would be okay. Because we're okay, we found the problem and it's not us."

The answer was an investment question, not a program question. That was pretty consistent. There were a lot of neighborhood programs and a lot of pilot programs they created, but the real goal all the time was to see what could be done. In some cases, in education, yes, the government had to give the resources because they weren't equally distributed.

But she didn't see that as welfare, she just saw that as giving people fair access to the same resources. I think the liberals thought she was one of them. Because it was like income redistribution, but she never believed you should sort of mechanically do that. It was <u>resource</u> redistribution.

From *DISCLOSURE #29* (June 1977)
Redlining—There Ought to be a Law

In January all four regulators – the Federal Reserve Board, the Federal Deposit Insurance Corporation, the Federal Home Loan Bank Board, and the Comptroller of the Currency – were presented by NPA leadership with an outline of reinvestment regulations.

- Outlawing redlining – or geographic discrimination in lending. That regulators inform banks and S&Ls that they may not refuse to make a mortgage loan, or impose unfavorable terms (higher down payment, under-appraisal, shorter term, etc.) because of the neighborhood in which the house is located.
- Examining each institution's disclosure data and identifying neighborhoods that can be considered part of that institution's service area that are receiving no or very few loans.
- Requiring that institutions aggressively solicit loans from these underserved neighborhoods by various required affirmative

lending programs, i.e. with direct neighborhood advertising, contacts with realtors, etc. In other words, develop a marketing plan designed to solicit home loans and home improvement loans—the way they now do for suburban areas.

- ♦ Require that institutions clean up the application process. Many people never get to fill out written applications because of verbal refusals or discouragements emanating from the bank or savings and loan, or the institution has such a bad reputation for lending locally that even approaching the bank or S&L is considered an outright waste of time. Frequently buyers are advised not to apply by real estate brokers who tell them such-and such an institution in the neighborhood or all institutions in the neighborhood are not worth going to because of their past record. Another discouragement method is cropping up in Illinois and California. Institutions are asking for anywhere from $65 to more that $100 as an "application fee" to be paid up front at the time of applying. This makes it an expensive process to shop for a loan, especially when an institution is negative about the possibility of granting the loan.
- ♦ That the regulators impose severe sanctions against institutions who don't comply, even lifting their charter.

This is a rational, straightforward outline for solving the problem. Everyone accepts now that redlining exists. Congress, bankers and savings and loan officials, and even President Carter, who pledged to outlaw redlining when he was elected.

From "The Next Move" in the same issue

Gale Cincotta: For twenty-eight issues of *DISCLOSURE*, I have been using this column to share with you my thoughts on the issues that confront our neighborhoods. Now we are approaching our sixth annual conference and I don't think it's necessary to talk specifically about the issues this month. You all know the issues and why these issues have brought you from your neighborhoods across the country to be together here in Washington.

What I would like to share with you are my feelings as we come together again. Every year the conference becomes more and more like a reunion of good friends or an extended family. And in one sense that is precisely what we are—an extended family of neighborhood people. Sure, our homes may be hundreds of miles apart, but the issues that threaten our very survival and the fruits of our hard-earned efforts have brought us together as a close-knit family draws together in the face of hard times.

At the first national conference in 1972, we called ourselves "city survivors" as we first realized the common enemies we faced. At the third national conference in 1974, we raised our voices as one with chants of "Full Disclosure." In 1976, we built the People's Platform: Neighborhoods First and brought our planks to Washington at the fifth annual conference. During these five years, we've tasted victory, we've face heavy opposition; but, most importantly, we've kept organizing.

And this ability to face adversity, frustrations, and bureaucratic run-arounds and still come out swinging with a vision of larger victories to come is what makes our family so strong. And this strength is what makes the annual conference so much like a reunion where we are able to come together and revive that family strength from each other.

I still get goose bumps every time I see parts of the videotape from last year's conference. The spirit of the people cannot be broken. And this is what keeps me going. This is what fills me with optimistic anticipation about future victories and high expectations for action on our issues.

The movie "Rocky" has been used by many as an analogy of this or that aspect of American life. Well, perhaps "Rocky" serves best as an example of our organizing efforts. We've been going the rounds for five years now and we're still going the distance with the heavyweights against us. And going that distance has been a personal victory too for those of us involved and an even larger victory for the neighborhood movement.

But there are differences from the movie; there's no limit to the number of rounds; and no referee to stop the fight or award a split decision. We're in the fight all the way. The bell has rung for the next round. Together, let's come out swinging.

Michael Westgate: 2500 people came to Washington for NPA's 1977 "State of the Neighborhoods." In her "Next Move" column following the conference, Gale described the mood as angry. "Throughout our former conferences, people were angry because they did not expect the Nixon-Ford administration to do anything for their neighborhoods and they knew they had to push! But this year the level of anger is even higher because our expectations of Carter are higher... When we were in Washington, he had not yet appointed new regional or area HUD directors, despite the fact that Carter had called HUD the nation's biggest slum landlord during his campaign. Now two weeks later we have new regional directors, but we still are stuck with area HUD directors who have been in the middle of all the HUD scandals of the last eight years... When it comes to nominating officials for such agencies as the Federal Home Loan Bank Board, Mr. Carter certainly could find someone more sensitive to neighborhood needs than his old Naval Academy buddy,

Robert McKinney, chairman of First Federal Savings and Loan Association of Indianapolis. We don't need redliners regulating the lending industry...

Last year when we invited then-candidate Carter to address our conference, one of his staff apologized for Mr. Carter's inability to attend and asked us to 'Give Jimmy another chance.' But this year neither Carter or Mondale saw fit to address our conference."

HUD was in the process of dropping its requirement that 75% of Community Development funds be allocated to benefit low and moderate income persons under pressure from city halls and despite the strong support of neighborhood groups. HUD had no recommended theme for presidential action. So President Carter refused at that time to commit additional funds to help the cities since his experts in urban affairs had not yet developed a satisfactory urban policy. Robert Embry, HUD Assistant Secretary for Community Development and Planning, was asked to come up with a national urban policy through the Urban and Regional Policy Group (URPG). A Dec. 25, 1977 *Washington Post* article described a presentation at the White House which portrayed Carter as "livid" with URPG's report.

Mary Lee Widener: Gale was a real visionary. She had less faith in this country than I did. She just never, never, never believed people were going to do the right things for the right reasons when it came to community investment – never, never, never on this earth. I always felt that you could eventually change people's hearts and their style and they would do the right thing.

One of the reasons I felt that is because we had been so successful in our small way before CRA. With NHSA and the Neighborhood Housing Services organizations, we found that we could build those partnerships. It took the communications workshops and all that spadework to get people on the same page, but we were succeeding in getting them on the same page.

But for Gale that was just all too, too, too, too slow. She saw the financial industry headed in the wrong direction, that these were crumbs compared to what they needed to be doing and the attitude they needed to have. She set out to get a permanent solution, a public policy change, the CRA Act formed. It took a lot of organizing, a lot of passion, a lot of commitment, but she was central to that. I was not a part of the organizing for that, so I don't know the roles and relationships inside that effort, but obviously we were supportive of it. I was supportive of it. You got your sign-on letters and you got your this and your that to support it. But it took some passionate organizing to get that done and Gale was in the middle of that.

Michael Westgate: The Community Reinvestment Act passed remarkably quickly. Due to Senator Proxmire's adept handling, it was adopted in Conference Committee, without prior action by the House, in early

October, then approved by the Senate and the House. On October 12, 1977, Jimmy Carter signed it into law.

From Case Study by Hallahan (11/7/91)

Kirk Hallahan: Since 1975, Congress has taken action three times to strengthen the HMDA's disclosure requirements. (20)… The most significant of these was the Community Reinvestment Act of 1977, which was drafted by Proxmire's staffers to require lenders to delineate the markets they serve and to affirmatively make known the availability of their services. Regulators were to take an institution's performance into account when considering applications for new branches, new services or mergers and acquisitions. The Home Mortgage Disclosure Act was made permanent in 1988, and the scope of the reporting requirements was expanded. In 1989, the CRA was further strengthened to require regulators to rate institutions on their performances on 12 broad performance measures and to make these ratings public. HMDA's legacy has been to provide a vehicle through which more than 6,000 community groups now actively monitor lending performance. (20 – Footnote)

From *DISCLOSURE #31* (Sept. 1977)
Dynamics of Organizing

Shel Trapp: One of the criticisms of community organizing is that we too quickly move from one issue to another. It's called "claiming the victory and getting out of the fight." From this issue of *DISCLOSURE*, it is evident that many local groups are continuing the fight on significant victories for their community. Much like a boxer who sees his opponent stagger against the ropes and moves in for the knockout punch, these communities are hitting hard to maximize their victories.

With the climate of the country being what it is today; with financial institutions being very sensitive to their image thanks to our past efforts and more recently to Bert Lance [Carter's Director of the Office of Management and Budget], now is a fantastic opportunity for community organizing to heat up the redlining fight. By mounting an attack on local institutions and continuing the pressure on city officials and state regulators, many communities will be able to gain significant victories for their neighborhoods.

Although it may be an "old issue", now is not the time to "claim victory and get out of the fight." Rather, now is the time to push harder locally so that we can be sure that increased amounts of mortgage and rehab money will be coming to our neighborhoods. After ten to twenty years of redlining our communities, financial institutions must be forced to make large long-term commitments toward the reinvestment of our neighborhoods.

Now is the time for the knockout punch. The bankers are on the ropes.

Michael Westgate: Passage and signing of CRA on October 12, 1977 occurred with surprisingly little fanfare. Newspaper coverage was very limited and *DISCLOSURE* itself did not run a major article on CRA until April 1978.

The law became effective on Nov. 6, 1978 and its implementation would depend on regulations to be issued by the federal agencies charged with enforcing it, the actions of the 6,000 examiners involved, and the vigilance of the community groups.

CHAPTER 13

"In a tidy sleight of hand, the four federal banking regulators have attempted to gut the Community Reinvestment Act."

IMPLEMENTATION OF CRA

Michael Westgate: In a document issued in February 1978 based on S&L reports made public because of HMDA, the National Training and Information Center stated that large areas of eight cities were virtually without conventional home mortgage credit. "Even with all the evidence of strengthening urban housing markets, it continues to be inconceivable to many lenders that qualified buyers exist who want to invest in these neighborhoods," the report charged.

Allen Fishbein: My first recollection of Gale was attending this meeting of the National Neighborhoods Commission that was being held in D.C. and had a series of public hearings. I'd just joined the staff of the Center for Community Change in 1977.

I went with my colleague Jeff Zinzmeyer to this public hearing and I got a chance to meet her. I'd heard a lot about her.

Gale was described to me as the "mother of the anti-redlining movement." She wasn't particularly friendly at that moment. I mean there was a hearing going on. But more importantly I remember watching her in operation and getting her points in, making sure. Because the commissioners would have a chance to ask various people that they had called questions. She was just relentless in making sure that her perspective was getting represented there. And, if the discussion was going in a different direction than she wanted, she would reach back and ask a question and bring it back.

She was just <u>relentless</u> about that. That's a first impression of Gale, but it's an accurate one, that I carried with me through the whole time that I knew her. I never met anybody who was as resolute and just had the ability to stay on message, and just wear down anybody who was in her way. It was wearing down.

Gale would say, "No. This is the way I think we ought to do it." "Well, that's very interesting, Gale, but I think if we did it this way perhaps we'd be able to involve different..." "No. I think this is the way we ought to do it." And her position wouldn't change. You could be in that room for five hours, and her position was the same in hour five as it was when you started off. Meanwhile your position is totally changed. You're now saying, "Well, can't we have like at least one half-hour session, where we touched on that?" And even then, you weren't sure she was going to say "yes" or "no."

John Taylor, President of National Community Reinvestment Coalition (NCRC) in Washington, DC: CRA never would have existed without Gale. But you can follow a graph that shows 1977 to about 1990, CRA basically flatlined in terms of bank commitments. Any commitments that did occur were because of Gale and a handful of groups that she had and a few other organizations. But it was basically about $5 billion of written CRA agreements a year. And then you get to 1992 and that line goes like this. [Motions a sharp increase.] And you follow that line, that growth, with the Community Development Corporations (CDCs) and the Community Development Financial Institutions (CDFIs). They just follow that line in terms of their growth, the amount of money invested in those organizations and in underserved communities.

The fear from the Washington groups and from Gale was that NCRC would displace them, rather than understanding that the whole universe grew. And most important of all is that communities would prosper through an enhanced activism, organizing effort to engage more community groups in this effort. And that's indeed what happened.

Allen Fishbein: Gale never was mistaking that for her separate orientation. She knew these groups were fundamentally different. They were policy wonks. They represented different sets of concerns and constituencies. It was situational that they were on the same side. So when you say John Taylor tried to get her to join his board at the National Community Reinvestment Coalition, she was not going to join a coalition. It was kind of interesting; it was the other way around.

Gale was very selective about what boards she would be on. She would have a certain affinity for certain types of organizations. Like Neighborhood Housing Services in Chicago was a pet project of hers, and she was really active on the board of that organization. So she would do some of that. But when all was said and done, we would be doing things that NPA and NTIC thought we ought to be doing, not necessarily what the staff and others on the board at CCC thought we ought to be doing.

She had a clear idea, she had clarity about what she wanted to accomplish. Some people might say at times it was wrong, it was stubborn, it wasn't reflective of the right kind of analysis that was needed. But she was clear, she had this clarity of vision, and the relentlessness to get to that point. A lot of her success was attributable to those qualities.

You have to put yourself in the times. The audaciousness of this anti-redlining movement – challenging corporations and corporate decision-making and the experts with ragtag bunches of neighborhood folks who were not financial experts and couldn't argue the intricacies of mortgage finance underwriting -- required that kind of relentlessness and persistence.

Ultimately a lot of the success was lenders being pragmatic and recognizing that it was much better to figure out some rapprochement, some settlement, with these folks than to continue fighting them, even if they felt they had the prospect to continue to keep them at bay. Often movements and organizations take on the personality of their founder and their leader, and the culture of NTIC now is that persistence that is still filtering throughout the organization. And whether you're dealing with Gale, or you're dealing with any of her colleagues and staffers, they're almost all like that. There is that kind of persistence and kind of single-minded view of things.

She had great distrust of Washington organizations. When I think about Gale, she was a true kind of economic populist. That's what really intrigued me and attracted me to her. It's just something that was in her genes. She just had a real citizen average folks' view of things. It took her a long way. And she kept that.

Cal Bradford: To me NCRC is a good example of why Gale didn't go to Washington. She said it right from the very beginning. It's true. Now that's the organization Washington and Congress will look to say, "You're the representative of the neighborhoods on these issues." And, yet, even though you've got community people on your board and stuff, you're really run from Washington. You're run by people who were moving their careers around in Washington.

All the things that she was afraid would happen to the group have happened to NCRC. It has a lot of visibility, a lot of recognition, and it has no power. It poses absolutely no threat. They can write nasty letters about federal regulations and stuff like that, but they don't pose any threat. They particularly don't pose a threat to anybody who goes home to their community. Even though there may be a member of NCRC in the community, membership is more sort of corporate, economic development issues. That's fine. That's of value. Somebody has to do the daily work of economic development in communities or whatever else the organizers do is wasted. So it's not that I don't feel respect for that.

Allen Fishbein: I knew Gale for almost 30 years. I saw her regularly during that time when she came to Washington. I worked very hard at cultivating a relationship with Gale. I said very hard because you worked very hard with her. She wasn't going to help you out, in part because she had this distrust for Washington groups. CCC, as a result of work that Andy [Mott] and Pablo [Eisenberg] had done, had a relationship with her. It was kind of a bumpy one.

She basically thought they – NTIC – were the movement, and that organizations like CCC ought to be, if not exclusively, then predominantly about just following them, helping them and supporting them. Anyone who knows Pablo Eisenberg knows that Pablo, who is probably the preeminent fundraiser in the nonprofit world, helps everybody, even people he doesn't fully agree with in what they're trying to achieve.

It seems he never could quite help Gale enough.

So there was this stormy relationship. Since I became the community reinvestment person at the Center, over time the relationship worked its way over to me. I knew I just had to figure out a way of developing a rapport with this woman, getting her to respect what I could accomplish. It meant that I couldn't meet her halfway. I had to go a considerable distance to establish that rapport, and it was something that I just learned to do. I don't know whether I ever appreciated it. People started telling me about it later, like Bud Kanitz. Because Gale wouldn't give you the benefit of a doubt by saying, "Allen, I trust you." She would never say something like that. But you knew that she'd started putting at least some credence in what you had to say by listening to you, by asking you a question and listening. She would never say, "You're right." You'd never get the benefit of that from her.

But over time we developed this relationship where she did call me up and ask me questions and, for the Washington crew, trust my judgment. She wouldn't trust my judgment about organizing, but she would trust my judgment about what the Washington national organizations take on an issue was going to be, on a policy. Or she would ask me from time to time to help organize a meeting among Washington groups, to talk about CRA or the Home Mortgage Disclosure Act when they were under attack, or things that needed to be done, knowing that I knew these people, dealt with them daily. So I would be useful to her in that way, as being that contact point, so she didn't have to deal with 20 organizations. But I had to work at it and it was very affirmative.

CCC thought that NTIC and NPA were extremely important organizations, and wanted to do everything as practicable as they could do to support their work. My area at CCC was working on the implementation of the Community Reinvestment Act. The Center put together what we described as a "working group" right after CRA was passed in which we convened a whole range of organizations with an interest in reinvestment, including NTIC as well as groups like ACORN and other organizing groups, the national housing groups, and organizations along that line. So I knew Gale was going to be a very important part of that process and she was.

We spent a number of months working on the *Citizen's Guideline to CRA*, which was basically a recommendation to the regulators for the type of regulation that we wanted to see implemented. It was a very important document for a lot of reasons, because we brought a fairly diverse group together to see if we could reach a consensus. There were a lot of different ideas about what the emphasis of CRA ought to be and how it out to work. So reconciling those differences and reaching a consensus on them was a daunting task. It took us longer than we wanted to.

Then we sent it to the regulators. We had some influence on the shape of the regulation and on the outcome. And, of course, that was adopted by the regulators in 1978 and served as the mechanism for making CRA work until new rules were put into effect in 1994.

When I talk about her populist orientation, I'm reminded of the stubbornness about NTIC never wanting to open a Washington office. They'd thought about it. But ultimately NTIC and NPA felt that they were better, that they represented different and unique viewpoints by not being in Washington, and that Washington would compromise their view, and maybe make them more "accommodationist," and get sucked into the kind of compromise that's involved in a lot of Washington. Whereas, if they flew in from Chicago from time to time, they'd be mercifully ignorant of the political realities that people might be viewing as political realities at the time. That then was a better position to be in. Reflecting on that, this was probably a smart thing to do. Not to be viewed as another one of the mix of groups, but something different and unique from these other advocacy groups that were involved in these issues…

Gale just didn't want to really go that route. So that was one of the useful functions I could serve for her, being the eyes and ears about things. If I heard something that I thought was relevant or useful for her, I'd call her up, I always could get direct access to her—very, very accessible. She would always take my call if she was around. And she knew I didn't call her to chat about where she was going on her next vacation. So she knew usually if she was hearing from me, it was some news that she needed to hear.

Over the years, Gale developed a more complex view of the world, to reflect the changes that were going on in community reinvestment, and really the outgrowth of some of the successes. So back in the 70s, you were talking about a lending industry that was pretty uniformly redlining, that was not engaged in community development and revitalization efforts, and it was pretty easy to paint the world in those black and white terms. I think that suited Gale in a lot of ways. But as this world changed and matured, she started acknowledging that different entities operated differently.

Some critics might say, in part, that was based on the relationships that NTIC developed with these companies, that if they forged partnerships, her view would change about what they were doing. She recognized that ultimately, while she had a populist distrust, always, about the financial world, she recognized differences between the different players, and forged some personal relationships. She was savvy and sophisticated enough to have a measure of distrust about it, but she could put them in different categories, in different buckets.

Obviously she had physical problems as she got older, and it made it very difficult for her to get around. It was almost painful, in the last few years – she would come to town – to watch her go into these meetings and trying to walk the halls of Congress. Then the wheelchair, which made it difficult to get around, just probably sapped some of her energy, so she seemed just more tired there in the last couple of years. But tired until something would trigger her reaction and then you got full...

Ann Vick-Westgate: Gale force.

Allen Fishbein: Gale force came out. Exactly. So maybe she was a little more measured and selective about where she would use her energy. But that anger, that energy, that relentlessness I always saw there, right up until the end, maybe just a little more targeted as the years went by.

People, when she came to Washington, would think of Gale as this kind of mono-dimensional force concerned about redlining, the state of neighborhoods, and this was her entire life. I spent enough time with Gale to know that she took this great pleasure from the vacations she took, and she liked to gamble, and all these kinds of things.

In the early '90s, when CRA was under attack, Gale and some of her leaders were able to get a meeting with Allan Greenspan over at the Fed. You know there's a long history, obviously, with Gale having one of the only demonstrations in recent time outside of the Federal Reserve Board. Here she was meeting with Allan Greenspan and she asked me to come to the meeting.

We were in a fairly small room. It was six or seven people. We're waiting for the Chairman to come in. He was delayed. We were there making small talk with some of the Fed staff. Finally he comes swishing in the room and he says, "Oh, hi, Gale. It's good to see you." And she goes, "Do you really mean that?" And, without missing a beat, Greenspan says, "Oh, about 50%." That was a classic moment. That was an honest answer. It was just boom, boom.

Ann Vick-Westgate: Did she elicit honest answers from people?

Allen Fishbein: Well, she would certainly try to do that. We were involved again, in a meeting with the banking regulators, right after Clinton had been elected into office, like in early '93. We were meeting with the FDIC Acting Chairman at the time and the outgoing Comptroller of the Currency.

We came in at the beginning of the meeting and we're sitting down, talking about some CRA enforcement issues. And they started talking about who they are and Gale cut right through and she said, "Well, you're not going to be around for very long." That was Gale. She had this way of just deflating power, cutting through it, and not being willing to buy into their exalted status, or their self-importance. But it was often part of the Washington scene, "We're up here and you're just the folk." She would just have a very instinctive way to cut through all of that.

On the other hand, I also remember her going into meetings with people she viewed as allies and friends on Capitol Hill and turning on the Cincotta charm...

Ann Vick-Westgate: Nobody has talked to us about her charm!

Allen Fishbein: Her charm in the way that she would try to do it with some people like Bill Proxmire, whom she felt affinity for. You saw it some with Jack Kemp. People where she felt she had a certain rapport with them, there would be a lot of smiling. And she definitely would use a very different approach in talking with them than she would with most of the people that she met in Washington, whom she was very leery and distrustful of. She had the ability to change with the circumstance.

Bud Kanitz: When Jack Kemp came in as Secretary of HUD, Gale threatened to go to his house. I know this because I got the assignment from Shel Trapp to scope out his house. So I did the reconnaissance. But essentially what happened was that Kemp's daughter was getting married or there was a reception.

Anyway, Kemp got wind that NPA was gonna be in town and they might visit him, so he called Gale and sent his right-hand man, Tom Humbert, who came to the NPA Conference and promised they would have a meeting the next day with Kemp. Again, that started as a confrontation, but then Gale and Kemp got along famously. She really liked Kemp and he did some good things to reform FHA. But nothing as much as what happened when Bill Apgar was FHA

Jack Kemp, Secretary of HUD, and Gale learned to work together.

Commissioner during Clinton's years. Gale really worked well with him. Bill Apgar is now at the Joint Center at Harvard.

Gale said, "We're having a meeting with the new FHA Commissioner, Bill Apgar." Apgar showed up all by himself at the hotel. No aides-de-camp, no bodyguards. They had never met before. They hit it off. They had a long meeting and basically Apgar kept saying, "Hmpf; um-hmmm, um-hmmm." He'll probably tell you this. "She's right, you know, um-hmmm, um-hmmm." And so they had a fabulous partnership to clean up FHA.

Allen Fishbein: There was a certain organizational rivalry that existed between CCC and NTIC in those years, because we were working with some of the same organizations around the country, and NTIC was very turf-oriented. CCC was a different kind of an organization, where we had a lot of pride in working with virtually anyone out there in any circumstances, groups that were part of networks, groups that were independent, and all sorts of networks that we worked with, the ACORNs and the NTICs and the Gaudette networks. Whatever they happened to be we had a lot of pride in being able to work with them.

This relationship was interesting because in Washington, it was a good one: mutual respect and trust. She appreciated my opinions, whether she agreed or not, and saw me as being useful and helpful to her, in getting some access and entrée to organizations that she didn't have lines of communication with. But part of my work was also providing technical assistance out in the field with some of the same groups that NTIC worked with. Not so much with Gale personally, but with her staff, there was a real rivalry.

That was a source of conflict over the time and I have to believe it emanated from Gale. Some of it might have been more emblematic of Shel Trapp. But often that kind of attitude starts at the top. It has a way of filtering down. In one or two cases, actually NTIC staff were calling up groups and asking them to disinvite me after I had been invited to attend. But again that did happen, and running in connection with a national Washington matter, it would not go over very well.

One of the real areas that forged a relationship for us in the CRA area was in the early '80s when interstate mergers in banking began. Up until then banks were basically limited to the states in which they were chartered. CRA was premised on that system of these state-chartered banks, where opening up a new branch would be very important to them because that was their way of attracting new deposits, and the lifeblood of their business operations. So by requiring regulatory approval of a branch expansion request where community groups could raise issues about the funding record of these institutions and file what's called a CRA protest, it was thought that was the normal way it worked. All of a sudden, as a result of some interpretations by the U.S. Supreme Court, that started breaking down and you started getting these interstate mergers.

And that was a whole new ballgame, because that wasn't opening a new branch. That was two, what could be very large, corporate entities actually merging with each other and having to file a request with their regulators to get approval, but it was in a very different ballpark. In a regulatory sense, it was a more complicated procedure than the branch-opening request was. I'm a lawyer and I had studied the regulatory procedures and got to know them, at that point, probably as well as anybody from a community standpoint.

When those interstate mergers started, Gale really reached out to me, and her staff did, and relied on me to give them advice and insight about the procedures, and how they should go about analyzing these protests, and the points of vulnerability of the institutions, and things like that. That put our relationship on a different level. They obviously, after a while, developed their own set of expertise in that area, because merger activity just kept proliferating and proliferating. And probably, when people think of CRA mergers, breathed this life into CRA to make it a big-time regulatory concern for the banking community. It's one thing about getting denied on your ability to open a branch in a neighborhood; it's a very different thing about being held up, if not getting an outright denial, for a merger of two large institutions, which can affect the stock prices in the negotiated trading. A lot of the so-called "CRA agreements" which Gale and others became very expert at doing really owed their origins to those interstate merger activities that began in the early '80s.

So there wasn't a lot of expertise around that. You could probably get everyone in a single room around three or four tables that had some real knowledge of the CRA process and the regulatory process back in the eighties. We provided a helpful technical assistance role to NTIC that we hadn't really provided before. So that helped round out the relationship. And we had quite a bit of communication with each other, particularly during that early period of the mergers that helped forge that relationship as well.

Michael Westgate: It was quite a learning curve going from the neighborhood S&L, single institution, where you could mobilize the customer base within one square mile or something like that, to statewide and then ultimately nationally, even internationally.

Allen Fishbein: Yes. That was important. Just the politics of organizing coordinated community input was a lot more complicated because often there could be a number of states involved in these merger activities, a number of different markets. Often they involved institutions that could be at two ends of the United States. It really brought it into a whole different level of sophistication that was required and, in part, led to the increasing sophistication and professionalization of community reinvestment that has occurred over the years. Now that's a whole separate discussion. Some people might think something was lost along the way as well. But it was required, because you were dealing with large institutions and had to learn about different aspects of corporate finance and corporate decision-making that was way beyond what people knew about it before.

From *DISCLOSURE* #33 (Dec. 1977)
FHLBB Regs—Another Victory for Comment

The new chairman of the Federal Home Loan Bank Board (FHLBB) Robert H. McKinney announced with much fanfare on November 8th new regulations to increase the flow of mortgage money to older neighborhoods by cracking down on discriminatory redlining. At a White House news conference, Vice President Walter Mondale, filling in at the last moment for President Carter, called the regulations "the strongest action ever taken to counteract neighborhood redlining."

Michael Westgate: On November 13, 1977 *The New York Times* ("Government Moves Against Redlining") reported Chaiman McKinney's comment that the S&Ls were "going to be very upset" over the new regulations. "These regulations are tough, but they are not unreasonable. We aren't asking the industry to make unsafe or unsound loans."

Allen Fishbein: Gale wasn't a detail person, so she wanted to be able to get advice on what to do. It was very important for her to bring that in-house ultimately at NTIC. Because she wanted to really grow that organization and make it a truly national organization and not just be viewed as a Chicago-oriented organization. So she wasn't the detail person to do it.

Gale was this real embodiment of this populist instinct. What I learned from her was about always working to keep it simple. It was very easy for people like myself and others and this professionalization, as I call it, of community reinvestment, to turn this into something that was far removed from organizing, from involving neighborhood leaders in the process. She had this great instinct about keeping it simple. Whether it was in terms of CRA protests or even crafting legislation, this was always the guiding principle for her. I think she used to use the method that if she couldn't figure out and explain it to her friends and neighbors, then this wasn't going to work.

Ultimately, I'm not sure that vision has really been able to persist, because of the very different changes that have gone on in financial services. Increasingly it has involved higher and higher levels of expertise and sophistication. The challenge now – you talk about people who might be reading this book and going forward – is how you can be knowledgeable and cognizant of the very sophisticated financial operations that occur today, not just primary markets but secondary markets and securitization and Wall Street and the global economy, and still actually have a base, and still involve the folks that are affected by all of this in the process.

Because, as we all know, part of the whole community organizing orientation that Gale came out of – whether you call it Alinsky-style or whatever – was having neighborhood leaders be the front spokespeople and be comfortable and knowledgeable enough that they could sit down with financial leaders, and be able to hold their own. What's probably kept me involved in this field, and the most exciting recollections that I have, is when that stuff happened successfully, because it's great moments to watch. But it has become increasingly difficult for that same level of community leadership to be involved in the same way. It's become more of a technician's approach. At these conferences, you see a lot of "suits."

Michael Westgate: Gale dropped out of high school. Did you sense that held her back in any way? Or did that perhaps enable her to see things with more clarity?

Allen Fishbein: It probably was part of her distrust of the professionals and the lawyers. She had a great distrust of lawyers. In the early days of CRA, of course, there was a real question about how this law was actually going to play out. Right? There were a lot of different theories.

CRA involved a certain kind of legal process, this regulatory process. The orientation of community organizing was to move out of the litigation world, and to move it into direct action and direct negotiation and response. Rather than suing institutions, it was showing that you had community power to convince those institutions that they needed to deal with you—a very different orientation.

Gale had real concerns – because she always used to be bad-mouthing the lawyers – that the lawyers were going to take this over. That this was going to be these formal, administrative hearings in which the lawyers were going to be running the show. And the community organizations would maybe be clients, but have a very secondary role in the process. She was very distrustful of that. We didn't know how it was going to go in the early days of CRA. In fact, I was brought on board as a lawyer in part because CCC felt that there was going to be a lot of these formal challenges to what was at the time bank branch expansions. We wanted to develop the expertise that we could provide guidance not just to community groups but also to Legal Services lawyers and other local counsel to help them with these proceedings.

Now probably one of the most fortunate things is that the agencies, for their own reasons, decided not to use the formal regulatory hearings process that they actually have in their regulations for different types of administrative proceedings. Instead, they decided to use a more informal, relaxed process that didn't have rules of evidence, didn't have the same kind of procedural rules. They basically allowed communities, with backup from community organizers and other staff, to make their case and not have to be filtered through, and channeled through, counsel. I recognized that.

Ann Vick-Westgate: The regulatory agencies decided this?

Allen Fishbein: Yes. I was, for example, providing legal representation to the first successful challenge that occurred under CRA which was the denial of a branch expansion in Brooklyn, New York against Manhattan Savings Bank. We had this decision about what role we should be playing in the proceeding. I was working through a local organization there that was affiliated with Gale, and also a local lawyer that was involved. We wrote the petition but then, in terms of the hearing, we were going to be sitting back "here" and they were going to be making their case from their standpoint. If some procedural question came up, they might turn to us because we were afraid the bank's lawyer might try to use some procedural devices to try to limit the case we were able to put on.

But no one knew how that was going to play out at that time. Gale's great fear was that this was going to become a litigious battle, battling lawyers that would go on for years and years. You'd win administrative proceedings, but it would go to court and there would be appeals and nothing would ever get decided. Of course, litigation as it affects organizing, we know, can be very deadly for keeping people involved and invested in the outcome. The pace of it is so different from the organizing pace. So that was a real concern. Gale was definitely happy that the community still stayed in that CRA process as it played out. Overall it was a good thing that it played out that way.

From *DISCLOSURE* #33 (Dec. 1977)
FHLBB Regs: Another Victory For Comment

The regulations are in two packages. The first set, published in the Federal Register on November 8th, requires savings and loan associations, insured by the Federal Savings and Loan Insurance Corporation (FSLIC), to maintain a loan application register which would list loan applicant information, amount of loan, location of property and disposition of application. However, these regs leave open the question of: (1) whether these records are public documents available for community inspection; (2) whether the definition of "application" which does include oral requests, also includes phone requests; and (3) what penalties exist for non-compliance.

The second package or regs, published on November 14th, would prohibit denials of loans and refusal of loan applications, and loan offers on less favorable terms, "because of the age or neighborhood location of a dwelling." This reg also requires members' institutions to have written underwriting standards which can be regularly reviewed to assure equal opportunity in lending. The regs require, in addition, non-discriminatory advertising and a review of marketing practices.

However, these regs face the problem of loose terms which must be more strictly defined before these regs are finalized. These terms include: "unfounded or unsubstantiated characteristics of neighborhoods"; "physical or economic characteristics of neighborhoods"; "specific neighborhood factors affecting its present or short-range future"; "current market trends"; and "credit demands." In addition, there is no provision that the underwriting standards will be made available to applicants.

The affirmative marketing section needs to be amended to establish guidelines for minimum marketing requirements, which would include a marketing plan that would specify how the institution intends to advertise, contact realtors and solicit loans in the community it serves. In addition, there should be criteria for institutions to make public performance reports each year which would include: savings and lending data; an analysis of improvement or lack or improvement in this record; and what further marketing will be undertaken if there has been poor performance. Finally, the regs' requirement that institutions' advertisements include an "Equal Housing Lender" legend fails to include discrimination on the basis of neighborhood location as an illegal practice. This oversight or intentional omission is ironic considering that these regs are prohibiting such discrimination...

National People's Action is urging Mr. McKinney to hold public hearings on the contents of these significant regulations before they are finalized in mid-January. Through such hearings, this first step on NPA's agenda can be carried further to not only end redlining but assure neighborhood reinvestment.

Michael Westgate: Meantime, other states besides Illinois were entering into the CRA fray. But while people were becoming more adept at marshalling statistics to prove that banks were not serving their communities, financial institutions fought back. When the New Jersey Banking Commission issued regulations requiring lenders to separately list all mortgage application, whether granted or denied, the New Jersey Bankers Association filed suit claiming "invasion of corporate privacy."

Ann Vick-Westgate: Within the regulatory agencies, either at the board level or within the staff, were there allies that you could identify or did they have any say within their agencies?

Allen Fishbein: There would be staff people that you could talk to. Bud Kanitz was at the Office of the Comptroller of the Currency (OCC). That was after a while. And that was actually, in a way, a certain recognition.

Gene Ludwig was Comptroller of the Currency. He was a "friend" of Bill Clinton's. He was a bank lawyer but a very progressive guy in his own personal views. When he was appointed and came on at OCC, he really made a concerted effort to reach out to community organizations—which was fairly unknown.

CRA was signed into law during the Carter years. But most of its history was under fairly adverse circumstances, with some regulators pretty openly hostile to having to enforce CRA at all. So all of a sudden you had this switch. You had a regulator that came on board, and he's reaching out and personally calling up community groups, meeting with them. Ludwig tried to have regularly scheduled periodic meetings.

So Bud coming in actually was a symbol that "I want somebody out of your world to give me advice in here about who I can be talking with and keep me on the straight and narrow." That was very unusual at that point. The regulatory agencies mostly hired from within, so it wasn't lost on someone like Gene Ludwig that he was hiring a Bud Kanitz, and Bud Kanitz had ties with people like Gale and other organizations. You started seeing that happen in some of the other agencies as well. It happened at the Fed. But these were very important symbolic victories when they started to occur. And it gave Gale an access to have someone like Bud to pick up the phone and talk to on a regular basis.

From *DISCLOSURE* #34 (Jan. 1978)
A Poll in Search of a Policy

"This survey by Gallup reveals a reservoir of untapped energy at the local level and pride in the qualify of neighborhood life. The Carter administration intends to use these resources in solving our dilemmas." -- HUD Secretary Patricia Harris, *The Christian Science Monitor*, December 23, 1977.

The Gallup survey, to which Mrs. Harris refers, was published as the first major "state of the cities" survey in the last installment of the *Monitor*'s twelve-part "A Nation of Neighborhoods" Series. According to George Gallup himself, "The survey suggests that the development of neighborhoods and neighborhood pride may underpin the whole reconstruction and renaissance of America's cities."

Some of the most interesting Gallup results – gathered from interviews throughout the U.S. in communities with population in excess of 50,000 – show that among urban residents:

  ◆ about 3 of every 4 persons favor "anti-redlining legislation at the state and federal level, which would require banks to base credit on the personal record of the individual rather than the

neighborhood geographical location where the person lives;"
- a majority (53%) do not want to leave their neighborhood and nearly seven in ten (69%) are certain they will be living in the same neighborhood five years from now;
- a surprisingly small portion (8%) said they would like to move from their neighborhood to the suburbs;
- more than four in ten (42%) belong to or would like to belong to a neighborhood group or organization;
- one-third have already participated in a neighborhood improvement effort and feel their involvement contributed to solving a problem;
- a majority are willing to take direct action in defense of their neighborhood when it is threatened.

From "1978—The Next Move" from the same issue
The Myths of Risk and Regulation

Gale Cincotta: As we enter the next year, there remain two myths which in their perpetuation threaten any advancements which have been made in confronting our urban problems. The first myth is that the lender's perception of risk in mortgage lending, based upon geographical location, is justified. The second myth is that the lending industry is already over-regulated by technocratic bureaucrats, who do not understand a free market economy.

In reality, the lending industry has reached a point in this country, where their perceptions of risk have become self-fulfilling prophecies, denying equal opportunity to credit, and where their lobbying efforts are able to circumvent any substantive governmental regulation.

Both these myths of risk and regulation have again been brought to our attention in the media on at least five occasions in the last few months. In only two instances were these myths even challenged. Yet, because of their ramifications, these myths certainly merit substantial public debate, not unchallenged repetition.

The first recent acceptance of these myths was to be found in a November 27th *New York Times* editorial, entitled "Maximizing Mortgages, Minimizing Risks." While attempting to present both sides of the redlining issues, the editorial accepted the lending industry's "perception of risk" as valid. Furthermore, the editorial characterized efforts to require savings institutions to lend a stipulated part of their mortgage money in distressed neighborhoods as "dangerous measures that would weaken banking standards." The reader was left with the impression that in order to maximize mortgages, we must minimize risk.

The second article, published in the "Personal View" column of the *Chicago Daily News* on December 12th, follows the risk myth to its own logical conclusion. This article, entitled "Key to rebuilding of cities: try to make it profitable," was submitted by Neil Hartigan, former lieutenant governor of Illinois and now president of the Real Estate Research Corporation, a wholly owned subsidiary of the First National Bank of Chicago. Mr. Hartigan insists that "to the degree that the risk exists or is perceived to exist, government is going to have to guarantee loans." He assures the reader that "with government policies that reduce the risks, private business will respond."

The myth of risk is at a very crucial stage in its perpetuation. The neighborhood movement shook this myth's foundation in our attacks against redlining practices to the point that new regulations of the Federal Home Loan Bank Board (FHLBB) prohibit redlining by savings and loan associations. Their regs have been promulgated at the same time that the S&L industry is attempting to resurrect its proposal for coinsurance whereby the federal government would guarantee 80% of loans made in certain geographic areas. The industry is subtly trying to tie their desire for coinsurance to their acceptance of the anti-redlining regs. "If we can't deny loans to a neighborhood, the federal government certainly should protect us against the risks involved" is the way the chorus goes…

The next article, to which I wish to refer, is the first instance in a long time that the media has questioned the myths surrounding four lending institutions. The December 23rd *New York Times* article, "Banks Lobby Called Strongest in Capital" was the last in a weeklong series on "Policing the Banks." According to reporter David Burnham, the strength of the banks and other financial institutions has resulted in a situation where to an unusual degree "banking sets the terms of its own regulation and stays clear of effective independent review." Furthermore, the bank regulatory bodies are funded by assessment of member banks, not by Congressional appropriations. The myth of over-regulation loses some of its impact in light of who pay the regulators' bills and the dollar figures bankers have contributed and lent to Congressional campaigns. Burnham quotes an unnamed lobbyist for one of the nation's largest banks as saying that "the bank lobby can almost certainly stop anything it does not want in Congress." That's not what I could call regulation.

Ann Vick-Westgate: What happened at the Fed? Who was it at the Fed that was opening the windows?

Allen Fishbein: Well, a fellow by the name of Jim Lowell, who came out of the community development world more than the community organizing world, who actually was hired because, before that, the Fed was clueless. This was like, "What is this world? All of a sudden we've got to relate to these people, and we don't even know who they are." So they got somebody who was out of Neighborhood Housing Services just so he could tell them the names of the players and give them the numbers and things like that.

That evolved and – if you want to talk about an interesting victory – there's a woman by the name of Sandy Braunstein who came out of a CDC in D.C. and now directs the Consumer and Community Affairs Division of the Federal Reserve Board and probably wrote Allan Greenspan's remarks that he's going to be delivering here in an hour at the 2005 NCRC convention. So these are all important recognitions.

But the reality is Gale was very distrustful of regulators and she didn't treat them very well. She didn't treat, in some ways, Gene Ludwig very well. He appeared at an NPA conference which, early on, wasn't quite happy with what he was doing, and they put some sign over him. I mean that was tradition. I'm sure you've heard it.

NPA was like, "We're gonna give grief." So what happened after a while was this became like short straw time. Nobody at the top of an agency wanted to come to an NPA convention for a while because they knew they were going to get a lot of grief, so they would assign their underling. Then after a while their underlings would assign underlings under them. It got down to I was waiting for some interns to show up at an NPA meeting. Right? Some of them laughed about it and acknowledged it was a rite of passage, I remember because they would joke to me. Then they'd be able to tell stories to each other.

Ann Vick-Westgate: "I survived NPA."

Michael Westgate: And figured they wouldn't be hit again for a few years.

Allen Fishbein: That's right. It's like, "Oh, that's nothing. You know, when I went they poured water on me!" That kind of stuff. It was a certain one-upsmanship, a fraternity-type hazing process that they went through. But some of them just would avoid it like the plague.

So Gale always kept that distrust of the regulators, with these few exceptions of certain people. It wasn't even clear to me; it wasn't always on policy. She was susceptible to praise and some of them were pretty good at going that way. But it was more than that, because there were others who would try to praise her and I don't think she would reciprocate. But there were some people that, for some reason, she would just feel a certain affinity with. Or at least think that she could influence them in some way that she would deal with them. But some of them were just people that you had to be very wary of because they were going to do you in, in one way or another.

You know HMDA is such an embodiment of her concept of the organization. Information is power, relatively simple information that you don't have to be an econometrics economist to be able to analyze, particularly when it started. People could, on the church floors, be totaling up numbers and doing some basic computations. Empowering folks directly, not through experts, being sort of the core concept. HMDA was constantly under attack. It was enacted in '75 with a sunset provision in it in 1980. And it was kept alive by temporary extensions.

It was something that the industry always had a complete distaste for and thought they would be able to kill. It took considerable effort. That's where Gale and I worked a lot on efforts to combine forces and try to get other groups involved, like the mayors and people outside of the neighborhood constituency, to come to the defense. HMDA survived. There was a vote in the Senate where it survived by one or two votes from basically being killed.

Michael Westgate: It's amazing HMDA got passed in the first place and that it survived when you think of the strength of the American Bankers Association and the savings & loan leagues and all the other vested interests.

Allen Fishbein: It was really a testament to the strength of these groups that portray redlining as being a problem, which they were able to do before HMDA, through the transfer research and basically going down to do the most laborious of tasks at the Recorder of Deeds offices, and trying to document the extent to which the problem existed. Unfortunately for the communities, fortunately for the organizing, it was so glaring. I mean we're talking about zeros. Not that they made a few loans here. Zeros! You didn't have to be a PhD economist to analyze the numbers zero and zero.

That's such an embodiment of Gale, HMDA, because it was simple, because people understood its value, people were able to use it. I viewed them as like the old patriots from the Revolutionary War time, the Minutemen. People, even if they weren't directly involved in community reinvestment, they were involved in some other area of housing or neighborhoods and they could join in when HMDA was under attack. And they did time and time again. That was her embodiment of keeping it simple. Having a law serve not just as an information source but an <u>empowerment</u> to people to organize around.

CRA, although she has a lot of credit for it, is less of her origination and more of a Washington creation. The genesis of it, as I understand it, was to model it after the Federal Communications law at the time, which had licensing renewal requirements for TV and radio stations, where the public could comment on whether they were fulfilling a public mission.

Ann Vick-Westgate: Ken McLean talks more like CRA came out of Washington.

Allen Fishbein: But Gale joined it and embraced it because she recognized that ultimately HMDA wasn't enough. You needed some teeth and enforcement mechanisms to take that data and have it impact on institutions beyond your pure organizing. CRA as it's worked out is also "regulation from below." I've used the term—I didn't originate it. I think I popularized it and I've written some pieces where I refer to it.

CRA is an embodiment of that because, when all is said and done, it says regulators might go off and do these regular exams of institutions to see whether they are in compliance with CRA – the ratings consistently show that almost every institution gets a satisfactory or outstanding rating – but it's not limited to the regulators. So the community in essence does its own rating. Regulators may think they're a satisfactory institution; the community may think they're less than satisfactory.

So this regulation from below, which Gale came to embrace, combined with HMDA, is just the embodiment of her philosophy, of what she wanted to see, and her view of what a good public law is. She worked in other areas, FHA obviously being a key area, and different housing assistance programs. But something that brings together the confluence of all that her approach was, was trying to achieve both of these laws. HMDA is a great example

Michael Westgate: And disclosure being the common theme.

Allen Fishbein: And disclosure. Information being power in a way that the industry never fully appreciated. The industry was looking more at the compliance part of HMDA. Not as much of the fight was "Uh oh, they're going to have this data and then we're going to have to respond." I don't think they were really aware how HMDA might be used. It was like "we've got to write these reports every year." Of course that was pre-computer days and meant somebody literally had to keep logs. So it was very unpopular. But, again, the staying power of HMDA and CRA through very adverse climates for long periods of time shows that, if you do have a law that is rooted in a constituency, and they really understand its value and its purpose, with a little luck, they could overcome even those adversities. It does take some luck. But with a little luck, you can overcome some of the adverse climate so that you have meetings like this NCRC convention where you have as many industry people sitting down and communicating and talking to people in the movement as community folks.

Michael Westgate: Gale had little sense of her role and how it would be seen historically. She kept almost no records herself.

Allen Fishbein: When Gale was in town, and she'd be talking about some piece of information that had come to her attention, she'd be pulling some paper out of her pocket, and it was all crumpled up. She'd say, "Look,

Allen, this will prove that point." I was wondering what was ever going to happen to that. She used to joke. She said, "You know, once it goes into the bag, the chances of anyone seeing it again are really negligible." So her staff would try to grab it from her.

Michael Westgate: In late 1977 Gale had a new hat as one of 20 members of the National Commission on Neighborhoods appointed by President Carter and sworn in at White House ceremony. Robert Kuttner, formerly on Proxmire's staff in the Banking Committee, was the staff director. The Commission was established by Congress to undertake "a comprehensive study and investigation of the factors contributing to the decline of city neighborhoods and of the factors necessary to neighborhood survival and revitalization." Their findings were to be reported in January 1979, but the Commission was expected to have direct impact on the development of President Carter's urban policy in the coming months.

The FHLBB was taking the lead in proposing regulations whereas the Fed was being obstructionist. Savings and Loans around the country decried the proposed regulations.

From "The Next Move ," *DISCLOSURE #35* (Feb. 1978)

Gale Cincotta: The voice of the neighborhood movement has again been raised in Washington. And this time, apparently some people were listening:

- FHLBB Chairman Robert McKinney invited NPA leaders into his new board room and promised tough follow-thru on his new regs;
- HUD Assistant Secretary Robert Embry reiterated his commitment to the 75% CD provision;
- HUD Assistant Secretary Lawrence Simons vowed to move quickly on rehabbing HUD's inventory of abandonments;
- Representative Bingham of New York is introducing a bill to match CD funds for rehab with more dollars for rehab;
- Senator Proxmire and Representative St. Germain agreed to consider legislation for more bank investment in home mortgages;
- FHA Administrator Gloria Jimenez announced that they will be holding hearings throughout the country on insurance redlining;
- Representative Conyers reaffirmed his commitment to make LEAA work; and
- A "Dear Colleague" letter will be circulated on Capitol Hill to designate the week of June 4-10 as Neighborhoods Week.

But there's one person in Washington who apparently, even if he was listening, still has not heard. President Carter has been working for months on his urban policy. First the issue was to be addressed in his January State of the Union message. Then, the date was to be March 15th. Now the grapevine has all these bureaucrats working hard to deliver by that date, but what's a few weeks if it turns out to be April? The few weeks would not matter so much if we were waiting for an urban policy that was designed to deal with our neighborhood issues.

Michael Westgate: If there were government programs, like FHA, Gale wanted them well run. But she did not see government programs as a replacement for the private sector. She wanted banks to be active and to have a stake in her neighborhoods.

Cal Bradford: If you screwed up, too bad. She had no sympathy for the folks who screwed up on their home loans if it was their fault. She was very conservative. To me, the main thing for people to see is was how conservative this whole movement was. Most people who looked at it never understood that.

They wanted CRA essentially to apply to everybody. It's a simple approach. I won't describe it as simplistic, but it was fairly simple. That everything would be transparent. It certainly makes sense in a democracy. I don't think it's a radical view at all. It's ironic that the Republicans always fought it. In fact, that ought to be totally compatible with their notion of a free and private economy because, if people don't have information, then the economy's not open. It's a very conservative idea, at least in theory. If you talked to a conservative economist, they would see no reason, except for the cost. Why shouldn't we all have perfect information? Then the economy would work more perfectly. So she'd be very upset today with how much gets hidden. She'd probably be pretty depressed about CRA and some of these issues about how the government has withdrawn.

In an odd way, I think people didn't anticipate. They began to understand when the regs were being written for the Community Reinvestment Act how much they depended on government, even though their notion was it was going to create resources that are being controlled by the people. It was the way the act was written. If the regulators didn't control the banks, nobody else could. There's no right to private action. You can't sue. So it's all up to the bank regulatory institutions. That was one of the things they were nervous about to begin with, the banking regulatory institutions.

So it got handed over to the people they didn't trust. And, right off the bat, the next battle after CRA was about making the exams public. It was always about making it public: show us more. That's still on their agenda. They're fighting for public disclosure of the fair lending exams, always trying to make information available.

Michael Westgate: Gale was fighting that those rights should be established proactively through the regulators, not after-the-fact through the courts. Banks were publicly supported resources, not private fiefdoms. Gale and others recognized that it would take a lot of effort to get the regulators on board. Passing legislation alone would not solve the problem of redlining.

From *DISCLOSURE #37* (April 1978)

Community Challenges

Even as the fight over the regulations continues, several community groups have begun to use CRA as a basis for challenging branch applications. The Northwest Bronx Coalition successfully fought a suburban branch request of a local bank on the basis of their redlining practices. Community groups in Washington's Adams-Morgan neighborhood won an agreement in a branch application of Perpetual Federal S&L to include loans to current residents as well as upper income people buying into their neighborhood. Missouri ACORN is in the process of challenging a bank acquisition demanding that an affirmative lending program be agreed upon before the request is granted by the Federal Reserve Board.

National People's Action is currently working with the Center for Community Change in Washington to coordinate community challenges to financial institutions' applications covered by CRA. This group will be providing technical assistance to local groups, so any organization interested in pursuing the strategy of challenges is encouraged to send NPA a list of their least responsive federal institutions. This list will be monitored by CCC and when an application covered by CRA is filed, local groups will be notified as to what recourse they have for challenging.

Bruce Gottschall: The biggest change due to CRA was when they stopped some mergers because of poor ratings in '89 or '90, which is when the enforcement got a little stronger. That helped us because we, NHS, were in the middle of it. We could use it to create a little more receptive climate... [But then] banks created some capacity to figure out how to do it, so it became just a piece of business, became a cost that they just factored into their ongoing stream.

Some people speculate that CRA pushed people to buy junky loans and that whole argument around sub-prime or predatory lending evolved out of the CRA push because lenders just needed loans. They didn't care what kind. I don't buy that. People really did discover, which Gale said, "There's a market out there if you figure it out." And it's not as profitable but it can be, okay. If you're maximizing profits, you're not going to go that route. But if you just wanted to get some profits, you can work this business and then figure out how to layer in other pieces.

So CRA was an approach that really in a sense fit Gale's mindset, which was, "We just want to get people into the system. We don't want to break the system completely because, hey, there are some benefits." So she was complimenting lending by saying, "We're beating the shit out of you because we want you guys doing work, doing business. So take this as a compliment. That's why we're hitting you on the head, because we want you guys to do business where we are! If we thought you were worthless, we wouldn't waste our time beating your heads." So she always saw that as a compliment even if they didn't always take it that way.

So the CRA fed into that mode, "Let's get these people figured out, how the hell they run these places, rather than write them off." And so in a sense the CRA approach was, "Get your thinking cap on and figure out how to do this. And let's figure out how to measure it." And so it was saying, "Take it up to the board. Here's the business plan. How's your business plan going to reach this place where you're not reaching?" And then the enforcement piece helped later on.

So CRA is still on people's radar scene. They've still got to deal with it. The regulated lenders are more responsive than the non-regulated lenders because they got this that they got to think about. Most of them have figured out a strategy to do it and be okay, or even better than okay, at least within the system.

It is a paradox that some of the banks, when they saw the business opportunities in the neglected neighborhoods, invested in unregulated operations. And it is in the unregulated lenders that the problems of bad lending practices began. Gale never wanted anyone to make unsound loans.

Some of [the banks] have just bought unregulated lenders. That's the whole affiliation, affiliates, mortgage bankers, whether they report or not. So there are clearly holes and loopholes and that kind of thing. But when you look at the comparison between a regulated and unregulated situation, the regulated ones are being more responsive.

Mortgage brokers now originate 60 or 70% of the loans. Those are unregulated in some ways. Eventually they may get into a regulated situation somewhere, but not on the origination part. So, yeah, there is clearly a vast amount of the business that is not regulated. Then there was the CRA push, but you got the problem of what is the problem now? Now the problem is the easy credit issue. So that is almost a tougher thing to regulate, how you deal with it. So it's a whole different situation.

From "The Next Move," *DISCLOSURE #38* (May-June 1978)
   Gale Cincotta: The next move, as usual, is ours. We have fought some hard battles in the past. We have won some major victories. But you

know and I know that we have a long way to go. I don't need to tell you that people are coming from all over the country to Washington because they know that their issues are not being dealt with by the Carter Administration and our Democratic majority in Congress. You and I knew that a Democrat in the Oval Office didn't necessarily mean that we had a neighborhood voice in Washington. We knew back then but we gave the man the benefit of the doubt. We waited for Carter and our neighborhoods are still waiting.

But if our communities are to survive, we can wait no longer. At our first national conference in 1972, we called ourselves the "city survivors." We have survived these six years to date in one way and one way only: WE'VE ORGANIZED. And that is the same way we've begun our seventh year: by organizing our neighborhoods and fighting together on the national level.

We told Washington in 1972 that HUD was destroying neighborhoods. In 1973, steps began to be taken to pass legislation to reimburse FHA homeowners who were sold defective homes.

We told them in 1974 that financial institutions were redlining our communities and denying us mortgages because of where we live. In 1975, Congress passed the Home Mortgage Disclosure Act, which made the lending record of institutions public by census tract.

We told them in 1976 that cities were misspending Community Development funds. In 1977, HUD proposed regulations which would have required cities to spend 75 percent of their CD funds in low and moderate-income neighborhoods.

So what do we have to tell Washington in 1978? We have to tell Congress not to pass an amendment to the CD Act that will limit HUD's ability to disapprove a city's CD application for failure to benefit low and moderate-income people. Banking regulators have to be told to implement regulations for the Community Reinvestment Act so that the large commercial banks can be held accountable. We have to tell the President and Congress that we literally cannot live with an energy bill that deregulated the price of natural gas. We have to tell HUD Secretary Patricia Harris that UDAG funds must be spent for neighborhoods and not just for downtown fantasies and luxury hotels. We have to let "Fannie Mae" and the whole secondary mortgage market know that reinvestment should be for current residents and not for fueling trends of displacement. We have to make sure that tenants are not denied their rightful subsidies from HUD for operating expenses. We have to obtain better health care for seniors. We have to get better police protection for our neighborhoods. We have to tell Washington that people must have jobs. We have to tell them because if neighborhood people don't, no one else will.

From *DISCLOSURE #39* (July 1978)
Bank Regulators Hem & Haw

NPA leaders met with representatives from two of the three federal bank regulatory agencies at Sunday morning's reinvestment workshop. From the FDIC came Sherwin Koopman and Roper Hood. Comptroller of the Currency, John Heimann, was the third government guest. The Federal Reserve Board did not accept an invitation to attend…

The three regulators present agreed with NPA leaders that CRA enforcement should be part of regular bank examinations not just in branch application requests. All panelists agreed as well that affirmative lending plans should be required under CRA.

On the issue of community involvement in the examination process, Comptroller Heimann recommended that CRA regulations require bank examiners to contact all community groups and individuals who have complaints on record against an institution or have commented on an institution's affirmative plan. According to Comptroller Heimann, President Carter has requested that FDIC, the Comptroller of the Currency and the Federal Reserve Board (FRB) make joint CRA regs. NPA leadership quickly pointed out the danger in this approach, in merging the positions of the three regulators, the final product will be watered down.

NPA contends that the Federal Reserve Board is the least cooperative regulatory agency and must be pushed hard by communities and the Administration to support strong anti-redlining regs. Because the FRB refused to meet, NPA went to the FRB's office Monday morning with the CRA demands for G. William Miller, Chairman of the Board. Although Mr. Miller was out of town, his counsel, Thomas J. O'Connell, was left with a clear message to relay to him—that NPA is demanding stronger reinvestment initiatives by the FRB…

In other reinvestment developments, NPA celebrates a savings and loan victory. The FHLBB, which regulates federally-chartered savings and loans and state-chartered savings and loans that carry FSLIC insurance, starts enforcing new anti-redlining regulations this July. These regs prohibit S&Ls from refusing to make a loan, or varying the terms of a loan, because of the location of the house or the age of the house. Community groups are urged to stay on top of S&L loan activity in their cities and make complaints if redlining still happens to the FHLBB in Washington or its district offices.

A second reinvestment strategy proposed by the FHLBB is a lower-interest loan program of 10 billion dollars to moderate-income redlined neighborhoods. Community groups should push their local S&Ls to get involved in this reinvestment program and commit some portion of this $10 billion to their neighborhoods.

Tommy Fitzgibbon was one of Gale's favorite bank executives as he provided thoughtful counsel and insights to her. In his work with Manufacturers Bank (now MB) Tommy was heavily involved with the Chicago NHS in the early days and continued to play a key leadership role in that organization: Yesterday there was a clients' workshop on Fair Lending. I mention in all of these sorts of workshops that Gale and others in the 1970s – before CRA and before CRA really had any teeth – knew and we know now, those of us who came out of that era, what the economic impact was. Because this is what Gale's whole philosophy about CRA is that it's about good business. It's about making good loans. It's about putting capital back in the neighborhoods and communities where they've been capital-starved for one reason or other.

As Dan Mudd [Chief Operating Officer] from Fannie Mae said the other night, it's opened the investors' eyes to the potential for economic benefit that comes out of changing things so that more people can qualify for a credit. Well, isn't that smart! The emerging market, the immigrant community, the people who transit through or stay in our modest-income, low-income communities are the economic engine for the future. Having capital available, enabling them to buy a house or start a business, both of those things are important and vital to the stability, the economic stability, the political stability of communities in the future. Sixty-eight percent home ownership rate in this community, some improvement in minority home ownership, which was substantial compared over previous years, those are things where the industry is waking up. That was all what Gale was about.

Michael Westgate: If all of the banks would invest in the neighborhoods, then they're safe loans. If only one bank will invest in that neighborhood, then it's not a safe loan.

Tommy Fitzgibbon: Right. Similarly, as we dealt with the issue, in Gale's last years, of predatory lending, those are bad loans. They're devastating to the institutions who for years and years have made investments in the community. So it's improvident for those kinds of credits to become available. It really is bad, bad for the community, bad for the people.

It erodes the equity and then you get foreclosures, abandonments, all those things that are just devastating. It was right here, down on the second floor, where Gale and Jack Markowski [Commissioner of Chicago Department of Housing] and Stacey Young from the City and Ed Williams from Harris Bank and the folks from La Salle Bank, and the small banks, Park Federal and others, sat around the table, in 1999, and said, "We're not going to take this."

So we came up in partnership with Legal Assistance Foundation, NHS and several other coalitions, Greater Southwest Community Development Company, Jim Capraro, who used to work for Gale many years ago, and said, "Okay. What can we do? What can the financial industry do?" So we put up capital and said, "NHS, we're going to pay you to go out and figure a way for these people to get out of these deals. And we're going to put up the capital so you can make loans to people so that they can get out of the problem." And it's a national model.

Why was it a national model? Because Gale sat there and said, "We're going to build a coalition. We aren't going to rail against the banks; we know the banks aren't doing this stuff. The banks are not participating in this. This is a rogue broker-led activity that's just ripping the equity out of our neighborhoods. We don't want to have that happen." So it was her ability to develop and measure and monitor coalitions to make sure that it happened. So NTIC and NPA could do what they needed to do on the legislative front, to sort of push the envelope in terms of the city ordinance and the state legislation, not only here, but in Cleveland and Cincinnati and other places, to try and build on the successful establishment.

So the legacy was that she never quit. In fact, I'd bring her up through the back elevator on her walker in her last days because she wanted to be here when this happened. It was inspiring.

From *DISCLOSURE #40* (Sept. 1978)
CRA – Seldom an "Encouraging" Word

In a tidy sleight of hand, the four federal banking regulators have attempted to gut the Community Reinvestment Act (CRA) of 1977. Instead of shouldering responsibility for getting redlining banks to shape up, the regulators have offered up a set of meaningless statements for banks to draft and then file away and forget. Involved are the Federal Reserve Board, the Federal Home Loan Bank Board, the Comptroller of the Currency and the Federal Deposit Insurance Corporation...

Each agency regularly examines the banks under its jurisdiction. CRA clearly states that the regulator must use its authority to encourage ongoing reinvestment. The proposed regs do not state how the regulators are to exert their authority to encourage reinvestment. Furthermore, they incorrectly interpret the law by implying that CRA evaluations will only happen when banks apply for deposit facility changes like branches or mergers.

What are the regulators supposed to do? Will they pray for the bank, trusting the Almighty that banks will see the light on mortgages and loans in low and moderate-income neighborhoods? Perhaps federal hirelings will not feel authorized to use prayer!

As it stands now, banks and S&Ls must draft CRA statements about what communities they will serve and what types of credit they will extend. These statements have to be kept in a public file, along with public comment, for two years. With annual approval by the bank's board of directors. Sounds tough, doesn't it? These regs completely miss the point. CRA places responsibility on the regulators to encourage reinvestment.

NPA is recommending that new CRA regs set down specific CRA examination procedures to be used in regularly scheduled evaluations which would be publicly disclosed. The regs must also include income-specific criterion for determining a community's credit needs and criterion to determine if the bank has met those needs. Finally, concrete policy for the regulators to "encourage" reinvestment must be spelled out.

Public pressure must be kept on the regulators to produce reinvestment programs. If the regulators remain deaf to the voices of the neighborhoods and keep their wet noodle regs, the next confrontation will be on examination procedures to be issued this fall. CRA makes it clear— redlining is against the law!

Mary Lee Widener: CRA, as much as I would like to think it was not necessary, it changed the face of America. A lot of companies would never have done the kind of investing in communities that they do if it had not been for CRA. A lot of companies would stop investing in communities the way they do were it not for CRA. I became a believer in that. Quite frankly, I didn't want to have to believe that. I tend to want to have more faith in our society than that. But I had to get in the real world and that's the way it is.

I came to that realization and accepted it, even though I'd been very careful to give all of our investors credit for being there before CRA. Sometimes that's misunderstood because sometimes it's understood as meaning "You don't think CRA is necessary." I say, "No, that's not what I mean. There are people who were there before CRA who were not motivated by CRA. They were motivated because it was the right thing to do."

So we need to constantly give people with good hearts and doing things for the right reason credit. But it doesn't mean that we could be as far as we are in this country without CRA, because we could not be. And if CRA were to go away, this country would be harmed. Now, fortunately, once we got CRA that became crystal clear across the aisle to both Democrats and Republicans.

So then it was time for me to move when CRA was threatened. I could move in with <u>my</u> style to help save it. My style is to try and go and get powerful people whose hearts I believe are in the right place and have them use their influence to try to move the environment in the right manner. So I felt that CRA was sort of on the ropes and I think it was Senators Shelby and Gramm who were going to try to get rid of it the year that Jack Kemp was Secretary of HUD. Do you remember Gramm really went after it in a very vicious way? Everybody knew that he had the horsepower to make that vote happen, so we needed at that point a way to get some Republican influence to blunt that whole effort.

I was then chairman of the Federal Home Loan Bank of San Francisco and therefore had access to the chair and vice-chair group of all the banks. We as a group had access to the Federal Housing Finance Board. We had the opportunity to ask for national forums. So I asked for a joint meeting of all the banks, of the chairs, the vice-chairs, the presidents of the banks and the entire Federal Housing Finance Board which included the Secretary of HUD. Jack Kemp personally participated in that forum.

I asked both Jack Kemp and Herb Sandler of World Savings if they would do a motion. Herb was going to make the motion; Jack Kemp agreed to second the motion that that body of all the banks, all the presidents, all the boards and the entire Federal Housing Finance Board, that that group pass a resolution to protect CRA. That the institutions, all the banks therefore, would have as a part of their legislative or lobbying policy protecting CRA. That the Secretary of HUD would be on record that he wanted CRA protected. That was the meaning of that resolution, if we could get it passed.

So my strategy was to get this meeting together, get that motion, get that second, get it passed. I started lobbying people ahead of time. It was easy for most folks. But the key was Jack Kemp. It was an easy job for Herb. But Jack Kemp agreed to do it. I think you know that he's very, very community development-oriented.

So the day that we had the meeting – I'll never forget – they went through their agenda and things went long and went long and it seemed we were never going to get to the point that we could do our resolution. Herb Sandler finally came over to me and said, "I have to go. I can't stay any longer." And I said, "Well, may I have your proxy?" because it wouldn't have carried the same weight for it to be my motion. So I asked if I could have his proxy and put the motion on the table on his behalf. And he said yes. So when it came time I did that and I said, "Herb Sandler had to leave and he asked me if I'd make the following motion on his behalf." I made the motion; Jack Kemp seconded the motion. The motion passed. We of course took that and ran with it across the system and across the field.

And the other group that was in the meetings, it was not just the banks, the chairs and vice-chairs and staff. It was also the Affordable Housing Council leadership from all of the banks. So we had the community development folks because they were members of the advisory council. It was pretty powerful to be able to put forth a resolution that represented all of the people on these advisory councils, which was a big part of the community development field, plus the lenders on the boards of all these banks, plus the presidents of all these banks, plus the members of the Finance Board. We have no way of knowing whether or not that's what blunted the momentum that Gramm had, but the bottom line is we did stop it. It was stopped. He was stopped.

Gale's role in that, for me, is that she had first the vision—the vision to know that such a policy was needed. She had the vision. We were all on board and pushing on HMDA. But I think that CRA was a very visionary, gutsy thing to think about getting through Congress. You think about that. You just think about that! HMDA, nobody's going to care about that. You're just reporting data. It lets people turn on the lights. You get eyes. But CRA is you're going to do something about this. And we, as a Congress, are going to hold you accountable for doing something. I really, quite frankly, never expected Congress to pass CRA.

HMDA provided the ammunition, the evidence, the information. Even though HMDA provided that, I did not feel that Congress would take that step in response to the information. Now maybe you all have a different memory of Congress than I have!

Just because they know there's an injustice in some part of the society doesn't mean they're going to necessarily do something that is that prescriptive for the business sector of society. That to me just never fit. The Congress tended to support business, support the other sectors of society, is the way I always read it. What happened for the underserved was just small potatoes compared to what happened for the larger society, so I just never, never, never expected Congress to do anything like that.

What that did for me was let me know that there is a larger possibility, a latent desire to do the right thing in a lot of folks, not just the nice people that we found through our workshop processes. Gale made a difference in what the art of the possible is. She made a difference on that point in my life generally because I started to believe in the art of the possible on a much broader scale. It gave me the courage to ask people to do things that I might not have had the courage to do otherwise.

Gale was visionary and quite gutsy to go after a solution that required Congress to put a hammer, to arm-twist, to force a whole segment of our business sector to behave in a certain way.

The thing that Gale and I last worked on, backboned together, was the whole FHA foreclosure issue in Chicago because I discovered when I was a member of the PMI Mortgage Insurance Co. board that the mortgage insurance companies also didn't want this rash of FHA foreclosures all over the country. Because two things happened in that process with regard to mortgage insurance companies, first, the mortgage insurance was FHA insurance, so that was a customer they didn't get. Second, the foreclosure by the FHA was a foreclosure on a mortgage insurance contract. So it could skew how insurance regulators looked at the risk that the private mortgage insurers were carrying. So it was not in PMI's best interest to have mortgage failures across the country by anybody because it then changes the perception of risk.

Of course, if an insurance commissioner says, "Half of Chicago is going down the tubes. Therefore all of your private mortgage insurance in Chicago is at a higher risk than you have judged. Therefore I'm saying you have to have x millions of dollars more of reserves," that's right out of their pockets. So there was an opportunity for working together and achieving a mutual objective. So, of all things, Gale became a good partner with PMI and they with her. I brought them together working on the same issue. So we talked a few times about that, to get that together. But that's just the last thing on earth you would expect, Gale and a private mortgage insurance company working on the same thing!

Anita Miller: One reason that they needed me to come to Washington then was because the CRA law had been passed but there were no regulations. The Comptroller of the Currency, and the head of the Credit Union Administration, and the people from the Fed and the Federal Home Loan Bank Board had been going around the country, having hearings about what should be in the CRA regulation. In the meantime, we had all kinds of pulls and tugs from Gale and other civil rights groups in Washington, and from the bankers and the [S&L] industry on the other side.

I was brought in to join the FHLBB Board to figure out what CRA regulations should be. The first thing I discovered was that it had to be done by all of the regulators together. At that time, there was a rotation of who would be chairman of the federal regulatory group that met in secret, always in secret. And John Hyman was the chairman at the time. We would have meetings, all of the top regulators together.

Michael Westgate: The fact the meetings were held in secret is a good indication of how unenthusiastic the regulators were about CRA.

Anita Miller: I was the Bank Board person. I would make headway and get them moving forward on what needed to be done. I knew that it needed to be an open process. Today they talk about transparency. It's pretty funny. I knew it had to be transparent. I knew that people at the top levels of the financial institutions and the agencies had to be involved. As it turned out until they really had a problem with CRA that wasn't the case. But at least it was there in the law, in the regulation. I knew that, whatever their CRA statement was, it had to be made public and that the groups, individuals, would have a chance to comment so that the examiners could take this into account when they examined the institutions.

But every time I thought we were getting there, the staff of the agencies – which were empowered to write up what we wanted and come back – changed it completely and came back with the most God-awful stuff you could imagine. I would say to my staff person, "What's going on here?" She'd say, "The Fed and the Comptroller's people and the FDIC people are changing it." So I picked up the phone and I called John Hyman who I knew very well – we were both from New York – and I said, "John, if this happens one more time, I'm going to take minutes of these meetings and publicize them." Because they didn't take any minutes either. That was part of the problem.

These were secret meetings with no minutes. Well, when the S&L debacle came about, those meetings no longer were going to be secret any more. He said, "Anita, you couldn't do that!" I said, "Yes, I will do that." Well, that's how come we got the regulation.

But the people who were against the regulation hated it and the people who were for the regulation hated it. So I knew that we had to have done a fairly good job. And, with all the changes that have occurred since, there are basic principles in that first regulation that have held – the openness of it, the penalties involved with it, making them public, having the boards of the institutions responsible sign off. They never took that seriously until they finally got declined on things.

The next step along the way was whether or not we should grant contingent approvals for mergers and branches – that were really supposed to be reliant on what their CRA rating was. So if their CRA rating was good, they could get the approval, they could merge, they could get the branch and so on. If their CRA rating was lousy, we were supposed to deny them.

Along come the first couple of big cases. And the decision was, "Do we deny them and teach the industry a lesson? Or do we give them a conditional approval, go back and look at it a year later and see what they've done to improve themselves so that we could then give them final approval?" My thinking was – this was a toughie – we want to get the money flowing. We want to get the lending going. I would rather have them break their backs, do the right thing, come back and get the approval. In the meantime, they would start. But, if they didn't do what had to be done, they wouldn't see another approval from us. It was working very nicely. We'd send the examiners in and they came back in and they reported.

Well, the National People's Action had this big meeting in Washington. And that was when they blew the horns and they hit the cymbals and they screamed and they yelled – as they still do. NPA had a panel on a Sunday morning with Irv Spray who was head of the FDIC, who was basically a very decent man, but very much at sea in this environment; John Hyman from the Comptroller of the Currency; Larry Connell, the head of the Credit

Union Administration; and I was representing the Bank Board. The Fed declined to go. The Fed was a problem until Volcker came on. There were a whole series of questions that they asked. That you know they're going to ask; the same process continues.

They get to the thing about conditional approvals and implementing CRA and the other guys stumble so badly. People begin to yell and scream. In the meantime Gale and Shel tell me they're very worried about me. They get to me and I really took a very strong position. I said, "You may scream and you may yell and you may blow the horns, and that's your right to do so. But it's my right to take the way I think is the best way to get the money flowing into your neighborhoods. That's why I have given a conditional approval. I will stay on these people's backs and I will give more." Not a peep, not a peep in the whole room.

That was it. I had a rationale for why I was doing it. Afterwards Gale and Shel came over to me and said, "Oh, we were so worried." You know, there was a loyalty that went both ways. I don't know that they agreed with me, but they were worried for me.

But that was the whole principle of doing it. It was very, very controversial at the time. I did believe that you regulate, you teach an industry by being a very tough regulator on the first case that comes along. That is the best way that the lesson goes out. Somehow or other I really felt that the argument for getting the money going into these neighborhoods was stronger and that that would be a lesson if we said, "It's conditional. You're accountable to us. If anything happens again, you're not getting any more. If you don't comply, you're not getting any more approvals without having a perfect record." I think that perhaps for the industry this was a better approach too. It was a little carrot and stick which seemed to work very well.

Of course, the whole regulation is so different now. The agency setup is so different now. Now the other thing that we did, we set up the whole system of loans from the Federal Home Loan Banks. We created the Department of Community Investment with Al Hershen from California as the head of it. He had been a lawyer with the nonprofit lawyer's group out at Berkeley. He was very good.

One of the things that we did was to set up this whole system of bank loans going at lower rates to support community investment programs. We put community investment officers in each of the Federal Home Loan Banks around the country. That is still alive and well today. It is still an important source of money for community revitalization.

Carter made a huge boo-boo when he was out visiting some of the neighborhoods while he was running. He talked about ethnic purity. That created a firestorm. It was such a painful thing. Carter didn't mean anything by it. He meant it in a positive way, but he got sensitized in a hurry.

When McKinney came in to be Chairman of the Federal Home Loan Bank Board, Carter said, "I want you to deal with redlining. Right away." But McKinney needed another person to serve with him on the Bank Board who could do that because clearly he didn't have an ally in the subsequent Republican or any Republican administration that followed.

So out of this bad thing that happened with Carter, something very good happened. Because McKinney was a banker and an industrialist and he didn't know anything about this stuff. But by setting up this Department of Community Investment and having me on the Bank Board, it really helped to move things forward. Then we became the leader for the Fed and for every agency. The Fed was just terrible.

Michael Westgate: In addition to pushing the regulators to enforce the CRA which they had just gotten through Congress, Gale and Shel worked with local groups around the country to keep up their offensive in getting banks to respond to community needs.

From *DISCLOSURE #42* (December 1978)
First CRA Victory Brewing In Brooklyn

Against Investment Discrimination (AID) and Bank on Brooklyn are challenging Greater New York Savings Bank's application for a fifth Manhattan branch under the Community Reinvestment Act (CRA).

The challenge has drawn the Federal Deposit Insurance Corporation (FDIC) to scrutinize the application. According to CRA requirements, Greater New York must show it is meeting the banking needs of the existing service area before expanding a new branch.

AID told FDIC that in four Brooklyn neighborhoods where the Greater New York Savings draws $594 million in deposits, only $7.5 million has been invested in local mortgages. 80% of the Greater's deposits come from Brooklyn but only 6.5% of the bank's investments are in the borough. 78% of all investments are outside of New York State.

Bank on Brooklyn spokesperson Diane Moogan said that in "our dealings with Greater New York Savings Bank we have always been met with a contemptuous attitude toward Brooklyn, the neighborhood that built their bank. We were told Brooklyn has gone down the tubes and no one in their right mind would invest there. It was referred to as burned out, bombed out buildings. Never did we hear a positive word about New York City."

Greater New York Savings Bank Chairman Albert J. Casazza and President Jerome Maroon claim there is little mortgage demand in Brooklyn. But the Brooklyn groups say the community's real needs cannot be measured because many persons are scared off by Greater New York's mortgage lending terms. The bank requires a 25% downpayment on one to four unit buildings, 50% down on five to eight unit buildings, and refuses to consider mortgages on buildings over eight units and those with rent-controlled units.

Greater New York Bank has also reneged on agreements made last January with AID, Bank on Brooklyn, and the Flatbush Mortgage Committee. The agreements, negotiated under the auspices of State Superintendent of Banks Muriel Siebert after a year of confrontations between New York anti-redlining groups and the Greater New York, called for: $25 million in city mortgages in 1978; $100,0000 to be spent on the advertising of mortgage availability; solicitation of mortgage applications from real estate brokers; and mortgage lending terms that would be "competitive." The bank's failure to keep the agreement prompted AID to call it "little more than a public relations gimmick."

AID chairman Herb Steiner is optimistic about the branching challenge. "FDIC was not impressed with the bank," he said. "They intend to make clear to the bank what conditions have to be met before they act on the application. Now that CRA is on the horizon the banks are frightened, terrified of being examined under CRA. Everybody in the country is looking to our challenge. CRA has finally given credence to our struggle."

From *Illinois Issues* (July 1979)
Redlining: A black and white issue?
By Joan N. Collins

The major effort during the past six years by community organizations concerned about redlining has been to obtain mortgage disclosure laws such as the Illinois Financial Disclosure Act, which was passed in 1975. It required banks, credit unions, savings and loans, insurance companies and mortgage banking companies to file semiannual statements of deposits and various types of mortgage loans and applications. Information was to be reported by census tract and zip code area for conventional and insured residential mortgage loans, home improvement loans and construction loans in counties over 100,000 in population. But the Illinois Supreme Court ruled in January 1977 that federally chartered banks don't have to comply with the state law, and, in May 1978, ruled the entire act unconstitutional.

Spurred by the leadership of Gale Cincotta, executive director of the Chicago-based National Training and Information Center (NTIC), community groups pushed through Congress the Home Mortgage Disclosure Act of 1975. Although still limited as a means of collecting enough solid information about lending practices to nail down the redlining hypothesis, the act is quite important. It makes explicit the obligations of savings and loan institutions to their local communities. Congress states in the preamble to the act that it "finds that some depository institutions have sometimes contributed to the decline of certain geographical areas by their failure pursuant to their chartering responsibilities to provide adequate home financing to qualified applicants on reasonable terms and conditions."

Because of the way this information is collected and filed, thorough analyses of lending patterns in various areas from all sources is quite difficult to obtain. The best analysis so far is contained in the 1978 report by the National Training and Information Center.

Using community organizations in eight metropolitan areas, NTIC was able to show that "large areas of all central cities get very few or no conventional mortgages and the bulk of conventional mortgage lending is concentrated in a few parts of each metropolitan area." The report concludes, however, that "the data available under the Home Mortgage Disclosure Act (HMDA) is insufficient to conclusively prove practices of intentional, arbitrary geographic discrimination in real estate lending. Rigorous scientific or legal proof would require more and better data than HMDA forces lenders to disclose."

In 1977 the Justice Department reached an out-of-court settlement with the American Institute of Real Estate Appraisers (AIREA) on the charge that the organization, along with three other real estate organizations, was requiring or encouraging undervaluation of homes in racially changing neighborhoods. In the settlement, the AIREA agreed to "stop operating with preconceived negative expectations about racially integrated neighborhoods."

The newest arrow in the quiver of tactics to increase urban area investment is the Community Reinvestment Act (CRA), technically known as Title VIII of the Housing and Community Development Act of 1977. The CRA required, by February 1979, that regulated financial institutions make available to the public a map showing the areas they serve and a list of the specific types of credit they are prepared to extend. It is of course too early to assess the impact of this strategy, but the underlying congressional intent is encouraging.

Congress stated in the CRA that "regulated financial institutions are required by law to demonstrate that their deposit facilities serve the convenience and needs of the communities in which they are chartered to do business. The convenience and needs of communities include the need for credit services as well as deposit services, and regulated financial institutions have a continuing and affirmative obligation to help meet the credit needs of the local communities in which they are chartered."

From *DISCLOSURE* (same issue)
Group Challenges

With the "application" denial sanction by the regulators under CRA, many groups are using CRA to stop local institutions from branching without fulfilling the existing community credit needs. So far, these groups have instituted formal branching challenges:

- Adams-Morgan Organization against Perpetual Federal Savings and Loan, Washington, DC
- Back of the Yards Council against Loomis Savings and Loan Association, Chicago
- South Brooklyn AID against East New York Savings Bank, New York
- Greater Toledo Housing Coalition against First Federal Savings and Loan Associating, Toledo, Ohio
- Missouri ACORN and the Manchester-Tower Grove Community Organization against Commerce Bankshares, St. Louis
- Massachusetts FAIR SHARE against First National Bank of Boston
- Metro Fair Housing Services against Community Federal Savings and Loan Association, St. Louis and Kansas City, MO
- Northwest Bronx Clergy and Community Coalition against Dollar Savings Bank and North Side Savings Bank, New York

"The real challenge has been thrown to the community," says NPA Chairperson, Gale Cincotta. "It is up to us to do our homework and push CRA to its fullest potential."

The Home Mortgage Disclosure Act and other state disclosure laws now make three years' data available to communities. The use of HMDA to monitor lending, and CRA to reform it, is the neighborhoods' one-two punch for reinvestment.

From "The Next Move" (in the same issue)

Gale Cincotta: As we approach the new year, this determination is going to be challenged on many fronts. There is the growing battle on insurance redlining that many of us have become involved with during the past year. Our present negotiations with Allstate and Aetna will be carrying into the new year. Sessions with members of the American Insurance Association are being scheduled for early in the year. The passage of the Holtzman amendments will hopefully lead to even more FAIR Plan reforms at the state and national levels.

As the economists talk about the coming recession of 1979, the greatest challenge we face is making the Community Reinvestment Act (CRA) work. For the first time in history, financial institutions will be held accountable for how well they are meeting community credit needs. But as usual, it will be up to us to hold the regulators accountable for implementing CRA.

As the economy worsens, financial institutions are going to develop lists of priority lending and I don't need to tell you where our neighborhoods will end up on that list. CRA gives us a tool to make sure our community credit needs are met and don't get lost in any economic reshuffling.

Michael Westgate: As evidenced by their leadership on HMDA and CRA, Senator William Proxmire and Gale Cincotta both believed it was the responsibility of the banking industry to lend and it was the government's role to level the playing field for borrowers. Neighborhoods needed bank loans if they were to remain healthy. Anyone capable of repaying a loan should be able to get one, and the banks should get a reasonable return.

The impact of CRA was far greater than the public realized. Without CRA, my agency, Chelsea Neighborhood Housing Services could not have gotten the loans we did in Chelsea, Massachusetts for projects of the organization itself – or for the homeowners among the 150 homes we rehabilitated. Multiply our experience by thousands of communities around the US, and Gale paved the way for thousands of banks to reinvest billions of dollars – safely – for hundreds of thousands of people to live in better housing than they otherwise could have afforded.

From the 1979 Rockefeller Public Service Awards (RPSA)
Statement of Achievement (Seven Awardees)
Revitalizing communities and neighborhoods

Gale Cincotta, founder and president of National People's Action and executive director of the National Training and Information Center, Chicago.

Starting with her own neighborhood group on Chicago's blighted West Side, Cincotta helped convene, in 1972, the first national housing conference bringing together 2,000 community leaders to discuss urban development issues. Under her guidance, the two organizations she helped found – the National Training and Information Center and National People's Action – have assisted community groups in their local rebuilding efforts while providing a nationally-organized movement for neighborhood action. Her work was a major factor in the enactment of the Federal Home Mortgage Disclosure Act countering the debilitating practice of mortgage "redlining" by lending institutions. Cincotta has played a critically important role in mobilizing both grassroots leadership and national policy to assure badly needed investment in deteriorating neighborhoods as the key to their survival and to the future of cities.

Cincotta's response: "In accepting this award I'm really representing the countless neighborhood people and community leaders, who in the cities, instead of running, decided to stay put and find some solutions to problems."

CHAPTER 14

"The policemen would end up going in and negotiating for 'em."

RECLAIM AMERICA:
The Battles of New Orleans, Chicago and Wall Street

From the *Congressional Record* (June 23, 1982)
CITIZENS ON THE MARCH TO RECLAIM AMERICA
Hon. John Conyers of Michigan in the House of Representatives:

Mr. Speaker, the issues that we as a Congress and a country are confronting today are issues that will affect, for generations, the vitality of our American ideal. They are social, economic, and political ideals that give sway only to the Constitution of this land. It is within this Constitution that we find the framework for the emerging Reclaim America movement taking place among the towns and cities of this country. It is a campaign steeped in citizen involvement, grassroots patriotism, and a willingness – a demand – to accept responsibility for the decisions that affect the well-being of our constituents and our country.

Sponsored by National People's Action, Reclaim America is a rallying cry for millions of people who have been economically discriminated against. This crisis has been brought about by anti-people policies coming out of Washington, including artificially high interest rates, artificially high energy costs, and Federal cutbacks in all social service and community development moneys. At the same time we are witnessing an acceleration in defense spending, the threat of nuclear war, tax breaks for big business, and deregulation that benefits corporate America – and an overall shift in priorities to make the rich even richer.

Reclaim America is a coming together of all people who hold this country and its democratic principles to be the responsibilities of us all and are more than willing to do their part as Americans to keep it so regardless of race, ethnic heritage, religion, age, or political affiliation.

I want to commend this action, for it embodies the idea of our democracy and the foundation of our Republic. I look forward to participating in NPA's Reclaim America in September and urge you to join me.

Michael Westgate: Reclaim America was a bold attempt by Gale and NPA to marshal many forces towards an inclusive pro-citizenry movement to combat the excesses of the corporate world. They wanted to expand beyond issues of housing, to confront Wall Street and Big Oil. They sought to empower people – average citizens confronted with rising prices for consumer goods and particularly energy costs. "Reclaim America" was a mixed success and was seen by some as a dilution of NPA's and NTIC's expertise in the housing arena. Others thought it was a brilliant way to broaden the movement.

Joe Mariano: "Reclaim America" was a crazy idea. It was the nadir of the neighborhood movement and it was starting to go downhill. Reagan gets elected, Gale says, "Well, it seems to me all these networks and all these groups, all these organizers are standing in the way of leaders. We got to figure out a way to reach out to other people and create a movement from all these different organizations that'll take on corporate power." I was like, "Gale, what are you talking about?" She said, "Oh, yeah. We could do a whole bunch of cities. We could do this freedom train across the country."

Helen Murray: After CRA gets passed and we get HMDA, then we have to fight to keep CRA. In the meantime, you're starting to do fights on CRA, trying to use CRA. So we started to have these wins, these CRA wins, and NHS as well. We had all these wins. And then BOOM, here comes Volcker. So it became real clear that we ought to hit Volcker. So we had a surprise hit on Volcker in D.C. And, boy, that was a surprise too. They did not know we were coming to the Federal Reserve.

It was really fun. We had a group in the Bronx at that time. See, Roger Hayes was one of the staff and he knew, up in Chicago, Bill Murray. So, because Roger knew Bill, we borrowed the Land Shark from *Saturday Night Live*. One of the other guys on the staff, who was a character in New York, he sat up above the door of the Federal Reserve in the Land Shark costume. Now this is like going to Rome, right, and calling the Pope a Land Shark. We had a lot of people. In fact there should be footage from NBC, CBS. All of the big [networks] were covering this. Of course that was my responsibility. Quite frankly, I was the one that really wanted to push, and Gale supported that a hundred percent, that we ought to go to the Federal Reserve. There was no question about that.

So we keep demanding that Paul Volcker come down and announce that he would meet with us. Right? So, anyway, he finally lets our leadership go up. A lot of the people never knew who was doing the staff stuff. The pride was you shouldn't know that.

So we go up and we're sitting on this carpet like an inch thick. What we won out of that was ten hearings in different cities and then we had to go out and organize those. So I organized most of those. And Shel always said, "Whenever you have a victory, you have a new issue." It's like, "Oh, shit. Now we got to do this." Ten hearings.

Volcker wouldn't come down. He was willing to set up hearings with the Federal Reserve Board in the ten cities where they have their local banks to hear from the grassroots about how Fed policies were affecting people and what could be done about that. And he would come down with the leadership and announce that, but only if the Land Shark came down. Ted Wysocki and this other guy who worked with us at that time superimposed the Land Shark back on top with the picture of Volcker in our newsletter, which was just our own little fun thing.

Michael Westgate: One of the secrets of Gale's success was controlling the interplay between local grassroots organizing and the centers of power in Washington.

Groups associated with NPA could show up in force at hearings around the country. Congressmen who gave lip service to national organizations in Washington had to be more responsive to pressures brought on them at home. Even the Federal Reserve, relatively immune to public pressure, could not deny issues when they heard the same complaints at hearings wherever they held them.

Helen Murray: Then we did have those hearings. I organized one at Faneuil Hall [in Boston].. We had <u>business</u> people coming in there, saying the same thing the grassroots were saying. There were varying—effective or non-effective—results. They were very effective in Richmond, Virginia. There was a good organization called Richmond United Neighborhoods (RUN). RUN really made it happen because they got a commitment from the Federal Reserve Board and they got a dollar commitment for some stuff.

We started to see the whole banking system crumble in this country. The S&Ls were starting to go under and so the Feds were taking a look. The Office of the Comptroller of the Currency (OCC) and the Federal Reserve Board were putting their heads together and saying, "Let's just <u>let</u> Citicorp buy First Federal Savings." Yeah. There's no such thing as interstate banking. It's not allowed. Hasn't been since the 1930s. But we're going to allow this. "It's not really going to be a branch of Citicorp." And, boy, we saw the nose of the camel getting in the tent.

I remember working with Gale and we were trying to get her on hearings. I remember writing testimony, "We cannot let them do that." I remember working real hard on that against Citicorp. "Do not <u>let</u> this first stuff happen." You just felt like it was the little story of the kid in Amsterdam, putting your finger in the dike all over. Right? Gale was amazing. She just never gave up—trying to keep NHS going, trying to keep these commitments going.

Meanwhile the whole shape of banking is changing in this country. We had a whole lot of people saying, "You know what? We've been wasting a lot of money in savings accounts all these years. Boy, that money ought to be used somewhere else." Because they used to have a law, a certain percentage of that money had to go back into housing. "Oh, that was a big waste," they said on Wall Street. Right.

Now we could see this stuff was coming and it was going to really kill us. But it was like, "We don't need to be setting that stuff aside. That's not a real good use of our resources, you know. We could use them better to develop oil wells in Iraq or whatever." Right?

Citicorp was buying First Federal. Then, little by little and, of course, it's now you name it. I go to Jewel [Supermarket] now and it's Bank of America at Jewel in Chicago. Disgusting. So the bottom line is there's less

Gail in her prime.

and less local commitment. And, of course, there's this whole globalization, and this whole distortion of what is the American economy, and what is American businesses' responsibility to the American people. All those things we grew up on, fighting, we can't fight those battles anymore. The structure's not there to fight those battles. We're on a team here, and you've got to play ball with us. The teams are totally different.

Michael Westgate: Part of the genesis of Reclaim America was Gale's recognition that the world was becoming more complex. Boundaries between financial institutions, in place since the 1930s, were coming down. State lines were also becoming less relevant. NPA had to undertake initiatives that engaged broader citizen interests if they were to succeed in battles against corporate interests which had spread across these boundaries. Local neighborhood groups would be outgunned if their tactics were restricted to battling local banks.

Helen Murray: So the division of work generally split along the lines of Trapp on the road, Gale getting on the phone with bankers. Trapp would never talk to the bankers. That would always be Gale's job. A lot of funders wanted to come in and see Gale. Somebody from Levi Strauss, a program officer from the West Coast, wanted to come in and talk to Gale, and she couldn't be here. So Ed Shurna and myself were delegated to talk with this guy. And this guy, he didn't want to talk to us at all, "Well, where's Gale?" But he was not interested. We went through the motions. Finally he said at the end of the meeting with us, "When is Gale going to be here? I wanted to talk to her."

Gale was like a star, a celebrity for some people. Because she would spin out these ideas and people would like them. Then we'd get stuck trying to deliver on them. She had convinced this guy from Levi Strauss that we could replicate the Aetna model. And the Aetna model was Aetna insurance put up this money for all these different cities, and then our staff went in and helped them rehab houses, or set up things to deal with abandoned homes. Somehow she had said that we could do a similar thing with Levi Strauss. Levi Strauss wanted to do it around where they had plants – in those days in the United States. San Antonio being one of them and I think Atlanta, Georgia. Wherever they were. Albuquerque, New Mexico….

And this was to be without adding staff. [There] was like in Texas, a couple plants. I didn't even know what that was supposed to mean. Like we're supposed to find examples of economic development and help these people do something. Levi Strauss thought this was a good idea and they could involve their employees and get their name attached to helping revitalize neighborhoods.

Gale would say, "Well, I don't know. For example, you and Ed could fly to Dallas, rent a car and drive around Texas." I said, "Gale, Texas is a big state. Drive around looking for what?" "For examples of economic development…that's what they want to do." I said, "Okay, we could do that but it's not going to work." Drive around Texas!!

So I remember going out to Albuquerque, in the city, looking for examples. And they said they'd be willing to do anything in New Mexico. So I found some woman that was raising sheepdogs for people that could raise sheep up in the mountains. And she said, "If I can raise x number of dogs, we can create jobs for so many people." It was pretty far fetched. I said, "Gale, the only thing I found in New Mexico that even resembles economic development is some woman that says she can create jobs by raising sheepdogs." Gale was saying, "Well, that's not exactly what we're going to do." I said, "Well, yeah."

So it was those kinds of things. And whatever we did, we attempted to link up some neighborhood groups. But funding comes in with, already, all these restrictions on the program, when they say, "You got to do it in these places." So that was an example of it. I don't think we got funded from Levi Strauss again. But at the time, they were in love with Gale, and thought they could do something like that, and we'd benefit.

Ted Wysocki: We had succeeded in the later days of the Carter Administration in getting what, briefly, was a very major federal contract out of FEMA to look at insurance redlining. And the contract was big enough that not only was it augmenting NTIC's research staff significantly with a couple of people, it was also strategically placing organizers in a half a dozen cities and a couple states. The irony was Gale had just succeeded in negotiating the first insurance reinvestment agreement with Aetna. I can remember that *DISCLOSURE* cover. It was just Aetna eating crow. That was the fun part of *DISCLOSURE*.

It was interesting to watch somebody transform from their initial adamant opposition to Gale, [and] through the course of several meetings really make a transformation, and finally "get" what it was that Gale was saying. And even using this Shel dynamic of demands, that these were actual solutions. These weren't just demands out of the air; these were actual solutions to the problem that she was identifying. It was their substantive problem, and she was bringing it to them because they were actually in a position to make a change that would make a difference.

In New York, we had the CEO of Aetna making this public pledge in the press, then we go back to Gale's room and she gets a phone call from an insurance lobbyist who, within six weeks into the Reagan administration, had the FEMA contract rescinded after four months.

Joe Mariano: I was at the Battle of New Orleans in 1979. That was wild. I was all over the place. We just went all over the city, to Longview Gardens, to the boats. Anywhere the bankers were, we showed up. That was pretty amazing. The big speaker at the ABA Conference in New Orleans was Henry Kissinger.

Helen Murray: I had applied for the VISTA program and went down to New Orleans and used every inch of what I learned earlier at OBA because I was doing real estate organizing down there out of a church. In New Orleans, people lived an integrated housing pattern. But then after the school desegregation law the whole structure changed. Before it was perfectly all right to live next door, from the white perspective, to a family that was black and your kids could play with each other. People who lived down there explained this to me. It was really strange to me because you had all these social rules.

But you could play with each other until you were six years old and then... Some fellow, an African American, said to me, "But then Susie or whoever, who you played with all your life, you couldn't speak to her again." And so you'd get to the corner and the bus would come for the white kids and the bus would come for the black kids. But then, when the school desegregation law came, housing was connected to education.

So when I went down to New Orleans, on my own, I found out about this place. It wasn't one of the VISTA placements. But it was like, "Oh my God, this is what's been going on at OBA!" The real estate tactics and the whole playing on people's racial fears... There was a nun who was a Dominican and she had started an organization bringing some families together, both black and white, from the parish, and they were fumbling with where to go. When I came in, I started really pushing to organize public meetings with the realtors. And so I did that for a year. New Orleans was integrated until school desegregation, then real estate tactics began like in Chicago.

HMDA passed in 1975, two years before CRA, and it was effective immediately of course. As soon as we got the HMDA, we wanted to get the information and then use the information to start a new battle. Right? Then we had to fight again for it because they had a five-year sunset clause in HMDA. They passed it but we had to start all over again in '79 to get HMDA passed again. And then in '77 we had the CRA passed. But the American Bankers Association decided they wanted to kill it, so we had to go after them. So we went down to New Orleans in '79 for the "Battle of New Orleans!" I was the lead organizer at NTIC for the American Bankers Association meeting in New Orleans, because I had lived down there. With my blue eyes and blonde hair I got to be the infiltrator.

I went down and did all the advance stuff and we were going to have very few people and there were a lot of bankers. So I worked with Tom Fox on it. He was a good strategist. I called him up from New Orleans and I said, "Look, Tom, we haven't got the numbers here. But I found out this and I found out that. What do you think if we do this a little differently?" And he says, "I think it'll work." So I felt real confident when he said that.

I decided we had to have more music. So I found this band and they told me where their other gigs were. They couldn't do it this time and they couldn't do it that time because there were all these bankers' parties. And I thought, "We are going to be nothing at the Hilton or wherever they were down there. We're going to be this little sideshow. But if we could go out to the party at this former old plantation, you can see how the hoity-toity lived in the 'grand old days of slavery'."

So we went after them, because I found out from these guys I hired for our party where a lot of these things were going on. So that became the tactic then. A bunch of the bankers were going to go on one of the boat rides. So we did that. That was really a lot of fun. I feel a lot of personal success on that one.

The ABA had rented a boat and we were waiting for them when they docked and they had to walk the gauntlet so to speak. We had two lines of our people. And they came off and they'd had a few drinks, these bankers and all their whatever. A couple of them were very rude to one lady, Marie Bryant. She's an African American woman from the South Side. She was a great lady in the early days. Oh, she was terrific. She's dead now. But, anyway, Marie Bryant just put the message out to people "Don't react." And so we were in good shape. "We want you to do this. Don't stop CRA. Dah, dah, dah." Our people were always good. Our people are not going to hurt anybody. So when the bankers had to run the gauntlet, coming off the boat, we had placards that said, "Don't kill CRA". And we'd be chanting little things. Joe Mariano made one up that was called "Bankers Suck Neighborhoods Dry."

We did a bunch of different stuff on their different parties down there. So we made our presence known. That's what we were there for. We were there to let them know that there was going to be a big fight if they tried to get CRA stopped. So we were very effective in getting our message across. We had a great time.

I hired a yellow school bus company through a guy I knew that I used to organize with down there. They were wonderful. Black business. I'm so glad I hired them because anyone else would have quit us. Those guys got parking tickets all the way through but they never dropped us. And those drivers came to that party and they listened to that music with us and they were just thrilled. They just felt so good about what we were doing. Because they know, they've lived the same experience.

So it was great. In fact I brought a bottle of champagne to my friend who found me that business the last night when I was there because those men were so fantastic. I didn't know they were getting all these tickets and stuff. But they did. They said, "It's okay. It's okay." That was really cool.

Ann Vick-Westgate: Who came up with the use of bands? That is powerful.

Helen Murray: That was probably me with my New Orleans experience. When we had the national conference, we said we were going to have this hit in New Orleans. We did this big kickoff at the end of the meeting on Sunday, "Okay, everybody get ready." We had umbrellas and we had somebody play the "Saints" in Washington. Because it worked it's still there [as part of the conferences].

You know I'd like to say that was my strategy when I went down there, but the reality was I figured it out when I was hiring the band. Right? It was fun. It was so much fun to be a troublemaker for good! As a good kid, I always had to do the right thing. I loved it!

And I could pass, man! When somebody wanted me to do something, these guys with their long hair and their beards or Gale, they'd say, "Go find something out." I looked like the girl next door, so I'd walk in. I could find anything out because they wouldn't stop me, because I had blue eyes and blonde hair, and I looked the way you were supposed to look. So I got to be the infiltrator. It was fun. It was fun. My life wouldn't be the same without it. And Gale taught me a lot.

Ted Wysocki: I was at the Battle of New Orleans too. The best thing about the Battle of New Orleans was – again this is Tom Fox, one of the NPA organizers at the time – getting the police to be interested and supportive of what the issues were. The police in New Orleans at the time were in disgruntled contract negotiations with the city. Consequently Tom struck up this relationship with the head cop and it was basically, "Well, as long as you're going to behave and you're going to tell us ahead of time where you're going, until we get to the actual formal convention day, just tell us what you're doing."

So consequently, whatever night it was where there was the ABA party on the riverboats, the police actually allowed us to set up a gauntlet, and all of the bankers had to walk through the gauntlet to get on the boat. Everybody behaved themselves. It was all jeering. Right? They all looked alike. "Oh, you have such a young wife!"

The cops just allowed that. What they did shut down was, they didn't let us anywhere near the convention hall. I forget whether it was Volcker or whoever was the big speaker at the actual formal proceedings. But they allowed us to go round doing all of these guerilla actions at hotels and events like the riverboat and stuff in terms of getting the issues out.

Gayle Brinkman: The reason New Orleans was chosen was to go down and deal with the ABA. We were normally accompanying Gale and we always had a police tail on us so it was very interesting. We were on the docks with huge numbers of people. And the bankers were on this party boat at the docks. And there were a lot of them staring at us and we were yelling at them and shouting chants and things like that.

Inez Killingsworth: I met Gale just as CRA was happening. It was right in the middle of that fight. That was fun. We call it the "Battle of New Orleans", when the bankers were having their convention and they was running away from us. Here we go again. You've gone through all of these tactics to try to get 'em to meet with you. And they were calling us crazy and trying to do all kinds of silly things to discredit us. So they were having their meeting in New Orleans and we decided we needed to go. Go and confront.

It was enough to make an impact. Our slogan is that "You can run but you can't hide. We'll find you." They were meeting on a boat to avoid NPA. We stayed in waiting for them to come. They had to come back. You got to come back. You can't stay. And so the Battle of New Orleans was a critical event in the CRA fight.

From *American Banker* (October 7, 1980)
Activist Gale Cincotta, Barred in '79, Named an ABA Panelist
By James Rubenstein

Gale Cincotta, head of a Chicago-based activist organization barred a year ago in New Orleans from addressing the annual convention of the American Bankers Association, is on the convention agenda this year as a panel member on community redevelopment.

At the 1979 ABA gathering, Mrs. Cincotta led a group of 200 demonstrators who heckled ABA delegates outside a New Orleans hotel and at other sites in the city to protest her being denied the right to speak to the ABA and present a list of anti-redlining demands. Mrs. Cincotta is chairman of National People's Action, an umbrella organization for 300 community groups which has lobbied vigorously in Congress – usually at odds with ABA – on housing-related legislation.

In an interview at NPA's Chicago office – adorned by a "souvenir" 1979 "ABA Welcomes Bankers" from the New Orleans convention – Mrs. Cincotta expressed dissatisfaction with ABA's handling of the convention disinvestment panel. She said the subject of community redevelopment deserves its widest audience possible and yet the panel will compete directly with a concurrent session on Federal Reserve Board pricing expected to draw a larger delegate gathering. Moreover the reinvestment panel format she said "leaves a lot to be desired" by giving community groups less visibility than they might receive in a formal speech by Mrs. Cincotta or Mr. Mott.

Ted Wysocki: One of the classic moments was the beginning of "Reclaim America" on Columbus Day when the ABA conference was in Chicago. The Chicago Police Department was not as cooperative as the New Orleans Police Department...

But at that point Gale was real pissed off. And it just made her speech even more dramatic than what the content already was. That's where the photo with her with the big "Reclaim America" banner was taken. That was always one of the fun parts. When I was doing the video, we were always in the front lines of the actions and stuff, making sure we were getting the great photos.

Michael Westgate: Andrew A. Leckey of the *Chicago-Sun Times* reported on community members being barred from entry to the ABA Convention and Gale's decision to give her speech outside. The resulting protest "included a high school marching band, several hundred demonstrators, a boat trip on Lake Michigan and an airplane with a streamer." ("ABA critic barred by bankers" – October 14, 1980)

Cal Bradford: Another example of Gale's character was when they did "Reclaim America." I'd go down to the office and the staff is organizing all the kits and what they're going to do. They told the City of New York they're going to have this big demonstration. They're going to start at Battery Park and they're going to walk all the way up to Wall Street. And they said, "Okay. We got to get a parade permit." They went through all the stuff and the police said, "And you're going to have to stay on the sidewalk." "Well, we got this huge crowd." "Those are going to be the rules."

So Gale gets down there. The whole crowd shows up, wall to wall in Wall Street [to] Reclaim America. They're all down there. There's a woman named Ann Divinney who's the leader of one of the groups in New York City, a wonderful, wonderful woman. And this crowd is coming up Wall Street with their banners and stuff. We've got the video cameras because that's the thing we're taping. It's this pretty good size crowd. Later we understand that Ann's son worked on Wall Street and everyone's over at the window, a crowd, and he's just sitting at his desk. And this one guy, a friend of his, said, "There's a big demonstration out here." He said, "I know, I know, I know." "No, no. It's a really big demonstration." "I know. And does one of the people leading it [have] this polka dot dress on?" "Yeah." "That's my mother!" Gale was so American in this wonderful sense. One son's an insurance salesman. She's got a son who's a police officer.

So they went to New York and, after this big demonstration on Wall Street, the crowd's out there chanting and everything. They wanted to go around the block and they were going to shut down Wall Street. And the police said, "You can't do that. You can't close down Wall Street, but we'll let you go around the block. But you have to stay on the sidewalk." And the organizers were really ticked off. Gale huddles with them and she says, "Nope. We are going to stay on the sidewalk."

It was very important to her. Only a couple times ever were people arrested at the demonstrations. It was very important to her that people didn't get arrested. She said, "This isn't about civil disobedience. This is about getting a meeting or moving business along. You can't move business along if you get arrested. That's a diversion. Everybody on the sidewalk." And these people didn't want to do it. They wanted to march down Wall Street. "You all get on the sidewalk." And they're all grumbling. But they did it and they did their demonstration.

Then they were going to hit the Standard Oil building, right by Rockefeller Center. So they took the subway because they figured people would see all the buses coming. So they come up through the subway system, right across from the building, in the front doors, and before anybody can do anything they got hundreds of people inside. Of course, the building guys in their panic shut down all of the elevators in this huge high-rise building so they couldn't get upstairs. Which was probably a terrible violation of all the fire codes. And they call the police. The police send their crowd control unit. Turns out to be the same unit that was just down on Wall Street. We're outside filming. I wish I had the tapes because we had some audio on it. This was this wonderful experience that, when you're there, you'll never forget.

This police officer comes in and he said, "Oh, I know these people. They're okay." So he goes inside. And one of us got inside. We had sort of walkie-talkies so we could hear both sides of this conversation. So one of our camera guys goes inside with him and we're outside. He goes in and Gale is saying, "We want to negotiate. We want to have a meeting with Standard Oil about high oil prices." This was when oil prices were sky high.

Then Gale says: "We just need some time to organize the meeting." And the officer says, "Well, they called me. I have to respond to this call. I'm gonna go outside. I'm gonna see if I can find the rest of my men. It's gonna take me a while." Just basically saying, "You got the building to yourself for a while." And he goes outside and he keeps all his men outside. They're just walking around outside until the whole thing is all done.

Well, Gale said, "The police officers know what your life is like. You just explain it to the police officers. They'll understand because they're probably suffering from the same thing you are." So this guy said, "Well, they're not going to hurt anything." He's outside and he's talking to other people on his walkie-talkie through our walkie-talkie. It was wonderful. He's just saying, "Well, it's our system. We're going to go in in a few minutes. We don't want to cause any trouble here. The group is basically peaceful."

A lot of times you'll find they ended up getting the police to negotiate for them. It was very common that, when the police were called, Gale would say, "We just want a meeting. You're right, officer. We're not doing anything illegal." You know, don't walk on the flowers. It's their house and all that stuff. "We just need a meeting. Would you tell them that that's all we want?" And the policeman would end up going in and negotiating for them.

And that was the payoff for walking on the sidewalk. So in our minds, it all pays off. They're all done and finally they get on the bus. And the police captain gets on the bus and he thanks them for being such a good crowd. He says, "You know, crowd control's a tough job here. We're glad you were here and we understand your issues." Thanked them for being on the bus!

To me that's the thing about don't get arrested. It's not about the police. It's about the banks. It's about the oil companies. It's about something else. To have the ability to take a crowd of five thousand people and manage them in a situation like that, that's a brilliance too. That happens out of respect. That happens because the groups know why they're there. They didn't come for a lark. All those people worked hard and spent money they didn't really have to get there because these people don't have much money. They respect their own leadership and their own organizers. So when people say, "This is what we're gonna do," they do it.

One of the things you'll notice is that these groups... There aren't five thousand people who came to that meeting caring about oil. There were probably two thousand who cared about FHA and another thousand who cared about the banks. But everybody goes on everybody else's hit. That's part of what building the base is, you understand people by working with them.

But that was a fundamental philosophy; that was part of her character. She wasn't particularly religious herself, personally. Yet it always struck me that the organization—aside from the lack of structure being the power—this is really useful, sort of a jujitsu notion of organizing. You use the enemy's power to create your power notion. And this notion that you're really converting people...

They're the enemy and it's always talked about being the enemy. Trapp always organized around the enemy. Maybe it's a difference between the two. Gale always saw them as this kind of redemption because she believed so much in herself and her neighbors and her friends. It's an interesting kind of a feeling. She also believed in everybody.

Michael Westgate: In a September 3, 1982 article in the *Chicago Reader* ("Walking to work: Chicagoans kick off 'Reclaim America Week'") writer Robert Ebisch outlined the plans for the Chicago launch of Reclaim America beginning with West Side groups marching six miles down Madison to the Federal Plaza to be met by other groups. It was estimated that 40 organizations would be participating, totaling 5,000 people. The crowd was to march "to the offices of the mayor, the governor, and the [Continental] bank's president [to] submit the same list of ten Chicago corporate heads with whom they want to meet. The object: to find means of helping the moderate- and low-income people who have been hit hard by unemployment, price and interest-rate increases, and government cutbacks. In the following days, Chicagoans will join demonstrators in similar actions in Cleveland, Philadelphia, and Washington, D.C., ending up September 14 on New York's Wall Street with a crowd of 50,000, according to the estimate of National People's Action (NPA)."

In the article Gale Cincotta outlined her reasons for launching the Labor Day to September 14 event: "All of the social program cuts and all of the problems we're having are mostly because of defense spending and corporate tax breaks. Corporations used to pay about 40 percent of the bill to run this country, and now they're down to 7 percent. We could have work programs in this country that would put most people to work. Everybody's talking about the need for repair of bridges, streets, sewers, and water works. We would like the major corporations to put money out into the communities – low-interest loan pools, rehabilitation programs, job creation programs. Loan programs for small businesses. Of all the jobs in this country in the last 20 years, 65 percent were created by small business…"

Marilyn Evans: My first hit was on Wall Street. It was the first one. Reclaim America. It was great because I'd never been to New York before. We all got on the buses and came across the country. And never seen Wall Street before so my interpretation of Wall Street was quite different than what it was when I actually seen it.

I expected all these business people to be out there like the stock market. You know where they're in the stock market? I thought that would be on Wall Street. I guess it was, but it was inside, it wasn't outside. It was interesting because we all came together, the unity of the leaders that came together to just demonstrate community. The people was so overwhelming that it felt good. I really grew from that. And from then on I think I wanted to hit this place and hit that place, because Reclaim America, it symbolized a whole hell of a lot for a young person like me.

The first time that I got involved with NPA and with Gale was when my director from Working in Neighborhoods (WIN) in Cleveland sent me as staff to NTIC training, and there I met Gale and Shel Trapp. Now you've got to understand the type of background I come from. I'm the oldest girl out of eighteen siblings. For a long, long time there I was the only female besides my stepmother, and in my household females didn't have any power. Matter of fact, I basically was told, "Power is bad; you don't want power." And then, as a female, "You don't talk. You don't have an opinion. Your opinion is my opinion. So when I say something, the only thing you have to do is nod your head."

My father was very stern and he held us to the strictest code of obedience. So as I got older and graduated school, I really wanted to start a childcare center. But then I went to University Without Walls where I came upon a professor that happened to be my core faculty advisor who was pretty well pissed off at me because I had had my sixth child. And he was saying, "Dammit, Marilyn, you've got to get your life together. What are you going to do? You've got to stop having these kids." So I'm really peeed off at him by now because he's a Presbyterian. He's a minister. He ain't supposed to be talking like that.

From the family I come from, we value children. It isn't one of those things where you use birth control or whatever. Children still are a blessing. So I was really peed off at him. Then I swung back at him out of anger and I said, "Well, I gotta find a job to organize myself." He said, "Marilyn, there is a job across the way there. Go over there and get an interview." I went there and I sat down and started talking why I wanted to be hired or whatever. But see in the back of my mind I just thought that was a neat idea to become an organizer and get paid for organizing myself.

I met Gale at the same time. Gale, she was kind of laid back. She kept smoking too. She would utter a word of support here or other during the training, but she really wasn't that forthcoming at that time. Trapp was. Trapp really boggled my mind. What in the hell is this man talking about? I mean never knowing anything about organizing I just couldn't figure it out. Should we go and insult people this way?

But 25 years later, I'm still not organized. But I've been organizing for the last 25 years. But 1979 is when my director sent me to NTIC for training to be an organizer. Some of the Christian values I grew up in sort of was enemy to my coming future. Because I didn't drink, smoke or cuss or any of them things, walking into the training was... Trapp really got on my last nerves because he never would pull his pants up. All you would see was the crack of his back and he would chain smoke like a... My, he just one cigarette after another... And anytime he took a puff it was "fuck this, fuck that". So he really got into my nerves. Cincinnati do things a little bit more on the milder side than Chicago people do. So when I got back to home, I told my director that if this was organizing I was out.

"I'm not gonna do it." I said, "I quit. I can't do this. This is just not very Christian-like. This is not where I want to be." So my director, being very smart as she is, had to debrief me into understanding what organizing was about, and how we organize in different places. So after she finished I said, "Okay. As long as we don't go visit nobody right now, I'm fine." So I stayed on.

But in the meantime, I kept coming back to Chicago for different types of events and training and different types of issues. That's when I begin to follow Gale around. Gale would take you with her, and put you in front of her so that you could learn, so that you could begin to understand how to open your mouth. Because one of the things she always told me, "Open your mouth. Talk." "I don't know what to talk about. I can't." No words would come out. And she says, "What? Go ahead. Talk. Say it. Is this right? What opinion do you have?"

Never in my life did anybody ask me, what opinion did I have. You know, in the heat of battle, "what opinion do you have? Should we do it this way? Should we do it....?" I'm looking at her like she done growed four ears and toes and things. She's been in the forefront like this. She knew what to do. Why was she charging around and trying to get me to interact? So basically Gale was the one here in Chicago that took me under her wings and began to direct me into talking, having an opinion and really interacting with the group because I was really shy and an introvert at that time and still am, if you could believe that now. I'm still a little shy.

I was thirty-four when I started organizing and I was still idealistic. I was still wearing rosy colored glasses where right was right, a lie was a lie, and the truth was the truth. It wasn't until I started getting into all this, that lies became gray, blue and green areas. You just can't really call people liars. You got to say they didn't tell the truth. But Gale said, "Phooey on that. They lied? They lied. Don't worry about it! Go for it!"

So she really helped me structure my development around who I am, what was my capabilities to what ever issue that we was fighting on. And I always, always, would hide behind Gale or get close to her so she wouldn't notice me, but it never worked. It never worked. She called me out every time.

So that was my first experience with Gale and Trapp. That was 25 years ago. Her determination was always there. Her commitment was always there. She was there to help empower low-income people or people who had injustice, and help us learn and grow to help others of the same magnitude. And the only way that I seen her change was she gotten sicker. Then she got back well again, then she got sicker. But her mind and all maintained a clear direction of what she actually believed in. And that was getting them crooks.

Michael Westgate: In an August 1982 column ("Citizens are out to reclaim this country for little guy") Ralph Nader saluted Gale and Reclaim America: "Cincotta has done what no other citizens group has succeeded in doing. She has had direct meetings with Paul A. Volcker, chairman of the Federal Reserve Board, on interest rates and another head-to head with members of the Business Roundtable. Apart from breaking important new ground, Cincotta wants these elites to know that there are real people out there who know what these powerful corporations are doing to them.

Cincotta is not just demanding. She and others with her are determined to exercise the responsibility that comes with greater civic power to shape the future. Reclaim America is new citizen energy. The participants realize that politics is the rearranging of power and they mean to be in on the allocation.

Many years of community organizing and experience will be represented in these marches and the work that follows. Unlike the reactionary political action committees which are pouring money into political campaign coffers, the Reclaim America committees will be building people power around the country.

In his typically earthy way, Studs Terkel asks: "Who owns America? All our lives, ever since childhood, we were taught it was ours – the people's. We know differently now. We know it is Corporate America's. That's why Reclaim America is so exhilarating an idea – to make our dream real!"

Joe Mariano: Shel was very practical nuts and bolts. He saw the need to do local organizing and build local constituencies. Gale saw that that was a good thing. But she was also thinking bigger about it. She would say to me, "You know, the stuff we're doing on jobs. It's way too small. We're not a welfare organization. We can't keep on beating around the job issue, being focused around job training or getting people off of welfare. That's a tiny piece. There's bigger things that we should be doing in drawing people in."

We talked about Motorola here. In Illinois Motorola got all these deals so they could move to Harvard, Illinois, this little tiny farm town. Create this giant factory. Cut all these deals. Get their power from Wisconsin, electrical power. Get workers to drive all the way the hell out there. Get the tax abatements. Free land. Then they moved to Mexico. Gale said, "You know this is something that people, anybody, can be pissed off at. You can be a worker there. You can be a taxpayer. That's the kind of thing we ought to figure out, how to get the handles on that. These are the things we need to be doing, because this is the kind of thing that's going to destroy this country."

And then Trapp would try to say, "Well, okay, what's our first step? Where we going to find the constituents?" Those things. Practical things. Whereas Gale would say stuff like, "Reclaim America." So that was the tension. Trapp would try to bring it back to the practical, and she would talk more the visionary

And she'd sit and talk to me about her theories on what was driving this economy. And then how housing drove the economy, and HUD was a job creation program; it had nothing to do with housing. It was interesting stuff she'd talk about. It was hard to follow sometimes, but it was interesting stuff.

Allen Fishbein: Well, one area that's been particularly of interest to me, and what I've tried to work on particularly in recent years, was there's been this tremendous change in the financial services area. I mean tremendous change. If you had gone off even five years ago, you'd been very involved, had gone off to Africa and come back and looked at it, you'd barely be able to recognize it. No area is probably greater changed than in the mortgage area.

You're dealing with a few giant institutions, not regional or local. CRA is significantly less important to these institutions, as more and more activity occurs outside of the CRA regulatory process. Automated underwriting takes away the discretion. Risk-based pricing presumably is based on some objective criteria.

It was very difficult for Gale to really accept these changes. We used to talk about this, about new strategies, and in some ways she kept hoping things would go back to the way they were. You know, there were S&Ls and there were banks... When I talked to her I would say, "It's not going to happen. What do we do beyond? How do we get more institutions under CRA? What new tactics are going to be used?" Unfortunately she didn't live long enough to bring her insights into this.

She used to talk about Reg Q, for example, and pine for the day... Do you know what "Reg Q" is? Reg Q did two things. It was the regulation that basically permitted the S&Ls to pay a slightly higher rate on deposits. It was a quarter percent more than the banks could pay on savings accounts. It also set certain limits because of that on what could be charged. That was the world she grew up in. It was like everything was kind of regulated. If you could somehow gain entry and access to that setting, everything was going to be clear for you. I used to hear her say that, "Aw, you know we didn't have that problem when Reg Q was in. The worst thing Congress ever did was get rid of Reg Q."

Well, people have different views on that. But in part that reflected the increasing nationalization and globalization of credit, that you couldn't wall savings or lending off into different niches because they're all basically this fungible capital world. She had a very difficult time accepting that. That limited her from really thinking about where the field was headed.

I understand part of that because I think the fundamentals still apply. You've still got to figure out what motivates people. You've still got to build around people's concerns and desires. You can get caught up in this world of high finance and Wall Street securitization. But she understood the difficulties of organizing people around issues like that.

"Reclaim America" was an attempt in part to focus attention on Wall Street. Remember, they had a demonstration on Wall Street to try to build education and inform her constituency at NPA that they needed to reach out.

But I think that was a challenge. I don't want to point to <u>her</u> as being limited. I think the whole field had really had difficulties with figuring out how to take this next step up, to have that level of sophistication, but not lose your ties to the local level at the same time. I don't think we've successfully come up with the solution. That's probably true not just in financial services and lending, but in lots of other areas in the economy as well.

You look at the field today and it's a much more professional field. Predatory lending has actually made the lawyers become a much more central part of the defense force here than they were when the issue was "how do we gain access to credit," because you need lawyers to defend people against losing their homes. So the world has changed and Gale was at the cusp of this when she passed away. And it would have been interesting to see in even a couple years how she would have been viewing it.

Tommy Fitzgibbon: I think Gale had this <u>strong</u> belief in the fact that human nature and the ability of common individuals to do the right thing was the gold, if you will, that was in our neighborhoods. What she did, and what her legacy at NTIC and NPA was, was to be able to mine that, and to help them in effect make improvements not only in their own lives, but also in the lives of their communities and the people who come after them.

Being a mom with lots of kids and struggling in a neighborhood that was going through some very bad changes, she needed to see if she could do something to turn that around, and finding early success and finding that her neighbors and her neighbors' neighbors were willing to take some chances to make things change... There's an inherent self-interest in everyone that there needs to be commitment to improve the schools. Gale kind of pushed the Mayor and pushed others into sort of changing the leadership on the school board, on how to makes things better.

The tactics were important because they were, frankly, a skill set of managing the movement of thought and getting people who had a stake in the outcome to understand different points of view. Whether it was a protest with yellow buses full of people or whether it was the quiet behind-the-scenes telephone calls that she would make to officials. Officials would return her calls, the HUD Secretary, others in the Governor's office. They would return her calls because they knew what she had to say and who she represented were important in terms of a voice for a constituency that was not necessarily well represented.

The phone calls on Saturday mornings to me or to Ed Williams at Harris Bank in order to say, "Here. We're thinking about doing... What's the impact? What is the Illinois Bankers Association going to think if I do this? Who are the people that we need to convince that this needs to go forward?"

It was that intelligence if you will that she was able to muster about how to execute change that made a difference.

So, even though she's most remembered for her bullhorn activities and the challenges, the quiet building of coalitions and the quiet building of communality of thought really probably had more to do with the outcome than the protests, although the protests, in effect, engaged the community probably more so.

She educated as much through the phone calls, if not more, than she did with the confrontations. She'd call, "Are you coming down to NHS? Can you stop and see me before you do?" "Tell me what you think about this person as a potential Assistant Secretary of HUD. People have asked me. Do you know him? Do you know her? What's her reputation?" So it was that aggregation of intelligence about people and organizations that I think made all the difference.

She knew where she was going. She knew how to gather momentum to bring things to a conclusion. She didn't win all the time. Nor did NTIC. Nor did the banks. Nor did the government. But certainly what it did was it moved or shifted the balance of legislation or regulation or capital or investment or approaches to things. Moved it more in the direction of where things needed to be for this country.

She knew what battles to fight. "I'm not going to fight on that. It doesn't help us to do that. Although it would be nice if we could win that, that won't contribute to the overall success. And may burn bridges that we'll need in the future." So she was very successful at certain judgments.

Bud Kanitz: Fannie Mae was one of the best demonstrations of how she had lasting impact… Gale also served on the Fannie Mae Advisory Committee which is kind of a blue ribbon group of folks from around the country. Last night at the NTIC 30th annual reception I was talking to one of the Fannie Mae folks and he said, "Yes, yes. We figured it was better to get Gale in the tent. So we got her on the Advisory Committee."

The Fannie Mae partnership is an absolutely excellent example of where Gale's confrontation tactics led to the partnerships that not only started with the big guy up at the top, but now have continued through Julie Gould. And continue and continue and continue. They continue to produce benefits for the folks in the neighborhood.

Gale knew how to operate in that kind of a corporate boardroom setting. She always was very effective. At one of the Fannie Mae meetings, there was a lot of yakkity, yakkity, yakkity, yak and finally Gale came out basically to the effect, "Well, let's cut through all this shit." And she just laid out the issue. Everybody's jaw dropped at how she nailed it. What a salient woman.

You never know exactly when to say it. If you said it too soon, you know, you wouldn't have the crowd with you. But she'd know the moment to do it. Gale had this ability to see three disparate things happen and see a trend.

Bill Dedman, a reporter up in Boston now, was very close to Gale because he wrote a series for the *Atlanta Constitution-Journal* on redlining called "The Color of Money" and he received a Pulitzer Prize in 1989. He got a lot of his information from Gale. I saw him earlier this year and talked to him and he was telling me how much information Gale had been able to provide him to do that series and also how much help she was overall. He went along on the action when Gale invaded HUD Secretary Sam Pierce's condo. He got pictures of that and he reported on that.

There was also an issue with the Treasury Department during the Clinton administration in '95 or '96. Gale had tried to get a meeting with Secretary Robert Rubin to give her perspective on how this public policy was going to affect neighborhoods. She couldn't get the time of day. She couldn't even get her phone messages returned by an assistant. So Gale and I and Allen Fishbein had a meeting in the White House with Gene Sperling, National Economic Council, to talk about this issue. Ellen Seidman worked for Gene Sperling, and Gale complained about, "I can't get a meeting with Bob Rubin." And so next thing they knew Ellen Seidman went out of the room and came back about fifteen minutes later and she said, "How about 4:30 today?"

Michael Westgate: I got a call from Joe Mariano in 1998 asking if Chelsea NHS, where I was executive director – returning full circle in a way, to where I had been in 1975, – would be interested in receiving a sub-grant from NTIC, from the Justice Department towards community organizing. Of course, I said yes. Joe paid us a visit. When Gale was invited to give the keynote address to the 1999 Annual Meeting of the Massachusetts Association of Community Development Corporations (MACDC) where I was a member of the Board, I asked for the opportunity to introduce her.

MACDC is a trade association of 75 CDCs statewide. It was the logical entity for me to channel my energies on redlining and similar issues that affected Chelsea more than most communities, given our high percentage of minorities. I was on MACDC's Community Reinvestment Committee dealing with the same issues Gale was dealing with. I had the opportunity to help draft the legislation which brought the Massachusetts insurance companies into a local version of CRA, requiring them to invest $200,000,000 over five years in Massachusetts low-moderate income communities in exchange for a change in Massachusetts tax law which would be more equitable for them.

MACDC was the forerunner among statewide organizations of CDCs. MACDC's Executive Director Marc Draisen stated that, at a national meeting of statewide organizations, they reported that collectively they had gotten commitments for over $210,000,000. About 95% of the national total was Massachusetts!

In introducing Gale, I gave the background of Chicago and its role as the biggest and best NHS organization in the country. I gave a lot of the credit for its success to Gale.

At the end of the evening she said, "You know, my plane doesn't take off until one o'clock. I've got to do something tomorrow morning. Can I be useful?" And I said, "Well, Chelsea's on the way to the airport. You could come over and maybe help inspire my staff." And she said, "Sure." I invited the board as well. Tuck Willis, the board president, and two others came.

She arrived and sat down. She was a great listener. She asked what some of the problems might be and how we were organizing. We said we had lots of problems but we hadn't pinned it on a single enemy. She said, "Well, the normal target is City Hall if you don't have any other. You've got to have an enemy." We said, "The only problem there is City Hall is on our board and most of our capital funding comes through City Hall." She said, "That won't do, will it?"

"Well, it doesn't sound to me like you've identified the enemy. The first thing you have to do is identify the enemy. If you don't have an enemy, you can't organize. Umm. Well, who else can you pick on?" "Well, the school system sucks and BU's running the school system." "Perfect. Perfect. BU's the enemy." It took her about ten minutes.

That was the last time I saw Gale. Her visit provided some of the motivation to write a book about her. She could see issues with such clarity— and see a way of dealing with them. If I could get her story across, that could provide inspiration to many people seeking to deal with problems and issues in their communities, as well as documenting the work of a remarkable woman who knew both how to lead and how to organize.

CHAPTER 15

"Getting such a call from Gale was like running a nice, quiet prisoner of war camp in North Vietnam and having Rambo drop in."

TRANSITION

Joe Mariano: Trapp didn't want to deal with Gale being weakened. He basically felt she couldn't walk any more, and it was getting to the point, "What are we going to do?" I said I'd talk to her about a wheelchair, how that would work, what it would look like, why it was important. How it wouldn't show weakness. Gale never wanted to be perceived as being weak, physically or in any way, shape or form. And I said to her, "Well, look, it's actually worse if people see you struggling to walk. I can get you in the back. I can even bring you up on the stage. Nobody will even know. We'll come out, go through the service entrance." So I plotted this out with her. I had the staff plot it out with the hotel, what we were going to do.

Then once we got through the first year and she liked the idea, that she wouldn't have to spend an hour, literally, walking from wherever she was to her room. That was a good deal. Just hop in the wheelchair and she'd get down there. She would literally have to leave and get there early, because she didn't want to have people see her. Very much like FDR.

Then the wheelchair thing happened, and that's all she wanted after that was the wheelchair. Trapp said, "What did you tell her?" "I don't think I said anything magic." Once we did that then I was in charge of rolling her down La Salle Street when we were hitting on predatory lending. Obviously she couldn't walk. I said, "Well, Gale, do you want to get a cab?" "No, roll me down the street." Rolling Gale down the street, it's not as easy as it sounds. This is in the Loop. But still it was a long hike and we had to get from here to there. Even though there's ramps on each of the corners now, it's still hard to go up and down.

The doctors would say, "Sure. We can do a knee operation. You got to quit smoking and lose weight." And Gail would say, "Well, I can't do both." "Well, you got to do both." That was the dilemma.

Alicia Mendoza: Gale left one day going home feeling badly, and then just never came back in. That was about two weeks before she died.

Joe Mariano: Anne-Marie said she looked like she was in a lot of pain. So that's when it all happened. Then she said she had to have an operation. Gale never told anybody about it personally. Became very closed at that point. You couldn't find anything out. So I wound up calling Gayle Brinkman and talking with her, "What's going on?"

Alicia Mendoza: That is what was so hurting – that we didn't know how very ill she was. She would come in even though she was in pain. She would tell us about her knees, of course, but there was much more to it than that. I feel she knew. A lot of people probably felt she knew, but didn't want to express it because she loved what she was doing.

She didn't want the doctor telling her she couldn't do it. The love of her work superseded the pain. She didn't want everybody worrying about her health. She wanted to keep on doing her work. Yet there were some times when I used to have a back problem, she would call me at home and see how I was doing and say, "Well, I hope you feel better. Take care of yourself." Even though I know a lot of days she didn't feel the best herself. She was just an amazing woman.

I often wonder myself where she got her strength. From time to time she would give me these little booklets that she would get in the mail. They had little prayers in them and when she had read them she would give them to me. To a certain degree she didn't have much organized religion—she was a spiritual person.

Marilyn Evans: Gale never did show her illness. I mean she was overweight; we knew that. And her knees was gone and it was a gradual descent. Because she was walking everywhere, then all of a sudden she went into the wheelchair. There were several things she could do, and several things she couldn't do as it got later on in her life. Understanding that she was in that condition, I wasn't prepared, didn't even know that she was as sick as she was. You never know people are as sick as they are. And Gale had a strong constitution. She wasn't going to let nothing hold her down. And that includes sickness, even up until her last breath. We weren't aware. I don't think people on the staff here knew.

Joe Mariano: So it never got to that bedside meeting because it became serious and she was in intensive care and it got worse. When the family said to me, "We're going to let Gale go," at first I thought it was – projecting my optimism – "Oh, she's out of the hospital." So I said, "Okay. Tell me what that means." "Well, we talked to the doctors and they agreed that she's not going to get any better. It's never going to get any better. These machines… It could be any time." So literally I said, "Wow. I appreciate the call. I know this has got to be hard."

Hung the phone up and I said to Anne-Marie, "We're going to the hospital." I said to the family, "Can I come?" They said, "No. Stay away." So I said to Anne-Marie, "I'm going to the hospital." Anne-Marie says, "I can't.

I can't go. I don't want to go." I called Trapp and I said, "Listen. I'm going out to Loyola. This is the situation." He went, "Jesus Christ. I can't deal with death. I don't want to deal with this." So I said, "Well, I"m going." So Alicia says, "I'd like to go." And I said, "Come on."

We just went in. You learn that at NPA. You don't take no. I went in and the nurse says, "Are you aware of the situation?" I said, "Yes, I talked to the family." She said, "Basically there's no hope." Alicia and I went in together. So it was hard.

Alicia and I drove in separate cars from the NTIC office and by the time we got to the Loyola Medical Center in Maywood – it was late in the day – maybe around 4:30 pm – and what surprised me was that there was no one there in the room – either from Gale's family or her close friends – maybe they had already said their goodbyes. There were tubes and wires coming from Gale to machines and monitors next to the bed. Gale seemed to be sleeping. I was uneasy with the scene in front of me and didn't know what to do.

Alicia started to talk to Gale about what was going on in the office and the meetings we were having on the issues which we were working on. We were also joking around – maybe more for ourselves than Gale – about going to gamble at the boats or whatever – talking about finding the enemy – the sharks who were destroying the neighborhoods with bad loans—and doing an NPA hit on them. All of a sudden it seemed that Gale's eyes opened – we realized that she did not have her glasses on – so we leaned in by her face. As I was watching her, I remember saying to Alicia in amazement "Did she just wink at us?" Alicia said that it looked like it to her. At that moment there was movement by her mouth – words seemed to be formed – some sounds made – and we heard ever so softly . . . "Get the crooks!" Alicia said to Gale . . . "Don't worry Gale, we will get the crooks!" Then nothing, just sleep or a comatose state again. We waited and waited . . . hoping for more but there was nothing more. . . .we sang softly. . . "When NPA . . . goes marchin' in. . . oh, I want to be in that number. . . when NPA comes marchin' in. . . ." and then decided to leave around 6:30 pm.

I told Alicia that I would be back at the hospital early the next morning. I also told Alicia that on my way home, I planned to stop by Gale's apartment building tonight to see Richard and maybe the Brinkmans to let them know I was there. The next morning, I got a phone call at home. . from whom . . . I can't remember . . . at around 7:30 or so . . . that Gale had passed away earlier in the morning.

Michael Westgate: Gale died on August 15, 2001. She received tributes from a wide variety of friends and even some who had considered her an adversary.

From letter to NTIC from Comptroller of the Currency (Aug. 16, 2001)

John D. Hawk, Jr.: Gale was an American original who developed the practice of community advocacy to a fine art. While some viewed her as a kind of urban terrorist, who could organize a boisterous demonstration in a campaign to highlight the plight of inner city neighborhoods, to others she was an inspirational leader, who knew how to get things done and pursued the interests of those she represented with all the vigor at her command. But however one felt about her, it is clear that no one in our time did more than Gale to raise our collective consciousness about the corrosive effects of redlining – a practice she viewed as her call to action.

Michael Westgate: The *Chicago Tribune* saluted Gale in an August 17, 2001 editorial, "An organizer for all seasons": Community organizers are constantly at risk of two occupational hazards. They may become so entranced by their own screaming and theatrics that they won't quit even when such tactics become counterproductive. Or they get co-opted by the politicians or the corporate 'suits' and cease to be effective. That effective combination of tenacity, style and realistic approach made Cincotta and her National Training and Information Center here a mecca for community organizers nationwide. It is also what kept her an effective fighter for neighborhood causes to the very end, long after lesser colleagues had faded from the scene.

From letter to NTIC from Fannie Mae (Aug. 17, 2001)

David Jeffers: In the community of housing activism, Gale never let us forget what it was all about. Every word she spoke, every stand she made, shook us from our complacency and kicked out from under us any self-satisfaction we may have been tempted to rest upon. She never took her eyes off who really mattered – the Americans whose rights to safe, decent and affordable housing have not yet been honored – and never allowed us to look away.

From eulogy for Gale, (Aug. 18, 2001)

Father Ed McKenna: Richard Hartnack, a senior vice president of the First National Bank of Chicago, once explained that his bank's agreeing to invest $120 million in Chicago's neighborhoods had begun with a call from Gale Cincotta requesting a meeting. Getting such a call, he said, was like "running a nice, quiet prisoner of war camp in North Vietnam and having Rambo drop in."

As Gale encouraged Fathers Mike Rocheford and Frank Phelan (Resurrection Parish) and myself, Ed McKenna and Charlie Tobin (St. Thomas Aquinas Church), pushing us out of easy rectory life into "street actions," so we and the Jesuit volunteers moved her into a "new being." No longer Aglaia, she became Gale (as in wind-force, natural, stormy, earth mother), as in earlier times a man named Saul became an apostle Paul. As President of OBA, she awakened the priests to "save Austin" from predatory realtors and absentee landlords and awful schools, so we awakened her to the supernatural grace of God that was within her.

Pablo Eisenberg: Twenty years ago you had some leaders who had vision, and they had passion, like Gale. They had courage. And they had a real sense of public service and commitment to the public good. Today? It's hard to find.

Part of it's the environment. But part of it is that there's just less value placed on public service. Now the movement to find the hybrid organizations that can span business and public and nonprofit is annoying because it's moving away from the fundamental issues. People are forgetting what is called correctly "nonprofitness" that is actually a quality of being different from profit.

Those are the qualities that Gale had, that young folks don't have. They have no role models for following. Our universities and academic centers do a <u>lousy</u> job. They're sort of training and developing real budget analysts and not leaders – people who don't know politics, who don't know coalition building, who don't have vision and courage. And because of that, there is a lack of leaders.

I'm on the board of the fellowship program funded by Ford Foundation called "New Voices." It came out of the needs of human rights organizations, with Ford putting in money every year for fifteen New Voice Fellows, particularly with a stress on people of color, who get funded. And they're mostly human rights, the legal servicey-type organizations. Since I've been on the board a year, I've been trying to get them to have kids stationed in community organizing groups, advocacy, issue groups and like that. They're going to move that way.

You have another one run by the Advocacy Institute, funded by Ford, that gives fellowships for people who are mid-career, 35-40s. You know, they're going to do well. And I argued hard with Ford, when they were doing it, "Put your money in kids in their twenties. That's where you got to get them." Out of school, in school. That's where you go to launch them. If you have to triage, you triage out the 50-year-olds. They're going to do what they're going to do. You can't really inspire a generation there, and you can with the 20-year-olds.

I have Marcy Kaptur come in to my classroom at Georgetown– the congresswoman who was a strong supporter of Gale – talking about the relationship between non-profits and politics, how she used to work for Msgr.

Geno Baroni, and how she evolved into being a congresswoman. They want to hear those stories and they don't get that. We don't start leadership or even have civic education in high schools any more.

George Knight: Some of the issues have shifted so much from those days to now. Gale was able to both deal with the specifics of injustice, particular things that could be cured, as well as understand the systems that allowed that stuff to happen. But now the systems are much more defended from a public relations point of view. To some extent we've almost cycled back, we have to rub raw the sores, because people aren't angry. People should be angry about being forced into taking an interest-only loan. It's just terrible that a pair of teachers can't afford to buy a home. What are we building by doing that?

And the anger is gone. That piece was easy for us. In Chicago, it was easy, particularly around the blockbusting. That was so patently evil for everybody. Blacks, whites, everybody lost in that process. That was so patently easy to organize against. It was scary at the time because some of the blockbusters did use physical intimidation and threats. But the anger was there and the sympathy of those uninvolved. They could identify with the situation. But now somehow we've got 35 years later and people don't identify with the problems.

When we went into Housing Court in Chicago and we'd have the pictures and the basement was filled with water and sewage, there were rats, there was a sense, a broad sense – even sometimes the landlords would concede – that conditions were intolerable and needed to be changed. That was usually their first offense. It bought them another 30 days. But some actually believed it. Actually did do something about it. I don't know now that people would even say that's unfair. They'd say, "Move to another house." We've lost a sense of what's fair. -

We've got to get away from referring to this as hellraising because our own rhetoric causes trouble. It's raising legitimate issues of economic justice. We didn't look at it as hellraising. To get the attention of one bank, a number of their depositors from their neighborhood just all happened to go in on a Saturday morning to make a one-cent deposit. The bank president suddenly was open to meeting with us about making mortgages in the neighborhood. Now it was frustrating to have to get to that point. The group had written letters and letters and letters and letters.

Ann Vick-Westgate: Where do you see NPA going in the future?

Inez Killingsworth: I see NPA living on. And so far as I'm concerned, I'm going to do all within my power to make sure it happens, that it continues to live on. It would be a sad story to just let it die out with all of the results, the things that has been accomplished because of NPA. CRA to me is our biggest issue, is our biggest victory, because the impact from that has just spread all over the place.

Ann Vick-Westgate: What about bringing in new leaders? Do you see a younger generation coming up that's going to continue to fight?

Inez Killingsworth: Yes. Yes, I do and I think that's very important because we don't want this to just fade out. This is something that's good, it's grounded, it's good, it works. So you have to keep reaching out to the younger people to develop those leadership skills. And now [that] we have a large youth group, we've been working toward getting that group. We've got some stable leaders. I've seen several young people that really are interested and they act it. They're working on the educational piece now. They've done some stuff on their own. So they love it.

So, yeah, I think the key thing is to teach 'em and train 'em the right way to do it. The way you can do it on a safe level without a lot of risk. We haven't gone to jail to do what we do because we are very disciplined. So we try to discipline people. Teach 'em when it's time to get loud and when it's time not to get loud and you listen and pay attention.

And if you do that on the local level, when you bring people to NPA your local people should be trained and know what to expect. You tell 'em this is what you do when the police come. So people are trained. That way, when you do the actions, it becomes fun. Not fun in the sense that you want to do it just to do it. But it takes the fear out of it. That's why we try to make sure that people are educated at the local level.

Michael Westgate: In terms of young leadership, can you identify them and train them as early as high school level or early twenties or late twenties? What's a good age to catch them at?

Inez Killingsworth: There are now youth groups, in some cities. In Cleveland, there's a youth group and they're all high school young people and they're very active. It's been an ongoing process. But with young people sometime they don't hang around, so we are trying to get some of those young people to grow up in the organization like Jimmy Cincotta did. Parents have their young people that are committed to the organization. What I see now are repeaters.

Ann Vick-Westgate: So what were the characteristics, the qualities, that Gale had that made her an effective leader? You mentioned she was a fantastic speaker. She was powerful.

Inez Killingsworth: Gale was very strong, had the strength of a lion. I would say it was God-given strength that she had. To me she was a born leader. And only the strength from God would give her the wisdom to continue to do what she was doing, to give of herself. See Gale was a very humble person. People may not realize because she carried this big stick. She would demand a lot of you. But she was a very humble person.

I worked with Gale on a real personal level and she had low points. When she would get to those low points, she would call and would say, "Inez, what the hell is going on?" I'd say, "Hell, I don't know. We don't know either." So we would talk time and time. We were just like at a crossroads. "So where do you go? How do you take this to the next level?" And we would just talk about it. She'd say, "Well, things is quiet." And that was probably one of the things she feared the most. When things got quiet and she wasn't hearing the rumbling. "What's going on? They're gone underground. Everything is quiet."

So I would say, "Hell, we don't know. It'll surface in a moment." And we'd feed off of each other like that. And humble in that sometimes when you get something for yourself, you don't remember the people that's still out there that's hurting. Gale never forgot that. She was always looking, no matter what the issue was if it affected people in a way, "Oh, hell, we got to find a way, we got to find a way to do it." And then sometimes people thought she didn't have a lot of empathy. She would say, "Damn, just do it. Just do it."

Joe Mariano: If there was a legacy, I think Gale would say, "I cared about the issues. I gave a damn about neighborhoods getting revitalized."

She would argue with us and say, "That's the problem with some of the other groups, the ACORNS of the world. They don't give a damn about the issues. They want to wield electoral power. They want to get in position so they can elect somebody, or unelect somebody, or get their people in there. That's the problem with Fair Share; they're all these organizers who want to run for office, who are using it as a platform for their own advancement." She would argue, "This office, we're working on these same issues that we started on, and if we have a new issue it's because it's come out of the neighborhoods, not because we thought about them."

So maybe that is a legacy. The unstated legacy was that "I don't want to be a famous politician. I don't want to do those kinds of things. I want people to be able to say, 'She cared about the issues. She made neighborhoods a better place to live.'" Maybe that's it.

George Knight: One of the criticisms was that Gale dominated NPA and never really let other people rise and be the focal point. The leadership succession has been an interesting struggle for them at NTIC.

I guess every saint has weaknesses. She didn't develop the next generation of leaders and really step aside and put them there. OBA withered and disappeared virtually after she and Shel left. It didn't hang together. NCO hung on for much, much longer and now it's gone, but it hung on for a much longer time.

Cal Bradford: Like all of us as we get older, Gale had a little less capacity to understand and engage new issues. She stuck with old issues even after they weren't the main issues to the organization anymore. But that's just the human thing. It's again an issue about not getting other leadership up to the national level or not restructuring while she's there. But I don't know how you could have. It wouldn't have happened. It wouldn't happen in any organization until after the leader is gone and you see what the loss is.

Gale felt the racial issue. She felt women's issues got shortchanged. She felt terribly disappointed in the women's movement. It lost its opportunities. It got lost and alienated the very people that she worked with, that she wanted to be a part of it. She was interested in that, but didn't see her organization having space to deal with it, so that was sad.

She got in some ways more involved with her family. She depended on them more. She needed more time with them. She enjoyed them more.

I don't think Gale enjoyed what she was doing as much in the later years. Part of it was the staff turned over so much, and it was frustrating to her. She couldn't look around the room and see people that she shared history with, except for Joe Mariano and Anne-Marie Douglas. She didn't have that same sense when she looked out there. There were times when she would ask someone who this other staff person was. She didn't have the energy to train people anymore. She wanted people who knew all the stuff. It took the energy away from her.

Gale was very bitter about the predatory lending stuff and was having a hard time dealing with it. You get to that point in your life – not that she figured she was dying next year – where you say, "God. We've done all this work and now this horrible thing comes along. I haven't got that much energy. It's bigger and more evil." Gale always used to say there couldn't be anything worse than FHA. And then predatory lending came along and it's worse. It was taking people's homes who had NHS homes. It was flipping those loans. It was screwing all the people they'd helped together over the years. It was a little overwhelming to her.

Michael Westgate: Gale had fought for a new concept—that neighborhoods had rights. Corporations have rights but they should not trump those of communities. Gale won major battles, as reflected in the Community Reinvestment Act (CRA) and its prerequisite, Home Mortgage Disclosure Act (HMDA).

Gale had slain many Hydra heads but more kept emerging through predatory lending, and they were eroding what she had accomplished. Paradoxically, she had shown the conventional lenders that there was money to be made lending in neighborhoods they had written off as too risky. Now the subprime lenders came along and ripped off the very people she was trying to help.

Cal Bradford: She didn't have the resources. She tended to slip back into the things she was familiar with. Even if they may not have been as important, it provided a little security. She sort of lost the cutting edge.

She was terribly concerned about Social Security and very concerned, even in her own organization, about focusing so much on home ownership. To her there was this big plot. The government was trying to get everybody to own their own home, and FHA was part of the plot. All these people were going to get their own home. Then they were going to cut back on Social Security and people were going to end up with only the equity on their home, and that was going to be your big thing, and that was going to get taken away from you.

She really had a vision. She saw no way of dealing with that. She saw it dealing with the predatory lenders. So she had no organizing base that was pushing real hard for rental housing and she more and more felt home ownership is just not the answer. It's difficult to maintain your home. We may have pushed that as far as we can. There's nothing on that other side. The government's trying to get everyone to own a home. She just thought that was horrible.

Joe Mariano: Gale wanted to win and that was her goal. Trapp said that too. He quoted Lombardi, "Winning isn't everything. It's the only thing."

Gale towards the end – because her energy level was low – was willing to win even at the expense of circumventing organizing. So where in the older days she was more open to, "Okay, let's organize," later, if she could cut a deal with somebody, it was a lot easier than her getting on a bus – her knees were worn out – and going to battle again. She was willing to do that but it was hard. You saw that in Chicago too. There was some tension around Richard M. Daley not delivering some stuff, and she never wanted to go to war with Daley. She'd rather try to cut some deals somehow. Of course, it's pretty hard to go to war with Daley.

Daley was a stumbling block on the predatory lending legislation. He wasn't convinced this was the way to go. So basically we said, "You got to call him and tell him he's full of shit." She always wanted to work it through his staff and do that that way, as opposed to taking Daley on head on. He is very stubborn so he's not an easy guy to move. So, yeah, she wanted to win. But in the later days she wanted to figure out maybe there's other ways we can win and maybe we don't need to fight so many battles.

The last NPA [Conference] Gale was at was 2001. We found in a master's thesis, where this woman had done the interviews, she quoted Gale specifically saying that she didn't care if NPA faded away after her. That's absolutely true. Trapp was always worried Gale was going to die at her desk....

He'd have to dispose of the body. And that was probably Gale's vision for herself.

Gale could hardly walk because her knees were shot. So if she had to go the bathroom she literally would hold on to everything. She had this trail of things that she could hold onto, so she could get to the bathroom. Trapp would like hide his head because he was afraid she was going to fall and hit her head. But that was never talked about.

Then when Trapp retired, Gale spoke to me, "Well, what's wrong with Trapp?" "Gale, he's retired." "No, he's not. He wants something. What does he want?" "I don't think he wants anything, Gale." "Well, if he wants to work one day a week, that's fine with me. He can do that." "I talked to him about that, Gale, and I don't think that's the case."

"Well, he'll get bored in three months and come back." I said, "Well, maybe he will, but he's not going to come back here on a daily basis." "Well, that son of a bitch. I thought he was…"

At one point she said to me, "He's just doing this. It's not real. He told me he wasn't actually going to retire. It was going to be a year later or something like that." Of course he said, "I never said anything of the sort." And she always would change the story. Whatever she wanted to hear, she believed it. I said, "No, Gale. I didn't hear him say that." She said to me, "I always considered him to be a partner in this. For him to do this, I don't know what's wrong with him." That was in September of 2000 that Trapp did that dastardly deed.

In December of 1999 he told me he was going to do this, and that it was a done deal. That he wasn't going to change his mind. So I knew at that point that it was going to happen and I said, "Well, who else knows?" "You're it." "Well, I want you to set up a meeting with Anne-Marie and myself as soon as possible to talk about this. I also want you to talk to her and you got to talk to Cincotta." "Well, I can't talk to her. She'd be going to try to talk me out of it." "Not if you don't want to be talked out of it." He put it off and put it off and put it off, and it may have been in the summertime.

Cal Bradford: NPA is not as powerful as it was in terms of federal policy. This is the part where loving something clouds your judgment. But one of the problems is that NPA stayed independent from other organizations. They would endorse sign-on letters sometimes, but they generally didn't do that, and they didn't join as a membership thing. They didn't want to lose their independence, ever. And in a way that was good because, as I said, NPA is a Brigadoon. It's not a real thing. And it would have forced them to create a structure that was unnatural to an extent.

But the organizing part is gone. I see NPA having lost a role in the play there. It goes back and reestablishes itself from time to time. Part of it's the dynamics and part of it's the failure, maybe, of Gale to move people in before she left. Because for a whole year, people just said, "Well, Gale's gone. We don't have to pay attention to them anymore." She became the organization and in people's minds, much too much.

As much as Gale didn't have an office in Washington, she really depended on Allen Fishbein and the Center for Community Change to keep her up on what was going on, and on Bud Kanitz to keep her up. And that connection is gone. The distance is greater between Chicago and Washington. The issues are more complex. Predatory lending is much more complex than FHA was. People you're going to go after are harder to identify. And they don't have that base and so that's changed.

They're getting into issues that are much more difficult to deal with. You can't deal with them by negotiating and selling something as much as you could in the past. A lot of the issues that I worked with them on were pretty straightforward. And, quite frankly, even though the organization was very powerful, and it changed the banking structure for a while and it changed a lot of things, the big focus initially was on FHA. And FHA is almost as horrible today as it was in the '70s. The strangest thing is it's been as hard to reform the government. They can be more successful at reforming the banking structure and the insurance structure.

Michael Westgate: Banking regulations changed dramatically over time as Illinois authorized branching, then federal laws permitted interstate banking and encouraged mergers into larger and larger banks. Decision-making previously made at the local neighborhood bank was made further and further away, some in North Carolina, some in the UK and elsewhere overseas. This was facilitated by ever-more complex financial instruments devised by Wall Street, to combine pools of mortgages, issuing bonds backed by them, then selling them or pieces of them to investors and banks worldwide. Quick profits on sale of these products became addictive both to the firms, whose stocks jumped with the increase profits, and to the staff, who were paid increasingly on an incentive basis.

This empowerment was accompanied by federal pre-emption of state statutes. Throughout the end of the 20th century and into the 21st, federal legislation and regulations increasingly provided that state statutes and regulations could not be applied to federally chartered institutions. Federal preemption was done under the rationale that it would be too great an imposition on institutions doing business in all 50 states to have to comply with different jurisdictions.

But it is my conviction that the states have the right and the obligation to provide needed protections to their constituents. The states, indeed individual cities, should have the right to supplement federal laws with ones appropriate to their own needs.

Federal legislation, particularly the 1999 Gramm-Leach-Bliley Act, repealing the Glass-Steagall Act of 1933, took down the legal barriers between banking, insurance and brokerage businesses, institutionally combining risk-takers with conservative lenders. Corporate greed took over as pressures for short-term fee-generating activity took precedence over long-term sound investments. Local lenders no longer retained responsibility for the soundness of the loans they originated.

Payment of bonuses reinforced short-term attitudes. Corporate boards of directors abdicated responsibility for the long-term soundness of their organizations. Federal regulators and Congress were also complicit.

Congress passed legislation that required regulatory agencies to relax standards. Traditional barriers established in response to the havoc leading to the Great Depression in the 1930s had prevented banks from merging with insurance companies or brokerage houses. These barriers were torn down, successively, under both Republican and Democratic leadership. Banks who had the choice were even encouraged to shop for the federal regulators who would treat them the most leniently.

Many people, including myself, argue that federal legislation should set a floor, not a ceiling, on consumers' rights. States know the needs of their communities and their constituents better than the federal government. This argument is not restricted to lending. In air quality, California's right to establish higher emission standards for car exhaust was recognized after many years, with other states following suit.

It has become too easy for lobbyists, well-financed by lenders, to influence federal legislation. Had the needs for community reinvestment—and solutions—not been proven in Chicago and Illinois before HMDA and CRA were introduced, it is doubtful that they would have been passed. Cities and states have proven to be useful and necessary laboratories for defining problems and experimenting with remedies at the local level before seeking national legislation or funding.

The institutional purposes of banks, insurance companies and brokerage houses are different, as are the kinds of people needed to run them. There should be firewalls and regulations ensuring that each function is run in a way that protects consumers, institutional assets, and the economy as a whole from inappropriate risk-taking.

Meantime, changes in federal bankruptcy laws in the 1990s, favoring lenders, were designed to make it more difficult for individuals or families to declare bankruptcy to avoid financial responsibilities. They also made it almost impossible for many who need this protection to hold on to their homes while they paid off huge medical bills in particular.

These changes in the financial landscape would make it very difficult today to mount the kind of local campaigns at which Shel and Gale were so successful. Fortunately HMDA and CRA were successful in slowing the merger process enough to get some commitments to continue serving local financial needs, and these laws still provide some measure of protection. The reporting requirements under CRA also forced bankers to focus on the loans they make, as well as those they turn down. Unfortunately, the requirements have not been consistently applied over the years.

Gale was in some ways cynical. Two of her biggest fears were that the federal government would shove too many people into a homeownership position, only to allow their homes to be foreclosed. The second was that Social Security would be privatized, only to see people's guaranteed income as elders evaporate. The first fear was realized in 2008-09 when millions of people saw their homes being foreclosed. The second was averted when Congress refused to enact proposals by President George W. Bush to privatize Social Security.

From remarks made by the Comptroller of the Currency before the Enterprise Annual Network Conference, Nov. 19, 2008

John C. Dugan: While not perfect, CRA has made a positive contribution to community revitalization across the country and has generally encouraged sound community development lending, investment, and service initiatives by regulated banking organizations.

CRA is not the culprit behind the subprime mortgage lending abuses, or the broader credit quality issues in the marketplace. Indeed, the lenders most prominently associated with subprime mortgage lending abuses and high rates of foreclosure are lenders not subject to CRA. A recent study of 2006 Home Mortgage Disclosure Act data showed that banks subject to CRA and their affiliates originated or purchased only six percent of the reported high cost loans made to lower-income borrowers within their CRA assessment areas.

Over the last ten years, CRA has helped spur the doubling of lending by banking institutions to small businesses and farms, to more than $2.6 trillion. During this period, those lenders more than tripled community development lending to $371 billion.

Overwhelmingly, this lending has been safe and sound. For example, single-family CRA-related mortgages offered in conjunction with the NeighborWorks organizations have performed on a par with standard conventional mortgages. Foreclosure rates within the NeighborWorks network were just 0.21 percent in the second quarter of 2008, compared to 4.26 percent of subprime loans and 0.61 percent for conventional conforming mortgages.

From website http://financialservices.house.gov, March 12, 2009
Director of the Division of Consumer and Community Affairs of the
Federal Reserve System

Sandra Braunstein: We have run data on CRA lending and where loans are located, and we found that only six percent of all higher cost loans were made by CRA covered institutions in neighborhoods targeted, which would be low to moderate-income neighborhoods targeted by CRA… You're going to find that CRA was not the cause of this loan crisis.

Marilyn Evans: One of the most important things to emphasize is Gale's commitment in empowering other people, her commitment to fight injustice. Not too many people would do it like Gale did it. Even though she just got involved because she got angry at what happened at school with her kids, it became a bigger thing than she was. So I think what will sell Gale's story would be, "Gale loved who she was."

She would bring us to Chicago once a year for the training and she would just take us to different restaurants because she knew we were not exposed to different cultures and things. So she took us to a full-course Chinese restaurant and we had the seven or eight courses. That was the first time a lot of us had ever been in a Chinese restaurant. Then she took us to a Greek restaurant. She <u>loved</u> Greek. She was Greek. So she just loved the food. You could see how happy she was with being in her surroundings. She <u>loved</u> who she was.

Gale loved the country of America and she expressed that all the time. This flag, the symbol, belongs to us, us poor folks, and not to let them take our symbols away and use it against us. That was the first time, with Wall Street and all, that I begin to understand America. And took some ownership in it because Gale exhibited <u>so well</u>. Here she was just like me or I was just like her. We didn't have riches. We didn't have money. We didn't live in the best of places, but what we did have was good people. What we did have, we loved it. We cherished it. We were committed to it. So if you bring anything out about Gale, bring that out: pride in who you are, pride in your community.

Communities that a lot of people might look down on, or that they're trained to look down on… They're always telling you, "Go someplace else. Go someplace else. You can do better here. You can do better there. Move into a better community." But Gale got back, "If you don't fix where you're at, the same thing will happen when you go someplace else." So you got to begin to have pride in what you are, who you are. And don't step back because of the injustice. Step forward.

That's my whole take. That's what I keep in my heart and my head and how I encourage others to get involved. Gale was consistent. She would stay on you. As you developed, she'd pull you on a little further and a little further. And she taught me how to do that with the leaders that I had.

Gale brought people together of all races, earlier and better than a lot of others. I didn't know it at the time, but our organization, Communities United For Action [in Cincinatti], is a multi-racial and multi-issue operation, and having to pull that together, I don't know how she did it because I find it very, very hard to do it at times. But it's like you straddle in between the two. You have to do acrobatics to do it.

You're juggling because one race wants one thing and the other race wants another. You've got to find common ground to bring them all in. And then you got to be a ventriloquist because you got to talk all these different languages. I don't know how she did it.

You have to speak the language. Keep looking down. Oh, God. Like I said, it is a hard thing, but, at the same time, it has a lot of benefits because these are the people that the system turns against each other. If we don't find some middle ground to where we can all come together, they will continue to divide and conquer us, and we still will have the injustices.

NPA and NTIC are unique. It took me years to figure it out. NTIC is National Training and Information Center and they provide to the groups, in the different cities, technical assistance and staffing and research. And they help training also, a lot of training, and maybe some financial funds through grants or whatever. Training for both the organizers and the leaders. So there's a lot of that going on. So that's basically what NTIC does. They do the grant writing and all that for different projects that we would need to have happen.

NPA [and its annual conferences] is a horse of a different color. NPA is made up of all the groups – and they don't pay no membership, no membership – that come throughout our country. When we come together for the first time and for leadership training, we discover or we develop an agenda of a common ground on different issues that we all can fight on and that we can all win on.

Inez Killingsworth: NPA is a full-body experience. Following Gale, they said, "Let's get on the buses." And I said, "If you ever get on that bus at NPA, you'll be riding forever!" It's an experience. It's the energy that you generate there. It was a coming together of people from across the country that really energized me. It's like we're not alone.

Ann Vick-Westgate: We were on the bus out to the Martinez house, the HUD Secretary, in 2003.

Inez Killingsworth: I was involved with Martinez the next morning in a meeting. Well, that hit was strictly dedicated to Gale. Because he had made a commitment to her before she passed that he would meet. Gale was a very powerful person. People may not realize it, but she really was. And when she spoke it was like speaking from the mountain, Moses speaking from the mountain. Because she was a big lady and she carried a big stick.

So when Martinez came in as Secretary of HUD, right away they go, "You've got to meet with NPA." So it was easy for him to make the commitment because he didn't want Gale to come after him. So he promised in writing that he would. So, after Gale passed, it was like, "Okay. She's gone. Bye. Boom. I don't have to do it." And each time we had written letters and we had done all of the things that we were supposed to do to get this meeting, he just totally ignored us. So we just had to go out and reinvite him with more people.

Well, when we met he introduced us to the coldest part of HUD. He put us in an isolated room, a room that was an old cafeteria that had been deserted. We had about fifteen people. But they outnumbered us. And they had police and all kinds of people in an old cafeteria, pre-arranged setting. That was fine. But then we were surrounded with policemen as if we were criminals, had broken into something. After being invited in, we were treated real cold. But that was okay. Then he wanted to yell at us for coming on his property. So we allowed him to blow off his steam. After he finished, I said, "And as I was going to say…" I went on with the agenda. The conditions may have not been the best, but the results from that particular meeting were great.

As a result, 700 homes or families were saved in Cincinnati. So it didn't matter to be in the cold room, we're soldiers. He made commitments in that meeting. He committed his staff to working with us. "They are to work with you." And he told them. He had them there. Because if they had been working with us, doing their job, maybe we wouldn't have had to go where he was.

So after that meeting, and the next meeting we had in July, it was a different setting, back in his office, back up in the nice conference room. It was another step added to that because we had never been able to access <u>all</u> of the staff. So all of the staff from each one of the different departments was there. So whatever question we had and needed, they were there to answer. So that was the commitment that he made. So far. That's the first one he kept.

Cal Bradford: Joe Marino [who became NTIC's director after Gale's death] was pretty brilliant in picking three people as leaders [Brenda LaBlanc, Inez Killingsworth and Emira Palacios] instead of just one. He tried a whole different structure. He didn't try and just repeat what you had. That's the challenge that comes along when a business reaches that crisis point. You've got to figure you're going to do it differently. He left the structure of NPA, its non-structure, its sort of philosophy, alone. He's got two old leaders and one new leader and a whole new issue which is a very hard issue, immigrant rights, for people to digest.

In these political times and everything, that's really courageous of Joe and he's got a good leader to do it. He's got a good person. But it's a hard issue, sometimes it drives against some of his own constituents. So it's kind of courageous. And maybe something they couldn't have done with Gale.

Honestly, you have to say Gale knew some issues really well because she'd grown up with them. When new issues came along, she didn't have the same identity. She gave people their space, and she saw the need for the organizers that were doing it. But she didn't have the same personal involvement and commitment and understanding. She, as a person, understood the banking and the housing and the insurance, some of those issues, better than she understood the education and jobs. It just wasn't part of her being. She knew the education because she started out with it, but the education issues had changed a lot today.

Ann Vick-Westgate: How hard was the transition?

Marilyn Evans: This organization was founded by Gale and Trapp. And Trapp retired before Gale died. So he had moved away a little bit. Even that was strange because all the time that I had spent with NTIC, Trapp was always there. If I didn't see Gale, I always seen Trapp. But when she died the transition was slow. It wasn't visible. It was interesting as far as I could tell.

It became visible when Joe Mariano stepped up to be the director. There was some doubt that he was going to be a Gale. People want the same thing that was there before. So we expected Joe to be like Gale or Trapp. But that was different too because Joe was here with the organization before. He left for a while and came back. He was young. So how could he be like Trapp? How could he be like Gale? So his ideas and how he was going to run the organization would be a little bit different. And that was slow in developing because people kept wanting Gale or kept wanting Trapp to come back. But Joe forged ahead, bless his heart. And we are still in transition...

I was coming for board meetings. Matter of fact, Trapp called and asked me if I wanted to be a board member. And he says, "Look, Evans, I don't want none of your shit. The only thing you do is say 'yes.' I don't want you analyzing anything. Matter of fact, don't say anything, just nod your head. And then eat. You think you can do that?" I said, "Sure. I like that kind of board meeting!" So it was fun coming to the board meetings and enjoying the company of a lot of the old leaders that's not around any more.

But hearing the wealth of experience and the ideas they had was great. I was glad that I was asked to be on the board. I was on the board for at least four or six years before Gale died.

When Gale died they elected me the chair of the board. Remember now, they started this organization, so they was the key element of keeping this organization going with ideas and all that. But when you lose the boat, it look like where are [you] going? And we lost Trapp too. But I'm a capable person who has ideas and who has the commitment against injustice and for empowering low and moderate-income folk.

Michael Westgate: Were there things that Gale would bring to the board for discussion? Did her ideas get influenced at all by discussions at the board?

Marilyn Evans: If you know Gale like I know Gale, Gale brought what she said was gonna happen and that's what happened! The board process is a little different now. We all share. And Joe brings his ideas in, we talk and we go from there. It's a lot different. Matter of fact, we use *Robert's Rules of Order* now! How about that! We done even changed the personnel policies, updated it and everything. It hadn't been updated, God, maybe since the beginning of the organization. And the board has did this. But if Trapp and Gale were still there, they would have did it.

Ann Vick-Westgate: How did NPA change after Trapp left and Gale died? What kind of transition was there?

Marilyn Evans: Well, it wasn't only Gale dying and Trapp leaving that helped change the focus of NPA. Staff left too, old staff that was there. Because when you have the founders and the directors that went on, then the people who followed them will leave too because they're kind of down. New administration, new staff. And they're trying to kill us. They're young. They got so much energy and just ideas all over the place. That's <u>how</u> things changed. It went back to maybe when I first came to NPA and went to Reclaim America. The energy, the variety, the commitment and the hype is back.

It's energized now. Now if we stay until we're about Trapp's and Gale's age, I think we will be still, maybe, in the same ideas and whatever. And there will be another generation.

Ann Vick-Westgate: So when Gale Cincotta died and Shel was retired, was there any discussion of ending what NTIC was doing? Or was it just that it was going to continue, and you guys were going to figure out how to continue?

Joe Mariano: Well, when Trapp retired, his question was, was I willing to take over his responsibilities? I said, "That's fine. I'll do that. I don't think I'm going to like this, but I'll do it because I'm having fun. I think that it's exciting… I need you to do x, y and z with Gale. And I'm going to talk to Gale too about how that'll look, how that'll work, and all that good stuff." That was as far as it went, with Trapp doing whatever he did with Gale and Anne-Marie too. Talking with Gale, my idea was that we were going to continue on.

The work needed to be done. It was a good thing the organization had never been built around one person. At one point they had divided up some of the funders. So Trapp had Allstate and Mott. Gale had nothing to do with the Mott Foundation. Trapp always kept that as his turf as well as Allstate. So those were the funders that he dealt with. And then Trapp also dealt with the Bureau of Justice Assistance. So I got Trapp to help me transfer some of those relationships. But as it turns out, some of those relationships changed 'cause foundation people left. Executives that we knew were gone. We really didn't do much, but we worked as best we could to transfer those relationships. But Gale had relationships also with other foundations that I could talk to her about. I'd try to get into meetings with her, with the banks in particular.

Then, before she died, we had meetings with Allstate [Trapp had retired] and some of the other big places, Fannie Mae. So I was in those meetings with her. Not that I played a big role because they generally wanted to be talking to Gale about it. So I was there, heard what was going on, added my two cents every now and then.

So my first year when Trapp retired, my goal was to really sit with Gale and talk through things, on how we were going to do it. So the first NPA without Trapp I had a role with Gale up front. Not a prominent role, but a small role. Previous to that, Trapp was still here.

So the relationship I had with Gale was just being developed, in terms of what she wanted. How she wanted to run NPA, strategy ideas. And it worked. So when we did NPA in March or April, we had a good experience in 2001. So I just figured, "Well, okay. This is a bump in the road. Gale's going to the hospital." It wasn't a good thing.

One round without Trapp. It served as transition time, but it also raised questions.

Michael Westgate: Trapp retiring a year ahead of Gale actually served to strengthen the organization. Joe took over Trapp's load and was more able to take on some of Gale's when she passed on. While never made explicit, the dynamics presumed there would be a continuing operation.

What are the possible explanations for Gale's never dealing with transition? Was she self-centered and dealing with the movement as her personal fiefdom? Did she think that the issues would change and the people needed would emerge to deal with those issues? Would it strengthen the organization to rise again from the ashes of her and Trapp leaving? Was she selfless in thinking it would be presumptuous for her to try to manipulate what happened after her death? Was it simply in keeping with her credo that, like NPA, the issues and the leadership would self-identify themselves, and it was a secret to success that no one, including her, could control the agenda?

Joe Mariano: Trapp retired in September of 2000. We really only had one NPA before she was gone, one Leadership Meeting and one NPA. So at that point I was getting used to this, and Gale was in hospital. I called her at the hospital once and she said, "Well, I'm going into surgery tomorrow." This, that and the other thing, whatever she said. I can't remember, some task thing. I said, "Okay. I'll deal with it."

So then things weren't good. They found whatever cancer they found. So I knew she had some kind of cancer and it wasn't a good picture. That she wasn't going to have more than two years is what the doctors had said. I said, "Okay, Anne-Marie. You and I have to go there and sit and talk to Gale and we got to figure some stuff. Whatever that stuff is in terms of funding, in terms of how we're going to handle this, what do we say in public?" I imagined, in my craziness, this bedside conversation on where we'd take it the next steps.

One thing that Trapp did do, he actually convinced Gale that it would be a good thing if he retired and then NTIC could continue on. I don't know if she bought it or not. Maybe she wanted to see what was going to happen to things.

That's why I told him he had to do it. He told me, "Gale's got this thing that NTIC has a shelf life and when she goes, it goes." I said, "Well, you got to talk to her about this, and you two are in it together, and this could be beyond her." So I did think he had that conversation and she was willing to do it for a while. She enjoyed it too much at that point.

Gayle Brinkman: She had cancer once before. We were coming home from the Dunes and she said, "I've got this nodule on my neck." I said, "Ah, it's nothing." So she went in and had it biopsied and it was Hodgkin's. She had six months of chemo. She didn't tell anybody. She went to work every day. She never had a perm because she didn't want to lose her hair. And she didn't.

She would rent these funny movies, like Charlie Chaplin. I would leave work and take her to chemo, take her home, get her in. She was up the stairs and she was heavy and it was very difficult for her. She would rest the rest of the day. Sometimes she'd be nauseous. Through the six months there were like three times when we got a call in the middle of the night. She had to go to the ER; her white cells were too low. And she just carried on. She just carried on. That was during the summer and we were scheduled to go China that fall, September '88. So she ended her chemo in about September and then we went at the end of April '89.

Pablo Eisenberg: Did Gale care about her legacy? She was thinking big picture, not just "when I'm gone, the hell with it all." I don't think she ever thought about the future after her death. She had a mission and she wanted to keep it alive. The whole idea of succession is always a real problem with nonprofits, and most of them can't deal with it. The interesting thing is what if NTIC had been started in 2002, where you have the age of celebrity, and you've got the corporatization of America, and you have the role of the all-powerful egomaniac CEO, who builds egos rather than institutions? It's a much harder climate today, to have a sort of what John Gardner calls "a team leadership," or collegial leadership.

How Gale dealt with building a strong institution that would outlive her, and even rise to bigger heights, I don't know. She and Shel were sort of almost two sides of the same personal coin...

There were a lot of issues that many of us never talked to her about. Never talked to her about them, partly because it was intrusive, and partly because our job was not technical assistance, although that was our job at the Center. Never said, "What's your view on building strong organizations?" or "Why don't you..."

There was a lot of turnover at NTIC. She had a couple of very strong VISTAs that were very loyal and good. They didn't have the authority. Her influence could have been even larger, had she had three or four outstanding people in whom she invested her authority, and could have gone on and done things on their own for NTIC and for the movement. It's very rare. Why should she be human? Right? I mean, as I look at the nonprofit sector, and the leadership problem today, it's very few that do that.

Michael Westgate: What advice would you have for somebody – a future Gale Cincotta, eventually – seeing a cause today?

Pablo Eisenberg: Oh, the advice would be: "Surround yourself with the very best people you can, people who will challenge you as well as support you, people who can replace you if you fall down the stairs or are in the hospital for a year. And have a diverse staff because you've got to bring in lots of constituencies."

Michael Westgate: Do you see things changing a lot in terms of the underlying dynamics or the tactics that are appropriate? Are the same kinds of tactics that have worked in the past appropriate today and for the future? At NPA with Gale being gone?

Brenda LaBlanc: People are getting smarter. They're beginning to catch on. I do see efforts from time to time trying to talk about one group against another, but you can usually say, "That's not the problem."

Ann Vick-Westgate: Tactics have to change somewhat. All this security stuff has changed where you can get and how you get in places. We've got some wonderful stories of how they infiltrated HUD.

Brenda LaBlanc: HUD is always a problem. The last couple of years we've been doing it out at people's houses partly because you can't get in the buildings.

Barney Frank, member of the U.S. House of Representatives from Massachusetts since 1981 and chair of the House Financial Services Committee from 2007 - 2010. Frank was chief of staff for Boston Mayor Kevin White, for whom Michael Westgate also worked, in the 1970s: I would see Gale from time to time when she came to Washington for lobbying purposes. The tactics that National People's Action used were useful. Getting attention worked. It said something, which is, private-sector people are more vulnerable to embarrassment than public-sector people. You know if you're in public office you count on 30-40% of the people voting against you. In fact you use the opposition of some to generate support from others. People in the corporate world are much less used to that. Gale fully understood that and exploited this vulnerability. Now some groups make the mistake of not understanding the difference and, in fact, use tactics against political people that don't work.

Gale did a pretty good job. This mobilization of the kind of public focus against private-sector operations was a good thing. Plus it was also important, from a fundamental point of view, just to get people from lower economic circumstances to feel empowered. And that was important. Obviously from my standpoint getting the vote is very important, but it's sort of hard to see the consequences of voting. So having things where people could really get a direct sense as a participant, and feel those consequences, that was very important.

CRA's been very important addressing the needs. Every organization I talk to agrees. You know it was obviously not everything we'd like. But in fact the most important thing we got to do with CRA was to extend it. It was typical that the conservatives tried to cut it back. We wanted to extend it, extend it to other institutions. It's a wonderfully flexible instrument and it really played a very important role. I literally hear from all kinds of organizations – economic development organizations, housing organizations and others – that think CRA is the single most important instrument they have.

We've gained ground in general since CRA was passed in '77. But here's the problem, you have this ebb and flow. With the Republicans in power, there've been problems. We have lost less ground under George Bush thanks to the existence of CRA than we would have in its absence. By the way, there's a letter from Lawrence Lindsay who was then the Federal Reserve

Governor in charge of CRA and who later became the Bush economic advisor. He wrote me a letter refuting the assertion that CRA somehow interfered with safety and soundness. I cited that on many occasions when the Republicans went after CRA. He said there was no evidence that this has hurt anybody. That loans given under CRA don't show up any worse than any other. In fact that was really the sign that CRA was so successful.

Phil Gramm hated CRA when he was chairman of the Senate Banking Committee and had this bill everybody wanted. He was determined to really cut back on CRA and he was very unsuccessful. Phil Gramm really went after it. It was a high priority. He wasn't able to get more than cosmetic changes in the thing. The failure of that effort showed that CRA has now become an integral part of the landscape.

It's also the case that it's become even more important now because of bank mergers. We didn't know how important it was going to be. But the time when it's most enforceable of course is when there are changes in ownership and control.

If we didn't have CRA, this wave of bank consolidation would have had even more negative effects on the local communities than it had. I mean when Bank of America bought Fleet Bank, CRA was our major leverage point for trying to get them to do things.

Michael Westgate: What do you see as the battles of today and tomorrow in terms of community reinvestment generally?

Barney Frank: Well, we've won the battle and we're holding. Now we need to extend it. The problem is that more and more financial activity takes place in institutions that are not CRA-covered. That includes for me credit unions and I think that we need to go after them. A lot of them will probably easily qualify, but it still should be done. But then there are various mortgage bankers, insurance. But the big battle now is we're in a holding period. If the Democrats take control of either house of Congress, we'll begin to expand CRA. Because the biggest problem with it is not the way it works, but that a pretty much smaller percentage of the financial transactions are now in institutions that are subject to it...

Certainly there should be no exemption for international banks. I think we have a worldwide problem – that's what CRA tried to address – that we are seeing more and more economic growth with an increase in inequality. Economic growth for a variety of reasons is happening in a way that exacerbates inequality. Unnecessarily. Some inequality is necessary for the capitalist system. But we've got measures in place that exacerbate it. We should deal with those.

Michael Westgate: Do you want to give some examples of how to address the inequalities?

Barney Frank: One is by putting worker and environmental standards in trade agreements so that you don't have this kind of race to the bottom. Secondly, it is important for the World Bank and the IMF when they deal with countries not to ask that they reduce budget deficits in ways that are regressive, but to do it in ways that are socially progressive. Third, one of the ways that we did help was with debt relief. That was a very important step toward diminishing inequality. That one we've been successful at.

Michael Westgate: How do you see developing future Gale Cincottas or others that will take the lead in a grassroots kind of way?

Barney Frank: I have no idea. Nobody developed her. She developed herself. But I think you want to have elected officials be available to work with groups. I find a very important part of what I do is to work with various community groups. But you know the particular combination of energy and commitment and personal charisma, there's nothing you can do about that but hope it comes along.

Ann Vick-Westgate: She was asked several times to run for office and chose not to. She felt her place was working in the neighborhoods. She also resisted getting an office for NTIC in Washington, feeling that her credibility was out in the neighborhoods and she didn't want to become a Washington-based group. She could exert more force by swooping in from outside than she could if she was part of the system. She also balanced her activism with being very active in Chicago's Neighborhood Housing Services.

Barney Frank: Yeah. Tip O'Neill's point that all politics is local is very important. She recognized that you want to get people activated politically. That insight was absolutely correct. In fact I have told some of the organizations in Washington that advocate for good things and they've got a consumer field that they are heads without bodies – that they give us good advice, but they don't help us get it adopted.

So in that sense she was right. Now that doesn't mean you can't have something in Washington. I don't think Washington infects you. But she certainly was right to recognize that leverage and the impact grew from having people in the districts of the members of Congress, that they were respected.

I don't think that's incompatible with having an office in Washington. But certainly the indispensable thing was to be able to mobilize people in the districts.

Gale Cincotta: I've never had a grand plan to build the ultimate organization; my intent has always been to win.

APPENDIX A

LIST OF INTERVIEWEES
Interviews conducted by
Michael Westgate and Ann Vick-Westgate as shown

ED BAILEY in CHICAGO, JUNE 24, 2003: Past President of Organization for a Better Austin (OBA) and the subsequent SACCC organization. Ed was a long-time resident and leader in the Chicago's West Side Austin neighborhood.

GEORGE BEHYMER at his family cottage, 60 miles NE of CINCINNATI, OHIO, MAY 22-3, 2004: George is a retired savings & loan president from Cincinnati, who was active in the US and American Savings & Loan Leagues, a founding member of NHS of Cincinnati, advisor to Urban Reinvestment Task Force and Treasurer of Neighborhood Housing Services of America (NHSA).

CAL BRADFORD in WILLIAMSBURG, VA, JULY 15, 2005: Long-time professional friend of Gale, from his early days in graduate school, involved at the founding meeting of NTIC, to his current role as public policy expert on housing and banking issues and board member of NTIC. Professor of Sociology. Cal enlisted the support of Northwestern University professors and students to provide statistical support for Gale's issues.

GAYLE BRINKMAN CHICAGO, AUGUST 17, 2005: Homemaker who was Gale's best friend from the Austin neighborhood. Gayle created and ran an ongoing rummage sale in one of the churches to fund the early days of the OBA organization. Remained one of Gale's closest friends and confidantes up to the time of Gale's passing.

JIMMY CINCOTTA in CHICAGO, OCTOBER 22, 2003: The baby of the family as the youngest son of Gale, who was involved from his time as a toddler through his teenage years in organizing. Gale often brought him in tow with her to meetings and actions. Now lives and works in Canada, where he was elected president of the Learning Disabilities Association of Ottawa – Carleton. He discovered he had a learning disability at the age of 21. He went on to complete BA and MA degrees in Anthropology and Education.

ROGER COUGHLIN in CHICAGO, AUGUST 17, 2005: Father Roger Coughlin, a Roman Catholic priest, was the retired director of research at Catholic Charities for the Archdiocese of Chicago and a staunch supporter of community organizing and the down to earth visionary leadership of Gale. Roger served on the board of directors of NTIC until his death in 2010.

KATHY DESMOND in ALEXANDRIA, VA, May 20, 2005: Kathy worked as a program officer for national Campaign for Human Development of the U. S. Catholic Conference of Bishops from 1976-83 where she first met Gale Cincotta. She was also a consultant working with community development programs in the U.S. and Brazil for many years. She was the wife of the late George Knight.

PABLO EISENBERG in GEORGETOWN, D.C., MARCH 18, 2005: Liberal Washington, DC activist, thinker, urban policy expert and visionary. As the founding Executive Director of the Center for Community Change, Pablo saw the genius of Gale and was instrumental in convincing the Stern Fund – a national foundation – to provide the initial funding for Gale's Housing Training and Information Center (HTIC).

MARILYN EVANS in CHICAGO, AUGUST 18, 2005: Started as a local public housing leader from Cincinnati's Communities United For Action and moved to the national level – working closely with Gale on the reinvestment issue. Marilyn became the President of the NTIC Board of Directors and continues her organizing work in Cincinnati, Ohio.

ALLEN FISHBEIN in WASHINGTON DC, MARCH 16, 18, 2005: While he worked as the chief reinvestment strategist at the Center For Community Change in Washington, DC, Gale spent a lot of time on the phone with him from Chicago, getting to understand the politics and legislative personalities in Washington. They would banter ideas back and forth on possible policy changes in banking and the regulation of the financial services industry to further neighborhood reinvestment. Later when Allen went to work at HUD, Gale would call him to better understand the workings of that agency – particularly around the administration and operation of the Federal Housing Administration (FHA).

TOMMY FITZGIBBON in CHICAGO, NOVEMBER 25, 2003: One of Gale's favorite bank executives as he provided thoughtful counsel and insights to her. In his work with Manufacturers Bank (now MB) Tommy was heavily involved with the Chicago NHS in the early days and continues to play a key leadership role in that organization.

BARNEY FRANK in NEWTON, MA, JANUARY 18, 2006: Member of the U.S. House of Representatives from Massachusetts since 1981 and chair of the Financial Services Committee in the U.S. House of Representatives from 2007-2010. Frank was chief of staff for Boston Mayor Kevin White, for whom Michael Westgate also worked, in the 1970s.

TOM GAUDETTE [Gaudette Tapes]: Veteran community organizer who founded the OBA. Tom moved to the OBA turf from his position as the founding community organizer, with Msgr. Jack Egan, of the Industrial Areas Foundation (IAF) Chicago organizing project called the Northwest Community Organization (NCO). At that time, he was still a part of Alinsky's IAF.

BRUCE GOTTSCHALL in CHICAGO, JUNE 26, 2003: Bruce began his career, after serving in the Peace Corps in Peru, as a community organizer hired by NCO Executive Director Robert Johnsen. Worked closely with Gale on reinvestment and redlining issues while he was at Bickerdike Redevelopment Corp, a spinoff of NCO. Gale recommended Bruce to Westgate who hired him as the organizer for what became the Neighborhood Housing Services (NHS) of Chicago. Bruce was then hired as its founding Executive Director by the new board of the Chicago NHS. Bruce and Gale continued to strategize until Gale's passing. Bruce was the first and only Executive Director of NHS of Chicago until his retirement in 2009. He remains on the NTIC, now NPA, board.

BUD KANITZ in WASHINGTON, SEPTEMBER 9, 2003: Started his organizing career in Chicago with the Northwest Community Organization (NCO). From 1982-97 he served as the Executive Director of the National Neighborhood Coalition in Washington, DC. Hired in 1997 as Director for Community Relations for the Comptroller of the Currency in Washington. Bud remained a favorite confidante of Gale who often engaged him in give and take conversations about reinvestment ideas and policy changes. He was always a solid supporter of neighborhood-based community organizing and held the record for having attended the most national neighborhood conferences with Gale in Washington, DC. Bud is now retired and lives in Wisconsin.

INEZ KILLINGSWORTH in CHICAGO, OCTOBER 23, 2003: A trusted member of Gale's national leadership team on banking and reinvestment issues, Inez provided continuing advice and support. She stepped up to follow Gale as a co-chairperson, with Brenda LaBlanc and Elmira Palacios, of National People's Action. She started in the 1970's as a local leader in Cleveland, Ohio's east side Union Miles neighborhood working on the issue of controlling stray dogs and shifted her focus to take on the need for that city's banks and S&Ls to reinvest in the inner city. Her organization's campaign and negotiation led to the first CRA agreement in the nation – done by a local neighborhood group – with Cleveland's Society National Bank. Inez is currently leading the community organizing fight – statewide – to keep people in their homes who were victimized by loan sharks – as the founding board Chairperson of Empowering and Strengthening Ohio's People (ESOP).

GEORGE KNIGHT in ALEXANDRIA VA, May 20, 2005: George met Gale when he was working at Northwest Community Organization (NCO). He founded the nonprofit Bickerdike Redevelopment Corporation which he ran from 1967-70. He then worked as an accountant and went on to become Finance Director, then Executive Director, of Neighborhood Reinvestment Corporation (now d/b/a NeighborWorks America) from 1990 to 2000. George held master's degrees in divinity and social work. He died in 2008.

BRENDA LABLANC in CHICAGO, AUGUST 17, 2005: Began her work with Gale on the national leadership team at the NPA meeting in the 1970's with Federal Reserve Chairman Paul Volker in Washington, DC on the very high interest rates. Brenda started her organizing work as a founding leader with the Des Moines chapter of Iowa Citizens for Community Improvement (CCI) on the reinvestment issue. She was a key national leader working with Gale in negotiations with big banks and as an NPA advocate in her work with members of Congress – educating them on the need for the Community Reinvestment Act (CRA). She followed Gale as a co-chairperson of NPA.

JOE MARIANO in CHICAGO, OCTOBER 23 and 24, 2003: Veteran community organizer since 1974 who worked at NTIC for 20 years, taking over as the second NTIC Executive Director after the passing of Gale in 2001. As the president of the Chicago-based Grass Roots Training Team, Inc. he now is consulting with community organization clients, such as Empowering and Strengthening Ohio's People (ESOP), on how to win and manage their success.

JUSTIN McCARTHY in CHICAGO, OCTOBER 23, 2003: Past president of OBA. Neighborhood leader who stuck with the Organization for a Better Austin – even though many white parishioners were moving out in the 1960's. He came into the organization through the social justice work in which he was involved at the neighborhood Catholic parish where he was a member.

KEN MCLEAN in ARLINGTON VA, SEPTEMBER 25, 2003: Chicago native and Senator William Proxmire's chief banking committee staff member who worked closely with Gale to write up the draft bill which would become the Home Mortgage Disclosure Act (HMDA). He also played a key role in the drafting of the Community Reinvestment Act (CRA).

ALICIA MENDOZA in CHICAGO, OCTOBER 23, 2003: Chicago Southsider who was hired by Gale in the early 1980's as her administrative assistant at NTIC. Alicia and Gale also socialized around a shared love for playing bingo and visiting the riverboat casinos to have fun and win some through Gale's good luck and skill at gambling. Alicia still works at NTIC and is the only staffer left who has the institutional memory of earlier days.

ANITA MILLER in WASHINGTON CROSSING, PA, MAY 18, 2004: Program Officer at The Ford Foundation. Anita became known as an "adventurous philanthropist". She sees Gale as doing more for American urban neighborhoods than anyone else in the past 50 years. Anita helped Gale hone her skills and delivered significant funding from Ford to National Training and Information Center (NTIC). Anita went on to become director of its South Bronx program for Local Initiatives Support Corp (LISC). Appointed to Federal Home Loan Bank Board by President Jimmy Carter where she served as Acting Chairman.

MIKE MOSKOW at the FEDERAL RESERVE BANK OF CHICAGO, JUNE 14, 2004: An economist appointed by President Nixon as Assistant Secretary of HUD, in charge of Policy Development and Research. He helped end Urban Renewal, shifting federal grants to Community Development Block Grants. Westgate and Whiteside negotiated with him a grant of $250,000 as the first federal funding for NRC towards its Neighborhood Housing Services programs, including NHS of Chicago. Mike went on to become President of the Federal Reserve Bank of Chicago.

HELEN J. MURRAY in CHICAGO, OCTOBER 25, 2003: Native Chicagoan who was one of the first female organizers hired by Gale. Her initial job was to put together the followup meeting in Baltimore MD after the first national housing conference. Helen was also active in organizing for the 1979 "Battle of New Orleans" against the American Bankers Association. She became chief organizer, staffing Gale during the national HMDA and CRA campaigns.

SHEL TRAPP in CHICAGO, OCT 23, 2003: Former Methodist minister. Tough-talking Chicago community organizer who broke with Alinsky's strict mandate that only males would be in leadership roles. Shel organized to get Gale elected the first woman president of OBA. He ended up as Gale's lifelong collaborator, colleague and fellow strategist. Shel took local community organizing on issues to the national level when he and Gale co-founded NTIC and NPA, where he worked until he retired in 2000. He died in October 2010.

MARY VOLPE in CHICAGO, JUNE 28, 2003: Veteran leader who worked with Gale at OBA on issues and later ran another neighborhood organization. Mary lived in the North Austin part of the neighborhood.

BILL WHITESIDE in WASHINGTON DC, SEPTEMBER 24, 2003: Hired by Preston Martin, chairman of the Federal Home Loan Bank Board, to be executive director of the Center for Executive Development. Bill identified Neighborhood Housing Services of Pittsburgh as the best model for drawing together neighborhood activists, lenders and the city to solve urban lending problems. He formed the Urban Reinvestment Task Force, hiring Westgate as Assistant Director for Administration and charging him with initiating a program in Chicago. Gale testified in support of Whiteside's program and its incorporation by Congress as the Neighborhood Reinvestment Corp. Whiteside ran NRC until 1990. Now known as NeighborWorks America, its affiliated NeighborWorks organizations are serving over 2300 communities and 4,000,000 residents.

MARY LEE WIDENER in OAKLAND CA, FEBRUARY 28, 2006: She shared a hotel room with Gale at the first workshop leading to the founding of NHS of Chicago, where they plotted together how to make it work. Mary Lee acknowledges that her own work was made easier because of Gale's. She was president of Neighborhood Housing Services of America (NHSA), NRC's non-profit sister agency in Oakland CA, from its founding to 2009. Mary Lee strategized with Bill Whiteside how to form the Urban Reinvestment

Task Force and later get it incorporated by Congress as Neighborhood Reinvestment Corp. Mary Lee founded the Social Compact, served as chairman of Federal Home Loan Bank of San Francisco and on the board of various financial services companies including PMI (Private Mortgage Insurance). NHSA was responsible for bringing over $1 billion in lending to needy neighborhoods including Chicago's, beginning in 1974.

ALICIA WILLIAMS at the FEDERAL RESERVE BANK OF CHICAGO, JUNE 14, 2004: Vice president for consumer and community affairs in the economic research department of the Federal Reserve Bank of Chicago. Alicia previously was in charge of bank examinations on compliance, including CRA.

ED WILLIAMS in CHICAGO, OCTOBER 21, 2003: Banker at Chicago's Harris bank, who negotiated with Gale— quickly signing and implementing one of the first and most successful CRA reinvestment agreements in Chicago. Ed had a mutually respectful relationship with Gale and was trusted by Gale to be an unofficial advisor on banking policy as it related to neighborhood issues. He even served as a reference for Gale on banking matters. Now retired.

TED WYSOCKI in WASHINGTON, MARCH 19, 2005: One of the initial staff of HTIC, Ted worked with Gale for twelve years and was the founding editor of *DISCLOSURE, the National Newspaper of Neighborhoods.* He penned the Congressional testimony used by Gale to promote the need for HMDA and CRA as well as many of her national speeches. Ted became CEO of the LEED Council in Chicago in 2002.

DESCRIPTIONS were provided by Joe Mariano, February 2009, updated by Michael Westgate, January, 2011.

CHRONOLOGY FOR GALE FORCE

1929
- Gale Cincotta born Aglaia Angelos.

1935
- Shel Trapp born.

1936
- Home Owners Loan Corporation (HOLC) publishes redlining map of Philadelphia.

1940 - 1958
- Samuel Alphonsius Cardinal Stritch serves as Archbishop of Chicago

1943 -1945
- Gale attends Marshal HS, Chicago leaving after 10th grade.

1945
- Gale marries Roy Cincotta (born 1904).

1946
- Tom Cincotta born.

1947
- Ted Cincotta born.

1948
- George Cincotta born.

1949
- Chuck Cincotta born.

1954
- Richard Cincotta born.

1958 - 1965
- Albert Gregory Cardinal Meyer serves as Archibishop of Chicago

1961
- U. S. Commission on Civil Rights finds that African-American borrowers are often required to make higher down payments and pay off loans faster than whites.

1962
- Northwest Community Organization (NCO) founded; Father Janiak is first president; funding provided by 22 Catholic parishes. Alinsky hires Tom Gaudette to run NCO "for three years."

1963
- Jimmy Cincotta born.

1964
- CA law requires state-chartered S&Ls to submit certain lending data to the Commissioner.

1965 - 1982
- John Patrick Cardinal Cody serves as archibishop of Chicago; Cody mugged in 1965.

1966
- Organization for a Better Austin formed, Justin McCarthy first president (1966-68). Gaudette hired to run Organization for a Better Austin; hires Trapp as organizer.
- Monsignor Egan banished by Cardinal Cody to Notre Dame University.

1967
- First OBA convention convenes; 1200 people attend, equal numbers black and white. Trapp meets Cincotta, organizing on PTA, and they begin working together.
- Cincotta holds various positions at OBA, 1967-72: Chair, Real Estate Practices Committee; Chair, Education Committee; Chair, Finance Committee; Vice President; Bud Kanitz works at NCO, 1967-71.

1968
- Cincotta elected second President of OBA, first woman, 1968-1969
  - Cincotta flies in plane for the first time.
- Housing Act of 1968 declares a national housing goal of "a decent home and a suitable living environment within the next decade."

◆ Pittsburgh NHS formed by neighborhood residents, bankers, city, first in country and model for Chicago and many other cities.

1969
◆ OBA, NCO and Our Lady of the Angels form West Side Coalition. Parish Real Estate Practices Committee formed, with Cincotta as coalition leader.

1971
◆ NCO hires Shel Trapp as its executive director.
◆ Bud Kanitz starts work at Industrial Council of Northwest Chicago.
◆ Serious funding of OBA by Catholic Church begins.
◆ Geno Baroni addresses Community Congress.

1972
◆ FIRST National Housing Conference convenes at St. Sylvester's Church; 368 community groups from 38 states send 1600 delegates.
◆ Organizing follow-up meeting held in Baltimore; form NPA and NTIC; first "Action" done against George Romney, Secretary of HUD, in Washington.
◆ NPA demands that FHA reimburse homebuyers under federal housing law sections #203 and 221 for cost of repairing structural defects.
◆ NTIC board votes to hire Cincotta as Executive Director, Trapp as Training Director, Anne- Marie Douglas as secretary.

1973
◆ NTIC and NPA open office on Division Street in Chicago.
◆ SECOND Annual National Housing Conference convenes in Chicago; June – Dec. Meetings held with FHLB-Chicago and FHLBB to force mortgage surveys.
Dec. Thirteen community groups form MAHA
◆ Cincotta formulates Chicago Laboratory:
I. Organize neighborhoods;
II. Form citywide coalition: MAHA;
III. Form national network.
◆ *Study of the Factors of Risk in Urban Mortgage Lending* conducted by FSLIC. Westgate is project manager.
Research conducted by Dr. Alex Williams at the University of Pittsburgh.

1974

- ♦ THIRD Annual National Housing Conference convenes in Chicago; 800 delegates from 25 states and 35 cities attend; Daley condemns S&Ls for having "followed negative and harmful practices which have undermined stable neighborhoods" and supports full financial disclosure; FHLBB Chairman Bomar admits, "FHLBB probably has authority to require full disclosure."
- ♦ Chicago Disclosure Ordinance passed requiring disclosure and anti-redlining pledges from banks seeking city funds.
- ♦ First issue of *DISCLOSURE* newsletter published.
- ♦ Housing Act of 1974 declares that nation faces "critical social economic and environmental problems arising in significant measure from inadequate public and private investment in housing."
- ♦ Equal Credit Opportunity Act passed.
- ♦ NPA reports FHA loans are replacing conventional lending.
- ♦ MAHA wins monthly "People's Court" day in Housing Court; twenty-five landlords repair buildings; Court backlog reduced from 5 years to 1 year.
- ♦ Cincotta appointed to Governor Dan Walker's Blue Ribbon Commission on Mortgage Practices.
- ♦ First NHS of Chicago workshops held at Lake Geneva; Westgate hires Bruce Gottschall as organizer and interim director, on recommendation of Cincotta.
- ♦ FHLB-Chicago presents consolidated data from member S&Ls by zip code.
- ♦ Illinois Legislative Investigating Committee holds hearings on redlining in Chicago.
- ♦ Illinois legislature passes laws prohibiting redlining and requiring disclosure.
- ♦ MAHA meeting held with Bartell (President, FHLB-Chicago) attempting to get his support for mandatory disclosure; frustrated, they picket his home, leaflet his neighbors.
- ♦ NPA announces Bomar, chairman, FHLBB, is "our target" in Washington. After two years of fighting FHA, NTIC declares victory: homebuyers under FHA's Sections 203 and 221 can be reimbursed for the cost of repairing structural defects as part of the Housing and Community Development Act of 1974; anyone who purchased a home with structural defects after August 1, 1968 has until August 22, 1975 to file a complaint with the Secretary of HUD for reimbursement for expenditures to correct any dangerous conditions.
- ♦ NPA begins holding regional housing conferences around the country.
- ♦ Cincotta and 30 community leaders, uninvited, enter a HUD "neighborhood conference" at Palmer House.

- Bartell declares, "Community people wouldn't know what to do with disclosure."
- Cincotta declares, "NHS is a breakthrough in our efforts to preserve Chicago's communities."
- Illinois amends its S&L rules & regulations to prohibit redlining, first in country; nine other states have disclosure and/or anti-redlining bills signed or in process.
- Cincotta cries for "FULL DISCLOSURE" to ring throughout the country.

1975

- Senator Adlai Stevenson (D-IL) assures MAHA/FHA Coalition leaders that he will draft legislation to curtail fast foreclosure practices.
- HUD had no forms for dealing with structural defect problems; NTIC prints some up and homeowners use them; HUD approves them.
- Proxmire becomes chair of Senate Banking Committee.
- Carla Hills becomes Secretary of HUD.
- Top-level leadership of Catholic Charities from sixteen cities strategize efforts to save their urban and rural communities.
- Chicago's City Ordinance takes effect regarding deposit of city funds; survey done by FHLB proves some banks make over 99% of their loans outside Chicago.
- Cincotta points out that HUD has reneged on its UDAG grants, supposed to be distributed 75% to neighborhood projects, were actually only 3%. NHS of Chicago incorporates.
- Justice Department files suit against nation's savings and loan associations, mortgage bankers and real estate appraisers for under-appraising homes in racially changing areas.
- FOURTH National Housing Conference convenes in Chicago; Bob Bartell, President FHLB-Chicago, states unwillingness to support HMDA; delegates demand a national disclosure law, as does a Catholic Charities leadership session led by Father Coughlin.
- Senator Proxmire holds committee hearings on S 1281, HMDA: May 5th for community people, May 6th for bankers, and May 7th for federal regulators.
- 150 NPAH leaders convene at 4H Center in DC to lobby for S. 1281 (HMDA).
- Mayor Richard J. Daley joins Cincotta and Chicago Planning Commissioner Lewis Hill and HUD Area Director John Waner, all testifying in Washington on HMDA.
- Cincotta testifies in support of S. 1724 to set up Neighborhood Reinvestment Corp.

- ◆ Cincotta testifies before Rep. St. Germain's sub-committee in favor of HMDA.
- ◆ Cincotta is only community person invited to testify on FHA abuses before US Senate's Committee on Banking & Urban Affairs and US House Committee on Banking Operations' Subcommittee on Manpower & Housing.
- ◆ Bankers testify in opposition to HMDA.
- ◆ Congressman Joe Moakley (D-MA) introduces HR 6596 to require both savings and lending data and adds mortgage bankers to list; replaced by HR 8024 by Rep. St. Germain (D-RI), Chairman of the House Subcommittee on Financial Institutions Supervision, Regulation and Insurance, which deletes Moakley's additions.
- ◆ Illinois passes Fairness in Lending bill making redlining illegal in the State of Illinois; legislation requires disclosure of savings and lending data and limits relocation of savings and loan associations.
- ◆ HTIC renamed NTIC, recognizing its scope as more than just housing. [Note: prior to 1975, NTIC was known as HTIC and NPA as NPAH.]
- ◆ US Senate passes S. 1281 (HMDA) after months of deliberation and a heated floor debate; defeats the Tower-Garn amendment, 41-40 that would have limited disclosure to a pilot study in 20 cities; HMDA, supported by community groups across the country, passes Senate 45 to 37.
- ◆ Oct. 31 House Passes Home Mortgage Disclosure Act HR 10024.
- ◆ Bomar quits as chair of FHLBB.
- ◆ HUD Hit Day held in 9 cities, including DC.
- ◆ NTIC convenes a national reinvestment workshop in Chicago; 340 delegates from 43 cities meet with goal to increase community participation in negotiation for neighborhood survival.
- ◆ Dec. 12 Joint committee approves resolved HMDA bill.
- ◆ Dec. 15 Senate passes resolved bill.
- ◆ Dec. 18 House Passes resolved bill.

1976
- ◆ Jan. 3 President Ford signs HMDA.
- ◆ NPA leadership presents "People's Platform" for neighborhood revitalization to Democratic Party hearings in Providence, later Kansas City and Denver.
- ◆ NPA confronts ABA in DC.
- ◆ NPA confronts ABA at O'Hare Marriott in Chicago.
- ◆ MAHA is now a loose organization of about 30 community groups from 15 Chicago neighborhoods and suburbs including Oak Park, Harvey, and Chicago Heights; NPA is a national network of community organizations like MAHA with groups in 39 states and 104 urban areas; both operate from offices at 121 W. Superior St. in Chicago.

- FIFTH Annual NPA Neighborhoods Conference convenes in Washington with 2000 delegates from 60 cities; National People's Action turns DC upside down; Paul Horvitz, Director of Research, FDIC, signs commitments to NPA, subsequently promoted; "actions" held against Garth Marston, Chairman of FHLBB, and David Meeker, Assistant Secretary of HUD for Community Planning and Development.
- President Ford announces formation of the President's Commission on Urban Development and Neighborhood Revitalization.
- Proxmire's proposed Neighborhood Commission (S. 3554) passes committee.
- Senate Committee on Banking, Housing and Urban Affairs holds hearings on the implementation of the Home Mortgage Disclosure Act; principal witness Gale Cincotta recommends additions to the regulations governing HMDA and calls for critical legislative amendments; Cincotta points out that the Federal Reserve Board to date has failed to issue regulations.

1977
- Community Reinvestment Act (CRA) legislation is introduced in Congress; hearings held.
- Federal limits (Regulation Q) on interest paid on savings accounts expire.
- CRA hearings held in Boston, Chicago, Atlanta, Dallas, San Francisco and New York.
- NPA pushes President Carter to declare June 12-18 "Neighborhoods First" Week.
- SIXTH Annual "State of the Neighborhoods" Conference held in D.C. with 2500 people from 108 cities; delegates are angry that HUD has made no new appointments to regional/area offices after Carter calls HUD biggest slumlord in country; "action" taken to occupy office of Patricia Roberts Harris, Secretary of HUD in Washington.
Representatives from 40 cities attend Insurance Redlining Panel.
- Dr. Paul Horvitz, Assistant to the Chairman of the FDIC, states openly that his agency is "incompetent" to develop any kind of reinvestment programs.
Other regulators take similar positions.
- President Carter appoints fellow Annapolis graduate, Robert McKinney, chair of First Federal S&L of Indianapolis, to chair FHLBB; Cincotta testifies in opposition to his confirmation at Senate hearings, as the worst lender in that city; Proxmire votes against McKinney's confirmation.

- Cincotta supports passage of bill to create the Neighborhood Reinvestment Corporation that will expand the Urban Reinvestment Task Force's Neighborhood Housing Services program nationally; campaigns to prod and entice private sector to invest in communities.
- Trapp declares "Now is the time for the knock-out punch. The bankers are on the ropes."
- Oct. 12 - CRA (S. 406) passes as Title VIII of Housing and Community Development Act, effective Nov. 6, 1978.
- Robert H. McKinney announces new regulations to increase the flow of mortgage money to older neighborhoods by cracking down on discriminatory redlining.
- Cincotta is one of 20 members of the National Commission on Neighborhoods appointed by President Carter and sworn in at White House ceremony.

1978

- Allstate Insurance Corp invests $1 million in NHS of Chicago. SEVENTH Annual Conference convenes; NPA occupies Carla Hill's HUD office for 12 hours.
- FHLBB commits to enforcing new anti-redlining regulations based on location or age of home and to spending $10 billion in Affordable Housing Program (AHP) monies in moderate-income neighborhoods.
- Regulators attempt to gut CRA by limiting regulations to simply encouraging financial institutions to meet the credit needs of the local community.
- Fourteen organizations in seven cities demonstrate against insurance companies.
- Lending industry starts drive to kill HMDA when it expires on June 28, 1980.
- Eight community groups institute formal banking challenges under CRA.

1979

- Mott Foundation funds NTIC as one of six intermediate service organizations.
- NPA and others push for renewal of HMDA.
- EIGHTH Annual National Housing Conference convenes; delegates protest against American Bankers Association; they march ABA President John Perkins out of hall, take over ABA boardroom, demand to be placed on ABA agenda in New Orleans.
- Battle of New Orleans takes place, nonstop hits for three days including surrounding convention hall.

- Aetna announces $15 million loan program in six NPA neighborhoods.

1980

- Shell-shocked from Battle of New Orleans, ABA announces to Senate hearing that it no longer opposes HMDA.
- Interest rates hit 20%.
- *Saturday Night Live* land shark appears over entrance to the Federal Reserve Bank, red tape strung on building.
- Volcker agrees to regional hearings in ten cities.
- NPA kicks off "Reclaim America" at ABA meeting, Chicago.

1981

- TENTH Annual National Housing Conference convenes; takes over office of HUD Secretary Samuel Pierce.
- Aetna announces its neighborhood reinvestment program.

1982

- Joe Mariano starts work at NTIC.
- Cincotta meets with Volcker; she is furious he will not listen to neighborhood experts; her leadership team walks out when he attempts to lecture the group.
- NPA "Reclaim America Week" bus caravan hits 5 cities in 5 days, 30 hits and actions; storms US Chamber of Commerce headquarters in DC, then travels to NYC; tens of thousands shut down Wall Street; Msgr. Baroni prophetically calls Reclaim America "25 years ahead of its time."

1984

- Tommy Cincotta (Gale's eldest son) dies in VA hospital in Chicago. Her husband Roy Cincotta dies. Cincotta's parents die soon thereafter.
- Cincotta involved in successful CRA merger negotiations between Harris and other banks.

1985

- Cincotta takes trip to Europe; visits Italy and Greece, including her father's hometown near Corinth.
- Cincotta honored by *Ms. Magazine* as a "Woman of the Year"

1986

- 15th Annual Neighborhoods Conference deals with renewal of HMDA, also Gramm-Rudman budget cuts, housing and community development.

1987
- Cincotta develops Hodgkin's disease, unknown to staff, undergoes 6 months of chemo treatment.

1989
- NPA takes first major CRA enforcement actions against Continental Bank and Decatur FS&LA.
- Congressman Joseph Kennedy initiates amendment to CRA making ratings public.
- Financial Institutions Reform Recovery and Enforcement Act (FIRREA) increased scope of CRA, requiring regulatory agencies to evaluate and make public banks' compliance with CRA as "outstanding, satisfactory, needs to improve or substantial noncompliance"; this enables community groups to focus banks' attention on the needs of their neighborhoods.
- Federal Home Loan Bank Board functions transferred to Office of Thrift Supervision. Federal Savings and Loan Insurance Corp. (FSLIC) functions merged into Federal Deposit Insurance Corp. (FDIC).
- Resolution Trust Corp. formed to deal with insolvent Savings & Loan Associations.

1990
- Congress passes Cranston-Gonzalez Housing Act dealing with foreclosures.
- Congress requires regulators to make individual lenders CRA evaluations and ratings public.

1992
- Congress issues CRA Status Report: "Status of the Community Reinvestment Act."
- ACORN signs CRA agreements with various banks in Brooklyn, Chicago, Dallas, Philadelphia, Phoenix, St. Louis, Washington during the 1990s.

1995
- First Chicago NBD Bank pledges to put $1 billion into Chicago's communities and other efforts; Cincotta and Richard M. Daley are both present when pledge announced.
- Fannie Mae, Freddie Mac agree to purchase 30% of loans from underserved markets and to change loan criteria to allow 75% credit of rental income to qualify loan applicants.

1996

- Marriott International agrees to implement jobs program demanded by NPA.

1999

- Cincotta delivers keynote speech in Boston to Massachusetts Association of Community Development Associations (MACDC), introduced by Westgate.

2001

- Aug. 15 Gale Cincotta dies in Chicago.

APPENDIX C

ACRONYMS

ABA	American Bankers Association
ACORN	Association of Community Organizations for Reform Now
CAPS	Chicago Alternative Policing Strategy
CCC	Center for Community Change [national]
CCHR	Chicago Commission on Human Relations
CCI	Citizens for Community Improvement [Iowa]
CD	Community Development
CDC	Community Development Corporation
CDFI	Community Development Financial Institutions
CHD	Campaign for Human Development [of the Roman Catholic Church]
CRA	Community Reinvestment Act
FDIC	Federal Deposit Insurance Corp.
FEMA	Federal Emergency Management Agency
FHA	Federal Housing Administration
FHLB	Federal Home Loan Bank [of Chicago unless otherwise stated]
FHLBB	Federal Home Loan Bank Board, Washington, DC
FHLMC	Federal Home Loan Mortgage Corp. (Freddie Mac)
FIRREA	Financial Institutions Reform, Recovery and Enforcement Act
FNMA	Federal National Mortgage Association (Fannie Mae)
FRB	Federal Reserve Board
FSLIC	Federal Savings & Loan Insurance Corp.
FS&LA	Federal Savings and Loan Association
HMDA	Home Mortgage Disclosure Act
HOLC	Home Owners Loan Corporation, Washington, DC
HTIC	Housing Training & Information Center [precursor to NTIC]
HUD	Housing & Urban Development, U.S. Dept. of
IAF	Industrial Areas Foundation [Chicago]
LEAA	Law Enforcement Assistance Administration [U.S. Dept. of Justice]
LISC	Local Initiative Support Corporation
MACDC	Massachusetts Association of Community Development Corporations
MAHA	Metropolitan Area Housing Alliance [Chicago area]

NCO	Northwest Community Organization [Chicago]
NCRC	National Community Reinvestment Coalition, Washington
NHS	Neighborhood Housing Services
NHSA	Neighborhood Housing Services of America [Oakland, CA]
NPA[H]	National People's Action [on Housing, originally]
NRC	Neighborhood Reinvestment Corporation (d/b/a NeighborWorks America)
NTIC	National Training & Information Center
NWO	NeighborWorks Organization [member of NeighborWorks America]
OBA	Organization for a Better Austin [Chicago]
OCC	Office of the Comptroller of the Currency
PICO	People Improving Communities through Organizing [national]
PMI	Private Mortgage Insurance Inc.
PTA	Parent Teachers Association
Reg Q	Federal regulation of interest paid by banks to depositors
RERC	Real Estate Research Corp. [Chicago]
S&L	Savings & Loan Association [state- or federally-chartered]
SACCC	South Austin Coalition Community Council [Chicago]
SMSA	Standard Metropolitan Statistical Area
THA	Town Hall Assembly [rival organization to OBA]
TWO	The Woodlawn Organization [Chicago]
URTF	Urban Reinvestment Task Force
VA	Veterans Administration
VISTA	Volunteers In Service To America
WIN	Working in Neighborhoods (WIN) [Cleveland]
WSC	West Side of Chicago
501(c)(3)	Non-profit designation by Internal Revenue Service (IRS)
501(c)(4)	Non-profit designation by IRS allowed to lobby more directly

APPENDIX D

BIBLIOGRAPHY

Advisory Committee on Regional Barriers to Affordable Housing, Report to Bush and Kemp *(1991) Not In My Back Yard: Removing Barriers to Affordable Housing,* Washington: GPO

Ahlbrandt, Roger S, Jr and Brophy, Paul C. (1975) *An Evaluation of Pittsburgh's Neighborhood Housing Services Program,* Washington: U.S. Department of Housing and Urban Development

Ahlbrandt, Roger S, Jr. and Brophy, Paul C. (1975) *The Neighborhood Housing Services Model: A Progress Assessment of the Related Activities of the Urban Reinvestment Task Force,* Washington: U. S Department of Housing and Urban Development

Algren, Nelson (1983) *Chicago: City on the Make,* Introduction by Studs Terkel, Chicago: University of Chicago Press

Alinsky, Saul D. (1946) *Reveille for Radicals,* Chicago: University of Chicago Press

Alinsky, Saul D. (1971) *Rules for Radicals: A Pragmatic Primer for Realistic Radicals,* New York: Vintage Books

Anzer, Thomas C.; Gould, Laurie; Peattie, Debra A. (1996) *Chelsea Neighborhood Housing Services: The RENT TO OWN Program,* unpublished research paper for Entrepreneurship in the Social Sector, Harvard Business School

Ash, Jay (2001) *State of the City Address,* Chelsea MA: City of Chelsea

Aspen Institute (2002) *Voices from the Field II: Reflections on Comprehensive Community Change,* Washington: The Aspen Institute

Austin, James E; Strimling, Andrea L; Elias, Jaan (1996) *Leadership In Action: The Cleveland Turnaround, Case Series,* Boston: Harvard Business School

Banfield, Edward C. (1968) *The Unheavenly City: The Nature and Future of Our Urban Crisis,* Boston: Little, Brown and Co.

Belsky, Eric S.; Lambert, Alexander; von Hoffman, Alexander. (2000) *Insights Into the Practice of Community Reinvestment Act Lending: A Synthesis of CRA Discussion Groups* (Moderated by Nicolas P. Retsinas), Cambridge: Joint Center for Housing Studies

Belsky, Eric; Schill, Michael; Yezer, Anthony (2001) *The Effect of the Community Reinvestment Act on Bank and Thrift Home Purchase Mortgage Lending,* Cambridge: Joint Center for Housing Studies

Block, Peter (1993) *Stewardship: Choosing Service over Self-Interest,* San Francisco: Berret-Koehler Publishers

Boyer, Brian D. (1973) *Cities Destroyed For Cash: The FHA Scandal at HUD,* Chicago: Follett Publishing Company

Boyte, Harry C. (1980) *The Backyard Revolution: Understanding the New Citizen Movement,* Philadelphia: Temple University Press

Boyte, Harry C. (1984) *Community Is Possible: Repairing America's Roots,* New York: Harper & Row

Bradford, Calvin (1975) *Mortgage Lending Practices,* Chicago: Urban-Suburban Study Group, Northwestern University

Bratt, Rachel G. (2002) *Housing for Very Low-Income Households: The Record of President Clinton, 1993-2000,* Cambridge: Joint Center for Housing Studies

Bratt, Rachel G.; Keyes, Langley C.; Schwartz, Alex; Vidal, Avis C. (1994) *Confronting the Management Challenge: Affordable Housing in the Nonprofit Sector,* New York: The New School for Social Research

Bunnell, Gene (1977) *Built to Last,* Washington: The Preservation Press

Cannato, Vincent J. (2001) *The Ungovernable City: John Lindsay and His Struggle to Save New York,* New York: Basic Books

Case, Frederick E., editor (1972) *Inner-City Housing and Private Enterprise, Based on Studies in Nine Cities,* Westport, CT: Praeger Publishers

Castle, Robert W. Jr. (1968) *PRAYERS from the Burned-Out City,* New York: Sheed and Ward

City Council of the City of Chicago (1974) *Ordinance requiring data on residential lending information from banks holding deposits from the City.* Chicago: City of Chicago

Chicago Public Library, Special Collections
Austin High School Records, 1879-1971, 2 lineal feet, 17 photos
Austin Community Collection, 1860-81, 7 lineal feet, 300 photos, 19 oversize folders

Austin Newspapers, 1876-1997, 13 lineal feet Videotape collection

Cincotta, Gale, "Redlining and FHA: New Research Proves Dual Home Financing in Chicago Neighborhoods"—Testimony presented on behalf of Metropolitan Area Housing Alliance before Congress on May 5, 1975

Cincotta, Gale (1991) "Statement about Harris Bank and its CRA rating," cited in *Consumer Bankers Association Newsletter*

Cincotta, Gale, Testimony as Panelist at Public Hearing on Home Equity Lending, Federal Reserve Bank of Chicago, August 16, 2000

Cincotta, Gale, *From Redlining to Reinvestment, the Need for Eternal Vigilance,* Paper presented before the 4th International Conference on Financial Services panel on "European Monetary Union and the Regional Responsibility of Financial Institutions towards the Consumer;" Strasbourg, France, Sept. 27, 1996

Cisneros, Henry G.; Kemp, Jack F.; Retsinas, Nicholas P.; Colton, Kent W. (2005) *Opportunity and Progress: A Bipartisan Platform for National Housing Policy,* Cambridge: Joint Center for Housing Studies of Harvard University

Clark, Ramsey (1970) *Crime in America: Observations on Its Nature, Causes, Prevention and Control,* New York: Simon & Schuster

Conte, Joanne (1998) *A Case Study: Contrasting the Building of Grassroots Community Organizing Coalitions in Denver and Chicago,* unpublished Master's Thesis, University of Colorado, Denver

Coughlin, Roger J. and Riplinger, Cathryn A. (1999) *The Story of Charitable Care in the Archdiocese of Chicago, 1844-1997,* Chicago: The Catholic Charities

Daigle, Marc and Adelberg, John (1992) *Neighborhoods of Tomorrow,* Watertown, MA: The Center for Collaborative Communities

Delgado, Gary (1994) *Beyond the Politics of Place, New Directions in Community Organizing in the 1990s,* Oakland, CA: Applied Research Center

Diamond, Jared (2005) *COLLAPSE: How Societies Choose to Fail or Succeed,* London: Penguin Books

Diers, Jim (2004) *Building Community the Seattle Way,* Seattle: University of Washington Press

Farrell, John A. (2001) *Tip O'Neill and the Democratic Century,* Boston: Little Brown & Co.

Federal Reserve Bank of Chicago (1999) *Profitwise: Social Compact makes an impact on Chicago,* Chicago: Federal Reserve Bank

Federal Reserve Bank of Chicago (1999) *Mortgage Credit Access Partnership, Progress Report,* Chicago: Federal Reserve Bank

Fisher, Robert (1994) *Let the People Decide: Neighborhood Organizing in America,* New York: Twayne Publishers

Fleming, Ronald Lee and Halderman, Lauri (1982) *On Common Ground: Caring for Shared Land from Town Common to Urban Park,* Harvard, MA: Harvard Common Press

The Ford Foundation. Selected documents, pamphlets and files of The Ford Foundation are listed here, together, in chronological order. Author made copies of the relevant files which are on microfiche in the Foundation's archives:

- All archives relating to grants requested from and made to NTIC, including internal foundation staff memos
- Longstreth, Bevis and Rosenbok, H. David (1973) *Corporate Social Responsibility and the Institutional Investor: A Report to the Ford Foundation*, New York: Praeger Publishers
- *HTIC Technical Assistance Proposal* (March 5, 1975)
- *Letter from Ford Foundation Program Officer Basil Whiting* (Division of National Affairs) to Richard O. Ristine, Vice President and Secretary of the Lilly Endowment (January 8, 1976)
- *Program Action document:* Recommending a $125,000 grant over two years to the Housing, Training and Information Center from Ford's National Affairs Division "to strengthen the research, technical assistance and training components of a program focused on neighborhood preservation" (January 12, 1976)
- Kolodny, Robert (1977) *A Monitoring Report: The National Training and Information Center*, prepared at the request of the National Affairs Division of the Ford Foundation (unpublished)
- Nevin, David (1981) *Left-Handed Fastballers: Scouting and Training America's Grass-Roots Leaders, 1966-77*, New York: The Ford Foundation
- The Ford Foundation (1989) *Affordable Housing: The Years Ahead*, New York: The Ford Foundation
- Joint Center for Housing Studies (2002) *The 25th Anniversary of the Community Reinvestment Act: Access to Capital in an Evolving Financial Services System*, Prepared for the Ford Foundation (unpublished)

Forrester, Jay W. (1969) *Urban Dynamics*, Cambridge: MIT Press

Friend, Irwin, editor (July 1969) *Study of the Savings and Loan Industry*, Washington: Federal Home Loan Bank Board

Friend, Irwin (Sept. 1969) *Summary And Recommendations: Study of the Savings and Loan Industry*, Washington: Federal Home Loan Bank Board

Frisbie, Margery (1991) *An Alley in Chicago: The Ministry of a City Priest*, Kansas City, MO: Sheed and Ward

Galbraith, John Kenneth (1967) *The New Industrial State*, Boston: Houghton-Mifflin Co.

Galbraith, John Kenneth (1973) *Economics & The Public Purpose*, Boston: Houghton-Mifflin Co. Boston

Gans, Herbert J. (1962) *The Urban Villagers*, New York: The MacMillan Co.

Garr, Robin (1995) *Reinvesting In America: The Grassroots Movements that are Feeding the Hungry, Housing the Homeless, and Putting Americans Back to Work*, Reading, MA: Addison-Wesley

Gaudette, Tom, selected papers from archives of the Von Der Ahe Library at Loyola Marymount University, Los Angeles [copies made by author]

Gladwell, Malcolm (2000) *The Tipping Point: How Little Things Can Make a Big Difference*, New York: Little Brown & Co.

Gladwell, Malcolm (2008) *Outliers: The Story of Success*, New York: Little, Brown & Co.

Glickman, Norman J. and Servon, Lisa J. (1998) "More than Bricks and Sticks: Five Components of Community Development Corporation Capacity", article in *Housing Policy Debate*, Washington: Fannie Mae

Greeley, Andrew M. (2005) *The Bishop in the Old Neighborhood*, New York: Forge Books

Green, James (2006) *Death in the Haymarket: A Story of Chicago, The First Labor Movement and the Bombing that Divided Gilded Age America*, New York: Pantheon Books

Greenwood, Davydd and Levin, Morten (1998) *Democratizing Research: An Introduction to Action Research*, Thousand Oaks, CA: Sage Publications

Grier, George (1971) *The Baby Bust: An Agenda for the '70s*, Washington: The Washington Center for Metropolitan Studies

Hallahan, Kirk (1992) *The Mortgage Redlining Controversy, 1972-1975: National People's Action Takes on the Lenders and Wins Anti-Discrimination Legislation in Congress – A Case Study in Social Problems and Agenda Building: The Role of Reformers, Lawmakers and Media in Public Policy Making* Paper presented to Quantitative Studies Division, Association in Journalism and Mass Communication, Montreal (unpublished)

Harrington, Michael (1962) *The Other America: Poverty in the United States*, New York: Simon & Schuster

Hayes, Christopher, "The Good Neighbor: Community activist Gale Cincotta's work was never done" in *The Chicago Reader* (December 21, 2001)

Heise, Kenan and Frazel, Mark (1993) *Hands on Chicago: Getting Hold of the City,* (Sixth Printing), Chicago: Bonus Books

Holli, Melvin G., and Jones, Peter d'A. (1995) *Ethnic Chicago: A Multicultural Portrait,* Grand Rapids, MI: Eerdsmans Publishing Co.

Immergluck, Dan (2004) *Credit to the Community: Community Reinvestment and Fair Lending Policy in the United States*, Armonk, New York: M.E. Sharpe, Inc.

Jacobs, Jane (1961) *The Death and Life of Great American Cities*, New York: Random House

Jacobs, Jane (1970) *The Economy of Cities*, New York: Vintage Books

Jacobs, Jane (2007) *Block By Block and the Future of New York*, New York: Princeton Architectural Press

Johnson, Philip, and Burgee, John (1969) *The Island Nobody Knows*, New York: City of New York and State of New York [Roosevelt Island, where Westgate was interim Project Manager in 1970]

Kansas City Temporary Advisory Commission on Housing Report to The Mayor and City Council (1973) *A Housing Policy for Kansas City*, Kansas City MO: Kansas City Development Department [Westgate met with authors while performing initial field work leading to formation of NHS in Kansas City.]

Joint Center for Housing Studies at Harvard (2005) *The Changing Structure of the Home Remodeling Industry: Improving America's Housing*, Cambridge: Joint Center for Housing Studies

Kayser, Vicki, editor (1978) *Boston's Triple Deckers*, Boston: Office of Program Development

Kerner, Otto, Chairman (1968) *Report of The National Advisory Commission on Civil Disorders*, Washington: GPO

Kilbridge, Maurice D.; O'Block, Robert P.; Teplitz, Paul V. (1970) *Urban Analysis*, Boston: Harvard Graduate School of Business Administration

King, Mel (1981) *Chain Of Change: Struggles for Black Community Development*, Boston: South End Press

Kirchner, David E. (2001) *Challenging Private Power: Neighborhood Opposition to Redlining in Three Midwestern Cities*, Doctoral Dissertation, Washington University, St. Louis, MO (unpublished)

Kratovil, Robert (1965) *Real Estate Law*, Englewood Cliffs, NJ: Prentice-Hall

Lindsay, John V. (1969) *The City: New York's Mayor reports firsthand on the struggle to make a livable city*, New York: W.W. Norton & Co.

Listokin, David (1985) *Living Cities: Report of the Twentieth Century Fund Task Force on Urban Preservation Policies*, New York: Priority Press Publications

Lord, Richard (2005) *American Nightmare: Predatory Lending and the Foreclosure of the American Dream*, Monroe, ME: Common Courage Press

Luquetta, Andrea Caliz, and Thrash, Tunua (2000) *Insuring The Future Of Our Communities: The First Progress Report on the Massachusetts Insurance Industry Investment Initiatives*, Boston: Massachusetts Association of Community Development Corporations

Lukas, J. Anthony (1985) *Common Ground: A Turbulent Decade in the Lives of Three American Families*, New York, Alfred A. Knopf

Marshall, Jeffery (1992) *Staying ahead of CRA: What Financial Institutions must know to win at community reinvestment*, Homewood, IL: Irwin Professional Publications

Martin, Preston and Epstein, Lita (2003) *The Complete Idiot's Guide to The Federal Reserve*, Indianapolis: Alpha Publications

Mason, David Lawrence (2004) *From Buildings and Loans to Bail-outs: A History of the American Savings and Loan Industry, 1831- 1995*, Cambridge, England: Cambridge University Press

McAuley Institute (1999) *Women as Catalysts for Social Change: A Study of Women-led Community Development Organizations*, Silver Spring, MD: McAuley Institute

McKnight, John (1995) *The Careless Society: Community and Its Counterfeits*, New York: Harper Collins

Medoff, Peter and Sklar, Holly (1994) *Streets Of Hope: The Fall and Rise of an Urban Neighborhood*, Boston: South End Press

Meizhu, Lui; Robles, Barbara; Leondar-Wright, Betsy; Brewer, Rose; Adamson, Rebecca with United for a Fair Economy (2006) *The Color Of Wealth: The Story Behind the U.S. Racial Wealth Divide*, New York: The New Press

Merrill, Charles (1986) *The Checkbook: The Politics and Ethics of Foundation Philanthropy*, Boston: Oelgeschlager, Gunn & Hain.

Metzger, John T. (2000) *Planned Abandonment: The Neighborhood Life-Cycle Theory and National Urban Policy*, East Lansing: Michigan State University Press

Mishel, Lawrence and Bernstein, Jared (1999) *The State of Working America, 1998-99*, Ithaca: Cornell University Press

Monroe, Albert (2001) *How the Federal Housing Administration Affects Homeownership* Cambridge: Joint Center for Housing Studies

Neighborhood Housing Services of America (1994) *20 Years of Investing in the American Dream*, Oakland: NHSA

NHS Stories (2002) *NHS of Chicago Annual Report*, Chicago: Neighborhood Housing Services of Chicago

National Training and Information Center (NTIC), Selected documents, pamphlets and files of NTIC and NPA (formerly HTIC and NPAH) are listed here, together, in chronological order:

- *DISCLOSURE Newsletters* (all issues, 1974-78; selected issues, 1979-2003)
- *REPORTS* (1981-2003)
- Press clippings file (1974 - 2003)
- *The Grass-Roots Battle Against Redlining: From the Streets to the Halls of Congress* (1975)
- *How to Use the Home Mortgage Disclosure Act of 1975* (1976)
- Fox, Tom (1976) *The American Nightmare: Federal Housing Administration,* with quotes from George Bliss and Chuck Neubauer, investigative reporters for the *Chicago Tribune* [They were 1975 Pulitzer Prize winners for their reporting on FHA.]
- Trapp, Shel (1976) *A Challenge for Change: Selected Essays on Community Organizing, Leadership Development and Citizen Participation*
- Naparstek, Arthur J. and Cincotta, Gale (1976) *Urban Disinvestment: New Implications for Community Organization, Research and Public Policy,* Chicago: National Center for Urban Ethnic Affairs and the National Training and Information Center (a joint publication)
- *Neighborhoods First: From the '70s into the '80s—Highlights from Disclosure (1977)*
- Przybylski, Michael; Murray, Helen; Page, Philip; Wysocki, Theodore (1978) *Perceptions of Risk: The Bankers' Myth – An eight city survey of mortgage disclosure data*
- *The Community Reinvestment Act (CRA) Handbook,* Second edition (1979)
- Trapp, Shel (1979) *Who, Me a Researcher? Yes, You!*
- Keenan, Gerald (1979) *Insurance Redlining: Profits vs. Policyholders, Insurance Redlining and Reinvestment, Directions for Change,* Report on Conference at Continental Plaza Hotel, Chicago, held March 22-23, 1979, Chicago: NTIC and the Illinois Advisory Committee to the US Commission on Civil Rights (joint publication)
- *Pass the Buck…Back! The Community Reinvestment Handbook,* 3rd edition (1979)
- *Why Displacement?* (1979)
- Benedek, Vera (1980) *CRA: Ten Fights for Reinvestment*
- Schachter, Rob (1981) *Insurance Redlining—Organizing to Win!*

- Przybylski, Michael; Gardner, Joseph; Shurna, Edward (1981) *Controlling Neighborhood Development: A Manual for Community Groups*
- Trapp, Shel (1986) *Blessed be the Fighters, Reflections on Organizing: Collected Essays*
- *The Silent Bomb: FHA Devastation of Neighborhood – A manual to help communities organize against the abuse of the FHA Program* (1994)
- *Twenty-five Years, Neighborhood Dreams, Issues, Organizing* (1997)
- Obituary File for Gale Cincotta (2001)
- *The Next Move: In Remembrance of Gale*, booklet prepared by NTIC for Gale's memorial service at the Chicago Fine Arts Exchange (November 1, 2001)
- *Organizing to Win* (2001)
- *Taking Our Neighborhoods Back,* (2nd edition, 2002)
- *This Old Reg: The Community Reinvestment Act Needs Renovation* (2002)
- *Celebrating 30 Years of Organizing Neighborhoods* (2003)
- *Banking and Housing Post Conference Report, August 17-19* (2005)

O'Rourke, Lawrence M. (1991) *GENO: The Life and Mission of Geno Baroni,* Mahwah, New Jersey: Paulist Press

Osterman, Paul (1989) *In the Midst of Plenty: A Profile of Boston and Its Poor,* Boston: The Boston Foundation

Parzen, Julia Ann (1992) *Credit Where It's Due: Development Banking for Communities,* Philadelphia: Temple University Press

Peck, M. Scott (1987) *The Different Drummer: Community Making and Peace,* New York: Simon & Schuster

Pierce, Gregory F. Augustine (1984) *Activism that Makes Sense: Congregations and Community Organization,* Chicago: Acta Publications

Powledge, Fred, (1970) *Model City: A Test of American Liberalism – One Town's Efforts to Rebuild Itself,* New York: Simon & Schuster [about New Haven]

Proxmire, Senator William (1980) *The Fleecing of America,* Boston: Houghton Mifflin

Reader, John (2004) *CITIES,* New York: Atlantic Monthly Press

Retsinas, Nicolas P. and Belsky, Eric S., editors (2002) Low-Income Home-Ownership: Examining the Unexamined Goal, Washington: The Brookings Institution Press

Robinson, Michael A. (1991) *Overdrawn: The Bailout of American Savings – The Inside Story of the $2 Billion S&L Debacle,* New York: Penguin Books

Rosales, F. Arturo (1996) *Chicano: The History of the Mexican American Civil Rights Movement* (based on the Public Broadcast Service Series of the same name), Houston: Arte Publico Press, University of Houston

Royko, Mike (1971) *Boss: Richard J. Daley of Chicago,* New York: Penguin Group

Russell, John R., editor (1974) *Cases in Urban Management*, Cambridge: MIT University Press

Santagate, Guy A. (1999) *State Of The All America City Address,* Chelsea MA: City of Chelsea

Satter, Beryl (2009) Family Properties: How the Struggle over Race and Real Estate Transformed Chicago and the United States, New York: Henry Holt and Co.

Schnell, Suzanne C. (1997) *Profiles of Partnership Achievement: Street-tested Strategies for Strengthening Neighborhoods,* Chevy Chase, MD: Social Compact [The partnership between Chelsea Neighborhood Housing Services (CNHS) and Citizens Bank was a 1995 Finalist for the National Social Compact Award. Together CNHS and Citizens designed and implemented the RENT TO OWN Program for triple-deckers in Chelsea.]

Squires, Gregory D., editor (1992) *From Redlining To Reinvestment: Community Responses to Urban Disinvestment,* Philadelphia: Temple University Press [Chapter 9, "The Legacy, the Promise, and the Unfinished Agenda" was written by Cal Bradford and Gale Cincotta.]

Squires, Gregory D.; Bennett, Larry; McCourt, Kathleen; Nyden, Philip (1987) *Chicago: Race, Class and The Response to Urban Decline*, Philadelphia: Temple University Press

Squires, Gregory D., editor (2003) *Organizing Access To Capital: Advocacy and the Democratization of Financial Institution*s, Philadelphia: Temple University Press

Stegman, Michael A. (1972) *Housing Investment in the Inner City: The Dynamics of Decline,* Cambridge: MIT Press

Sternlieb, George (1972) *The Urban Housing Dilemma: The Dynamics of New York City's Rent Controlled Housing,* New York: City of New York Housing and Development Administration

Sternlieb, George and Burchell, Robert W. (1973) *Residential Abandonment: The Tenement Landlord Revisited,* Piscataway, NJ: Rutgers University Press

Sternlieb, George and Listokin, David, editors (1981) *New Tools For Economic Development: The Enterprise Zone, Development Bank and The Reconstruction Finance Corporation,* Piscataway, NJ: Rutgers University Press

Terkel, Studs (1972) *Working: People Talk About What They Do All Day and How They Feel About What They Do,* New York: Pantheon Books

Thomas, Kenneth H. (1998) *The CRA Handbook: Strategies, Exam Reviews, Case Histories,* New York: McGraw Hill

Trapp, Shel (2004) *Dynamics of Organizing: Building Power by Developing the Human Spirit,* Chicago: Self-published

Tullberg, Kathleen (2000) *A Progress Report II: Initiatives by Massachusetts Bankers and Neighborhood Leaders to Meet Community Credit Needs, 1990-2000,* Boston: Massachusetts Community & Banking Council

U.S. Senate Banking Committee (1980) *Analysis of HMDA data from three SMSAs: Chicago, Buffalo, San Diego.* Washington: Government Printing Office

Van Horne, James C. (1968) *Financial Management and Policy,* Englewood Cliffs, NJ: Prentice-Hall

Van Order, Robert, and Zorn, Peter (2001) *Performance of Low-Income and Minority Mortgages,* Cambridge: Joint Center for Housing Studies

Von Furstenberg, George M. and Greene, R. Geffery (1974) *The Effects of Race and Age on Mortgage Delinquency Risk, based on data obtained from Alex O. Williams and James L. Kenkel of the University of Pittsburgh,* Bloomington: Indiana University Press

Von Furstenberg, George M. and Greene, R. Geffery (Spring 1974) "Estimation of Delinquency Risk for Home Mortgage Portfolios" in the *American Real Estate and Urban Economics Association JOURNAL,* Washington

Von Tscharner, Renata and Fleming, Ronald Lee (1987) *New Providence: A Changing Cityscape,* San Diego: Gulliver Books

Von Hoffman, Alexander (2003) *House By House, Block By Block,* Oxford: Oxford University Press

Warren, Mark R. (2001) *Dry Bones Rattling: Community Building to Revitalize American Democracy,* Princeton: Princeton University Press

Westgate, Michael (1971) *Redevelopment of Urban Waterfront: Problems and Opportunities,* unpublished thesis at Harvard Business School

Westgate, Michael (1980) *Fisheries Development Opportunities for New York,* New York: City of New York

Westgate, Michael and Bergman, D.A. (1986) "Plans for a Demonstration Photovoltaic/ Wind/Pumped Storage System Integrated on an Island in Boston Harbor," article in *Energy for Rural and Island Communities IV,* Oxford: Pergamon Press

Westgate, Michael (1995) *Beyond the Bricks and Mortar: Chelsea Neighborhood Housing Services, Annual Report,* Chelsea MA: Chelsea NHS

Westgate, Michael, *Testimony before the Federal Reserve Bank of Boston*, July 7, 1999

Westgate, Michael (2003) *Customer Satisfaction Survey of NeighborWorks Organizations Doing Business with Neighborhood Housing Services of America,* Boston: Education & Resources Group, Inc.

Westgate, Michael and Vick-Westgate, Ann (2004) *Honoring the NeighborWorks System and Friends Who Share the Dream*, Oakland: Neighborhood Housing Services of America [30th Anniversary of NHSA]

We've Found the Enemy (undated) an anonymously written document found in the Gaudette Papers, Loyola Marymount University, Los Angeles, CA [Interviews with Tom Gaudette]

Whiteside, William A. (undated) *Neighborhood Housing Services Handbook (draft)*, Washington: Urban Reinvestment Task Force

Williams, Alex O. and Kenkel, James L. (1974) *Study of the Factors of Risk in Urban Mortgage Lending*, conducted at the University of Pittsburgh, Washington: Federal Savings & Loan Insurance Corp. [Westgate was project manager on behalf of FSLIC.]

Williams, Alex O.; Beranek, William; Kenkel, James L. (Fall 1974) "Default Risk in Urban Mortgages: A Pittsburgh Prototype Analysis," in the *American Real Estate and Urban Economics Association JOURNAL,* Washington

Winnick, Lou (1995) *Going to Scale: The Ascent of Neighborhood Housing Services,* unpublished

Wright, David J. (2001) *It Takes A Neighborhood: Strategies to Prevent Urban Decline*, Albany, NY: Rockefeller Institute Press

APPENDIX E

INDEX

This index is intended primarily as a guide to the strategies Gale employed. It also identifies individuals who are key to the events in this book. In the interest of brevity, the numerous references to NTIC staff and those interviewed as sources for the book are not included in the index. Major events are listed in the Chronology. Photos are indicated in italics.

AUTHOR

Michael Westgate worked with Gale Cincotta and others from 1973 to 1975 establishing Neighborhood Housing Services (NHS) of Chicago. Begun with a lot of energy and guidance from Gale, NHS of Chicago grew to be the biggest and best of the NeighborWorks organizations in the US, lending almost $500,000,000 to meet the housing needs of almost 30,000 households of otherwise underserved people of Chicago. Gale regarded NHS as an important laboratory where her ideas could be tested and solutions implemented.

At the time Westgate worked with Gale he was Assistant Director for Administration of the Urban Reinvestment Task Force (URTF) in Washington, responding to the crisis in lending in neighborhoods in Chicago and other cities around the country. He was the URTF's project manager for Chicago. The Task Force, sponsored by the Federal Home Loan Bank Board, evolved into the Congressionally-chartered Neighborhood Reinvestment Corporation, since renamed NeighborWorks America. Westgate was responsible for the Bank Board's liquidation of Republic Savings & Loan in Washington in 1971-73 and was project manager for its 1973 study, *Factors of Risk in Urban Mortgage Lending.* He conducted a 2003 study and report on the billion-dollar impact made nationally by Neighborhood Housing Services of America (NHSA) in Oakland, CA, the non-profit secondary market for NeighborWorks Organizations.

His professional work has included three years as Executive Director of Boston's Economic Development Industrial Corporation (EDIC) under Mayor Kevin White. He was responsible for the development of three industrial parks, including Boston Marine Industrial Park. He previously served as Assistant Commissioner of Ports & Terminals in New York under Mayor John Lindsay, helping to found South Street Seaport Museum.

Westgate kept in touch with Gale and, as a member of the Community Reinvestment Committee of the Massachusetts Association of Community Development Corporations (MACDC), helped craft a version of the Community Reinvestment Act for the insurance industry in Massachusetts. It required insurance companies to invest and lend $200 million for low and moderate-income housing and economic development in Massachusetts. He also served on the Massachusetts Community & Banking Council.

He writes from the perspective of 40 years of community development work at the federal, state, city and neighborhood organization levels, including 12 years as Executive Director of Chelsea Neighborhood Housing Services.

He holds a B.A. from Swarthmore College and an MBA from Harvard Business School.

He now lives on Cape Cod with his wife Ann Vick-Westgate, who has collaborated with him in the interviewing for, and editing of, this book. He serves as Treasurer for the Cape Cod Commercial Hook Fishermen's Association and its Cape Cod Fisheries Trust.

His children, Ramsay and Katherine, live with their spouses and daughters in San Jose, CA and New York City respectively.

ACKNOWLEDGEMENTS

This book would not have been birthed or completed without the inspiration of my wife, Ann Vick-Westgate. Early encouragement and guidance also came from Joe Mariano and Bud Kanitz, who also took the time, towards the end, to critique the entire manuscript.

Everyone who participated, enthusiastically, in the interview process are the ones who made this book possible. There are two people to thank in particular: Gale's youngest son, Jimmy Cincotta, who provided the context of her family life, and the late Shel Trapp, Gale's indispensable partner over the years, always figuring out together how to galvanize people around the issues. Shel was enthusiastic about the publication of this book. Many thanks to the late Lou Winnick of The Ford Foundation for providing entrée to their archives. The photos came from Gale's son Richard Cincotta, Gale's close friend Gayle Brinkman, and Neighborhood Housing Services (NHS) of Chicago. I also want to recognize Marie Williams at Watermark, in Chatham, for her care and expertise in the design of this book.

There are many who provided financial support, covering some of our expenses during the eight years required to produce this book. Special thanks to the following in particular:

Depositors Insurance Fund
Drumcliff Foundation
NeighborWorks America

Barry Black, Michael Dukakis, Norman Edmonson, Lansing Fair,
Allen Fishbein, William Fitzhugh, Bruce Gottschall, Bud Kanitz,
Joe Mariano, Michael Moskos, John McMullen, Mike Sananman,
Mark & Nancy Simonitsch, Sue Turner